AF573937

From Pop

SELECTIONS FROM THE Sonnabend Collection

to Now

From Pop

SELECTIONS FROM THE Sonnabend Collection

to Now

INTRODUCTORY ESSAY BY CHARLES ASHLEY STAINBACK, CURATOR

EDITED BY MARGARET SUNDELL

CATALOGUE TEXTS BY RACHEL HAIDU

THE FRANCES YOUNG TANG TEACHING MUSEUM AND ART GALLERY AT SKIDMORE COLLEGE

This publication accompanies the exhibition "From Pop to Now: Selections from the Sonnabend Collection," organized by Charles Ashley Stainback, Dayton Director of the Frances Young Tang Teaching Museum and Art Gallery, Skidmore College. This exhibition and publication have been made possible by the generous support of Mr. and Mrs. Edgar J. Wachenheim III, Beverly Beaston Grossman '58 and Felix T. Grossman, the Edward J. Noble Foundation, the AT&T Foundation, and the Friends of the Tang.

Library of Congress Control Number: 2002104980
This publication was produced in conjunction with the exhibition "From Pop to Now: Selections from the Sonnabend Collection," curated by Charles Ashley Stainback

Exhibition itinerary:

The Frances Young Tang Teaching Museum and Art Gallery at Skidmore College
Saratoga Springs, New York
June to September 2002

Wexner Center for the Arts at Ohio State University
Columbus, Ohio
November 2002 to February 2003

Milwaukee Art Museum
Milwaukee, Wisconsin
February to May 2003

First edition 2002

Edited by Margaret Sundell
Designed by Bethany Johns
Lithography and printing by GZD, Ditzingen-Heimerdingen, Germany
Distribution by D.A.P. / Distributed Art Publishers
155 Sixth Avenue, Second Floor
New York, New York 10013-1507
T. 212.627.1999
F. 212.627.9484

ISBN 0-9708790-7-5

CONTENTS

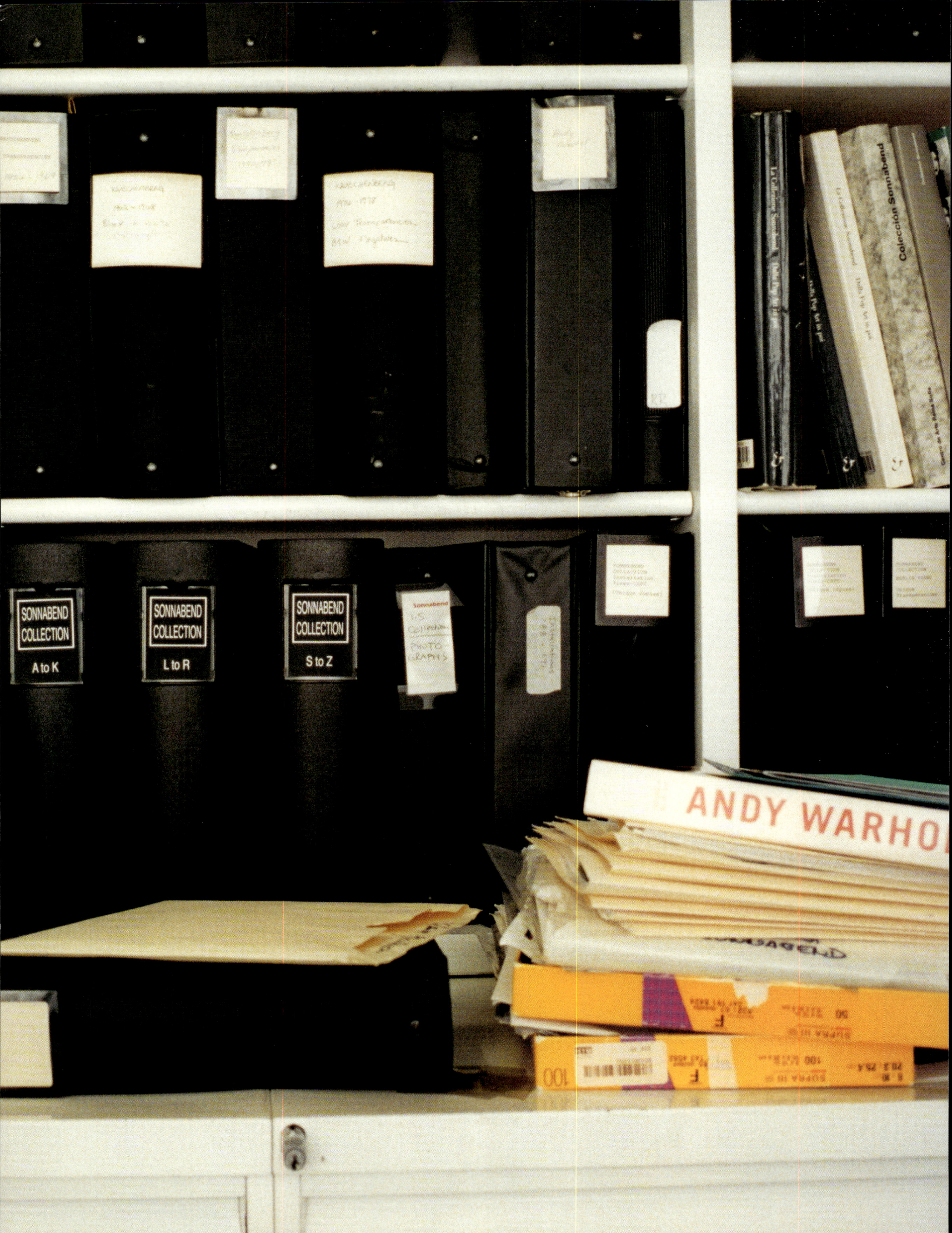

SONNABEND
COLLECTION
A to K
SONNABEND
COLLECTION
L to R
SONNABEND
COLLECTION
S to Z
Colección Sonnabend
ANDY WARHO

NO IDEAS HAVE ENTERED THIS INTRODUCTION[1]

> "Every passion borders on the chaotic, but the collector's passion borders on the chaos of memories."
> —Walter Benjamin, "Unpacking My Library"[2]

> "I am not really a dealer; I am an amateur, a word I use in the French sense: 'one who loves.' In this case it's a love of art."
> —Ileana Sonnabend[3]

To visit a museum exhibition of the Sonnabend Collection is to experience the life of Ileana Sonnabend. Contemporary art is, and has been for almost half a century, central to her life. The studio visits, the gallery exhibitions, the enduring friendships with artists, the ongoing business, the white walls, the openings, the press, and the ever-changing cast of museum curators, collectors, aspiring artists, and gallery visitors are the substance of her memories. They are also part of each and every artwork in the collection. And while her gallery has been instrumental in launching and shaping the careers of many artists, it is Ileana Sonnabend's collection that has been called her most impressive legacy.[4]

With the fortieth anniversary[5] of the Sonnabend Gallery's first exhibition in Paris just a few months away, "From Pop to Now: Selections from the Sonnabend Collection" celebrates this remarkable life's work with eighty-one artworks by fifty-four artists. This memoir-as-art-collection is illustrated with iconic works and constitutes a veritable who's who of the contemporary art world from the late 1950s to the present. But even as it features many stellar artworks, it is nonetheless defined by the implicit framework—focused and inherently personal—of one individual's aesthetic. Throughout the curatorial process, a dialogue became evident—between recent art history and the distinct eye of the individual—that forced my own reexamination of the history of the avant-garde and recent artistic innovation. The already difficult challenge of making discerning aesthetic decisions was compounded by the desire to accurately convey a vision that has been at the vanguard of artistic activity. To reflect the true spirit of this important collection without letting one's own prejudices, vision, or understanding of contemporary art interfere isn't easy. The trick was to select the best of the best.

Pop art, Conceptualism, Minimalism, neo-geo, postmodernism, *arte povera*, video, performance, and photography are the signposts of avant-garde activity of the past four decades, and in ways both large and small, Ileana Sonnabend has provided greater visibility and appreciation for this new art.

Bookshelves, Sonnabend Gallery offices, New York, spring 2002.

Viewing, let alone collecting, contemporary art in the past few decades not only has challenged most museum or gallery visitors, but the viewing experience is also continually being reinvented by its authors. Since the 1960s, a variety of artistic activities—including Happenings and performance art, Conceptual art, and Earthworks—have run counter to the notion of the collectible object and, in turn, the economics of the gallery and private and institutional collections. Undaunted by this shifting landscape, Ileana Sonnabend has been drawn to those ideas and artists and the subsequent debate and discussion that has defined art from Pop to now.

It is difficult to pinpoint when Sonnabend's passion for contemporary art began. Clearly, it occurred well before she became a dealer—or "amateur"—and serious collector. Sonnabend emigrated to the United States during the turmoil of World War II with her first husband, Leo Castelli, and their five-year-old daughter Nina in 1941. She enrolled at Columbia University in 1942 to study psychology. There she met Michael Sonnabend. The Sonnabend Collection as it exists today began in earnest in the late 1950s when, with Castelli, she visited Jasper Johns's studio and immediately bought a painting, *Figure 1*. But this was not the first artwork Ileana had acquired. A Matisse watercolor (purchased on her honeymoon with Castelli) and paintings by Arshile Gorky, Willem de Kooning, Jackson Pollock, and Jean Dubuffet had once been part of her collection but had been sold just as that first Jasper Johns eventually would be.

After her breakup with Castelli and marriage to Michael Sonnabend in 1960, Ileana's unique dialogue with contemporary artworks and artists intensified with a move to Paris. The Sonnabends' notion of opening a gallery in Paris was meant to showcase the American artists who were little known at the time in Europe—Johns, Rauschenberg, Andy Warhol, Tom Wesselmann, George Segal, Roy Lichtenstein, Robert Morris, Lee Bontecou, and Bruce Nauman. The gallery was a sensation but also created much consternation among the cultural elite. French critic Otto Hahn referred to Ileana as the "ambassador of American art"[6] for her seemingly endless support of "her" artists. Soon she was buying works by many of the artists shown in the gallery. But by the early 1970s, it became clear that the focus of the international art world had shifted to New York, and the couple decided it was time to return to the United States and open a gallery there. Showing many of the artists in New York with whom they had established relationships in Europe, including Gilbert & George, Bernd and Hilla Becher, Anne and Patrick Poirier, and Christian Boltanski, as well as younger American artists—Vito Acconci, John Baldessari, Mel Bochner, to name a few—the Sonnabend Gallery quickly became a major force in the international art world.

The Sonnabend Collection naturally reflects a long-term commitment to artists who have been featured at the Sonnabends' galleries in Paris, Geneva,[7] and New York. (Most but not all of the works in the exhibition are by Sonnabend artists.) The association with the so-called cutting edge of the art world continues today with a still-growing roster of new artists and additions to the Sonnabend Collection. The move of the Sonnabend Gallery to Chelsea in 2000 marks the sixth iteration of the gallery and the continuation of a tradition that to date has featured the work of more than two hundred artists.

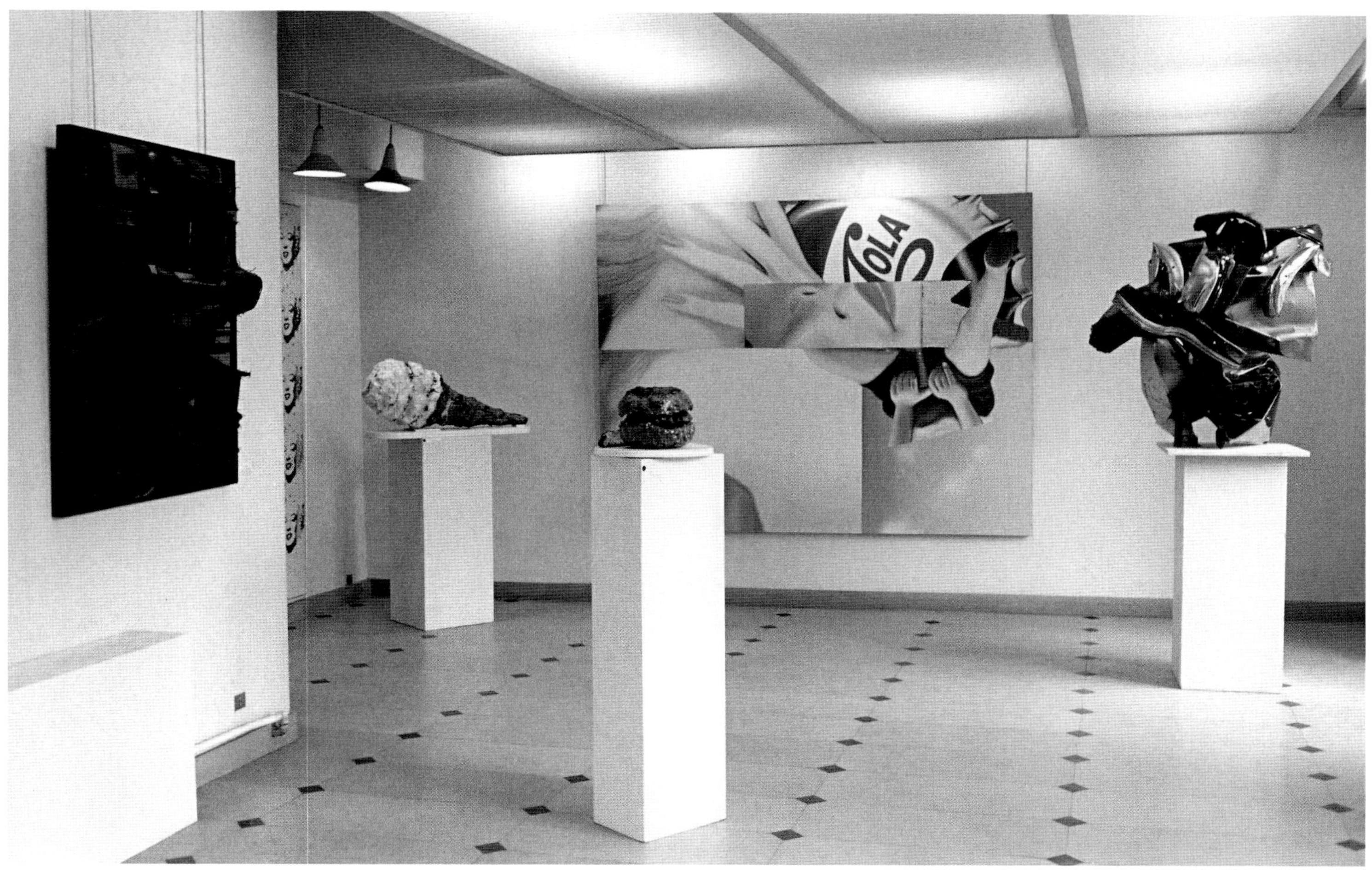

Installation view of the exhibition "Pop Art Américain," Galerie Ileana Sonnabend, Paris, 1963. Artists include **Lee Bontecou**, **Andy Warhol**, **Claes Oldenburg**, **James Rosenquist**, and **John Chamberlain**.

To collaborate with Ileana Sonnabend and Antonio Homem (director of the Sonnabend Gallery since 1968) on the selection of works for this exhibition was not unlike the experience of unpacking one's library. With each question, each request, every binder of transparencies, every visit to New York during the two years of planning, it became clear that it would be impossible, in one exhibition, one catalogue, and one medium-size museum, to even begin to reveal the true scope of the Sonnabend Collection. Acutely aware of how little could be shown (for instance, there are dozens of Anselm Kiefer paintings in the collection and we had space for only one), the challenge was to find a logical premise linking artists to decades and decades to the collective whole. Like any library's organizational system for shelving books for easy retrieval, a museum exhibition requires a narrative logic for the visitor to follow from object to object, gallery to gallery. The answer was to feature artworks that symbolized the artist's move off the easel, out of the studio, away from the unique handmade object to works that increasingly were mechanically reproduced, namely photographs.

Ever since Pop artists—Warhol and Rauschenberg among others—began to appropriate photographic imagery for their paintings, the photograph has assumed a central role in the contemporary art world. Try imagining any part of daily life without photographic or video images and it is easy to understand why they have become critical in recent aesthetic practice. The notion that photographs

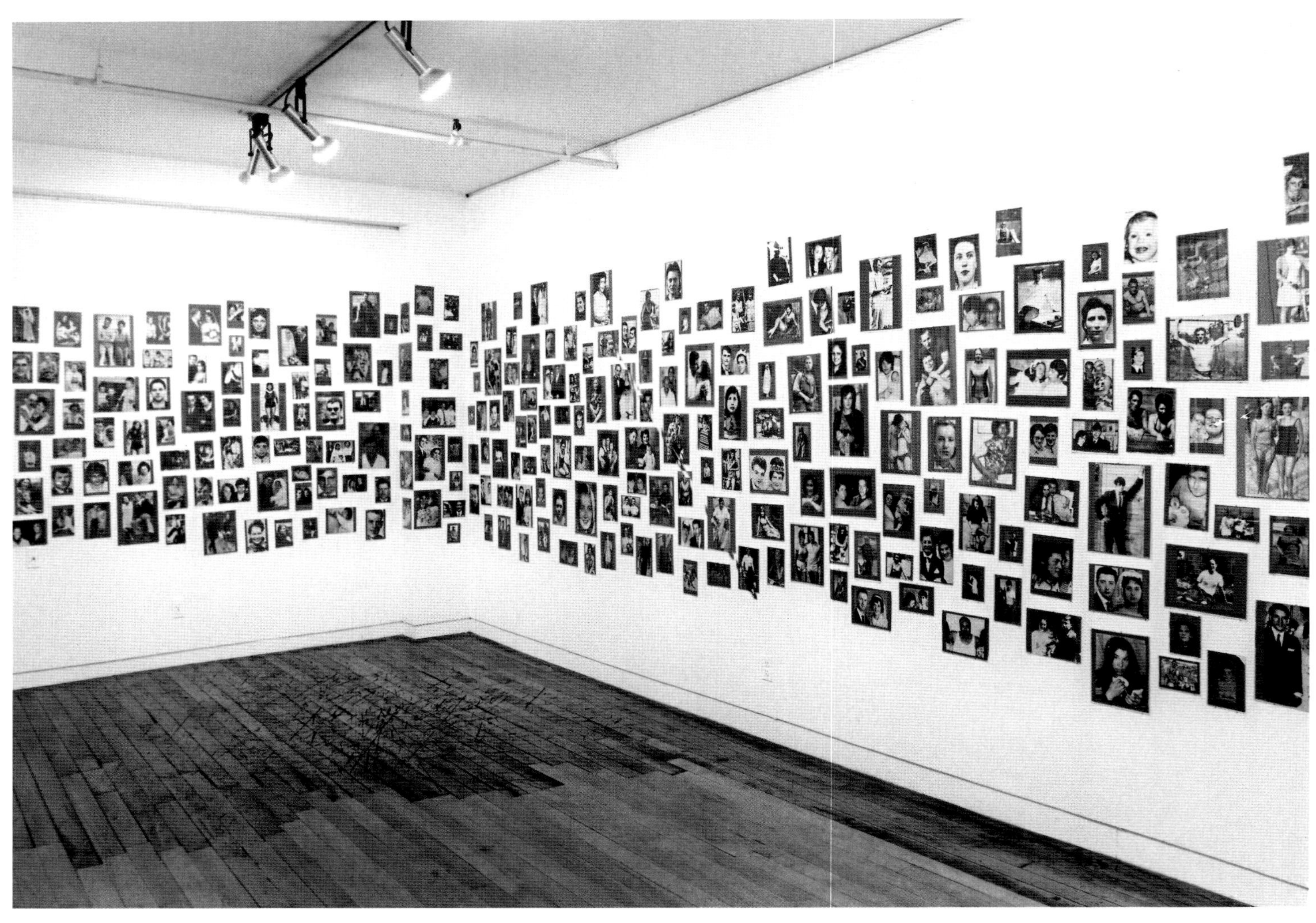

Installation view of **Christian Boltanski**'s *Detective*, 1972–73, from the exhibition "Christian Boltanski," Sonnabend Gallery, New York, 1973.

were little more than mechanical reproductions of conventional subjects began to change dramatically in the 1960s and '70s. Artists such as Ed Ruscha, Baldessari, the Bechers, Boltanski, Nauman, Bochner, and William Wegman began using cameras to make images that often confounded previous notions of appropriate subject matter—water towers, parking lots, found and rephotographed vernacular photographs, a pet dog. For these artists, the camera-made image—photography as well as video—could address broader and more complex issues than those with which traditional media, and especially traditional "photography," were engaged. The subtle visual thread of photographically based works throughout "From Pop to Now" allows maximum exposure of many of the great artists and artworks in the collection while foregrounding a medium that has been pivotal to the artistic landscape of the past few decades.

Though art historians and critics disagree on the seminal artistic achievements since Abstract Expressionism, the impact of Ileana Sonnabend and her gallery on the contemporary art world is indisputable. And the Sonnabend Collection itself has remained virtually unseen and little known. Not until "From Pop to Now" has the collection been shown in such breadth or depth in the United States.[8]

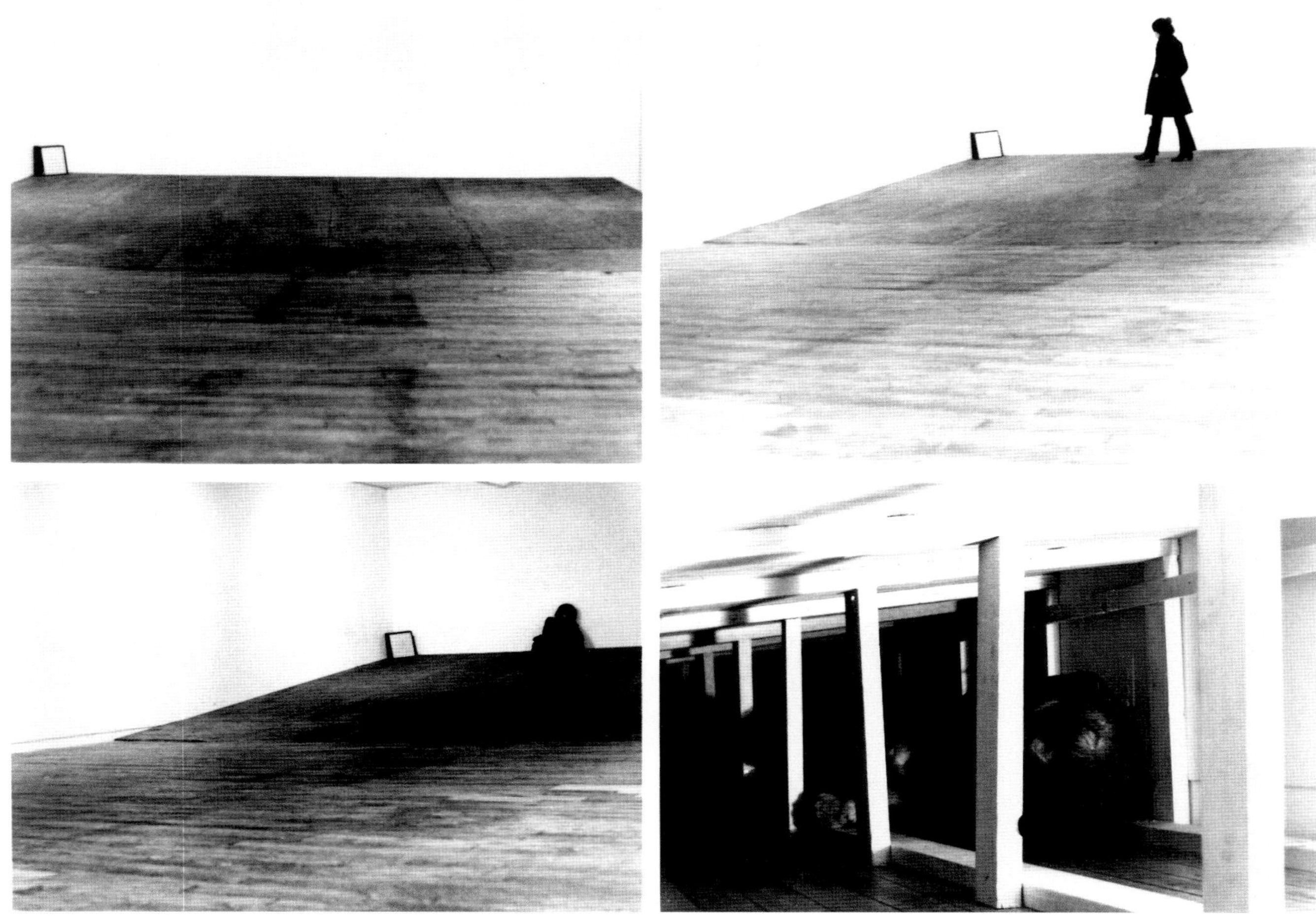

Installation views of **Vito Acconci**'s *Seedbed* performance at Sonnabend Gallery, New York, 1972.

Given Ileana Sonnabend's search for innovative and "outlandish"[9] artists, it seems fitting that this major survey is being organized and shown initially at a young museum dedicated to the new and challenging.

As any art historian will tell you, time is the truest test of artistic achievement. But forty years is an eternity when one considers what has transpired in the contemporary art world. Ileana Sonnabend has been remarkably prescient in perceiving the early genius of an artist long before he or she has fully emerged in the art arena. Johns's use of iconic images and symbols; the appropriation of mundane consumer images by Lichtenstein, Warhol, and Rauschenberg; early uses of the camera by Wegman, Nauman, Boltanski, Boyd Webb, Bochner, the Bechers, and Baldessari; performance pieces like Acconci's *Seedbed*[10] or Gilbert & George's "Singing Sculptures"[11]; the Italian *arte povera* artists Mario Merz, Pier Paolo Calzolari, and Jannis Kounellis, who embraced an artmaking process of open-ended experimentation; and the work of Jeff Koons and Haim Steinbach, who appropriated consumer culture even more directly than the Pop artists of a generation before—all share a remarkable commonality: Ileana Sonnabend and the Sonnabend Collection. In much the same way that the artistic activity of

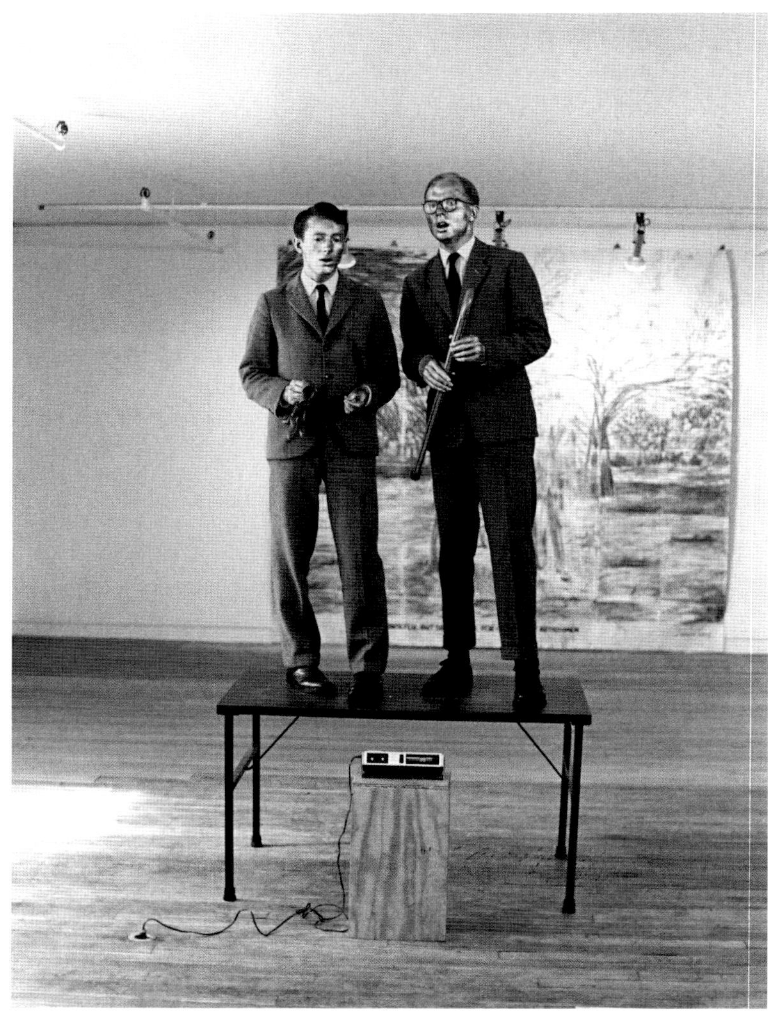

Installation view of **Gilbert & George**'s *The Singing Sculpture* performance at Sonnabend Gallery, New York, 1971.

Marcel Duchamp's time influenced much of the art of the 1960s and '70s, the era of Pop, Conceptualism, Minimalism, performance art, video, and the emergence of the use of the photograph—all in the 1960s—has shaped the art of today and what is yet to come.

Because of the complex—or, for the uninitiated viewer, seemingly unintelligible—notions that many contemporary artists are trying to communicate, the contemporary art collector is most likely the least understood or appreciated of art collectors. Indeed, in 1964, Arthur C. Danto, the respected American writer and intellectual, patented a common theme that still resonates today for the public's thinking about contemporary art. In a review of a Warhol exhibition at New York's Stable Gallery, Danto stated: "Warhol brought the history of art to an end with his Brillo boxes by demonstrating that no visual criterion could serve the purpose of defining art: Why were these boxes art when their originals were just boxes?" [12]

Such questions ultimately arise when we think about the audience for contemporary art. Here, a lesson from Marcel Duchamp—himself an irascible poser of the unanswerable question—is worth recalling. It was Duchamp who, at the beginning of the twentieth century, gave modern art a slap on the behind shortly after birth, teaching us that it is the viewer who completes the work of art. Once the artist/author releases a work, it enters the realm of the art world, waiting to be completed.

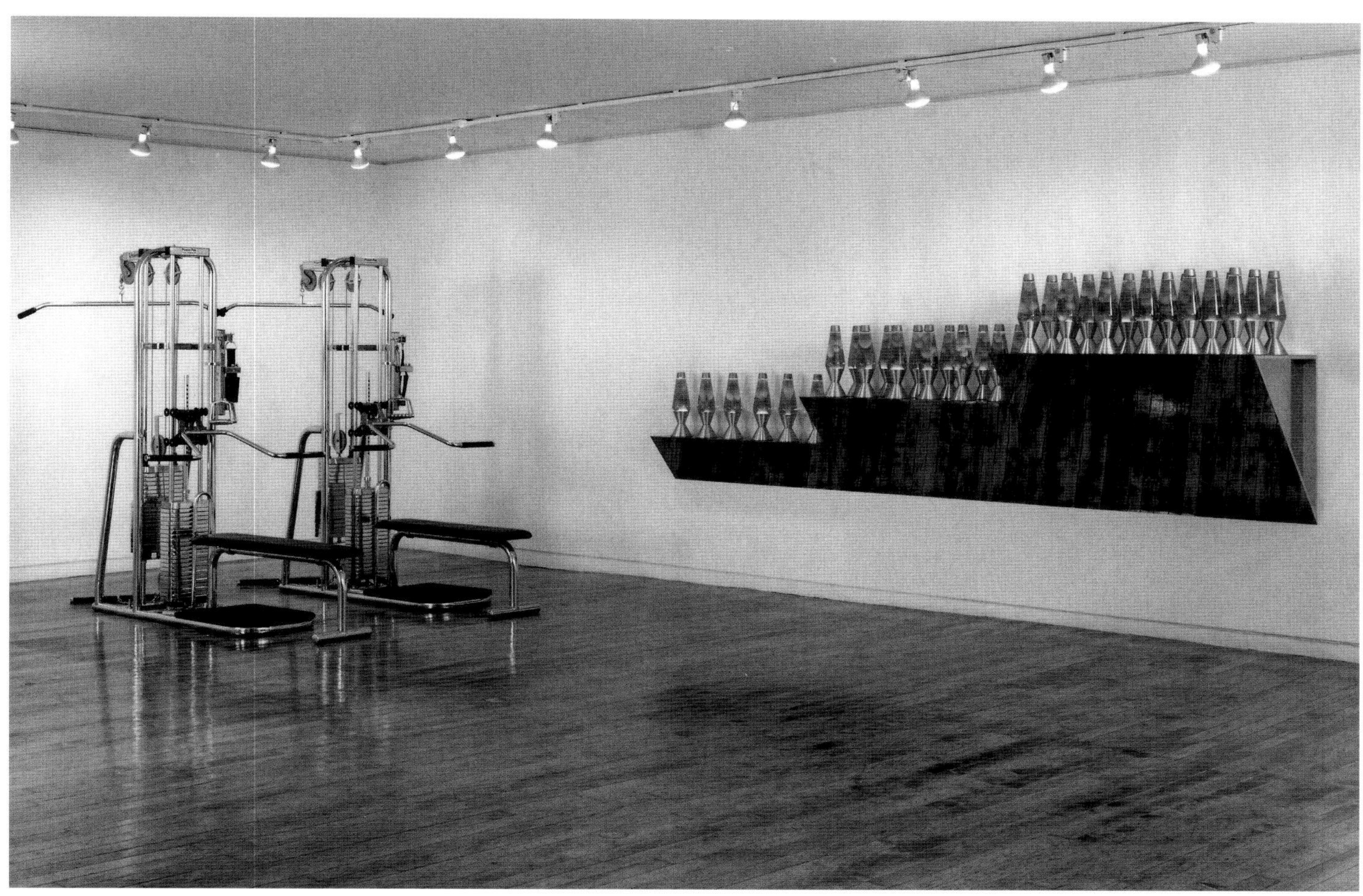

Installation view of **Haim Steinbach**'s *Spirit 1*, 1987, from the exhibition "If You Smoke," Sonnabend Gallery, New York, 1987.

However, looking at an artwork, as even Danto later acknowledged in a review of the Warhol retrospective at the Museum of Modern Art in 1989,[13] does not guarantee full appreciation, understanding, or acceptance of the artist's intent.

That distinction is not unlike the chasm between living through history and reading about it—between what is or isn't art. The critic, scholar, or historian, I am sorry to say, ultimately does not define what art is—those who make it, the artists, define it. Arguments about the critical function of art and society's fixation on uniqueness and innovation will continue with the critics, scholars, and those individuals who can devote much more time (and ink) than I can here. Their written histories will agree, nonetheless, that any avant-garde art challenges, criticizes, and agitates the status quo, pushing, prodding, and eventually breaking down the boundaries of what is acceptable. Not surprisingly, the history of twentieth-century art will ultimately be measured by great moments of avant-garde activity. And in that survey it is no coincidence that Ileana Sonnabend's presence is always near.

"From Pop to Now" is not a definitive survey of the past four decades of artmaking—no single exhibition could claim to be that. However, it reveals much of Ileana Sonnabend's answer to the question of art's raison d'être while simultaneously representing one of the most important art collections of the last half century. The love of contemporary art is a passion that Ileana Sonnabend has brought to her collection. No matter how the works are "completed" in Duchampian terms, as the Sonnabend Collection they complete an important part of recent art history. Even today, almost four decades after Mr. Danto proclaimed "the end of art"[14] with Warhol's agitation of the status quo, viewing contemporary art can be difficult. At its best, contemporary art demands that one think, question, relinquish preconceived notions of what is good or bad, beautiful or ugly, intelligent or dumb, and ultimately consider "what is the purpose of art?"

Art from Pop to now, if nothing else, is about change, redefinition, experimentation, and an ever-expanding notion of what constitutes the avant-garde. And while the avant-garde by definition fights against established notions of tradition—collector, museum, gallery, audience—it is reassuring to be reminded that this frequently strained relationship has fostered many of the past century's most important artistic contributions. If we accept Walter Benjamin's logic, the passion for collecting contemporary art therefore must rely on one's ability to decipher an ever-changing chaos of change. Far from resisting, Ileana Sonnabend has embraced change. In the process, she has preserved a crucial piece of history and, more important, her memories.

1. John Baldessari's 1967–68 painting, which reads EVERYTHING IS PURGED FROM THIS PAINTING BUT ART; NO IDEAS HAVE ENTERED THIS WORK was the inspiration for this title. I hope, however, that the reader can locate at least one idea before the end of the essay.
2. Walter Benjamin, "Unpacking My Library: A Talk about Book Collecting," in *Illuminations*, ed. Hannah Arendt (New York: Schocken Books, 1969), 60.
3. Laura de Coppet and Alan Jones, *The Art Dealers* (New York: Clarkson N. Potter, 1984).
4. Calvin Tomkins, "An Eye for the New," *New Yorker*, 17 January, 2000, 54–64.
5. Ileana and Michael Sonnabend opened Galerie Ileana Sonnabend in Paris on November 15, 1962, with an exhibition of Jasper Johns's paintings.
6. Otto Hahn, quoted in "Les Galeries d'Ileana Sonnabend" by Michel Bourel, Collection Sonnabend (Bordeaux, France: CAPC Musée d'Art Contemporain, 1988).
7. Galerie Sonnabend in Geneva at 14, rue Etienne Dumont was in business from 1974 to 1975. Galerie Sonnabend in Paris moved to larger quarters on the rue Mazarine in 1966 and continued until 1980.
8. Past Sonnabend Collection exhibitions in Europe and Japan: "Sonnabend Collection," curated by Jean-Louis Froment and Marc Sanchez and organized by CAPC Musée d'Art Contemporain, Bordeaux, toured from 1987 to 1991 at Centro de Arte Reina Sofia, Madrid; CAPC Musée d'Art Contemporain, Bordeaux; Art Cologne; Hamburger Bahnhof, Berlin; Galleria Nazionale d'Arte Moderna, Rome; Museo d'Arte Moderna e Contemporanea, Trento, Italy; Musée Rath, Geneva; Sezon Museum of Art, Tokyo; The Miyagi Museum of Art; The Fukuyama Museum of Art; The National Museum of Modern Art, Kyoto. "*Sammlung Sonnabend: Von der Pop-art bis heute; Amerikanische und europaische Kunst seit 1954*" at the Deichtorhallen Hamburg was shown in 1996 at Bayerische Staatsgemaldesammlungen, Munich.
9. De Coppet and Jones, *The Art Dealers*.
10. A performance by Vito Acconci held in January 1972 at Sonnabend Gallery, New York. This was Acconci's first solo show at the SoHo gallery. His goal was the production of "seed," and the means to this goal was masturbation, continuing throughout the day, so that a maximum of "seed" was produced.
11. A performance by Gilbert & George held at the opening of the Sonnabend Gallery, 420 West Broadway, New York, on September 25, 1971. *The Singing Sculpture* consisted of Gilbert & George standing on top of a small table singing along to a recording of the Music Hall tune "Underneath the Arches." This performance was replicated by the artists at the Sonnabend Gallery in 1991.
12. Arthur Danto, "The Artworld," *Journal of Philosophy*, no. 61 (1964): 571–584.
13. Danto, "Art," *The Nation*, 3 April, 1989, 458–461.
14. Danto, "The Artworld."

Installation view of the exhibition "From Pop to Now: Selections from the Sonnabend Collection," The Frances Young Tang Teaching Museum and Art Gallery at Skidmore College, 2002.

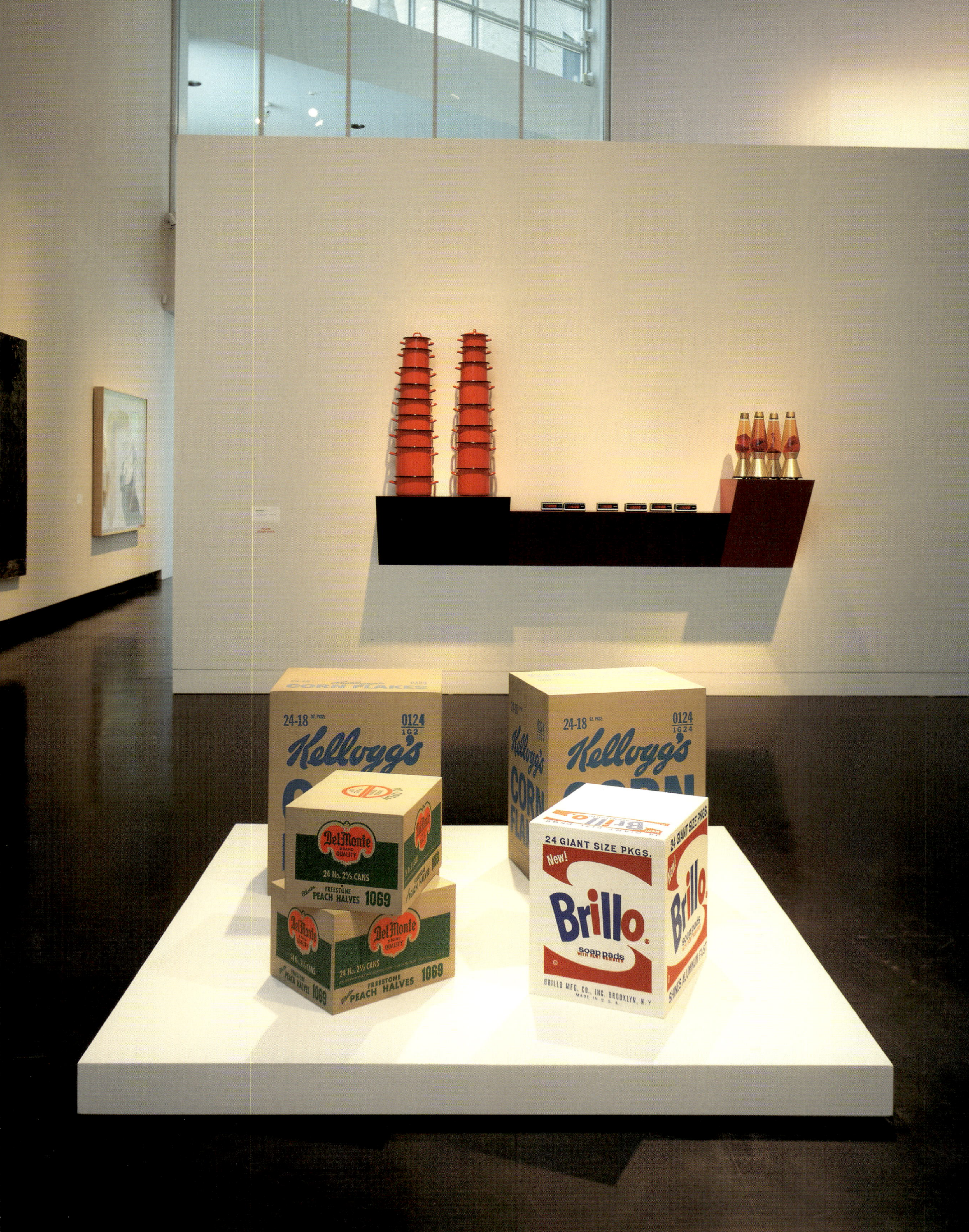

CORN FLAKES
24-18
0124
1G2
Kellogg's
24-18
0124
1G24
Kellogg's
CORN
Del Monte
BRAND
QUALITY
24 No. 2½ CANS
FREESTONE
PEACH HALVES
1069
24 GIANT SIZE PKGS.
New!
Brillo
soap pads
BRILLO MFG. CO., INC. BROOKLYN, N.Y
24 GIANT SIZE PKGS.
SHINES ALUMINUM FAST

SELECTIONS FROM THE SONNABEND COLLECTION

Jasper Johns
Tom Wesselmann
Robert Rauschenberg
Andy Warhol
Claes Oldenberg
Arman
Jim Dine
James Rosenquist
Roy Lichtenstein
Cy Twombly
Clay Ketter
Hiroshi Sugimoto
Christian Boltanski
Gilbert & George
Richard Artschwager
William Wegman
Bernd and Hilla Becher
Elger Esser
Peter Fischli and David Weiss
Vito Acconci
John Baldessari
Mel Bochner
Robert Morris
Dan Flavin
Sol LeWitt
Bruce Nauman
Donald Judd
Barry Le Va
Giovanni Anselmo
Michelangelo Pistoletto
Gilberto Zorio
Jannis Kounellis
Pier Paolo Calzolari
Keith Sonnier
Mario Merz
Anselm Kiefer
Robert Yarber
Ashley Bickerton
Haim Steinbach
Jeff Koons
Mathew Weinstein
Wim Delvoye
Rona Pondick
Anne and Patrick Poirier
Boyd Webb
Candida Höfer
Lawrence Beck
Andrea Robbins and Max Becher
Clifford Ross

Jasper Johns

Figure 8, 1959
Encaustic on canvas
20 1/16 x 15 in.

In 1959, the same year Jasper Johns painted *Number 8*, he made the following statement: "I am opposed to painting which is concerned with conceptions of simplicity."[1] This declaration might at first seem to be contradicted by this work's "simple" subject matter: a stenciled, painted number eight. But it reveals the acute sensitivity of Johns's approach. Familiar, oft-repeated forms can offer both artist and viewer an interest so profound as to render irrelevant any comparison with allegedly more complex or "original" motifs. By infusing ostensibly plain graphic symbols with intense visual incident and play, Johns's work points to the inadequacy of this conventional opposition.

Encaustic, a mixture of hot beeswax and pigment that was used in ancient Roman frescoes and American craft alike, is the pasty medium of *Number 8*'s extraordinarily worked-up surface. Dense patches of vibrant Crayola primaries—deep blue, true red, and orange yellow are interspersed across the sinuous curves of the numeral. Underneath the patchy, whitish background lie traces of these same primary colors and a few isolated clippings of matted-down newspaper. Throughout his work with numbers, letters and other familiar symbols, Johns conserved the appearance of traced stencils and copied-out figures. In *Number 8* some of the brushstrokes just outside the eight echo its lines and curves very closely, as if to suggest that the artist had repeatedly traced the figure. But at the same time, several white vertical drips appear like frozen brushstrokes—an effect heightened by the use of encaustic, which hardens into a thick, pasty consistency as it dries. Like the Abstract Expressionists who dominated the New York art world when Johns began showing in 1958, his painting technique stresses the immediate, material reality of his medium. But the introduction of subject matter and the use of encaustic—a medium that requires meticulous care—distance Johns's work from the spontaneity and abstraction of the New York School.

Since the beginning of his career, Johns has experimented with generic forms familiar to almost any viewer: flags, maps, numbers, letters, and targets. Instead of representing objects from the world and using painterly devices such as perspective to create the illusion of three-dimensional space, Johns paints symbols and signs directly on the canvas. There is no "original" number eight that served as a model for his painting. Johns thus subtly but irreversibly alters the function of artistic subject matter by using it to encourage us to reconsider precisely those things we thought we already knew. Johns was the first to fathom the potential richness of a range of familiar and even mass-produced visual forms. He has since produced four decades of supple experimentation with his medium and a rich and exacting dialogue with his viewers.

1. *Sixteen Americans*, ed. Dorothy C. Miller. (New York: Museum of Modern Art, 1959).

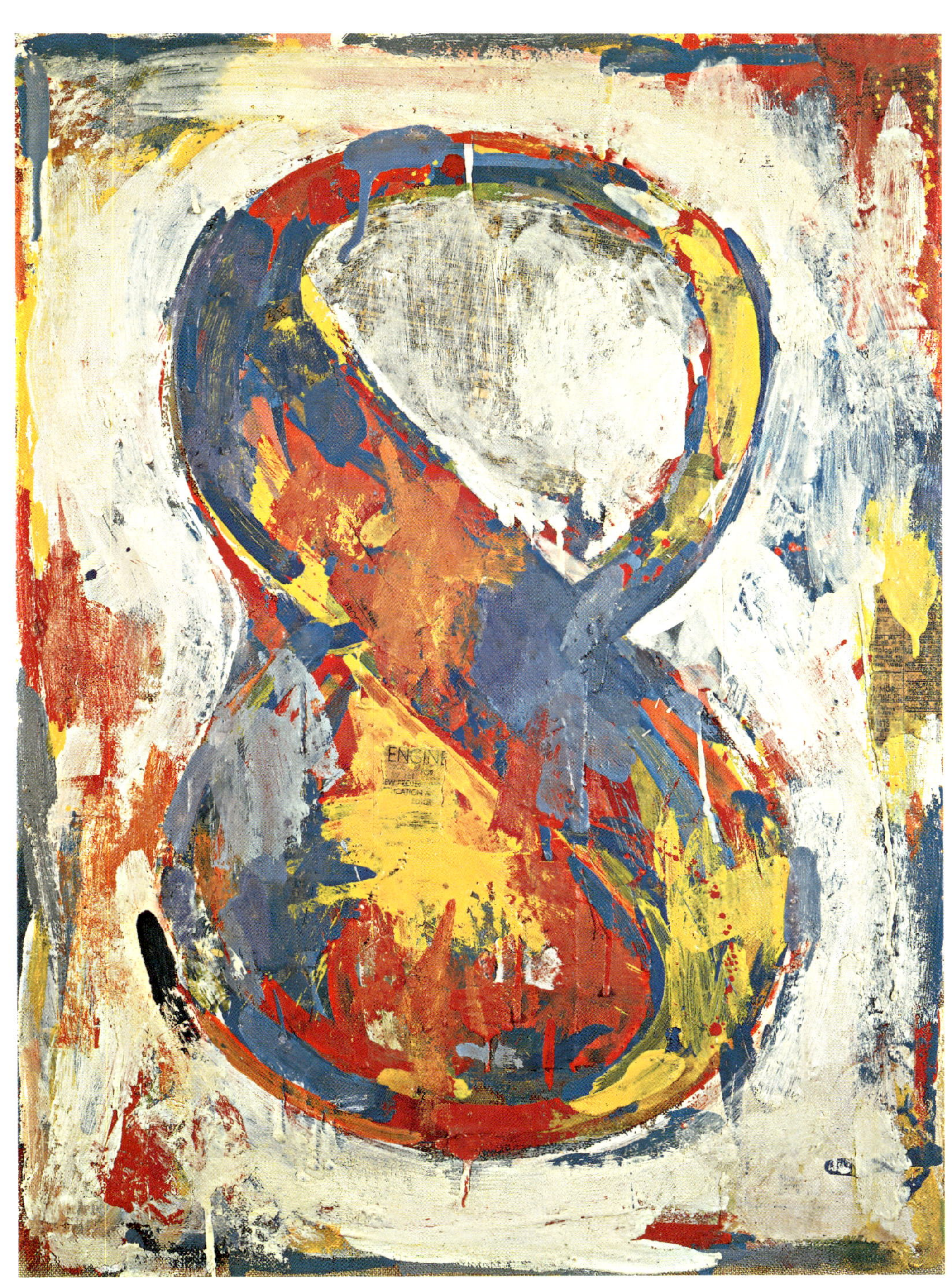

Tom Wesselmann

Still Life #45, 1962
Mixed media
35 x 48 in.

Tom Wesselmann's *Still Life #45*, a mixed-media work from 1962, first strikes the viewer with a powerfully iconic image then gradually reveals shades of complex artistic experimentation. A glistening roasted turkey is placed front and center, taking up almost the entire picture plane. It is set against a polychrome background composed of four Kodachrome hues—red, orange, yellow, and blue—painted in broad horizontal stripes across the entire width of the canvas. From the work's left edge peek three cutout roses, painted on a piece of board with the freehand loops of a practiced commercial style. The use of collage technique in Wesselman's work is unmistakable. The turkey—a vacuum-formed supermarket display—projects forcefully into the viewer's space, while the roses create actual shadows on the picture's surface. The initial effect resembles that of a photographer's preparatory staging—a dress rehearsal for a "real" painting, complete with color chart and proxy bouquet. But the lasting impression is of an artist profoundly invested in the formal issues of painting: composition, figure-ground relationships, and color.

Wesselmann's two best-known groups of work—the "Still Life" series, from 1962–64, and the roughly contemporaneous "Great American Nudes"—betray the idiosyncratic approach underlying his fascination with painting. His use of instantly recognizable subject matter and cool pseudo-realist visual style links Wesselmann to such Pop artists as Roy Lichtenstein and James Rosenquist. In fact Wesselmann's work is also profoundly indebted to the painterly innovations of Abstract Expressionists like Willem de Kooning, an artist he particularly admired. *Still Life #45*, for example, with its strong central motif balanced against an "allover" ground, echoes—with a decade's ironic distance—de Kooning's mid-1950s "Woman" series.

Seascape #14, painted a mere four years later, deals with many of the same formal concerns as *Still Life #45*, though this painting of a woman's foot against a haunting nighttime ocean view conveys a wholly different mood. Like a cartoonish cutout against a romantic vista, the foot is rendered with almost childlike or primitivist lines. Both an interruption and a focal point, it provides a central diagonal axis for the painting, yet its role is ambiguous. The foot has no identifying characteristics nor any obvious narrative role. By naming his work after the surrounding view rather than the more obvious choice of subject matter, Wesselmann again underscores the critical importance of formal issues and historical precedents in his art. Like the still life genre, the juxtaposition of a panoramic landscape and a strongly foregrounded object is an age-old painterly convention. Despite his deadpan humor, Wesselmann's careful reworking of such artistic tropes lends his work both internal consistency and historical sensitivity. Irrepressibly and unfailingly contemporary, he remains first and foremost a painter committed to his medium.

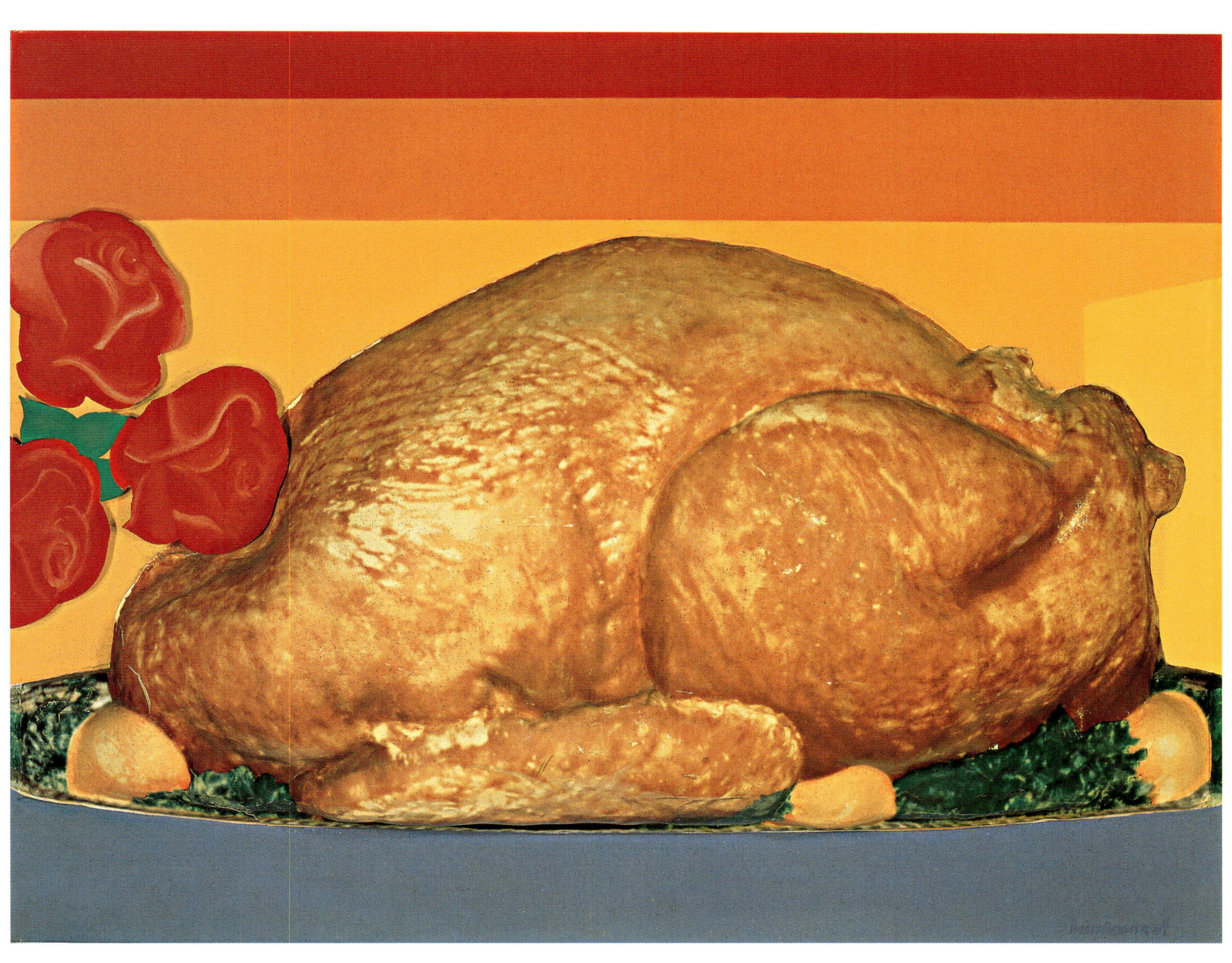

Robert Rauschenberg

Dylaby, 1962
Combine painting
109 1/2 x 87 x 15 in.

Dubbed "combines" by their author, the large-scale assemblages that Rauschenberg began making in 1954 are among his most celebrated works. *Bed*, 1955, features dramatic, gestural drips of paint across a patchwork quilt nailed to a stretcher. *Monogram*, 1958, includes a taxidermic Angora goat wearing a rubber tire around its middle. These works grew out of the incorporation of collage elements into Rauschenberg's otherwise abstract "Red Paintings" of 1953–54 and out of his intense dialogue with composer John Cage, choreographer Merce Cunningham, and fellow painter Jasper Johns. They testify to his exuberant embrace of all manner of "raw" material—as well as his sensitive dedication to the principles of formal composition.

In *Dylaby*, a combine from 1962, Rauschenberg begins with a large canvas tarp, half of which is attached to the wall and the other half left to drape in generous folds reaching the ground. A skateboard, a rusty Coca-Cola sign, and a few other tacked-up fragments create a spare, almost classical visual balance. Rauschenberg's recurring use of the color red imbues the work with a linear visual narrative, one that climaxes with a splotch of red paint outlined with black crayon as if for emphasis. The tines of dripping red that exceed this outline suggest a tension between design and artlessness, control and its opposite. Rauschenberg's handling of color also sets up a "call and response" dialogue between the artist's painted marks and the work's ready-made components. In *Dylaby*, the red, yellow, and white lettering of the Coca-Cola sign is echoed in two disks—one red, one yellow—set next to a large rectangular swatch of white paint. (In another nod to the self-conscious artistry underlying what at first appears a random configuration, a smaller blue disk above them invokes the familiar framework of the primary colors.) Then, two round stains in the lower center of the tarp echo the shapes of the red and yellow disks, so that one system of mimicry and repetition doubles another. Yet despite these precise compositional schemas, *Dylaby* has a spontaneous, almost slapdash feel. Its striking and inescapable heterogeneity—the rigor of its design contrasted with cheap or soiled discards, the elegance of its sculptural drapes contrasted with the spattered and dripping paint—is its defining feature.

Rauschenberg created *Dylaby* for an international exhibition of the same name. The show was held in 1962 at the Stedelijk Museum in Amsterdam and featured commissioned works from several young European and American artists. The exhibit's title was chosen by the curators to combine the two Dutch words *dynamisch* and *labyrinth*. Rauschenberg's own *Dylaby*, taking its cue from the exhibition's name, creates a microcosmic world of dynamic interactions, offering increasingly complex rewards to its viewers.

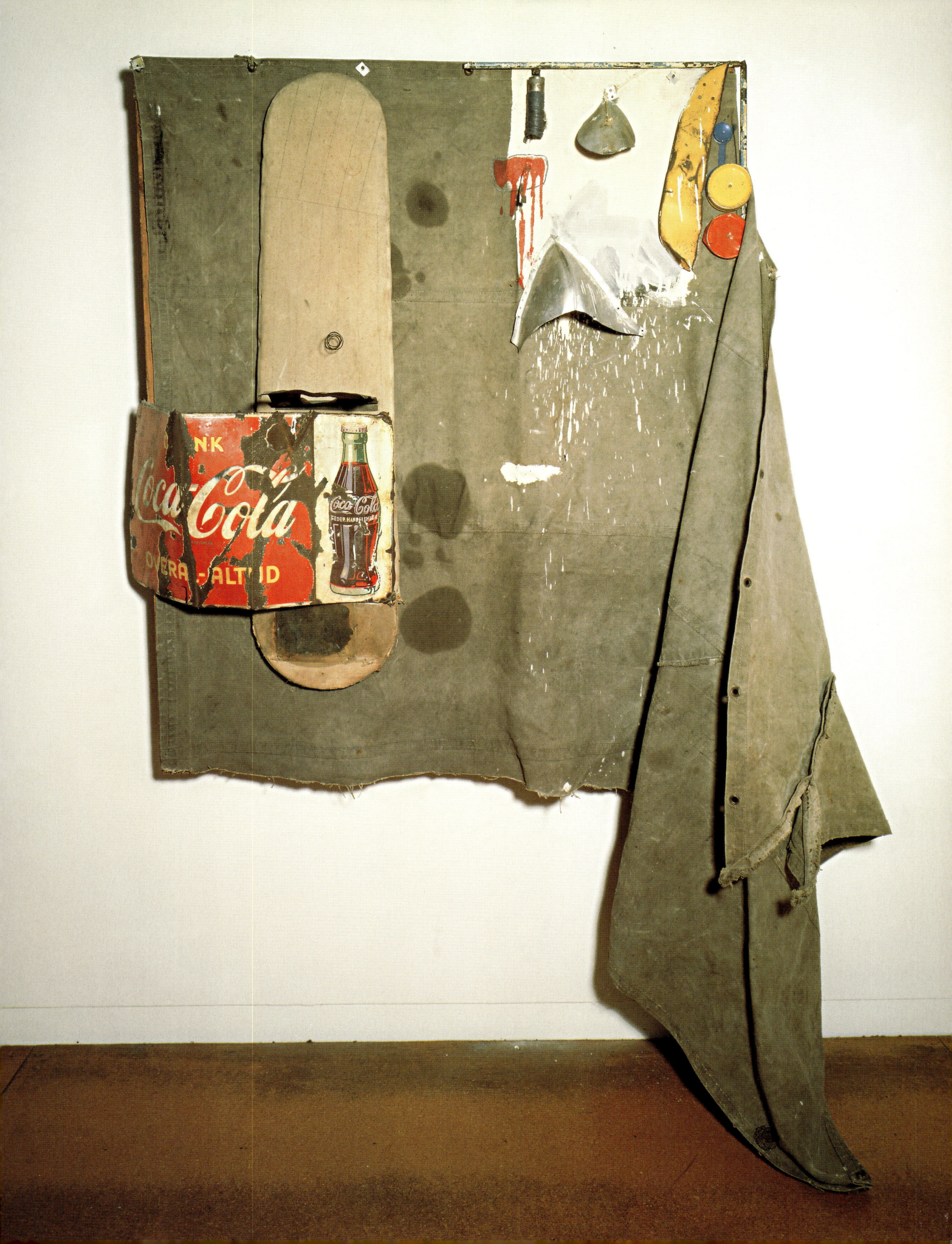
NK
Coca-Cola
OVERA -ALTID

Andy Warhol

Four Colored Campbell's Soup Cans, 1965
Acrylic and silkscreen on canvas
36 1/4 x 24 in. each
36 1/2 x 48 in. overall

Elizabeth Taylor's demure gaze stares out in each of Warhol's two silkscreen paintings from 1963: *Early Colored Liz (Turquoise)* and *Early Colored Liz (Chartreuse)*. If intimations of mortality seem to have seeped into the stagy lifelessness of Taylor's lipsticked grin, it is not accidental. Warhol began painting Taylor when she was critically ill, just as he first painted Marilyn Monroe after her suicide and Jackie Kennedy after her husband's assassination. It would seem that in Warhol's pantheon, beauty must be magnificently doomed.

The tension between an implied yet unknowable interior and a mask-like public persona marks all of Warhol's celebrity portraits, begun—along with his use of photo-silkscreen, originally a commercial technique—in 1962. Revealing the original newsprint image as an enlarged map of tiny dots, silkscreen functions as a photograph of a photograph, registering the artificiality of the original image in its new incarnation. Transformed by closely cropped compositions and bright washes of neon color, Warhol's silkscreens vividly illustrate both sides of America's fascination with celebrity: its vision of the "star" is simultaneously sentimental and garish, sensual and wholesome, intimate and untouchable.

Silkscreen remained a crucial technique in Warhol's inventory even as he moved into three dimensions. His *White Brillo Box*, *Del Monte Boxes*, and *Kellogg's Cornflakes Boxes* (all 1964) feature instantly recognizable commercial logos silkscreened onto white wooden cubes. In transforming everyday consumer products into sculptural units, Warhol drew a brilliant line of comparison with the Minimalist art of his day, from Sol LeWitt's clean modularity to Donald Judd 's strict geometric forms. When cast in more conventional artistic materials and left to stand alone, the cube serves as an imposing reminder of sculpture's most elemental and physically powerful capacities. Warhol's boxes, stacked haphazardly to reach nearly six feet, pit the power of such artistic forms against the clamoring advertisements printed on their sides.

Warhol enlarges both boxes and graphics to match the brands' aggressive claims, but adds nothing else—not a single trace of the artist's hand. This visual austerity parallels the "industrial" aesthetic of contemporaneous Minimalist work, in which steel, mirrors, and galvanized iron were borrowed from the field of manufacturing. Warhol thus deals two sets of claims at once: his works echo the visual appeal of advertising as well as the loftier ambitions of fine art. Through his simple gesture of mimicry, the distance between these two spheres emerges as an artificial and extremely fragile divide.

Nowhere is mimicry more famously exploited in Warhol's oeuvre than in his "Campbell's Soup Cans" series. In his 1962 installation at the Ferus Gallery in Los Angeles, Warhol remained faithful to the brand's iconic red-and-white color scheme and lined up thirty-two identically sized silkscreened canvases, each representing one of the brand's extant varieties, on a narrow shelf. The *Four Soup Cans* of 1965 present a single flavor—tomato—in four permutations. In yet another twist on assembly-line production, Warhol replaces Campbell's eye-catching red-and-white with a range of drab hues. Rendering suspect that which we think is most familiar, from the brand-name goods we consume daily to our cherished belief in art's originality, Warhol answers—even prefigures—the complex demands of contemporary society. His brilliant ability to make us see the germ of perversity inside our most commonplace habits and unexamined loyalties combines with his unerring aesthetic sensibility to create an art of inescapable relevance and allure.

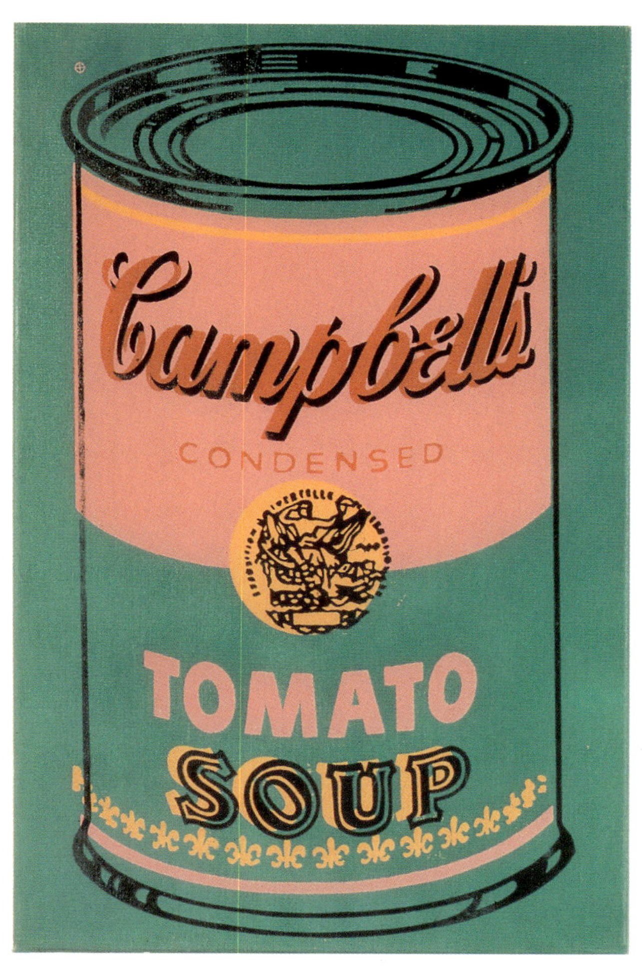
Campbell's
CONDENSED
TOMATO
SOUP

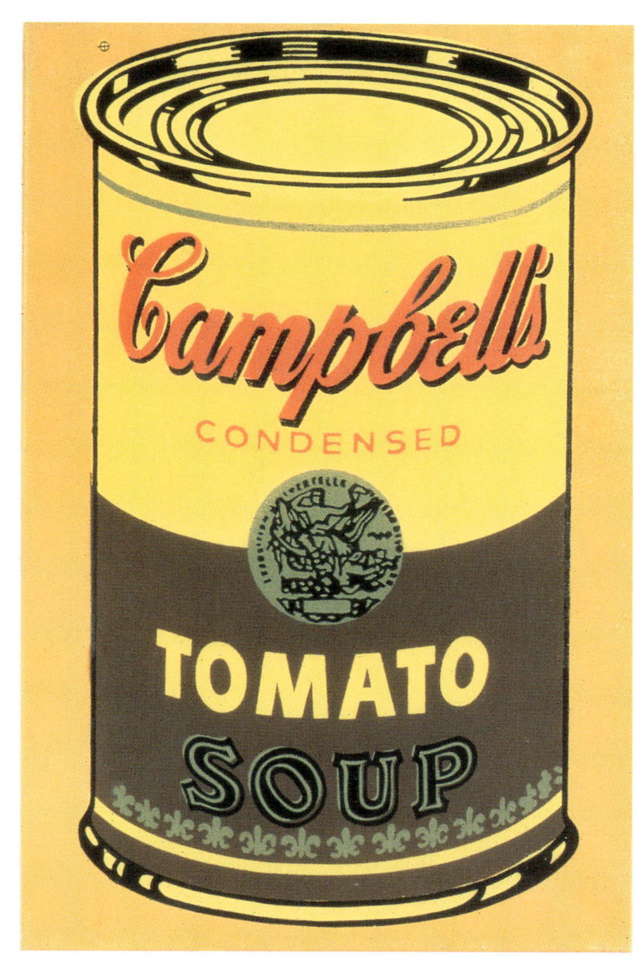
Campbell's
CONDENSED
TOMATO
SOUP

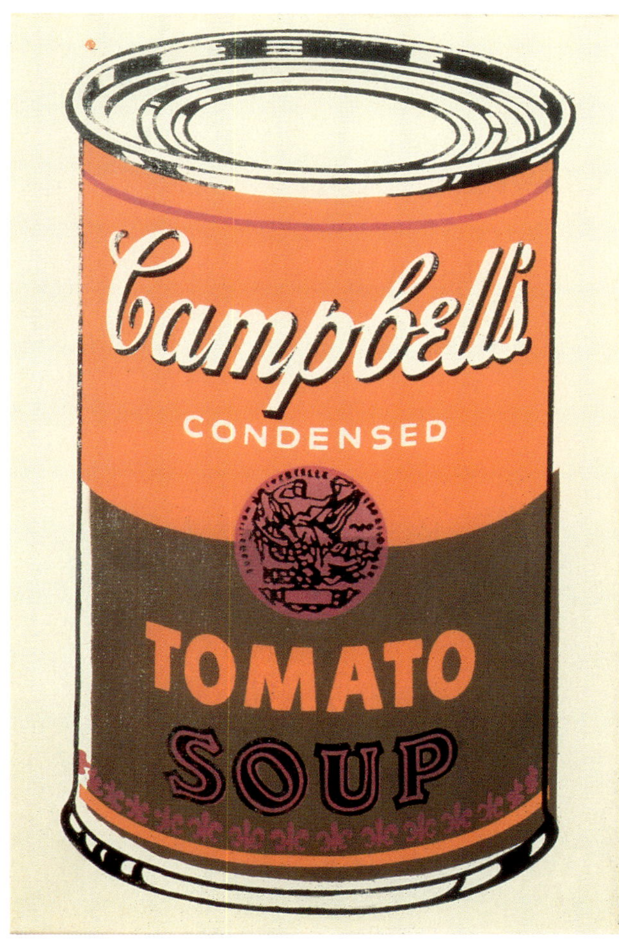
Campbell's
CONDENSED
TOMATO
SOUP

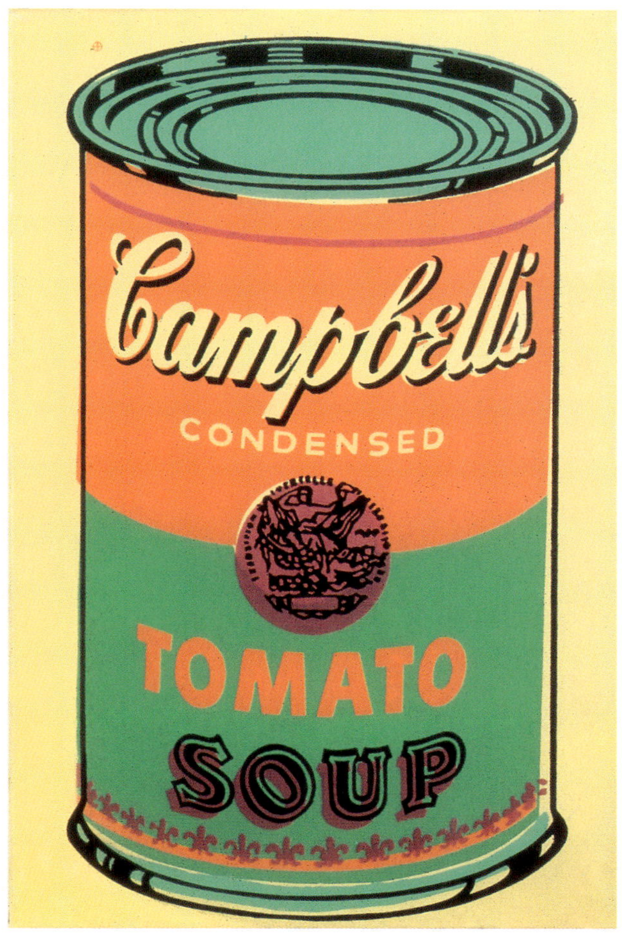
Campbell's
CONDENSED
TOMATO
SOUP

Andy Warhol
White Brillo Boxes, 1964
Silkscreen on wood
17 x 17 x 13 3/4 in. each
17 x 17 x 55 in. overall

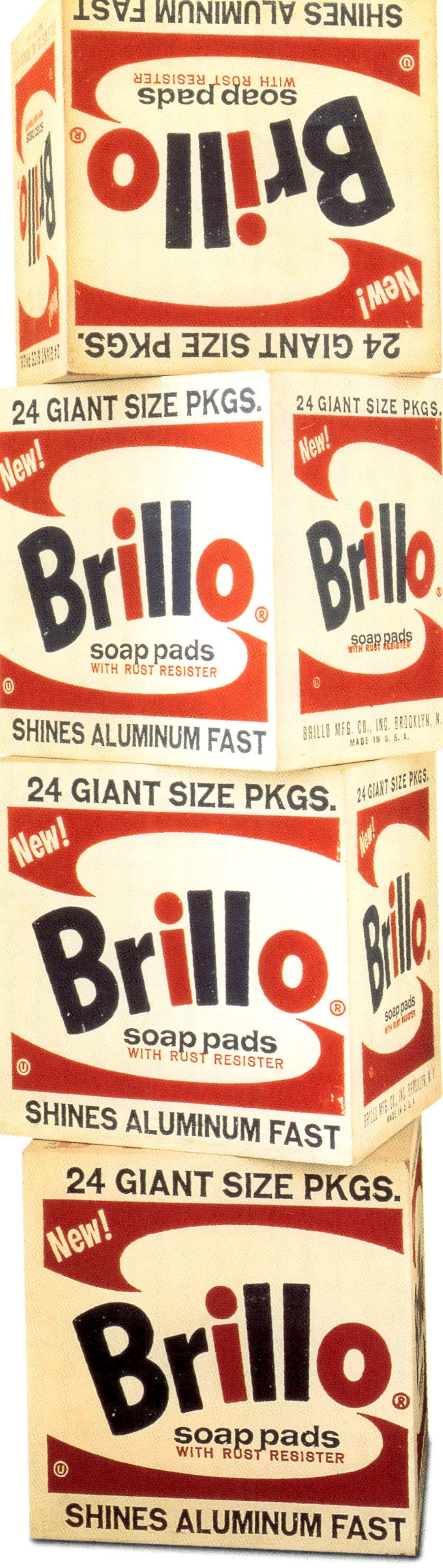
SHINES ALUMINUM FAST
Brillo
soap pads
WITH RUST RESISTER
New!
24 GIANT SIZE PKGS.
24 GIANT SIZE PKGS.
New!
Brillo
soap pads
WITH RUST RESISTER
SHINES ALUMINUM FAST
24 GIANT SIZE PKGS.
New!
Brillo
soap pads
WITH RUST RESISTER
BRILLO MFG. CO., INC. BROOKLYN, N.Y.
MADE IN U.S.A.
24 GIANT SIZE PKGS.
New!
Brillo
soap pads
WITH RUST RESISTER
SHINES ALUMINUM FAST
24 GIANT SIZE PKGS.
New!
Brillo
soap pads
WITH RUST RESISTER
SHINES ALUMINUM FAST

Andy Warhol
Early Colored Liz (Turquoise), 1963
Silkscreen on canvas
40 x 40 in.

Early Colored Liz (Chartreuse), 1963
Silkscreen on canvas
40 x 40 in.

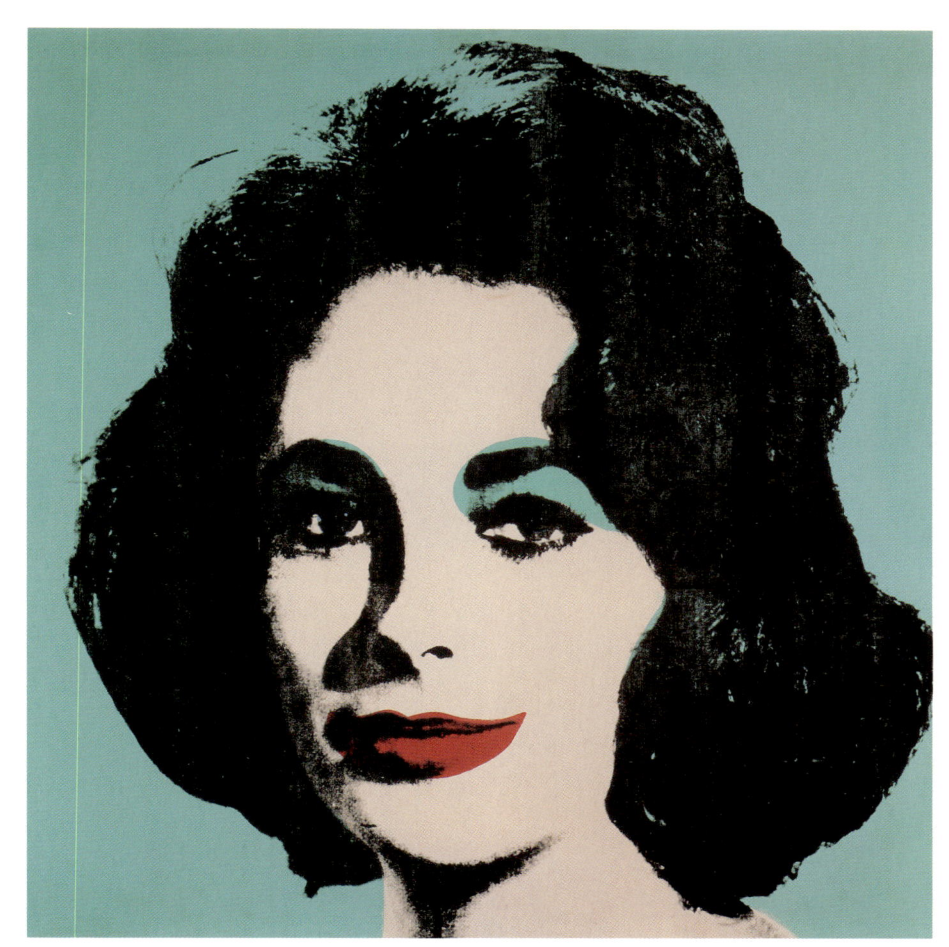

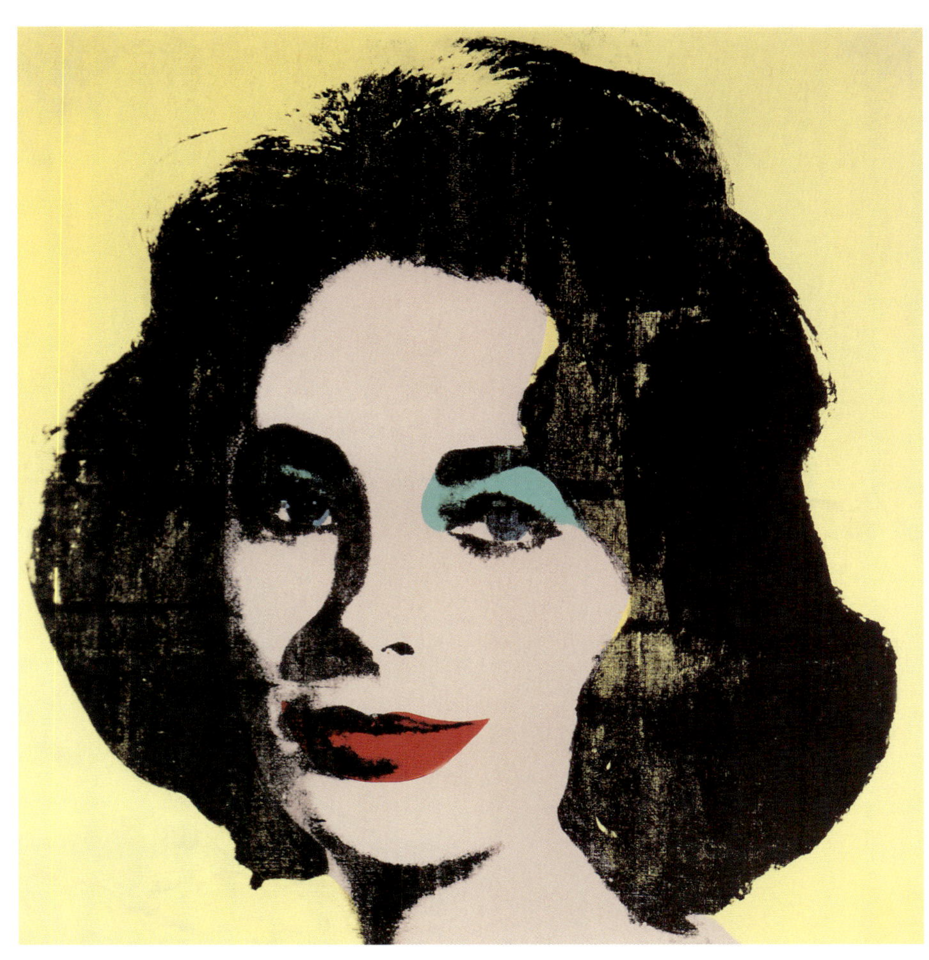

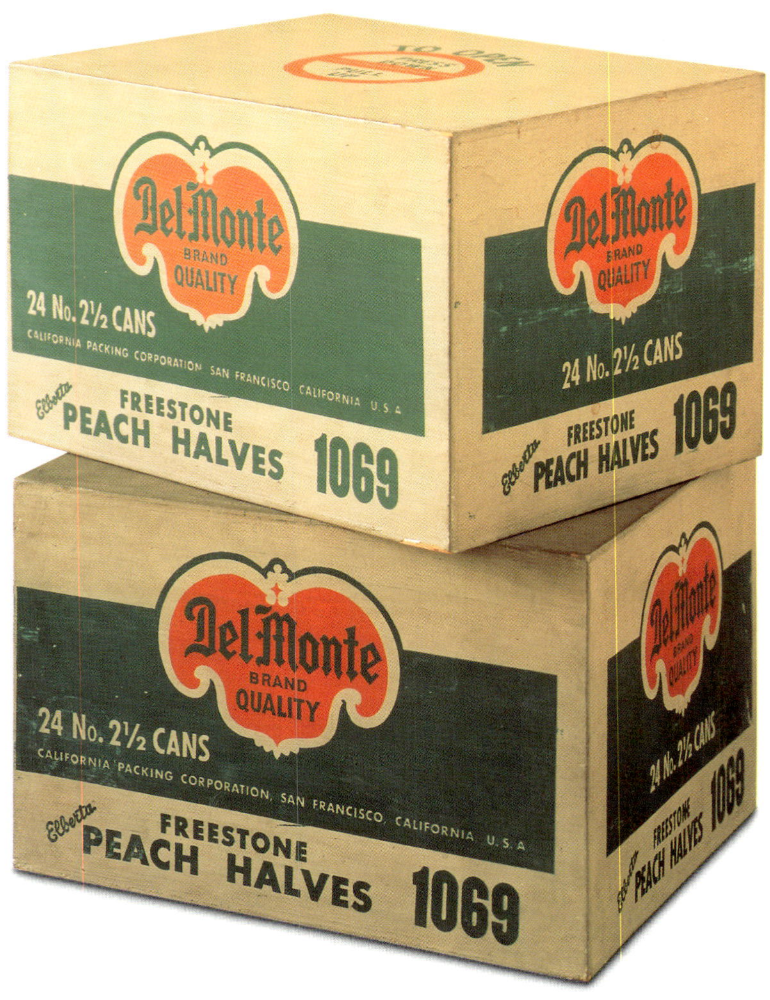

Andy Warhol
Del Monte Boxes, 1964
Two boxes, silkscreen on wood
9 1/16 x 15 x 11 3/4 in. each
9 1/16 x 15 x 23 1/2 in. overall

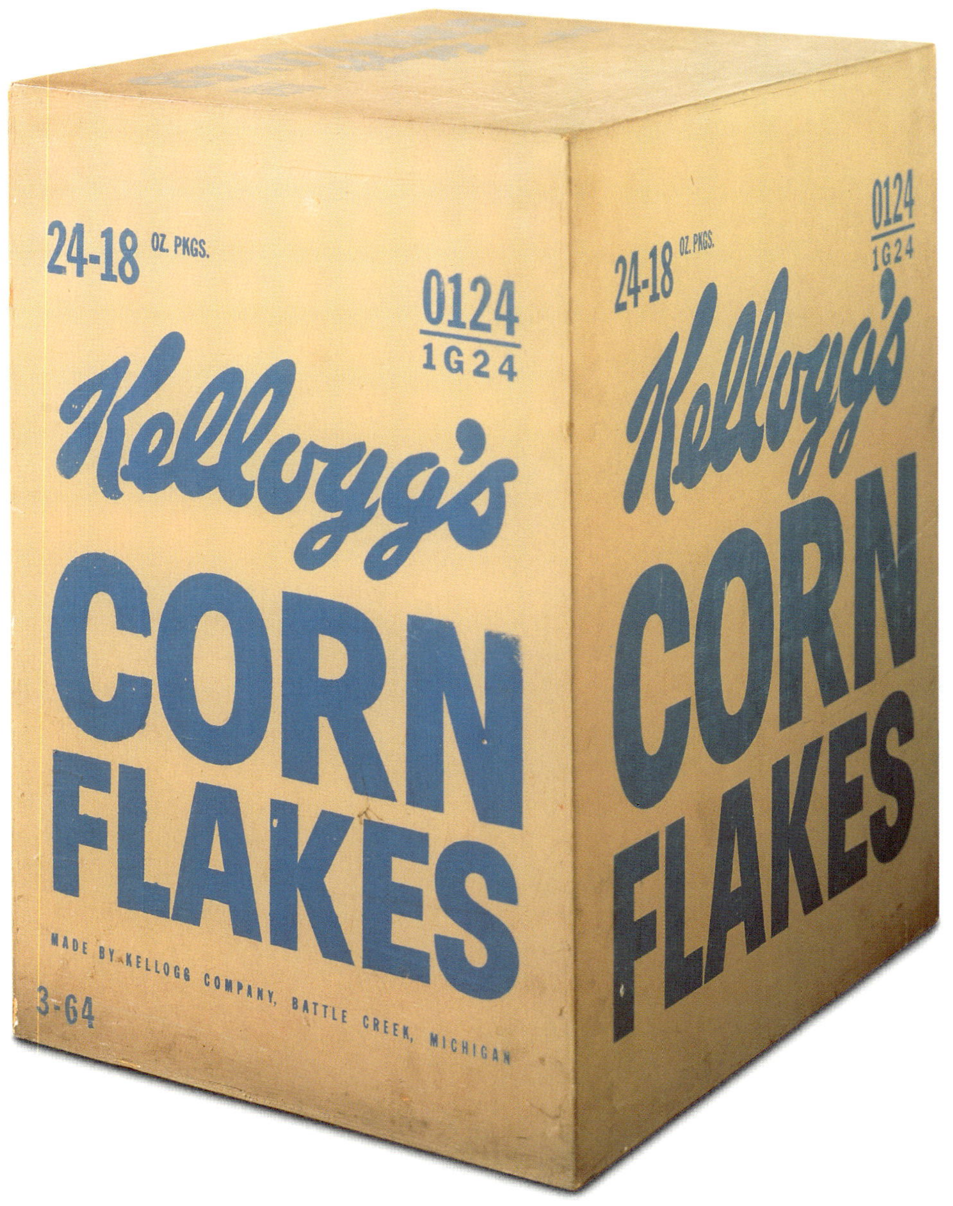

Andy Warhol
Kellogg's Cornflakes Boxes (detail), 1964
Two boxes, silkscreen on canvas
24 13/16 x 20 7/8 x 16 15/16 in. each
24 13/16 x 20 7/8 x 33 15/16 in. overall

Claes Oldenburg

Giant Ice Cream Cone, 1962
Enamel on muslin soaked in plaster
over wire frame
13 3/4 x 37 3/8 x 13 3/8 in.

Claes Oldenburg's "soft sculptures" of the early 1960s grew out of the props he made for his Happenings—the performance art genre that he and other artists including Jim Dine, George Segal, and Allan Kaprow produced at the time. From Kaprow's *18 Happenings in 6 Parts*, of 1959, which joined the careful choreography of simple everyday movements with music, lighting, and slide projections, to the vaudevillian tableaux of urban squalor in Oldenburg's *Ray Gun Spex*, of 1960, the Happenings epitomized the era's explosion of artistic energy. Enlarged to fifteen or eighteen feet, Oldenburg's props included airplanes and human figures, but it wasn't until *Store Days*, his 1961 storefront performance/environment/artwork in New York's East Village, that he began to think of these oversize sewn-together objects as sculptures. The "merchandise" in Oldenburg's store—painted plaster reliefs and soft sculptures—imitated such items as foodstuffs, typewriters, and telephones. Costing as little as $69.95, his pieces were "priced to sell." Garishly painted, grotesquely enlarged and misshapen, the works filled his store like so many dreams of everyday objects, full of pathos and wry humor.

Over three feet long and one foot in diameter, *Giant Ice Cream Cone*, 1962, was made on a scale that shrugs at sculptural convention, responding instead to what might be someone's idle dream of a gargantuan, sweet, dripping ice-cream cone. Its coloring—the gleaming dark brown cone, topped by a syrupy mix of white and yellow with green swirled in—is a nod to the hues of familiar commercial products rather than to standards of aesthetic beauty. Oldenburg also departed from artistic norms by incorporating aspects of domestic labor into the creation of his work. Most of his sculptures from the early '60s started with a homemade model from which Oldenburg made a stencil pattern on cloth. He then cut according to the stenciled shapes and sewed and stuffed them, usually using a wire armature. Either the fabric was soaked in plaster so that it would harden, as in *Giant Ice Cream Cone*, or was left "soft." Instead of building up clay or wax or cutting away a solid block of stone, Oldenburg constructed his sculptures from the outside in. His pneumatic forms owe their bulging and rutted contours to their irregular filling, while his surface textures, unlike modeled sculpture, betray no sign of the artist's hand. The objects' ungainliness reminds us that simple consumer products—even edibles that disappear in seconds—never, in fact, play a simple role in our lives. The sad, deflated folds of a "soft" typewriter might remind some viewers of the exhausting, creative, or routine labor of writing; the plaster-hardened muslin that straitjackets an ice-cream cone perhaps evokes the latter's unfaltering status as an object of collective desire.

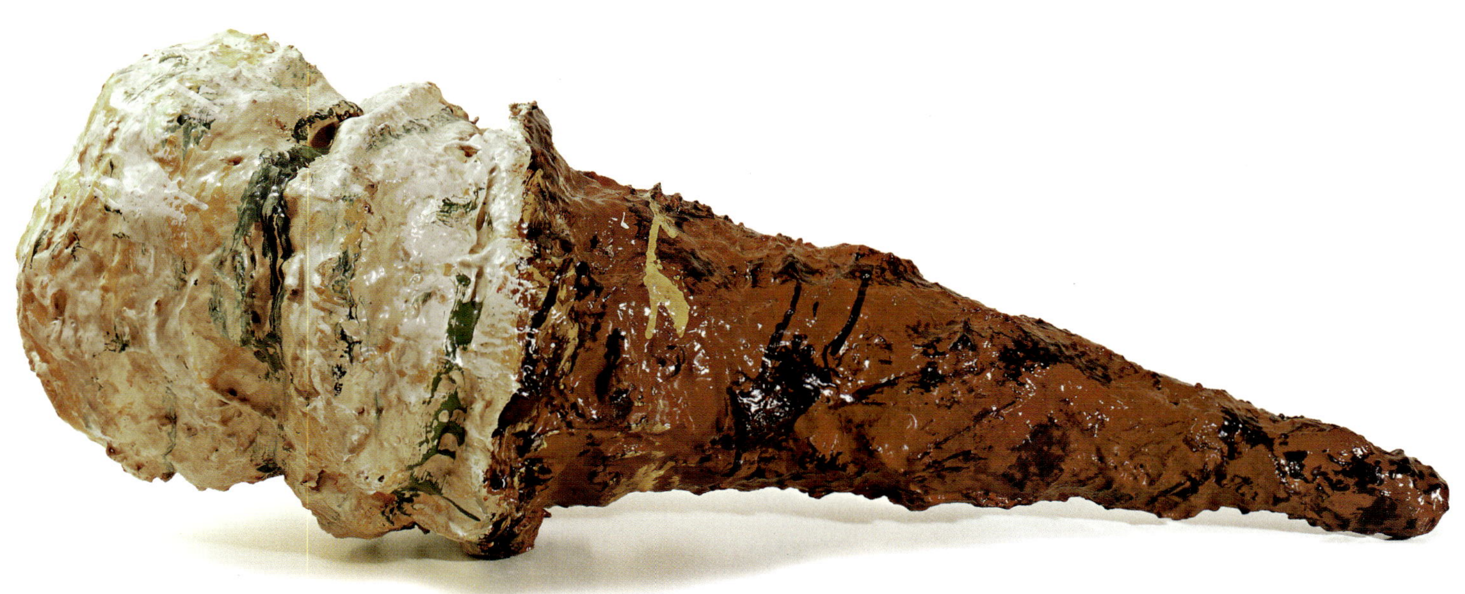

Arman

Grande poubelle, 1962
Accumulation in Plexiglas
49 1/4 x 24 7/8 x 24 3/8 in.

The "*Poubelles*," a series Arman began in 1960, are essentially his own collections of household or public trash, conserved in Plexiglas cases. Arman discovered this unconventional artistic form when, after experimenting briefly with the creation of assemblages using discarded debris collected from public spaces, he one day unloaded the entire unaltered contents of his mother-in-law's garbage into a glass container. Like time capsules or entombed relics, the *Poubelles* provide a record of local patterns of consumption. But unlike these analogues, the works have no obvious scientific or spiritual function. Rather, they testify to Arman's search for a new art, one that would not seek to *represent* objects from the real world, thereby affirming the age-old division between art and life. His art, instead, presents the passage of actual objects through society, bringing social life literally inside the artwork.

Grande poubelle, from 1962, has several crucial defining features. Strongly monochromatic, crowded with gray lint and cardboard brown papers, its most conspicuous elements are textual: a piece of paper with the handwritten heading "TO MY MUSE"; typed and handwritten word and sentence fragments; and packaging miscellany. Secondly, the trash is American, locating the site of its production outside the artist's native France. By 1960, Paris, so long the boastful center of avant-garde activity, had been marginalized, while New York claimed the spotlight after the war. But in the early sixties, an exchange suddenly opened up between American Pop artists and their European counterparts, culminating in several international group fairs and exhibits in 1962. *Grande poubelle*, replenishing Arman's French-born artistic concept with American trash, reflects this new international dialogue.

Also in 1962 Arman exhibited his "Automatic Garbage Cans," works to which gallery-goers and gallery attendants were invited to contribute their own garbage. Arman's *Poubelles*, formerly the results of his own private garbage collections, became dependent on viewer participation—"works in progress" that were far from realized when he installed them in a gallery. This provocative twist brought to the fore new aspects of the close rapport between art and consumerism, a relation that has fascinated twentieth-century artists from Kurt Schwitters to Andy Warhol. In Arman's case, this interest is coupled with a rejection of traditional aesthetic considerations such as composition and design: Arman refuses to alter or order his raw material and simply immobilizes it under Plexiglas. While garbage may strike us as too intimate or repugnant for public display, it is precisely the borderline between the public and private, the social and the aesthetic, that the *Poubelles* investigate. *Grande poubelle*, implacable and mute yet fascinating, invites us to examine what constitutes and defines aesthetic interest and its voyeuristic, sociological, or narcissistic counterparts and components.

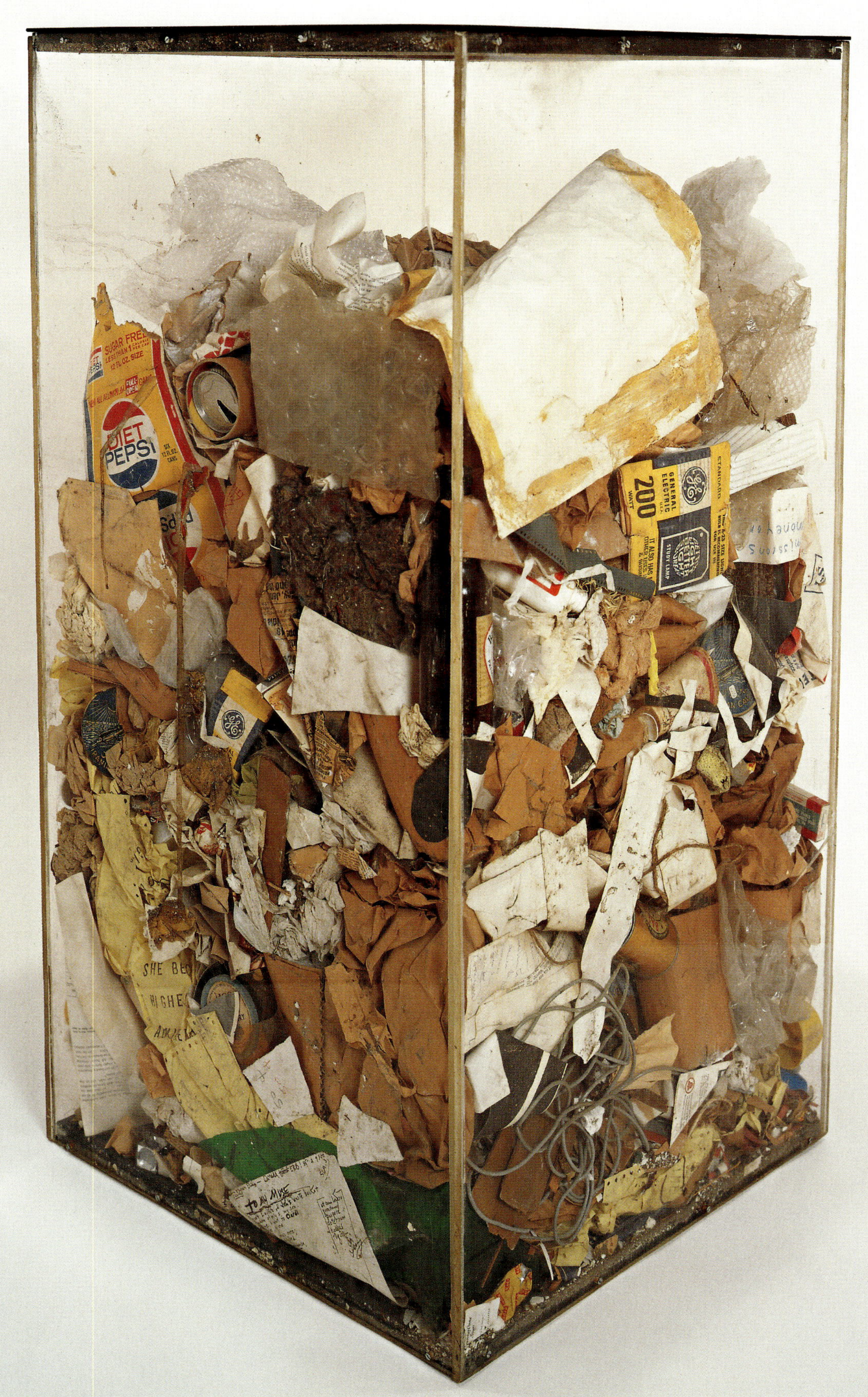
SUGAR FREE
DIET PEPSI
GENERAL ELECTRIC
200

Jim Dine

Proposed Still Life, 1962
Objects and oil on canvas
83 7/8 x 35 7/8 in.

Jim Dine's 1962 *Proposed Still Life* bears witness to the complexity of this artist's unclassifiable oeuvre. Though Dine came of age in New York together with such Pop artists as Roy Lichtenstein and Claes Oldenburg, and though his work shares some of Pop's familiar iconography, it delves into areas that in Pop were typically repressed. Most significant, many of Dine's works engage the associative powers of familiar or symbolic objects and can be seen in a profoundly autobiographical light. His extensive use of tools and other hardware-store staples, for instance, has often been linked to the teenage years Dine spent living with his grandparents after his mother's death and his father's remarriage. His grandfather owned a hardware and plumbing supply store where Dine worked while beginning his formal art training. This period is evoked symbolically in the small assortment of tools—pliers, hatchet, saw, and so forth—hung together from a single hook at the top of *Proposed Still Life*'s nearly seven-foot-high canvas. The "still life" is indeed only a "proposition," an idea or plan still unrealized—a fact signified by both the presence of the objects themselves and the childlike scrawl at the bottom: *THEN A GREY SCREW DRIVER, THEN A RED HATCHET, THEN A YELLOW PLYERS [sic]*, and so on. With its bitten-off beginning and repetitive, almost autistic syntax, Dine's text is both classification and fragment, a list that might serve as a clerk's ledger or a dream's slivered imagery. On one level it recalls a down-to-earth competence and on another, a suggestive lyricism. This inexorable duality, between the candid banality of much of Pop's imagery and an almost surrealist exploration of the complex relationship between word and image, runs through Dine's work.

A broad expanse of matte gray paint applied in sponged layers enlivened by patches of shiny brushwork, *Proposed Still Life* gives little indication of the vivid colors Dine "sees" in his list of tools. But the tools themselves are painted with splotches of lilac blue, primary red, and peachy orange, their vividness intruding on and even dominating the abstract canvas. Dine's treatment of these ordinary household objects gives concrete form to the effect that Marcel Duchamp's readymades have had on painting throughout the twentieth century. In 1917 Duchamp submitted an industrially manufactured porcelain urinal to an exhibition committee to be displayed as a work of art. The act of selecting a "ready-made," mass-produced object and proposing that act as an artwork in its own right suggested there was no need to actually paint a work of art again. Instead, artists of subsequent generations have taken up Duchamp's provocation, transforming it into a device that enriches their work. *Proposed Still Life*'s pileup of ordinary tools set against a highly textured and painterly field of abstraction irreverently challenges Duchamp. But, remaining true to his idiosyncratic project, Dine has also created a work that balances imposing, almost classical formal symmetry with unexpected playfulness and unusual psychological depth.

then a gray screw driver, then a red hatchet, then
a yellow pliers, then a blue vise, then a
green drill, then a violet C clamp, then an
orange level, then a flesh chisel then a

James Rosenquist

Balcony, 1961
Oil on canvas, mirror, Plexiglas
59 7/8 x 72 7/8 in.

Balcony, from 1961, is one of James Rosenquist's first works to contain materials not traditionally found in painting. It features a square mirror near the upper right-hand corner and a rectangular piece of Plexiglas in the center of the image. Starting in 1962–63, tin, clear plastic, aluminum, wood, and mirrored glass began to appear regularly in Rosenquist's almost mural-size paintings. These additions are in many ways comparable to Jasper Johns's and Robert Rauschenberg's experimentation with newsprint, fabric, and other elements from daily life. Rosenquist's use of recognizable subjects culled from mass culture also aligns him with Pop artists like Roy Lichtenstein and Andy Warhol. But the vast scale, cinematic feel, and distinctly suburban iconography of Rosenquist's painting set it stylistically apart from the work of his contemporaries.

In the shellacked curves of a woman's golden bouffant hairdo and the debonair flash of a man's cufflink—the two motifs that seem about to fit together like pieces of a puzzle in the center of *Balcony*—an entire, clichéd history of dry martinis, manicured lawns, and backyard swimming pools seems about to click into vivid motion. The flat, anonymous banality of Rosenquist's painting technique has an overtly commercial look, one that is often attributed to his early training as a sign painter. But employed in massive paintings this technique endows larger-than-life forms with a surreal, three-dimensional plasticity. Rosenquist heightens this otherworldly effect by using a white-lead base to mix his colors, which gives them a filtered, almost Technicolor appearance. Finally he fragments and juxtaposes the objects in his painting so that the apparently arbitrary combinations seem to follow an idiosyncratic, dreamlike logic.

In *Balcony*, the vacuity of Rosenquist's iconography—a panorama of the suburban banal—echoes in the void that is signified by the mirror in the corner. Depending on one's physical position, the mirror may also reflect the viewer's gaze, interrupting the act of viewing with a reminder of that act itself—along with other acts of viewing. For inside Rosenquist's massively scaled work are shards of an intimate, perhaps clandestine encounter, which also inevitably brings to mind scenes from movies and television. Rosenquist's painting thus suggests that in contemporary life the most public and private spaces of perception can never be completely separated. In *Balcony*, widely recognizable subject matter is closely coupled with the private challenge of contemplating Rosenquist's vast and cryptic image.

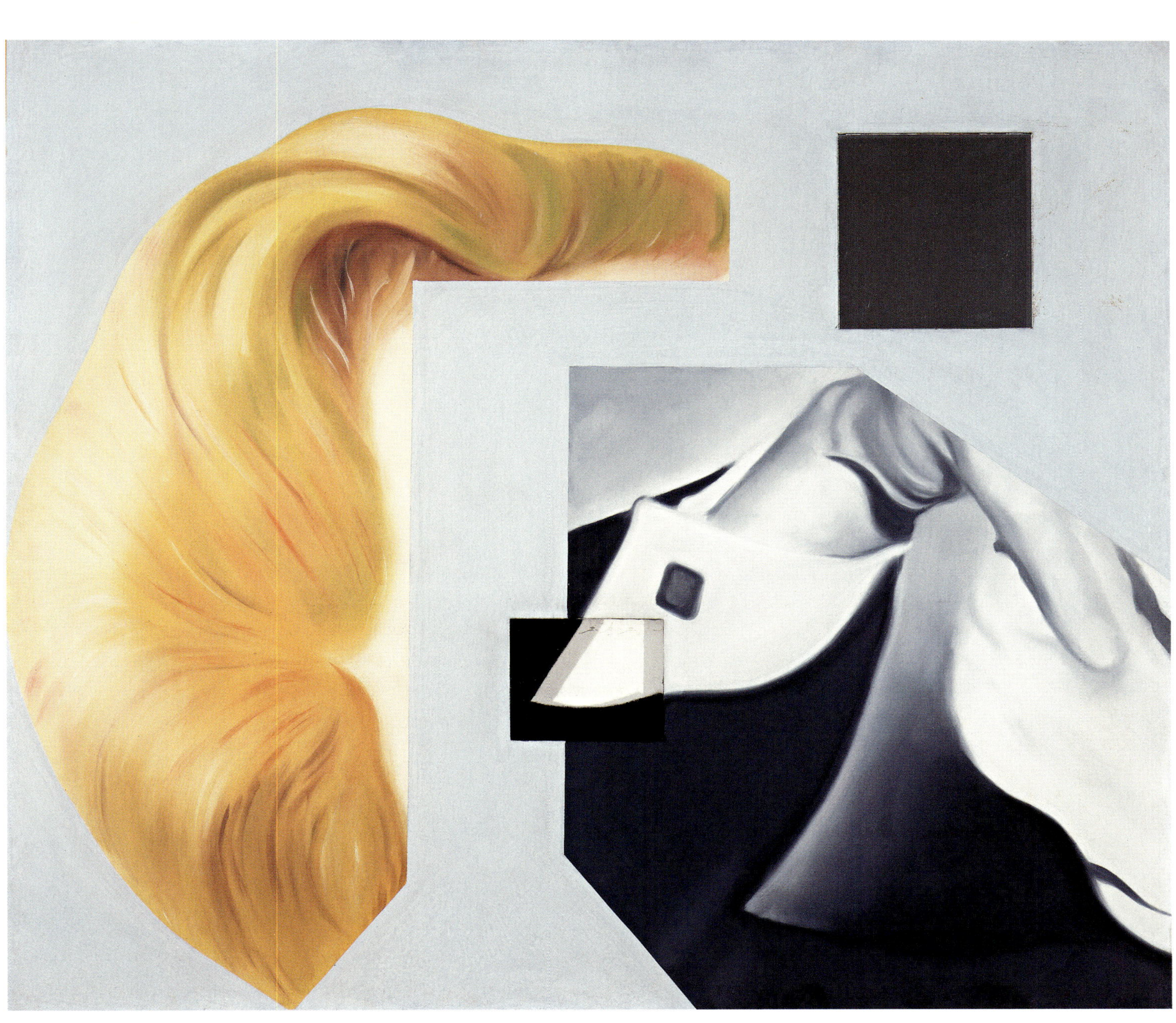

Roy Lichtenstein

Little Aloha, 1962
Acrylic on canvas
44 1/16 x 42 1/8 in.

Along with Andy Warhol, Roy Lichtenstein is one of the first contemporary American artists to have made commercial imagery the subject of his work. His paintings of the early and mid-1960s often feature comic-book characters and magazine reproductions of household objects. *Little Aloha*, 1962, for example, presents a sultry tropical beauty who could be either an advertiser's fantasy or a cartoon seductress. *Wall Explosion*, 1965, resembles a vividly imagined detonation from the Sunday supplement's comics, while *Large Spool*, 1963, magnifies an ordinary spool of hardware-store string. During this period Lichtenstein also turned his attention to famous works of modern art—the kind one might find reproduced and sold in postcard form at museum stores. Lichtenstein's "artistic" subjects include Monet's haystacks, Picasso's nudes, and Piet Mondrian's geometric compositions, which serve as the basis for *Non-Objective II*, 1964.

Lichtenstein not only appropriated the icons of popular culture, he also mimicked the techniques used to reproduce images on a mass scale. Many of his paintings contain rows of small dots, which resemble an enlargement of the almost invisible benday dots used in newspaper illustration. Dividing his compositions into broad expanses of either flat color or regimented dots, he imbued his paintings with a screenlike artificiality. Lichtenstein's technique also subtly reveals how contemporary technology affects our perception of the objects it represents. His dots give a milky opacity to *Wall Explosion*'s gray cloud, a glib velvetiness to *Little Aloha*'s expanse of skin, an exaggerated unreality to the all too ordinary cylinder of *Large Spool*. In *Non-Objective II* they add a witty twist to Mondrian's habit of replacing "pure" white with a range of slightly "off" neutrals, by likening those subtle shades to smudged newsprint. Into pop culture's apparently straightforward imagery Lichtenstein introduced a brilliant formal inventiveness; into the privileged realm of fine art he inserted a wry joke about painting's originality. In Lichtenstein's work, painting—including his own—becomes something that can be translated by the technologies of mass media, while the perceptual transformations wrought by those very technologies become the subject of Lichtenstein's explorations.

Although emulating the appearance of mechanical reproduction, Lichtenstein's works were all handpainted according to a time-consuming and rigorously methodical process. Starting with a cartoon or photograph, he would create a small drawing that sometimes combined aspects of several images. Then, projecting his drawing onto a canvas, he would redraw directly on the canvas, making precise formal modifications: In *Little Aloha* he cropped the original forms, producing a crowding-in effect that emphatically focuses our attention on the cosmetic high points of his subject's beauty: her kohl-lined eyes, manicured nails, and ruby red mouth. By dramatically reducing his tonal range—his palette in the sixties consisted of only four colors, plus black and white—Lichtenstein further distilled an impression of artificiality. His addition of a vaguely exotic floral pattern behind the woman's right arm conjures similar decorative elements used by Gauguin and Matisse. But the overall effect of the painting is that of an extremely simple and concentrated composition. Simultaneously magnifying and simplifying, Lichtenstein's work draws the viewer's attention to the rules of representation that have been endlessly refined by television, newsprint, advertising, and films. Giving them a new life in high art, his work exposes the creative possibilities latent even in the limits imposed by their technologies. At the same time, his pop iconography and supple visual sensibility furnished Lichtenstein with an utterly original means of painting.

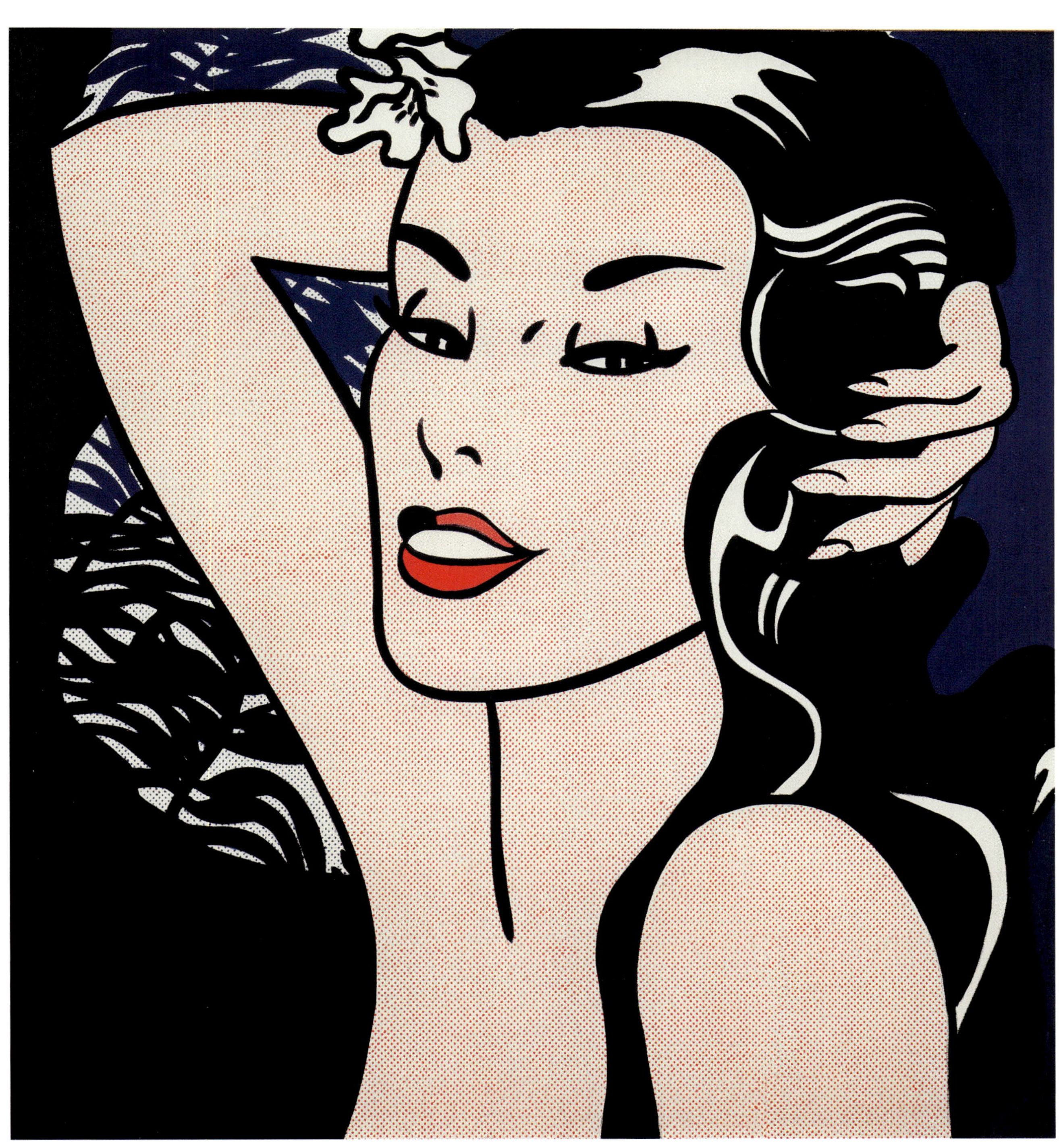

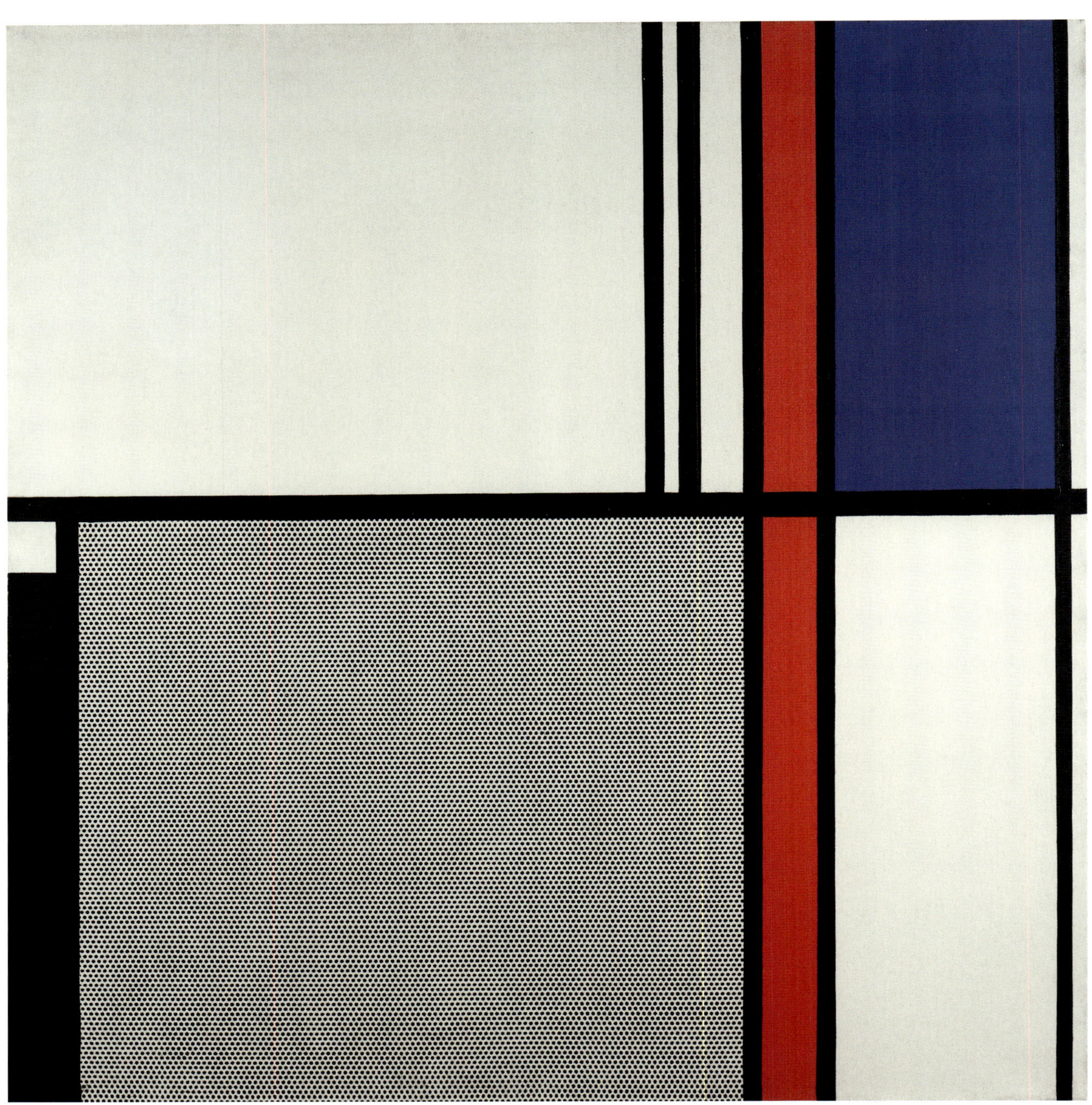

Roy Lichtenstein
Non-Objective II, 1964
Oil on canvas
48 x 48 in.

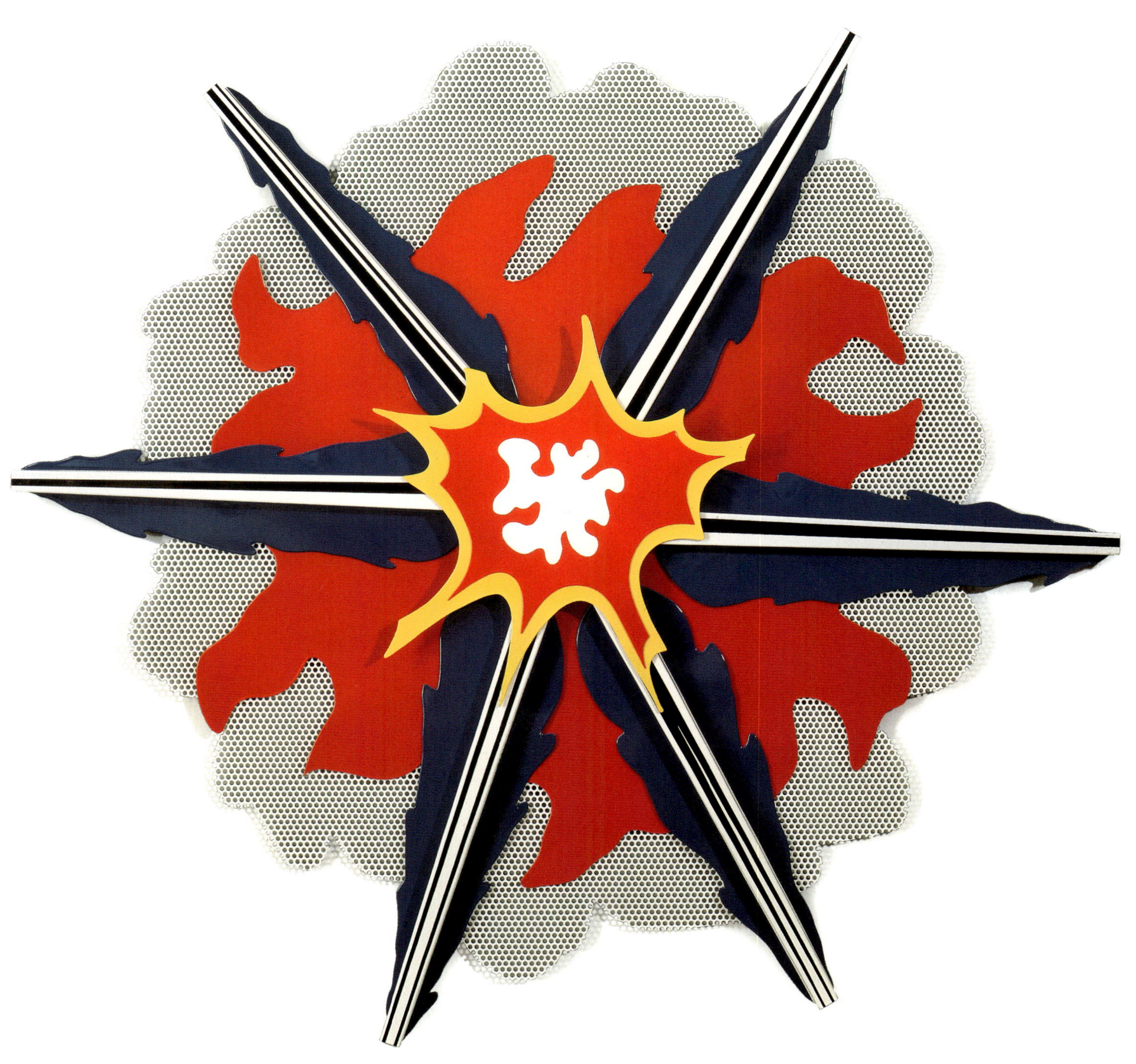

Roy Lichtenstein
Wall Explosion, 1965
Enamel on steel
76 3/4 x 83 3/4 in.

Roy Lichtenstein
Large Spool, 1963
Acrylic on canvas
68 x 55 in.

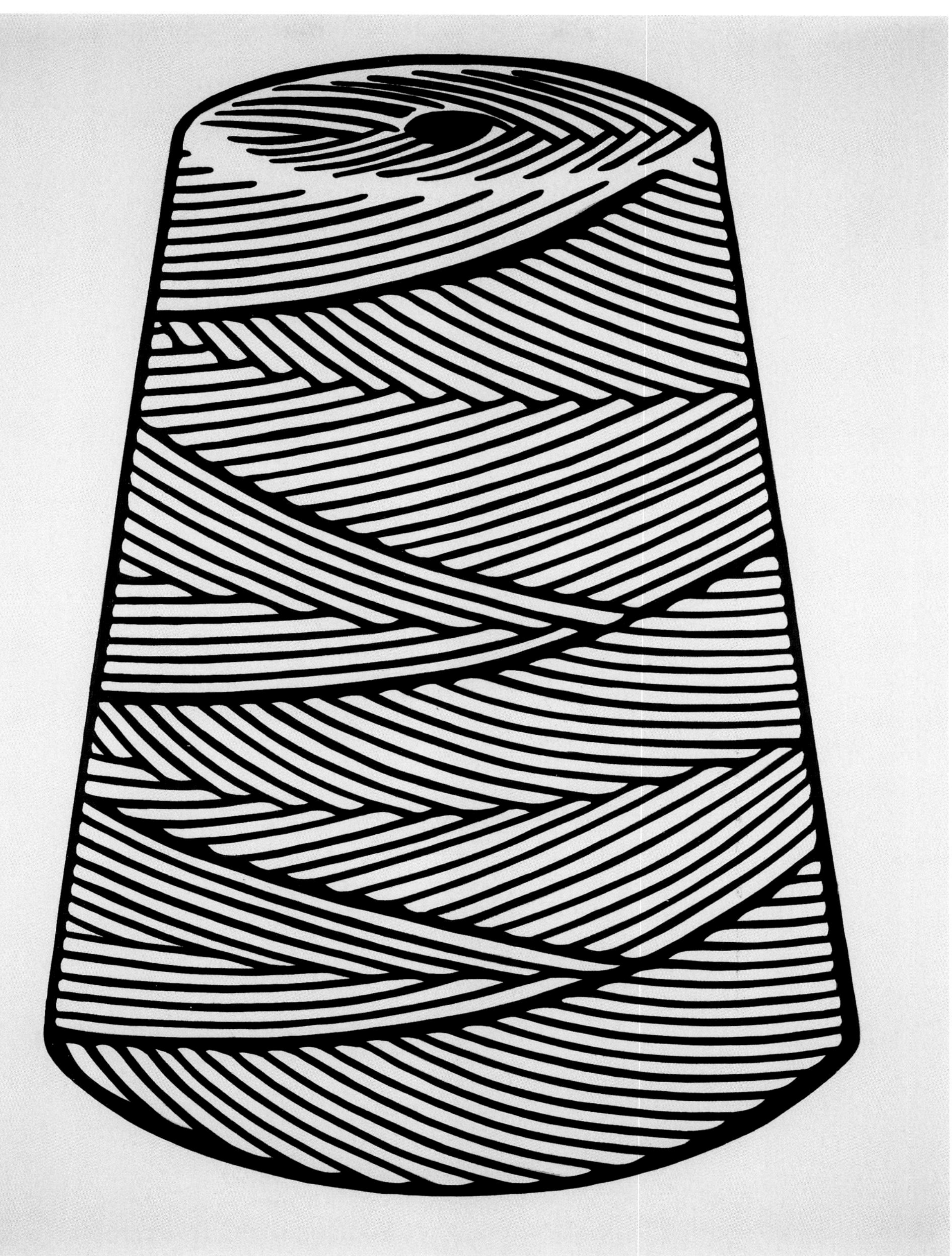

Cy Twombly

Untitled, 1956
Oil and crayon on canvas
48 1/16 x 63 in.

In *Untitled*, a work from 1956, Cy Twombly uses a distinctive technique that he developed in the mid-fifties. Applying pencil and crayon directly on wet paint—a highly unusual practice that produces the many layers and contrasting textures seen in *Untitled*—Twombly mixes a medium that is normally associated with canvas with those normally found on paper. The result is a richly varied work; from the grassy verticals at the bottom of the canvas to the slanting, rounded loops at the top, passing through the thickly compressed scribbles and erasures in the middle, *Untitled* is a picture with enormous movement and textural scope. The surface activity thickens as one "reads" the canvas from left to right, from the sparse left edge to the frenzied chaos of the right half. But *Untitled* also "goes deep": layers of half-erased lines and red crayon marks suggest a depth stretching behind the picture plane. This field of muffled, fading activity contrasts with the scratchy textures and vivid commotion of the work's surface.

Surface is an ambiguous notion in *Untitled.* The flatness of painting's natural plane was a crucial issue in the fifties, when emphasis on a medium's fundamental, inherent qualities was interpreted as the hallmark of modernism. But in Twombly's work, both flatness and the integrity of his medium are called into question. Heavy pencil lines move across slick patches of oily manila house paint, producing a discontinuous yet oddly uninterrupted surface whose flatness is far from apparent. In addition, Twombly uses pencil to make lines that are emphatically non-artistic—that is, lines that seem void of the skill and function that we associate with artist's sketches and drawings. Instead, they strongly recall scribbled epithets, frustrated marginalia, scrawled verse fragments. This graphic inundation, which recurs constantly in Twombly's work, produces a corollary realm to painting—that of writing and graffiti. The printed page, the public wall, and the work of art traditionally constitute three separate domains. Twombly's work, charged with the energy of disparate and opposing fields of representation, creates dynamic new possibilities for the medium of painting.

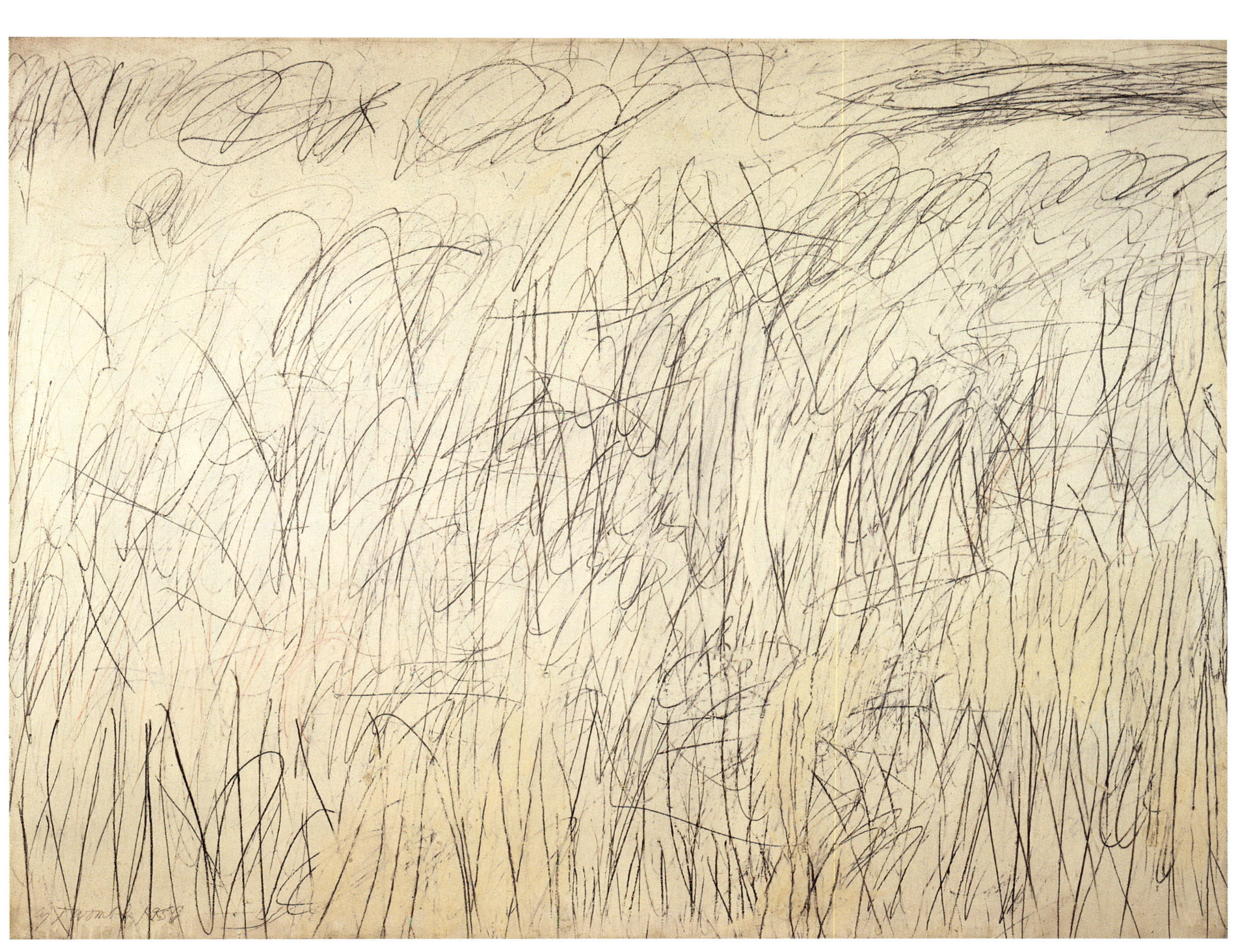

Clay Ketter

Surface Composite #6 (Totem), 1996
Melamin-coated particleboard, plastic laminate, stainless steel, and glass
82 11/16 x 23 5/8 x 23 5/8 in.

At first glance, Clay Ketter's *Surface Composite #6 (Totem)*, 1996, appears indistinguishable from an ordinary kitchen cabinet. A panel connects a small set of shelves placed at eye level to a slightly larger set below; the surfaces are white, smooth, and perfectly ordinary. Its resemblance to a commercially fabricated storage unit becomes only less certain upon close inspection. The interior shelves are perhaps slightly *too* recessed; the sheet of glass that rests on top of the lower unit is too fragile to serve as a countertop. Ketter's *Broom Closet Wall #1*, 2001, consists of interlocking panels of Masonite and wallboard painted in household enamel, edged in green-painted and plain wooden frames. The resulting geometric composition instantly evokes the precisely balanced grids made by Piet Mondrian in the first half of the twentieth century. Like Mondrian, Ketter employs a wide tonal range of whites that run from a thickly opaque cream to a more acidic, almost greenish wash. The contrast between such tones is emphasized by discernible white-on-white drips on the horizontal panel at *Broom Closet*'s bottom. Similarly, the horizontal rectangle at the center—a nearly perfect, absolute white—raises the question as to whether it shows us an "original" unaltered sheet of Masonite or wallboard, or a "finished" painted surface.

This contrast between raw material and a later level of finish lies at the heart of Ketter's work. *Broom Closet*'s precise compositional arrangement is less like one of Mondrian's obsessively perfected grids, while its temporary workmanlike surfaces resemble a cabinet under construction, awaiting a final paint job. The sheer uniform finish of *Surface Composite*, on the other hand, evokes the reliable, standardized precision of commercial surfaces. Construction—captured in various stages by these two examples from Ketter's work—is revealed to be a complex process: Inevitably, as a work in progress moves toward resolution, provisional stages disappear. The perfect finish of a surface—and the obliteration of the foregoing work process—becomes an end in itself. By showing distinctly different degrees and kinds of finish within a single work, Ketter draws our attention to stages of construction that are normally hidden or obscured in any process of physical transformation, artistic or industrial.

Mondrian, too, toyed with finish, continually revising his colored grids by minute increments. His working process can be seen as one that seeks not only a decisive aesthetic balance but the expression of a tension between the finished and the unfinished, between the idea of "finish" itself and the means used to attain it. Ketter's work, nearly a half century after Mondrian, takes these same tensions to another level. If artworks and design objects were to reveal more of the processes of construction they so often cover up, how would our notions of development and finish, change and resolution, be affected? Ketter's deceptively simple paintings and sculptures encourage us to consider precisely this question.

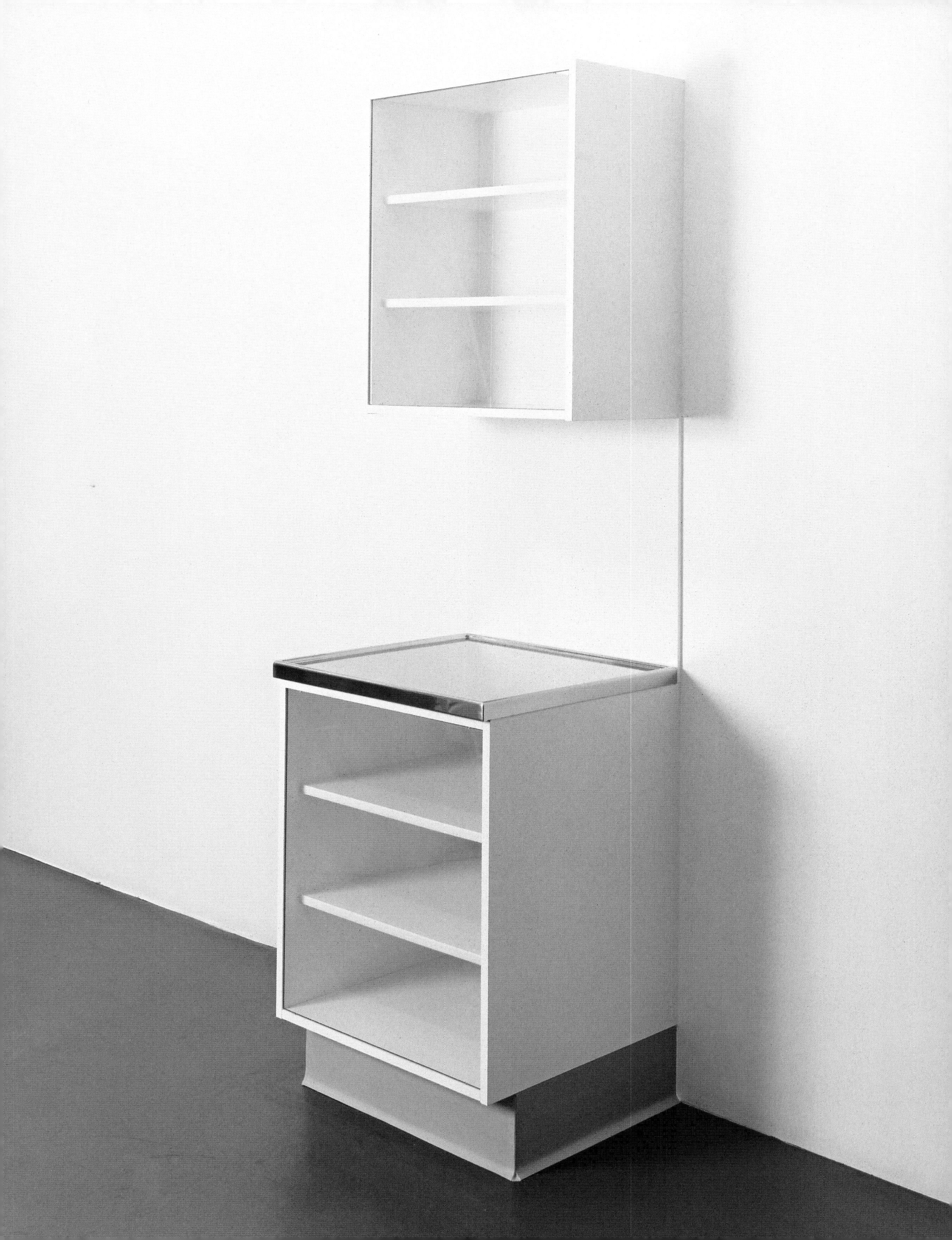

Clay Ketter
Broom Closet Wall #1, 2001
Household enamel paint, sand, and wallboard compound on Masonite; gypsum wallboard, steel corner bead, and wood frame
70 7/8 x 70 7/8 in.

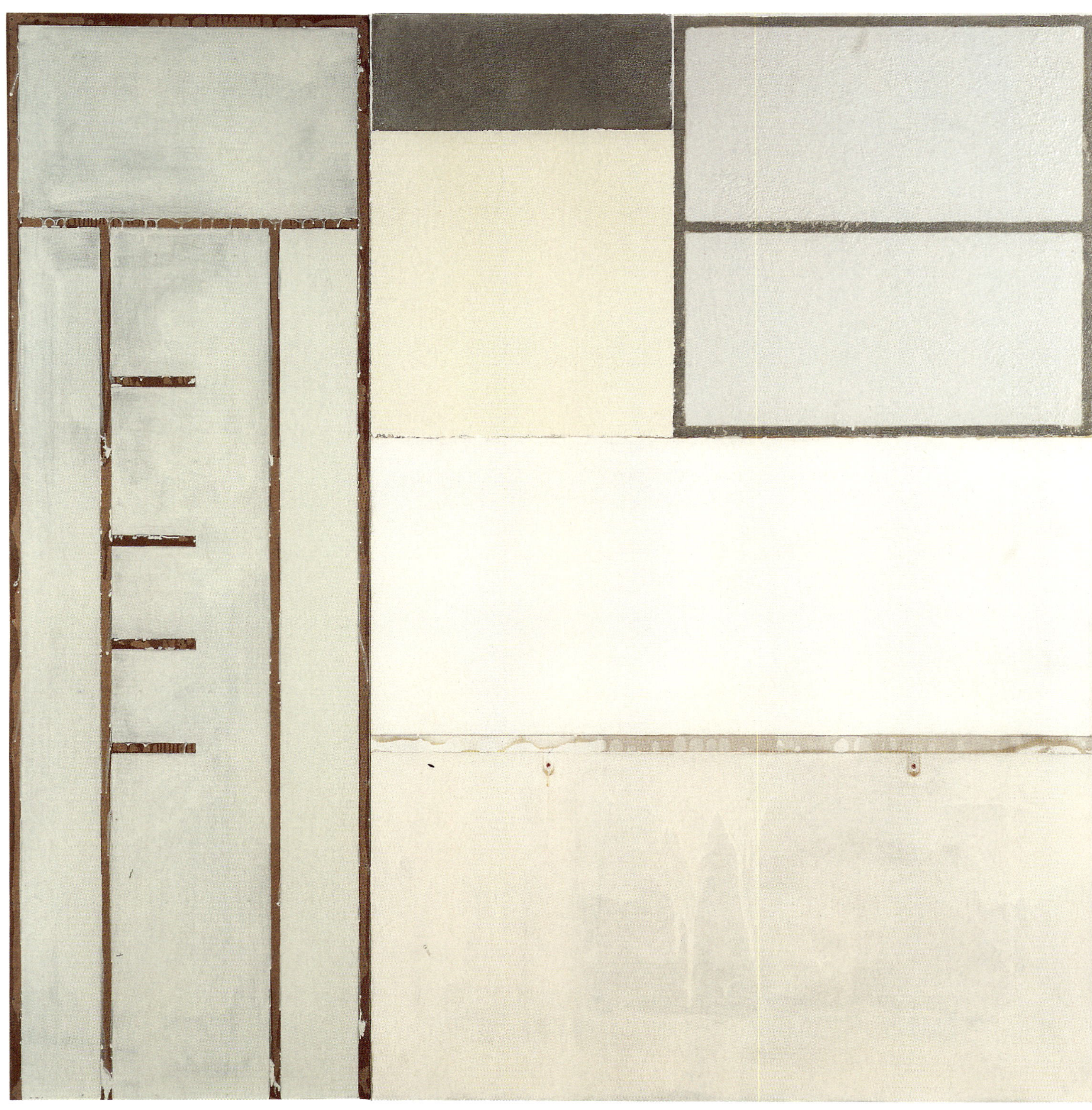

Hiroshi Sugimoto

Boden Sea, Uttwil, 1993
Gelatin silver photograph
20 x 24 in.

Archbishop Makarios III performed mass christenings, founded a seminary of Greek Orthodox faith in Kenya, and survived the Turkish invasion and coup d'état that forced him into exile from his native Cyprus. But Sugimoto's photograph, taken in 1999, is not a photograph of the archbishop, who died in 1977. Rather, it is an image of a wax effigy and is one of a group of large-scale black-and-white photographs, most of which were shot at Madame Tussaud's museums in London and Amsterdam. In these works, collectively titled "Portraits," Sugimoto treats each of his subjects with an identical format and distinctive portrait lighting. Some of the wax effigies, such as those of Queen Elizabeth II and Lady Diana, were modeled on contemporary photographs, but many, such as Napoléon Bonaparte's, were made on the basis of portrait paintings or even hearsay. The wax features of these older figures are perceptibly more unreal, a fact that Sugimoto's crystalline images inevitably register. It is in this sense that he photographs not—as it may first appear—the individuals credited with a role in making history, but the process of history-making itself and the role played by images in it.

Like the "Portraits," Sugimoto's "Theaters" and "Seascapes" are ongoing series. In "Theaters" Sugimoto presents the interiors of old-fashioned movie houses built in the "golden age" of moviegoing, when balustrades, columns, and other architectural ornaments extended the fantasy element of the audience's experience. For each image he shoots a single photograph whose exposure time lasts the duration of a film playing onscreen. The shifting images are registered by Sugimoto's camera as a luminous yet strangely vacant glow. It is as if an entire movie could resolve into a single eerily empty moment.

Images of sea and sky, the "Seascapes" are Sugimoto's most conceptually simple photographs, though they are also among his most technically demanding. For example, in order to determine the necessary exposure time for a nighttime seascape like *South Pacific, Tearai*, 1991, the artist had to calculate both the angle of the moon (predictable according to the season and the time of night) and the distance of his location from the equator. Some nighttime exposures can last as long as two or three hours; in all cases, the resulting images are of an uncanny, singular stillness. Seascapes shot in daylight produce similarly powerful and unexpectedly different effects: The silken texture of the sea in *Caribbean Sea, Jamaica*, 1980, contrasts with the waters of *Boden Sea, Uttwil* 1993, which seem almost empty, even ghostly. Though artists have been depicting the sea for centuries in all variety of media, never has it obtained the perfect immobility and subtle variety it does in Sugimoto's "Seascapes." Ocean fades imperceptibly into sky; their difference seems to be no more than that of air dissipating and releasing its own energy.

Although extraordinary planning is the hallmark of Sugimoto's technique, he eliminates all evidence of artistic intervention. No trace of the photographic process interferes with the viewer's experience of the subject at hand. The dramatic black folds of the archbishop's robes disappear into the background; a "Seascape" never includes the actual source of light—sun or moon—that is so essential to its atmosphere of serenity. But as we grow gradually aware of Sugimoto's sleight of hand, its gorgeously pure effects become, themselves, hauntingly unnatural.

Hiroshi Sugimoto
Caribbean Sea, Jamaica, 1980
Gelatin silver photograph
20 x 24 in.

Hiroshi Sugimoto
South Pacific Ocean, Tearai, 1991
Gelatin silver photograph
20 x 24 in.

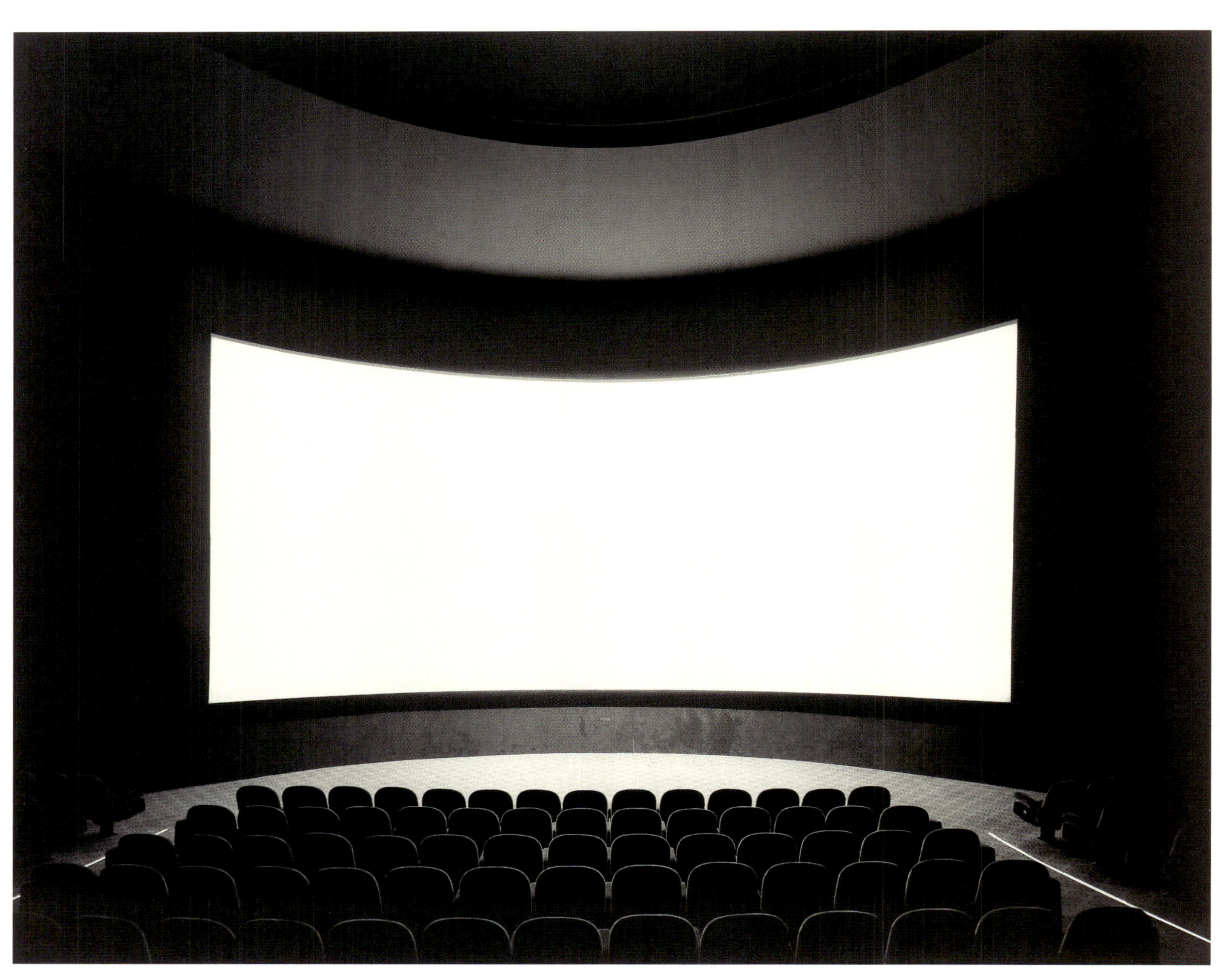

Hiroshi Sugimoto
Kino Panorama, Paris, 1998
Gelatin silver photograph
20 x 24 in.

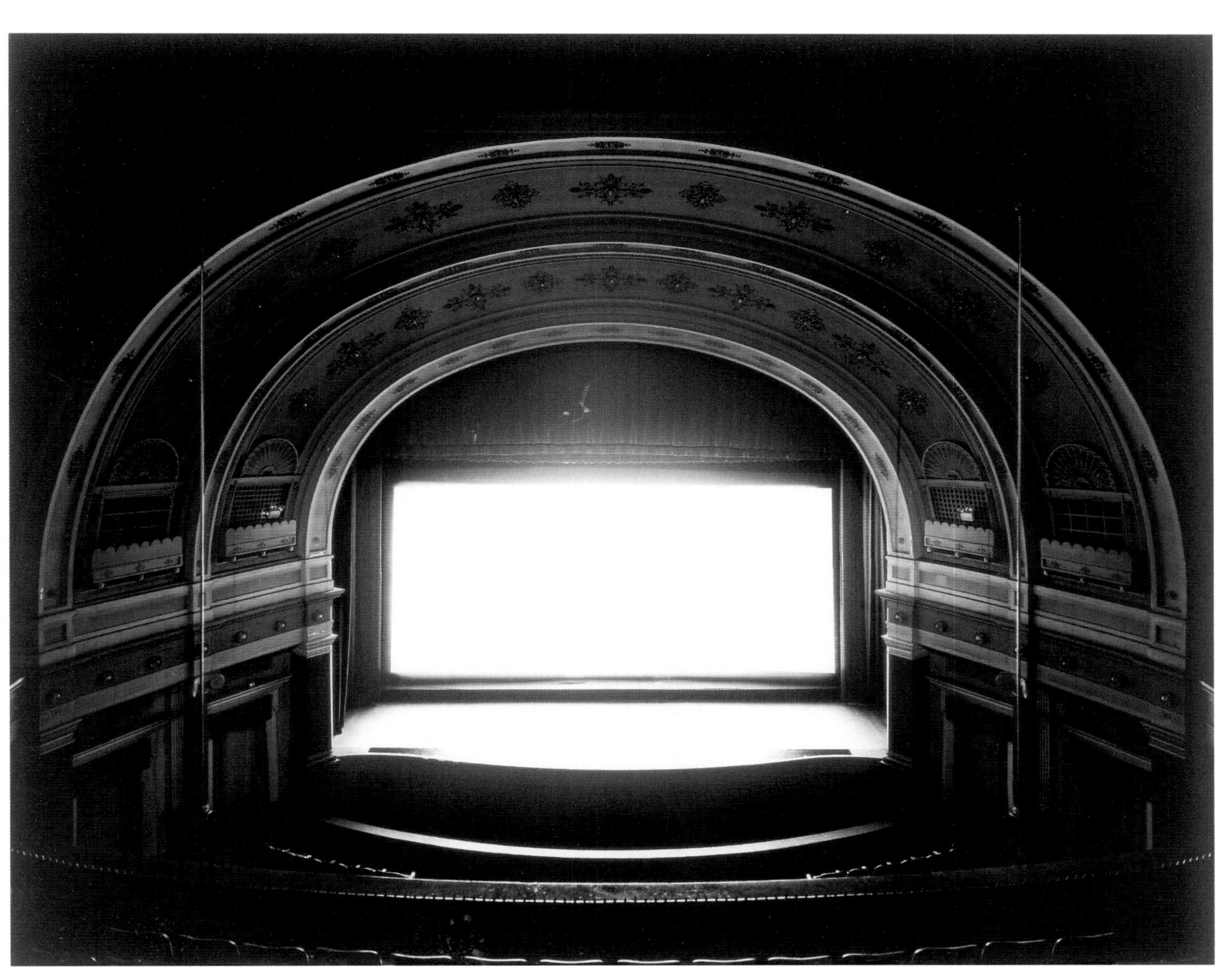

Hiroshi Sugimoto
Goshen, Ohio, 1980
Gelatin silver photograph
20 x 24 in.

Hiroshi Sugimoto
Archbishop Makarios III, 1999
Gelatin silver photograph
58 x 47 in.

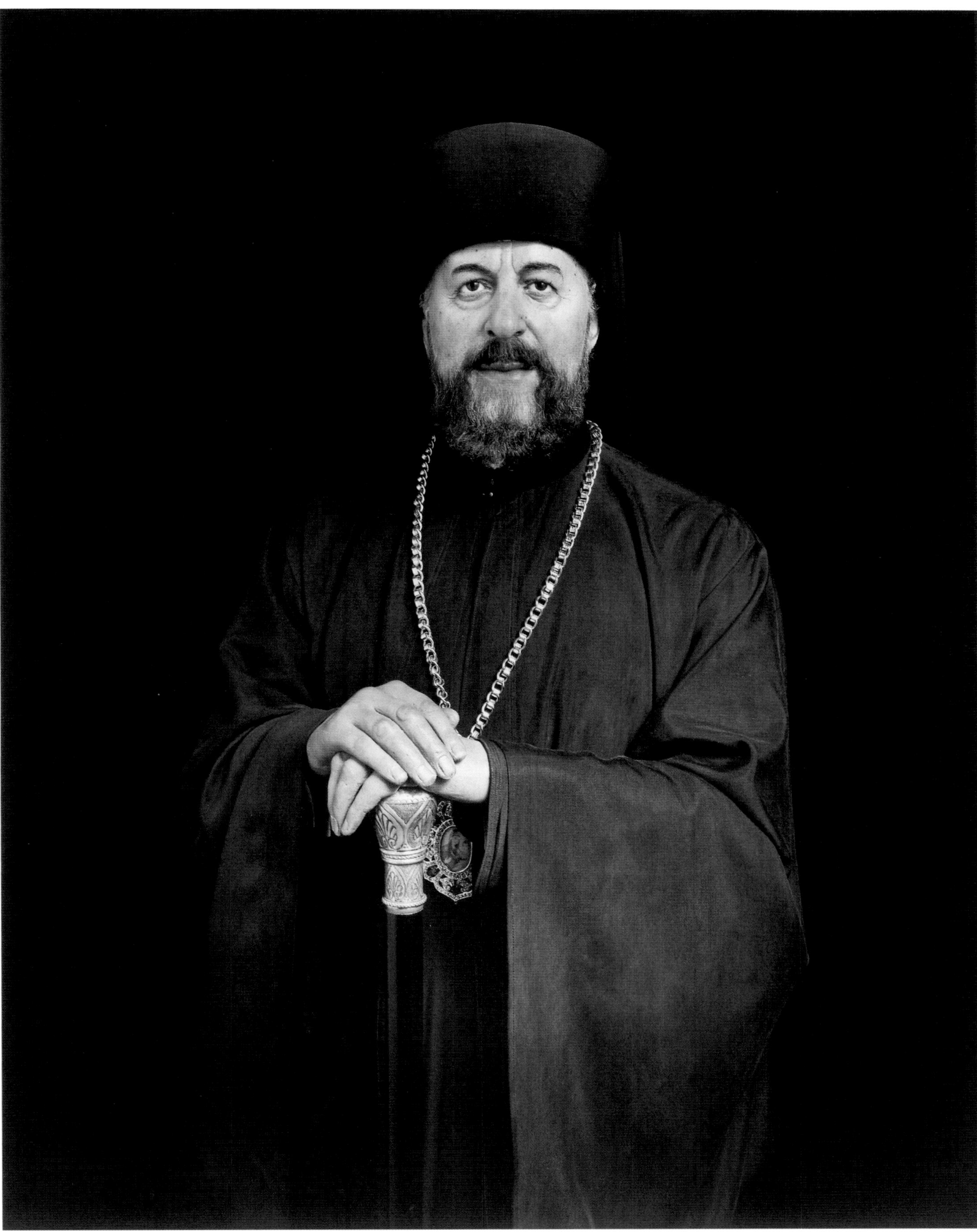

Christian Boltanski

The 62 Members of the Mickey Mouse Club in 1955, 1972
Sixty-two gelatin silver photographs
8 3/4 x 12 in. each
72 x 87 1/2 in. overall

For *The 62 Members of the Mickey Mouse Club in 1955*, a work from 1972, Christian Boltanski rephotographed, framed, and arranged sixty-two pictures from the 1955 edition of the club's annual magazine. In cropping and rephotographing each child's image, Boltanski continues a process of editing and reproduction that the children themselves initiated when they chose the photographs they felt represented them best. One girl is posing in her ballet tutu; a boy holds his dog. Most are simple head shots, but even within that straightforward format there is a vast range of variation. Indeed, if there is any real commonality among these subjects, it is the fact that their future remained entirely open to them in 1955—as it is unknowable to us today.

"I was eleven years old in 1955," Boltanski has said of this series, "and I resembled these sixty-two children.... Today they must be all about my age, but I can't learn what has become of them."[1] Boltanski's identification with the juvenile subjects of *62 Members* is echoed in his staged and often parodic explorations of his own childhood. In *Album photographique de Christian Boltanski 1948–1956*, an artist's book published in 1972, Boltanski had himself photographed with children, playing out activities described in such captions as: "This photo was taken on the evening of my birthday party. We were all exhausted." In each photograph the children with whom the adult Boltanski is pictured are stand-ins for his real childhood friends—just as his adult image is substituted for Boltanski the boy. While the events of the childhood he has "recollected" might be true, the album itself is, quite obviously, a fiction. This odd discrepancy—why restage a childhood?—raises several questions: What role does a photograph or any other visual record play in an individual's autobiography? How do such records come to substitute for the realities they represent in both individual and collective memory? What do our childhood memories mean to us? Photographic archives like the one Boltanski uses in making *62 Members* remind us of the fleeting nature of childhood itself. But in Boltanski's work, such remembrances are always linked to the artist's own persona as author, cataloguer, and autobiographer. Indeed, Boltanski's obsessive documentation of his own or others' childhoods is a grown-up version of the desire for self-discovery that motivates children's participation in groups like the Mickey Mouse Club. His work documents not his own childhood per se but this childlike yearning.

1. Christian Boltanski quoted in Lynn Gumpert, "The Life and Death of Christian Boltanski," in *Christian Boltanski: Lessons of Darkness* (Chicago: Museum of Contemporary Art, 1988), 58.

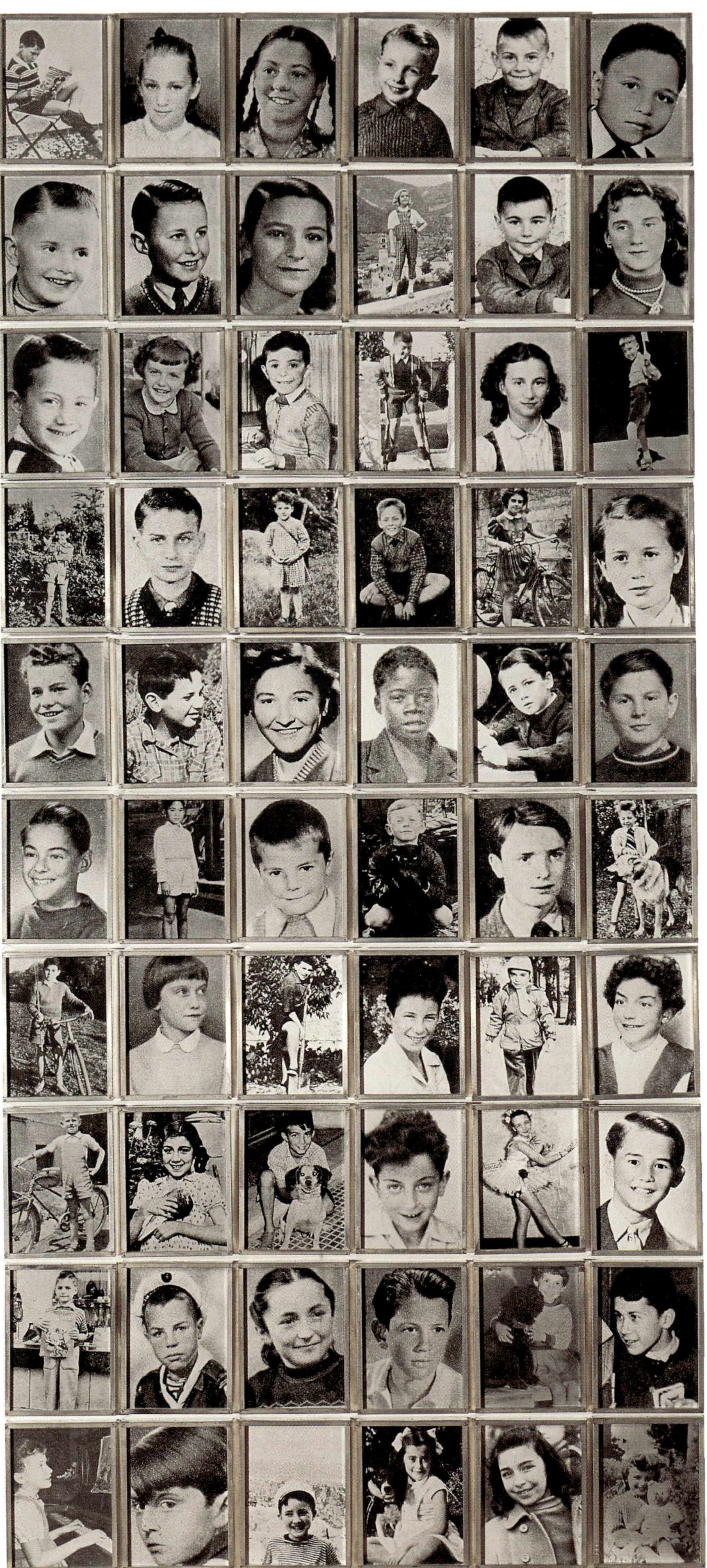

Gilbert & George

They, 1986
Performance still
95 x 79 1/2 in.

Since their meeting at St. Martin's School in 1967, Gilbert & George have operated as a single entity, making art inseparably and *out of* their inseparability. While their signature fastidious suits, refined grooming, and impossibly tony accents point to an all but obsolete English rectitude, their life-into-art partnership suggests a total lack of privacy and inhibition. Taking sociology's "minimal unit" and the notion of partnership to a radical extreme, Gilbert & George make no public appearances or statements separately, claiming that "it's more interesting to know what *we* think."[1] Their strictly regimented world, with rules governing everything from the decoration of their house to the timing of their meals, has become a generative force of much of their artistic oeuvre.

In *They*, from 1986, the artists assembled a grid of sixteen panels that, cumulatively, represent Gilbert & George—just as Gilbert and George, collectively, represent the artistic enterprise Gilbert & George. Flat lighting minimizes the differences between the facial structures of the two men, while the grid arrangement accentuates the permutability of Gilbert & George's "parts," as if to suggest the exchangeability of their very identities. Their blank stares, like the two pairs of hands placed candidly on their knees, reinforce the picture's generic, almost institutional look. This feeling of anonymity is a crucial aspect of their art, standing as the corollary to their own strongly expressed, very specific—yet collective—identity. "They," after all, can mean any set of others, depending on who is speaking, when, and where.

As a word that refers to a plurality of others, "they" points to the concept of collectivity that informs Gilbert & George's work. Used by the artists to title a self-representation, it also subtly raises the issue of otherness as it figures in modern social life. Since the 1960s, Gilbert & George have incorporated the identities of various misfits and social outcasts into their work in a dramatization of otherness that is particularly poignant in relation to their own artistic identities. From one of their earliest "Singing Sculptures," in which they performed a popular Music Hall ballad celebrating a tramp's view of life, to the early-1980s series *Modern Fears*, which juxtaposes pictures of the artists with images of the marginal or dispossessed, Gilbert & George have turned the characterization of the artist as a romantically destitute "other" inside out. *They*, simultaneously presenting the artists' otherness and togetherness in one work—and one word—forces the viewer to recognize the power of images and words to rationalize and reinforce distinctions between "us" and "them."

1. Gilbert & George with Andrew Duncan, "The Odd Couple," *Observer* (London), 28 June 1987.

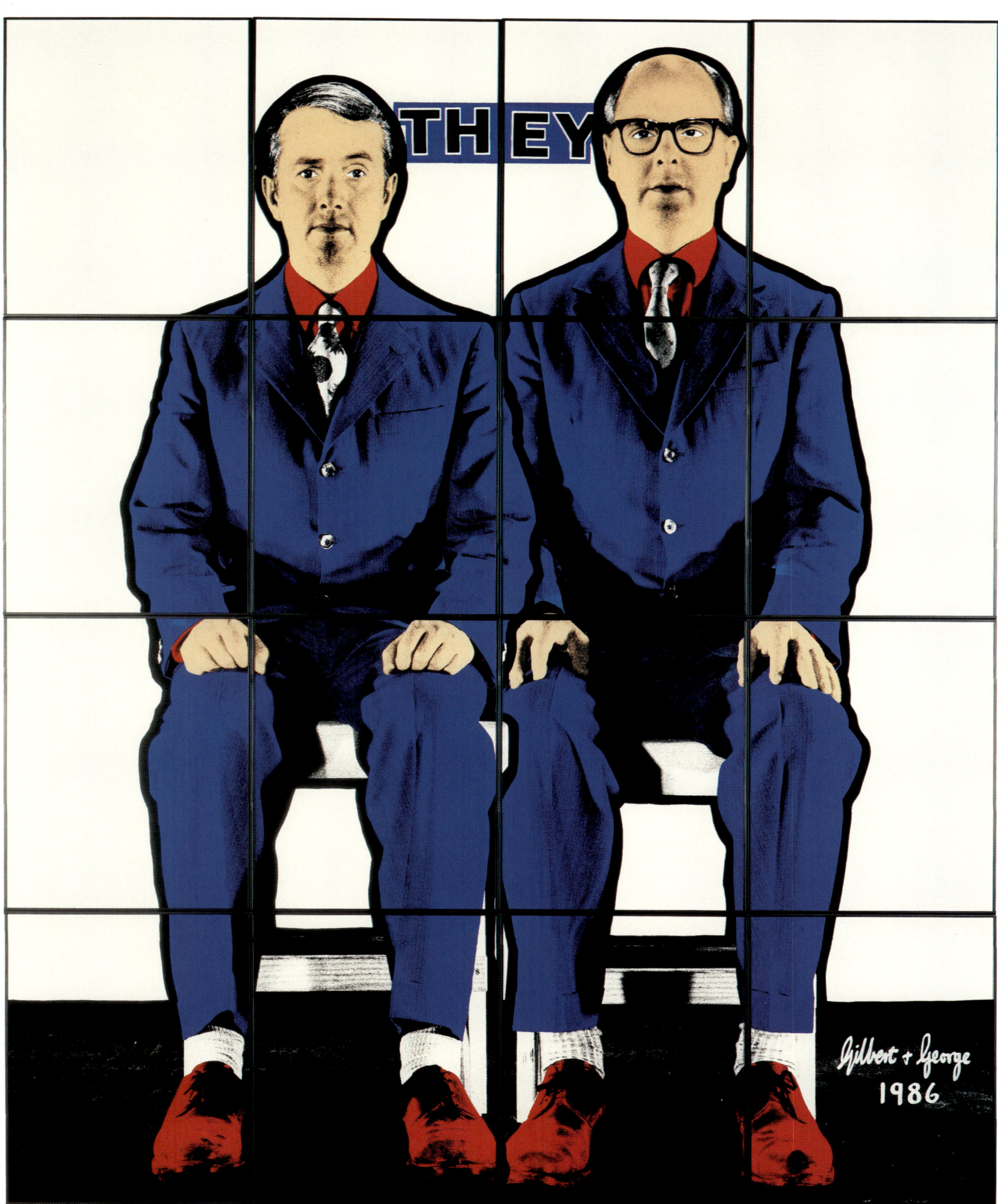
THEY
Gilbert + George
1986

Richard Artschwager

Double Dinner, 1988
Wood, Formica, paint, and rubberized hair
27 x 85 1/2 x 35 1/2 in.

At the outset of Richard Artschwager's career he worked as a commercial furniture maker while studying with the early-twentieth-century French painter and theoretician Amédée Ozenfant. The Formica paintings and "pseudo-furniture" sculptures that he debuted in the late 1950s combine the industrial materials of a contemporary cabinet-maker with the rigorously simplified forms of Ozenfant's Purist style. With them, the young artist developed an iconoclastic, pared-down version of Pop art that incorporated Minimalist sculpture's arresting physical effects on the viewer. The more recent generation of artists that includes Jeff Koons, Meyer Vaisman, Ashley Bickerton, and Haim Steinbach provides a somewhat different context for understanding Artschwager's work. Using a variety of technical means that include the purchase of consumer objects and the casting of ready-made industrial forms in "artistic" materials, these younger artists explore the different social and aesthetic positions and values accorded to artworks and commercial products. Artschwager's sculptural installations and trompe l'oeil painting similarly mine the differences between the allegedly separate realms of aesthetic objects and their "real-world" counterparts. His works reveal not only the subtle social structures embedded in each but the often uncanny, surreal effects that result from translating materials or forms from one realm into the other.

Artschwager's *Double Dinner*, 1988, belongs to the group of "Dinners" and "Diners" begun in the mid-1970s, composed of photorealist paintings of food on framed "plates" and installations that simulate "real" interior design. *Double Dinner*, a dining set constructed in wood and Formica and measuring nearly seven feet long, places two hypothetical diners an alienating distance apart. Even more disturbing is the wiry, scratchy, rubber-coated horsehair with which Artschwager covers the uninviting hard right angles of *Double Dinner*'s seats and table. Simultaneously evoking both inside and outside—the horsehair stuffing of mattresses and furniture, the hair shirt worn by biblical penitents—this material, which Artschwager developed in 1968 and has used intermittently since, lends a vaguely sinister air to a what could have been an ordinary, even banal domestic structure. When does something like a dining set cease to be a "simple" object and become a work of art? What is the difference between the indefinable feelings we can have for everyday objects and those responses we specifically label as aesthetic? What are the dimensions of consumer objects, their materials, and their forms in our private or interior lives? Artschwager weaves the intricate relations between these questions into a body of work imbued with wit and a discomfiting, subtle perversity.

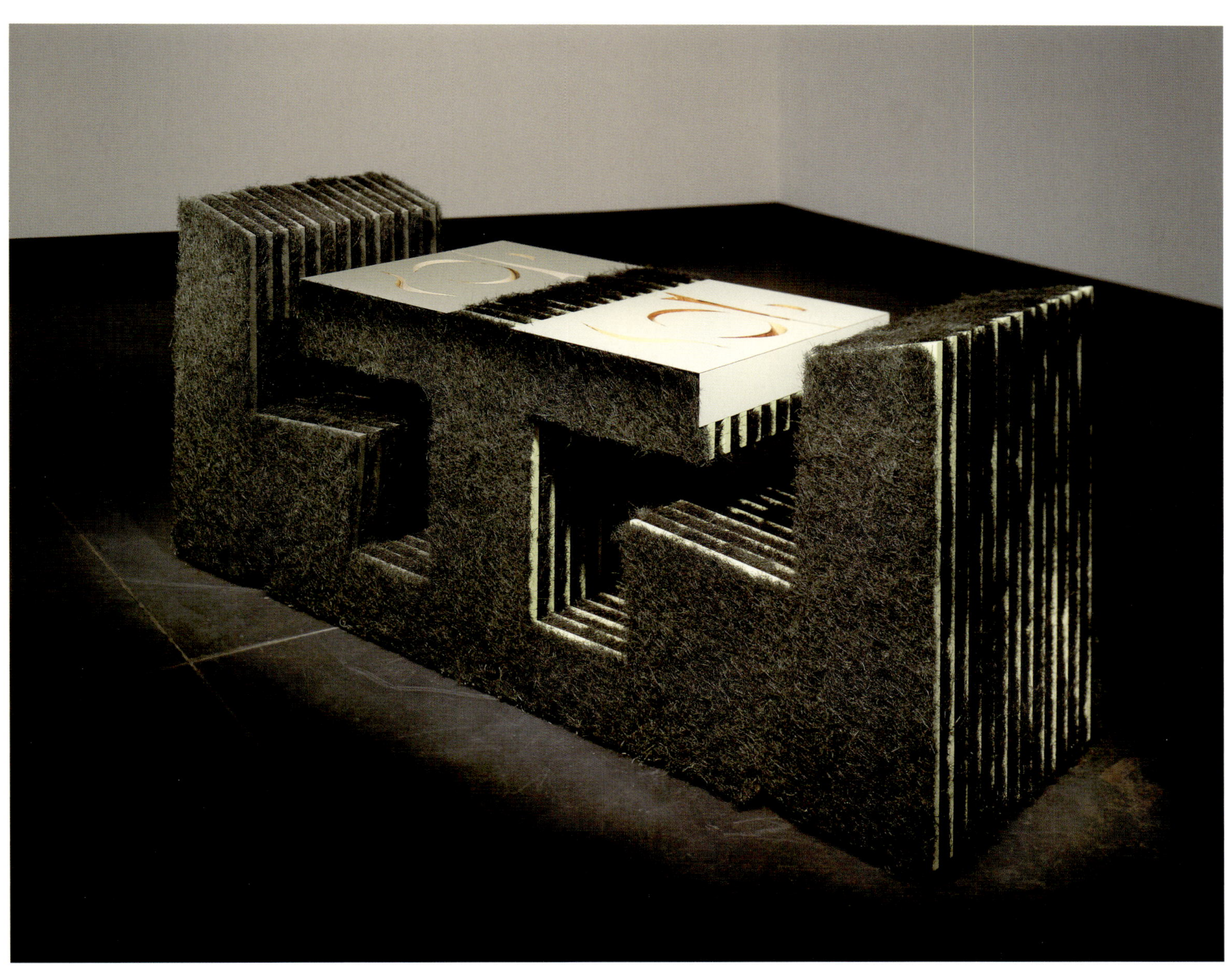

William Wegman

Stormy Night, 1972
Nine gelatin silver photographs
15 x 11 in. each
51 x 43 in. overall

Stormy Night, a 1972 work by William Wegman, is a grid of nine photographs of the artist's weimaraner, Man Ray, assuming nine positions on a white block. As the orientation of the block changes, increasing its height and the level of difficulty of Man Ray's postures, the grid begins to resemble an acrobatic how-to manual. What from a distance looks almost like nine graceful calligraphic figures turns out on closer inspection to be a witty circus of canine contortion.

"Can photographs of a dog be taken seriously?" Wegman's work seems to ask. In fact, *Stormy Night* rather pointedly references a crucial turning point in the history of both photography and science. In 1881 Eadweard Muybridge illustrated his book *The Attitudes of Animals in Motion: A Series of Photographs Illustrating the Consecutive Positions Assumed by Animals in Performing Various Movements* with photographs of dogs and horses. A decade later, Etienne-Jules Marey, a doctor by training, invented chronophotography, a means of recording motion over fixed time intervals. Marey's invention demonstrated, among other things, that the eye cannot see motion as precisely as technology can break it down. With its photographs of a dog cropped and centered, textbook style, *Stormy Night* alludes both to Muybridge's scientific ideals and to Marey's understanding that photography freezes motion with a crystalline clarity that human vision cannot match.

Nearly a century later, the early photographers' empirical approach was echoed in the efforts of American Minimalist sculptors to make viewers aware of the effects of time on the perception of their work. Their belief that human perception could be rationally quantified gave much Minimal art a didactic, even programmatic quality. Minimalism was a dominant force when Wegman began working in photography, performance art, and video, and his art can be seen as a reaction to its gravity. As a simple rectangular block—one of Minimalism's preferred forms—becomes a prop for Man Ray's antics in *Stormy Night*, we are reminded of the repressed comic element that can bubble up even out of rigorous aesthetic structures. *Portraiture/Portrait*, 1971, similarly employs humor to challenge Minimalism's literalism—an aspect that Frank Stella aptly summed up in his famous phrase, "What you see is what you see." *Portraiture/Portrait* consists of two photographs. On the left, the artist is shown taking a portrait of his wife; on the right, we see his wife alone. The work illustrates its title perfectly; one panel shows the act of portraiture, the other, the result—the final portrait. As the bare room and glumly expression-less face of Wegman's wife indicates, this portrait aims at little more than a visual reiteration of its title. But Wegman puts an absurdist spin on Minimalism's insistence on an artwork's literal meaning—that it "mean" nothing more than is self-evident and that it require nothing more from the viewer than unaided observation. For, as the viewer soon realizes, a second photographer "offstage" was needed in order to take the picture of Wegman photographing his wife. What might have been an all but pointless exercise becomes a witty rejoinder to Minimalism's austere ethos. Like Man Ray's lithe balancing act, *Portrait/Portraiture* reminds us of the essential need for whimsy and humility in even our most serious endeavors.

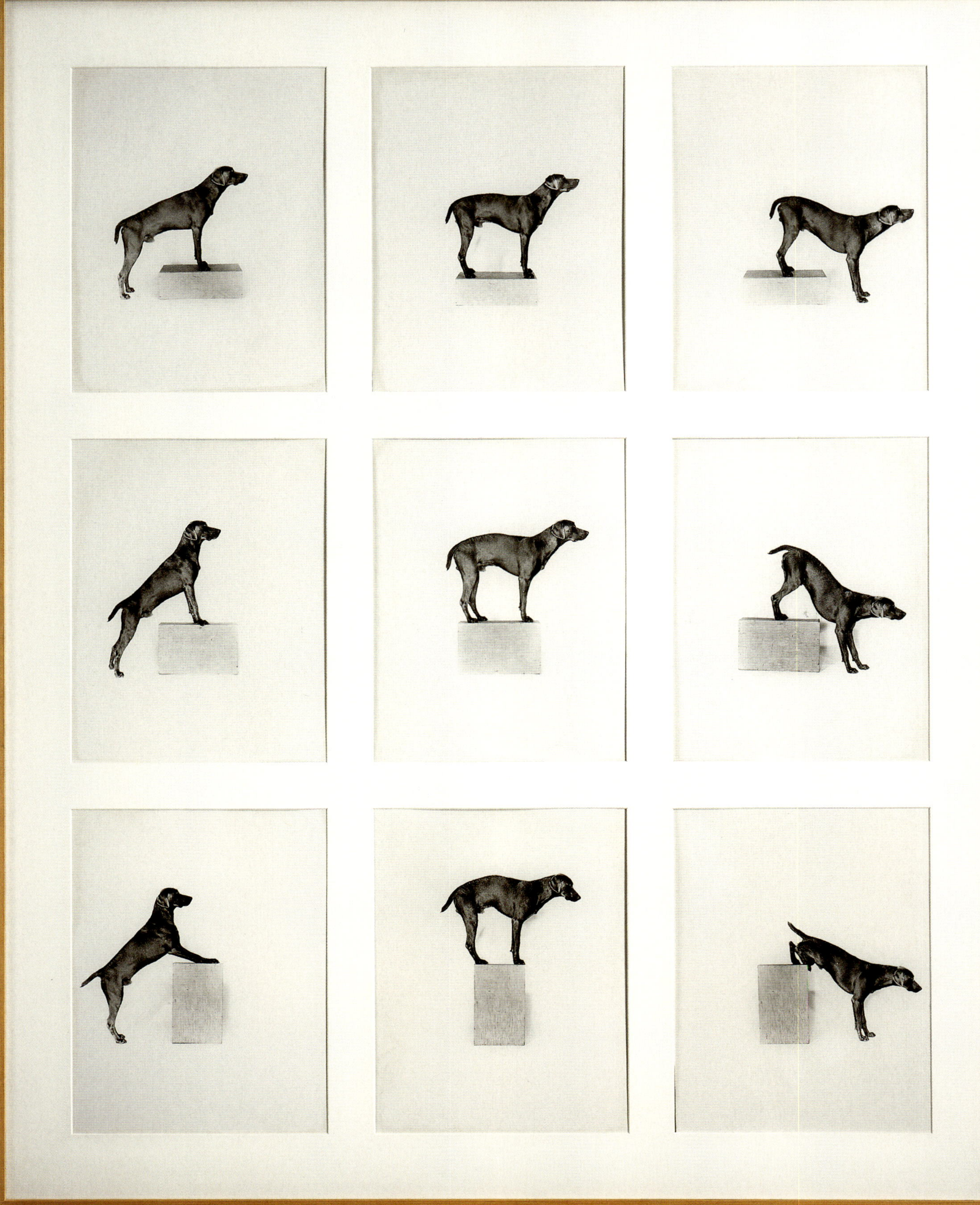

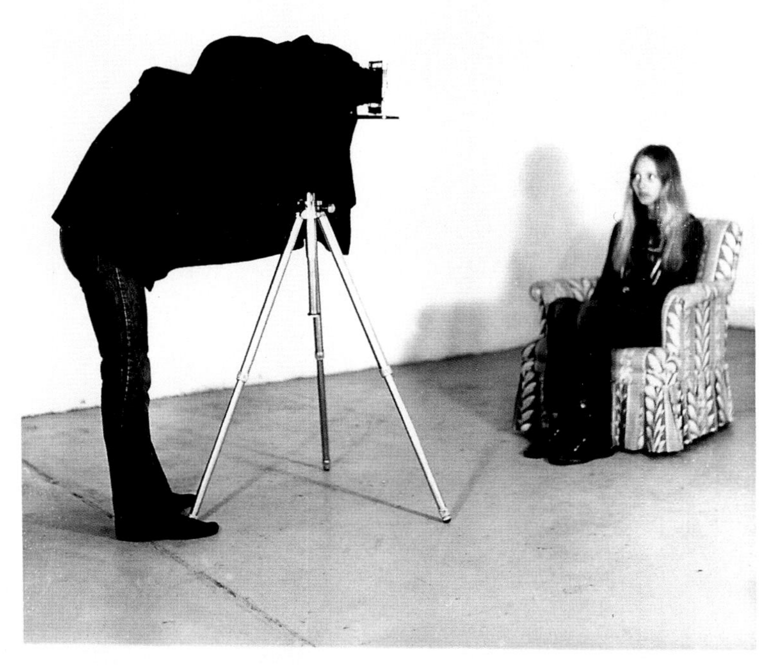

PORTRAITURE

William Wegman
Portraiture/Portrait, 1971
Two gelatin silver photographs
11 x 14 in. each
11 x 29 in. overall

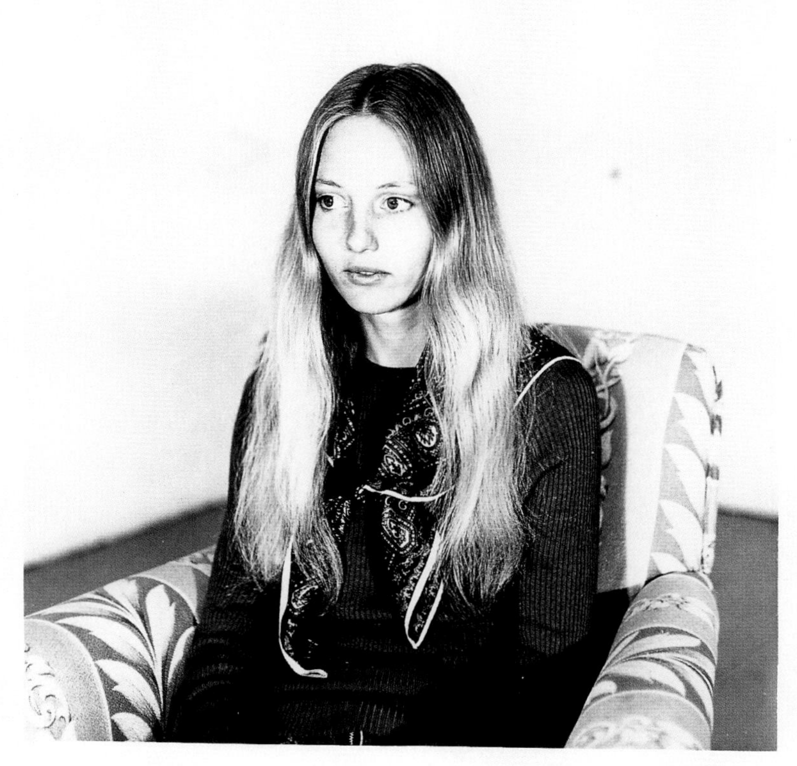

PORTRAIT

Bernd and Hilla Becher

Water Towers, 1988
Twenty-one gelatin silver photographs
16 x 20 in. each
67 x 129 in. overall

These two series of *Water Towers*—a 1972 work composed of nine gelatin silver photographs and one from 1988 of twenty-one gelatin silver photographs—testify to the extraordinary continuity that characterizes the work of Bernd and Hilla Becher. In 1959 they began documenting half-timbered workers' houses in historic industrial areas of Germany's South Westphalia. Since then the Bechers have photographed industrial structures across Western Europe and America including blast furnaces, grain elevators, cooling towers, coal bunkers, and factory plants. In the forty-three intervening years their approach has been unvarying. They photograph under uniformly overcast light so as to prevent any hint of shadow play or climatic variation; they show only the structure itself, including as little as possible of the surrounding area and avoiding bystanders altogether; and they center and tightly crop their formal frontal compositions, producing a sense of consistency over each gridded series.

This rigorous technique yields the subtly idiosyncratic moods that dominate each series, which the Bechers refer to as "Typologies." Each photograph is selected from their cumulative, ongoing, decades-long study of each type of structure, so that a given photograph may date from any time since the beginning of their work—and may even recur over the course of several typologies. The date assigned to a typology reflects the year in which the Bechers selected that group of images from among all of the photographs of a particular type of structure (such as a water tower). The aesthetic that might emerge over the course of a typology does not, therefore, necessarily reflect any geographic or temporal consistency; it reflects the artists' specific standards for selection in that moment. In the 1972 typology, the water towers' rounded forms seem to flatten almost completely, as if the photographs were vertical cross sections of the structures. The towers' streamlined silhouettes resemble champagne flutes, loudspeakers, and clarinets. In the 1988 series, the towers' designs are far more whimsical, featuring bulbous crowns with thatched roofs, or visible and even elaborate portals. The futuristic, hypermodern aspect of the structures from the 1972 series is replaced by a more down-to-earth, even nostalgic sensibility in 1988; in comparing the two, we witness two alternatives: a utopian vision of society seen through its architecture, and a desire to domesticate even these giant, odd, and somewhat otherworldly structures.

The grid that provides the Bechers' system for visual organization and display is a crucial feature of both modernist abstraction and scientific inquiry. Grids signify mechanized regularity and mathematical evenness and confer a sense of flatness and timelessness on their subjects. This neutral, ostensibly scientific aspect of the Bechers' work evokes earlier traditions within twentieth-century photography. Eugène Atget's photographs of old Paris and its denizens in the first quarter of the twentieth century and August Sander's enormous photographic archive of "types" of German people between the wars serve as the Bechers' historical antecedents. Both earlier projects pushed the function of photography beyond the strictly aesthetic, engaging the medium's "extra-artistic" uses in, for instance, criminology, statistical control, and archaeological exploration. Similarly, the Bechers use a gridded format to heighten their works' visual semblance to a scientific or historical archive. And indeed, their work does invite sociological, even political inquiry. The archi-

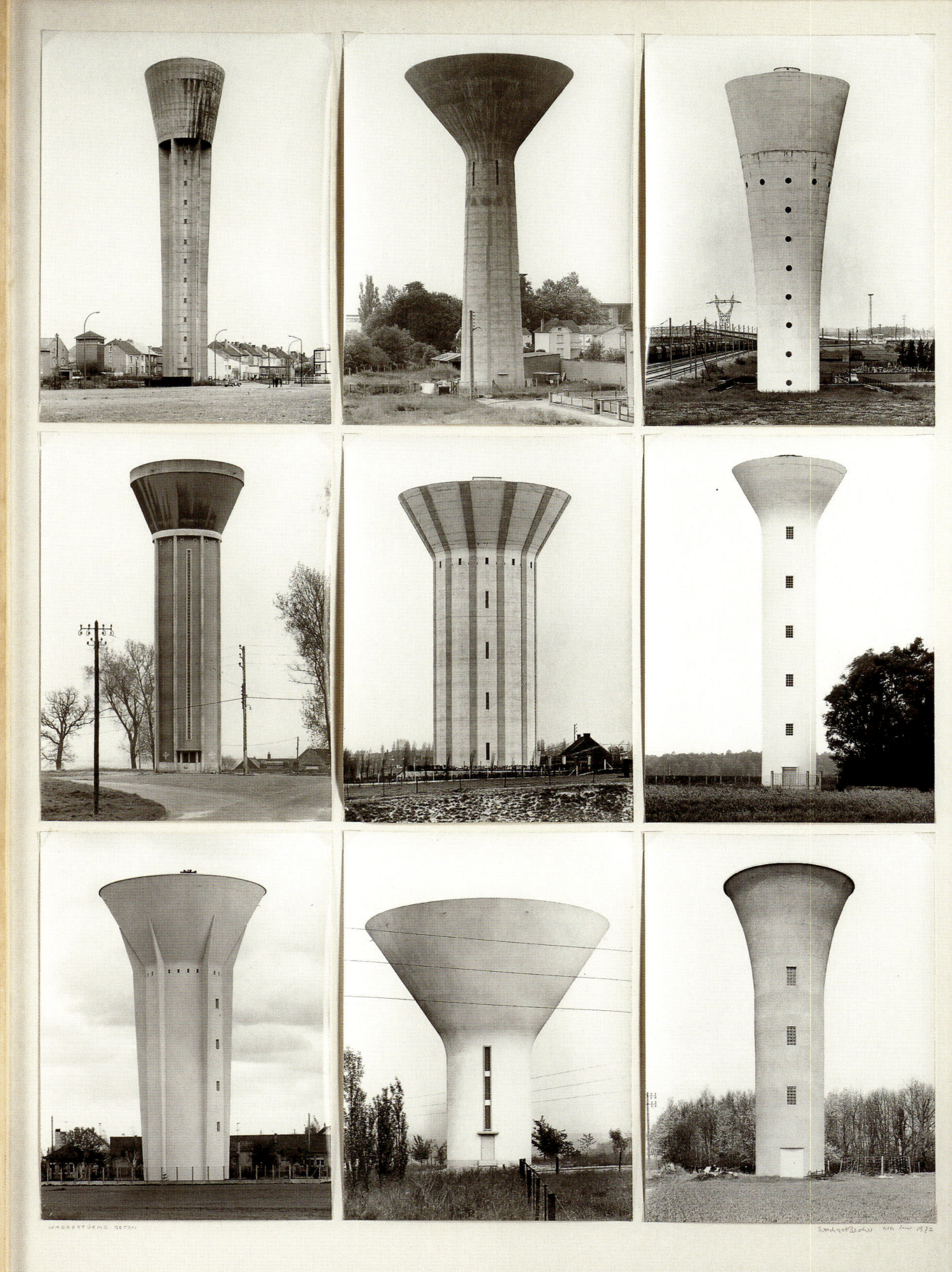
WASSERTÜRME BETON

tectural forms that the Bechers catalogue also disclose evidence of modern cycles of industrial manufacturing, in which productivity is inevitably followed by obsolescence. At the same time, their typologies are infused with a sly wit that subtly yet forcefully undermines any rigid idea of the role of documentation in analytic study. Sitting astride the barrier that conventionally separates "objective" scientific or historical truth from the "idio-syncratic" aesthetic or visual record, the Bechers' work seduces us into a world of the barely perceptible, the almost forgotten, and the nearly archaic. Indeed, in the Bechers' world, which we increasingly recognize as our own, such barriers become nearly as obsolete as the photographed structures themselves.

Bernd and Hilla Becher
Water Towers, 1972
Nine gelatin silver photographs
16 x 12 in. each
48 x 36 in. overall

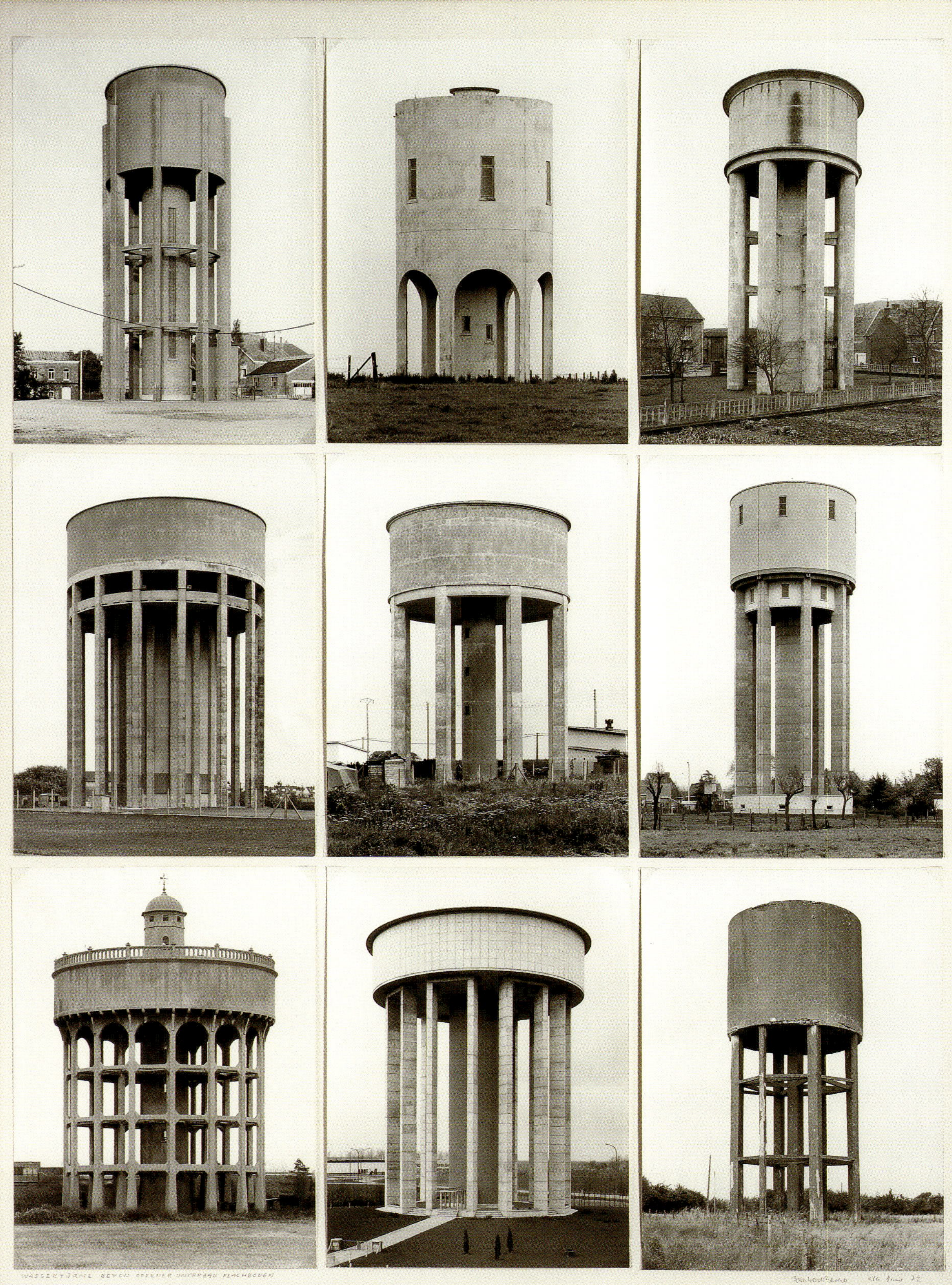
WASSERTÜRME BETON OFFENER UNTERBAU FLACHBODEN

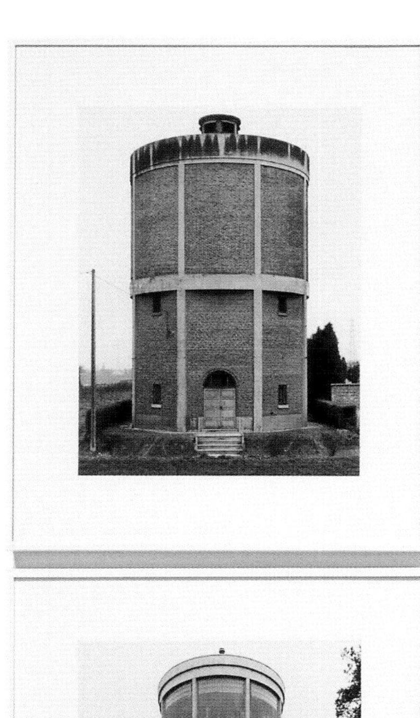
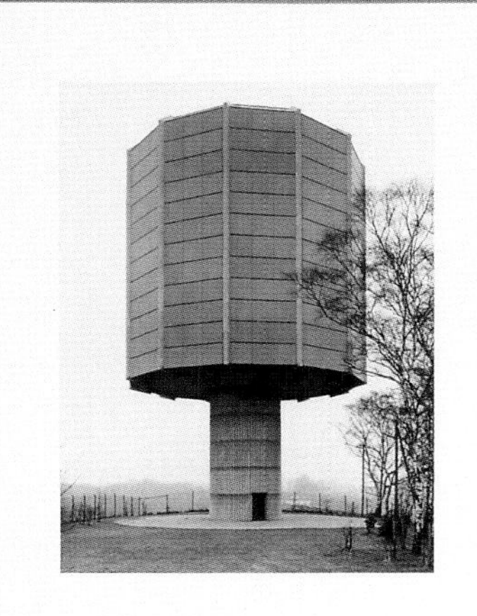
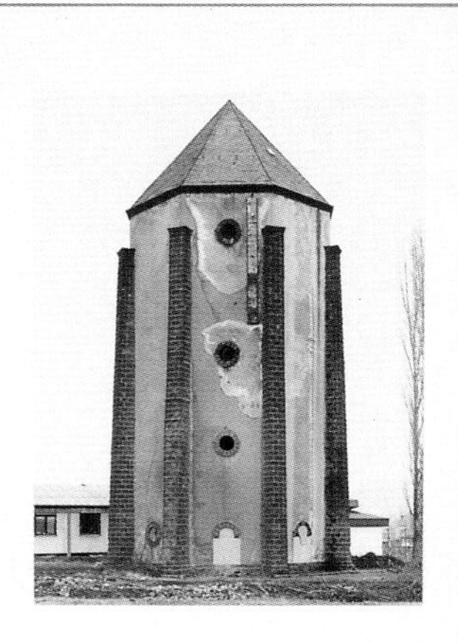
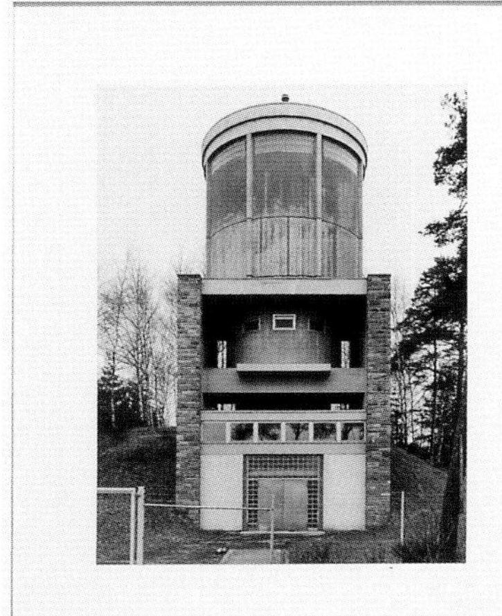
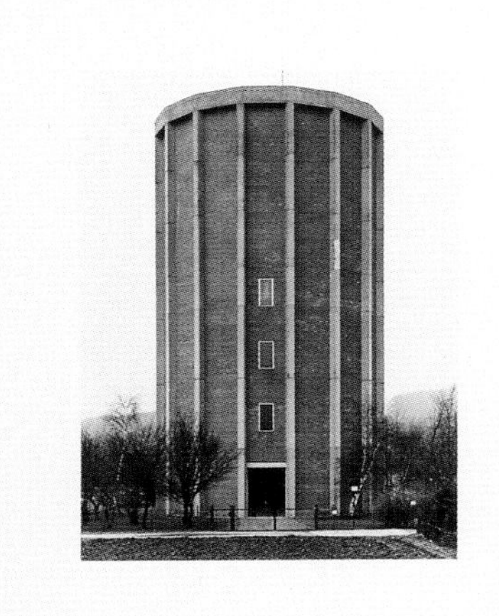
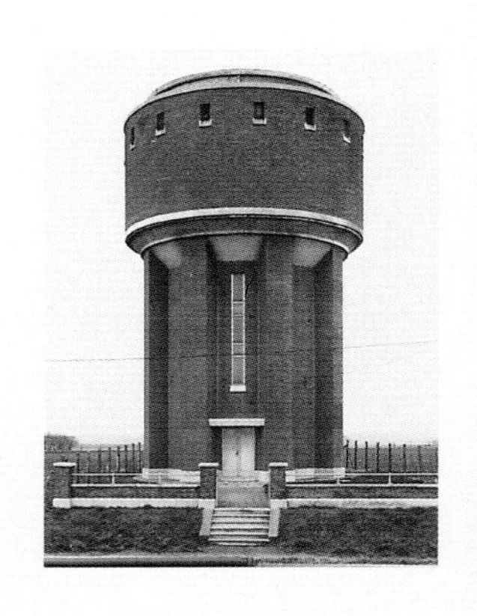
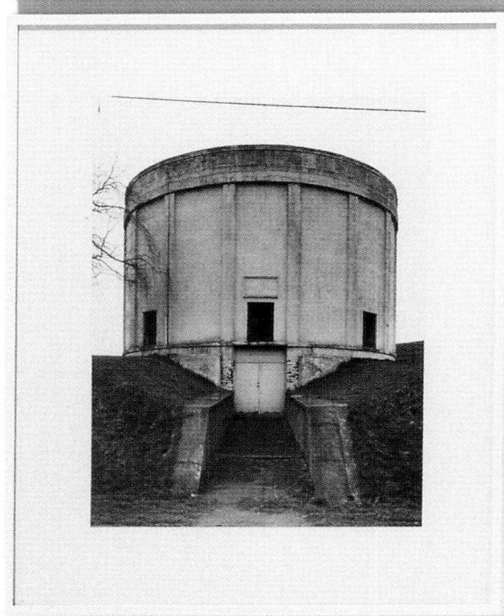
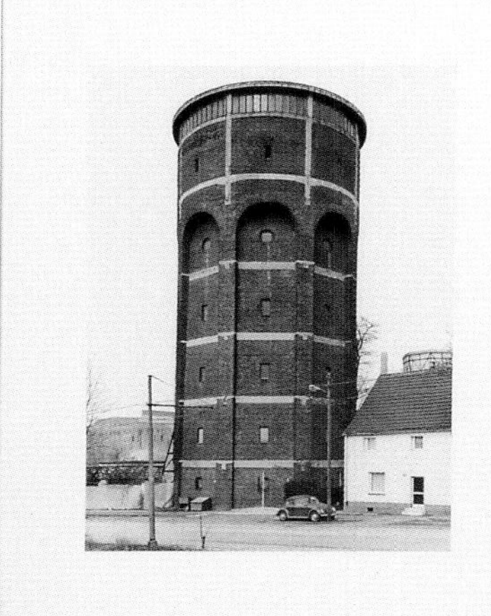
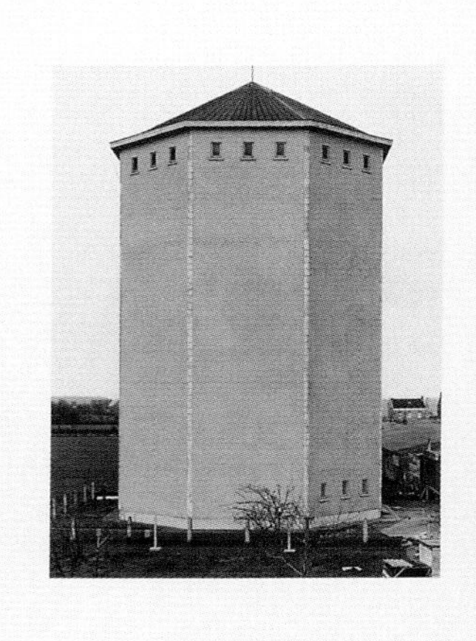

Bernd and Hilla Becher
Water Towers, 1972
Nine gelatin silver photographs
15 3/4 x 11 7/8 in. each
40 x 50 in. overall

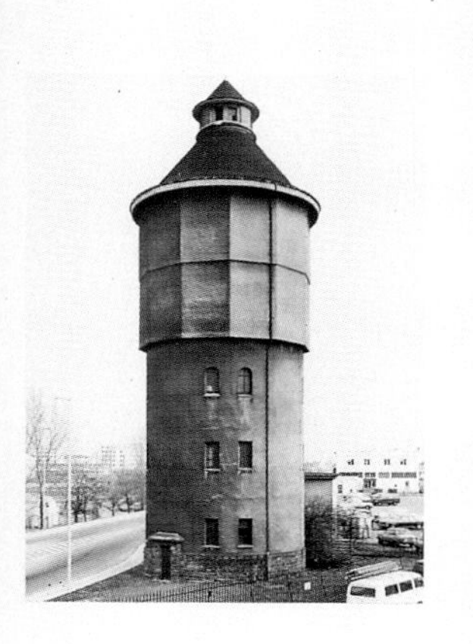
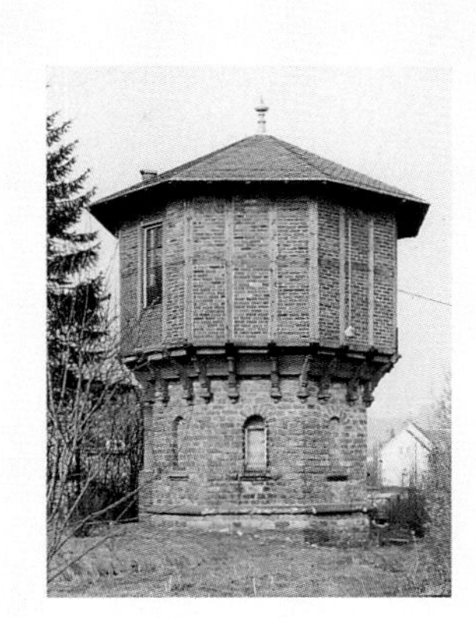
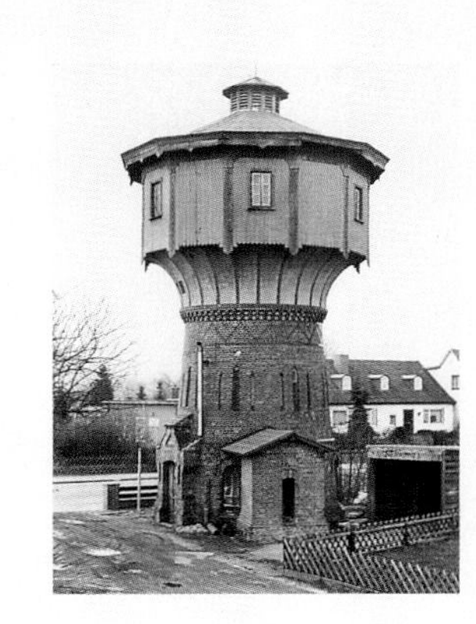
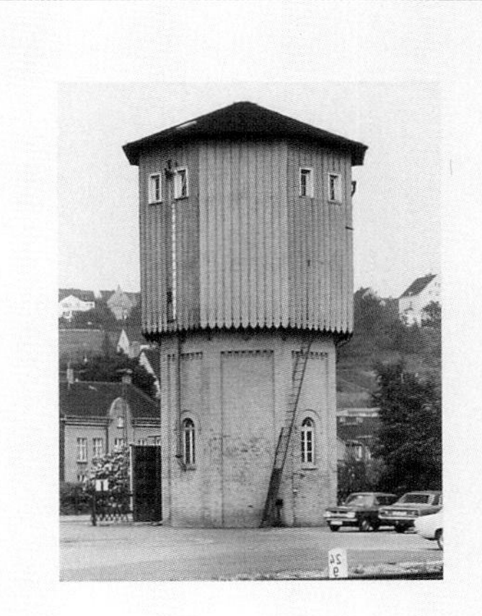
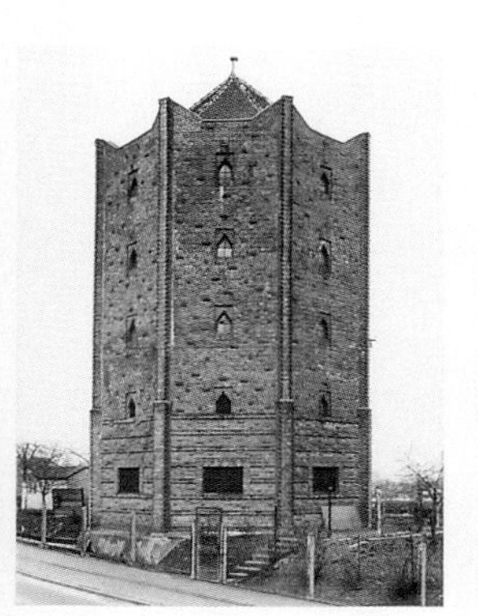
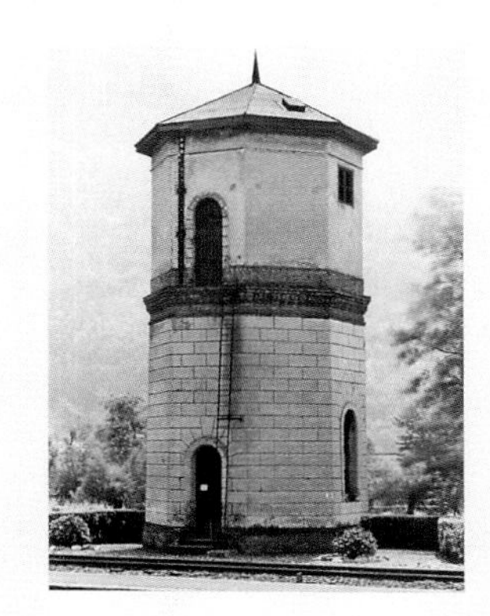
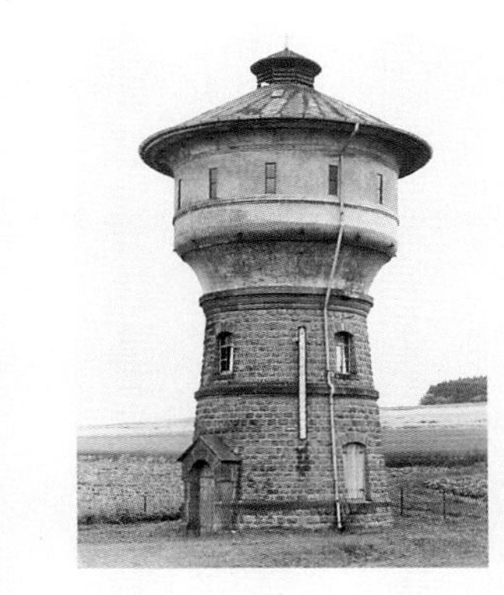
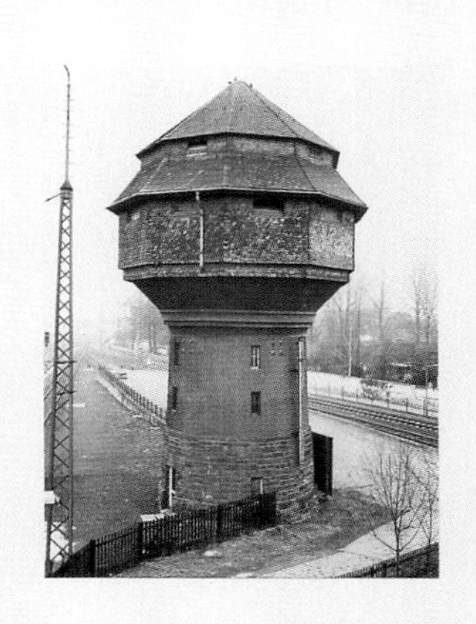
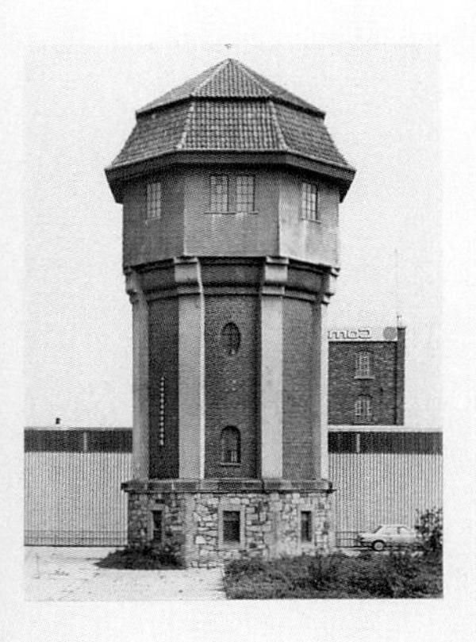
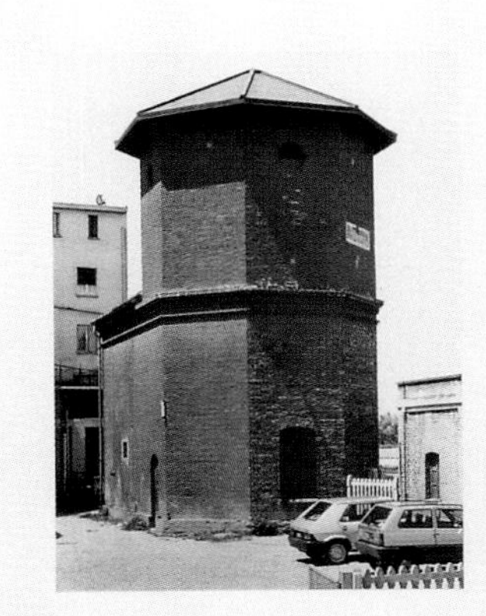
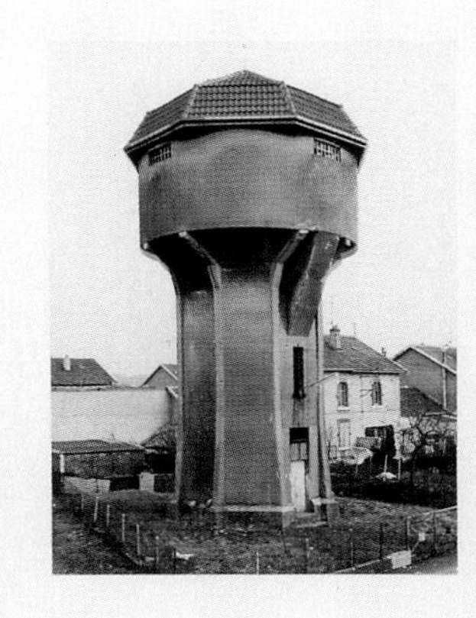
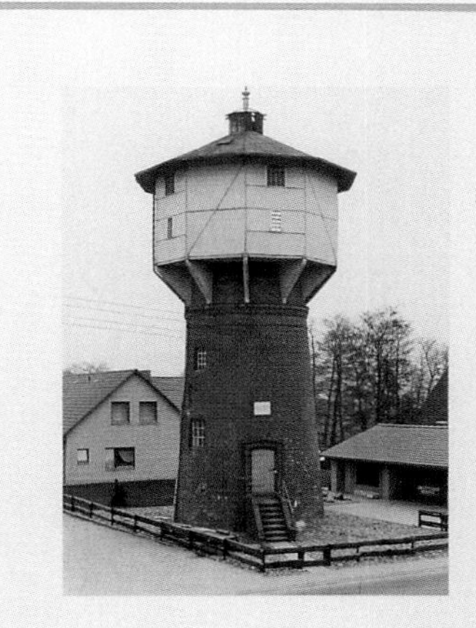

Elger Esser

Blois, 1998
Chromogenic color photograph
72 13/16 x 97 5/8 in.

Hauntingly beautiful, Elger Esser's *Blois*, 1998, presents a panoramic view of a French town with its eponymous royal castle dominating the Loire valley. The first stone fortress was built on this site in the thirteenth century to protect powerful local lords. It was only at the beginning of the sixteenth century, under the reign of Louis XII, that Blois was finally transformed into the luminous Renaissance château we see in Esser's image. It did not remain a functioning symbol of the newly consolidated French monarchy for long, however; a quarter century after Louis XII's ascendance, the crown deserted Blois and its castle.

Esser's photograph leaves an indelible impression of mute, almost motionless isolation. Though he brings an immediate, razor-sharp focus to even the tiniest detail of the castle and surrounding town, both appear wistfully lost to history, fundamentally unchanged by the intervening centuries since their construction. Gathering clouds above evoke a portentous romantic atmosphere, while a mossy, muted range of murky grays and ochres, stippled with the terra-cotta of the rooftops, intensifies a feeling of lyrical melancholy. The enormous size of the photograph, which measures six by eight feet, brings us directly into the landscape, almost as involuntary voyeurs, and reminds us of the contemporaneity of the photographic technology that Esser employs in contrast to his antiquated subject matter.

Esser is a student of Bernd and Hilla Becher, who practice a rigorous form of "straight" documentary photography. Although he has adopted their uncompromising technical standards, Esser is not averse to photo-manipulation and modifies the color saturation of his prints to achieve a pictorial effect. His panoramic views of celebrated sights, with their crystalline focus and dissolving golden hues, specifically recall the work of eighteenth-century painter Giovanni Antonio Canaletto. Canaletto's *vedute* (topographically exact records of his native Venice) often featured similarly thundering clouds and dilated spaces. Like Canaletto, Esser lowers his horizon line so that the sky becomes a vast expanse; the townhouses' turrets raking the sky replace the Venetian's regatta sails and church spires. Especially beloved by the generation of English "grand tourists" to whom they introduced Venetian monuments and culture, Canaletto's endlessly reproduced *vedute* lent such early tourism a sense of authenticity and romance. Esser, an artist based in Düsseldorf who grew up in Rome, positions himself like a latter-day tourist following in the footsteps of Canaletto by presenting sites already rendered familiar through painting. But the melancholy beauty of *Blois*—the exactitude of its rendering, the sensual heaviness of its clouds and colors—imbues a familiar format with the intimacy of a memory image, as if to preserve both the traditional artistic genre and the long-vacant castle for another use.

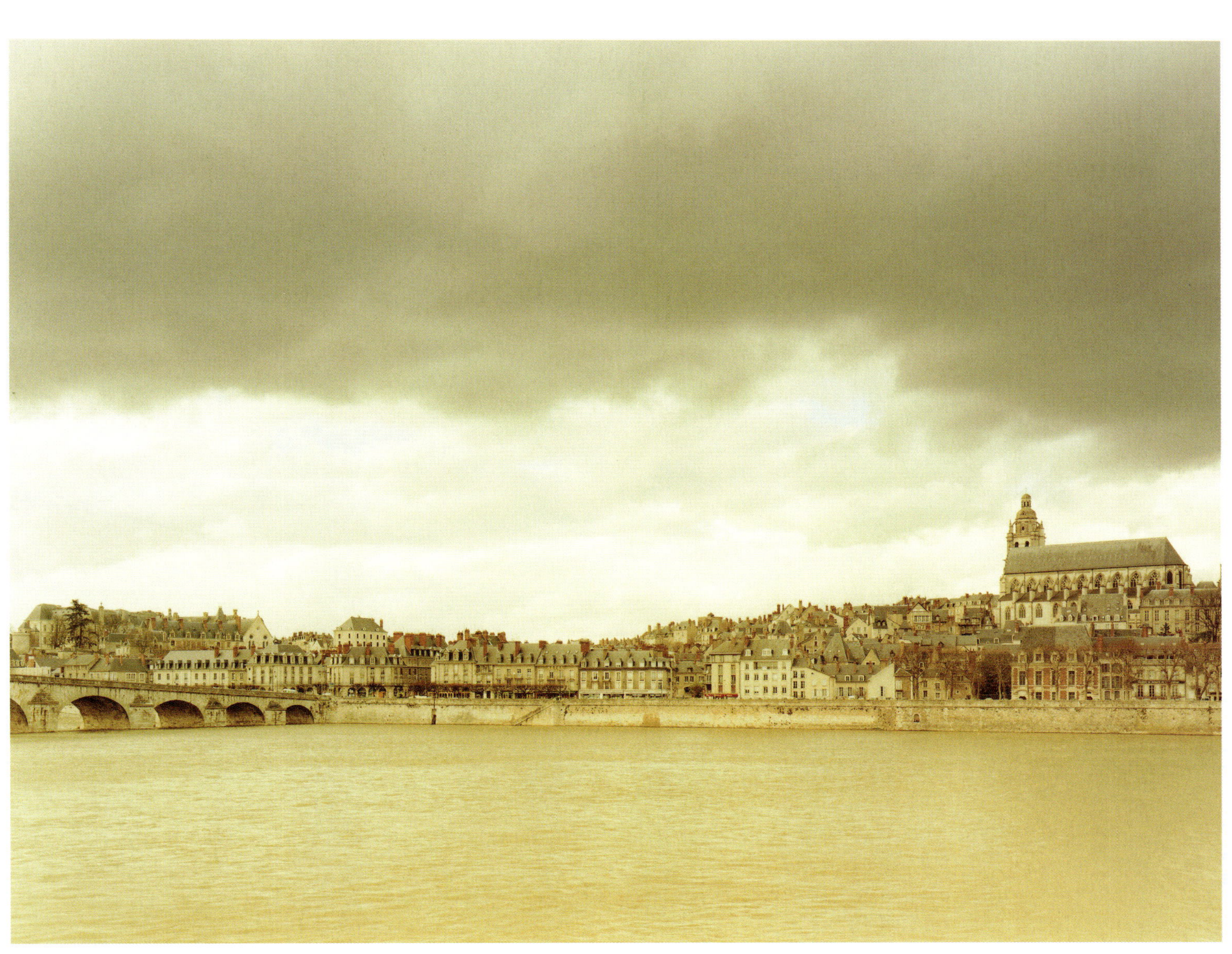

Peter Fischli and David Weiss

Dog Dish, 1987
Rubber
3 1/8 x 9 7/8 x 9 7/8 in.

Moroccan Ottoman, 1987
Rubber
11 1/4 x 22 1/16 x 22 1/16 in.

Uomo Intimo, 1987
Rubber
6 1/4 x 12 7/8 x 5 7/8 in.

Root, 1987
Rubber
22 3/8 x 18 1/2 x 14 5/8 in.

overleaf:
Untitled, 1993–94
Painted polyurethane
Dimensions variable

The Swiss artists Peter Fischli and David Weiss began working together in Los Angeles in 1979, when they collaborated on a short film. Their oeuvre has since grown to include photography, installations, sculpture, and video. Their works' dimensions can reach enormous scale, as in *Suddenly This Overview*, 1981, which consists of approximately 250 small sculptures in unfired clay. But regardless of medium or size, their projects explore a common theme: the relationship of what they call "trivial culture" to artwork.

For example, four sculptures from 1987, *Dog Dish*, *Morrocan Ottoman*, *Root*, and *Uomo Intimo* (whose title is a play on the name of the Italian men's magazine *Uomo Vogue*), are black rubber replicas of common objects displayed on white pedestals. Selecting their subjects from nature as well as from everyday domestic interiors, Fischli and Weiss produce a small "museum" of familiar objects in a material that, while mundane, also unsettlingly evokes the realm of sadomasochistic erotics. Their "museum's" expressive power resides in its unique combination of highly realistic rendering and sensuous tactility. Each object appears almost surrealistically, even fetishistically, individuated, as if the medium of black rubber had elicited the object's true nature. Each clammy, alien surface also delivers a surprisingly powerful invitation to touch; other sense responses—the taste of sweet licorice, the smell of incense or of tires permeated with gasoline—are also powerfully evoked. Like the real-life objects to which we grow attached, these works gain a character and aura all their own.

But in Fischli and Weiss' work, the sensuous reality of these black rubber statues is undeniably linked to the conceptual reality they assume as art objects placed atop white pedestals. As soon as they become "art," we examine them with an altogether different type of interest than we grant everyday objects. From Kurt Schwitters's collages to Robert Rauschenberg's combines to Andy Warhol's *Brillo Boxes*, the discarded and overlooked objects of daily life have provided modern artists with some of their richest source material. Fischli and Weiss's devotion to such "trivial culture" is also evident in *Untitled*, 1993–94, a photograph of one of their gallery installations from that year. The installation features objects such as a pallet, a paper coffee cup, and a small table, all of which Fischli and Weiss and their team of assistants have painstakingly replicated in painted polyurethane. Viewers entering the gallery encounter these objects as if they had been left behind by workmen. Indeed, according to the artists' instructions, the objects' arrangement need not follow any careful design or plan. Their display needs only to appear spontaneous, even careless. An extreme degree of subtle and precise control, however, underpins such "carelessness." For example, Fischli and Weiss alter the display according to the country in which it is exhibited; paper coffee cups are only common in America, for instance, and are therefore not included in European exhibits. The artists' attention to such details helps them achieve an uncommonly high standard of fidelity to the objects and situations their work represents. Yet it is precisely such clear-cut distinctions—between the real and the simulated, the conceptual and the sensuous, the significant and the "trivial"—that their work calls into question.

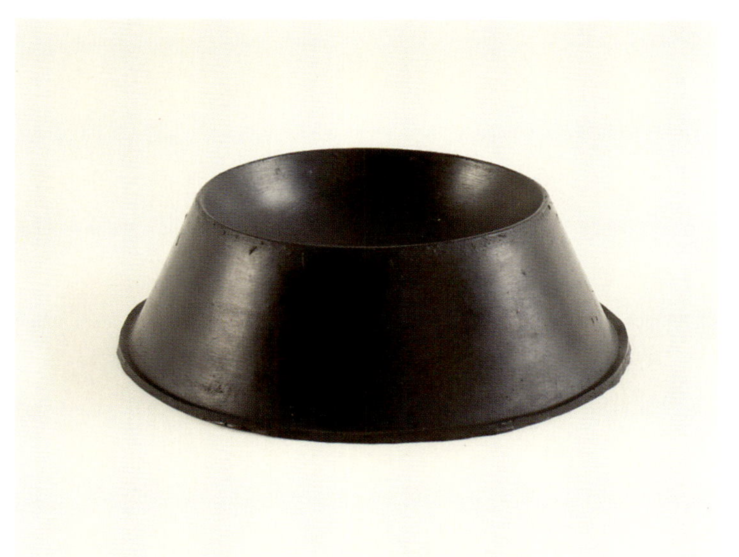
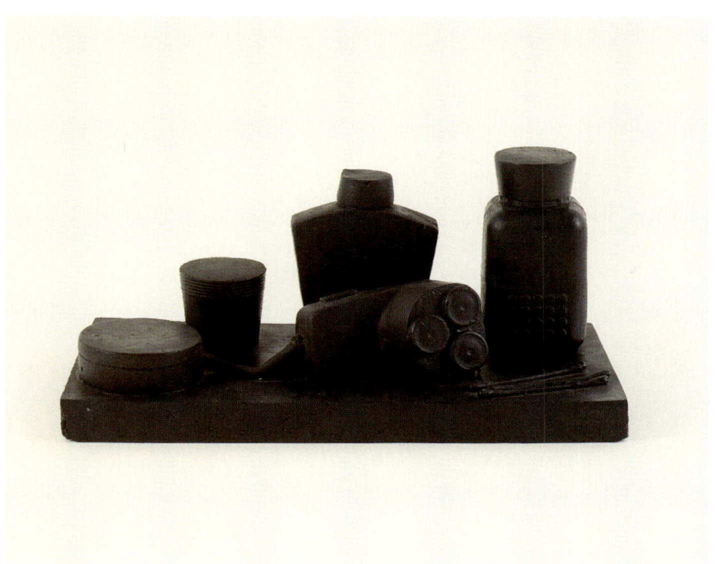
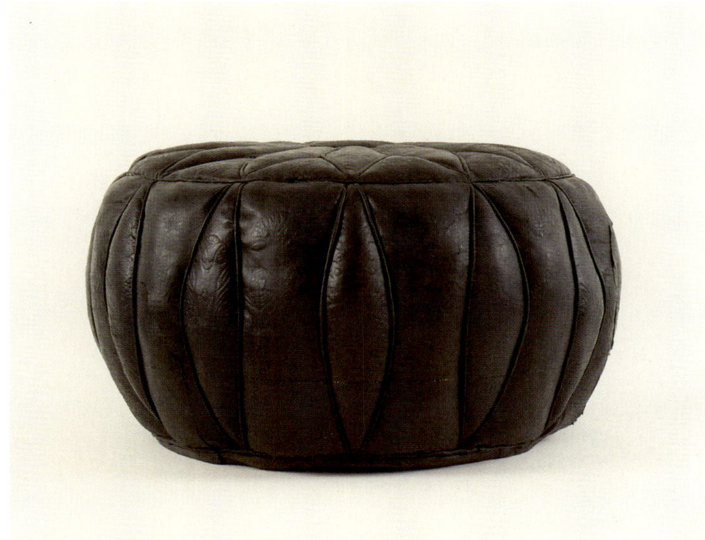
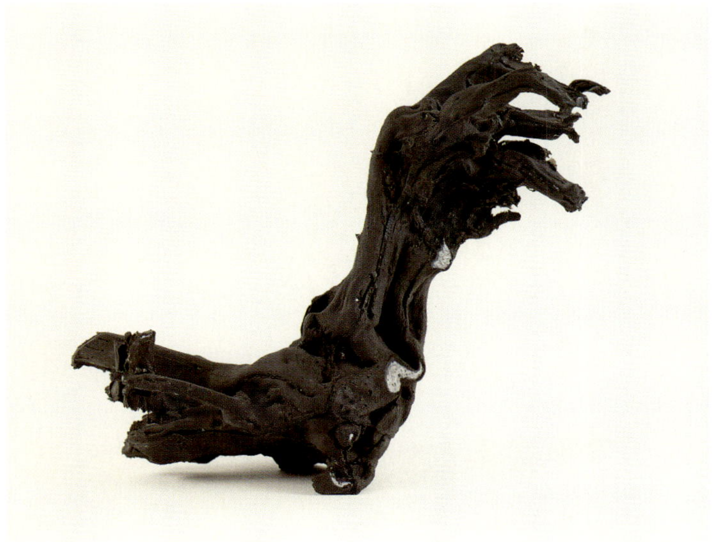

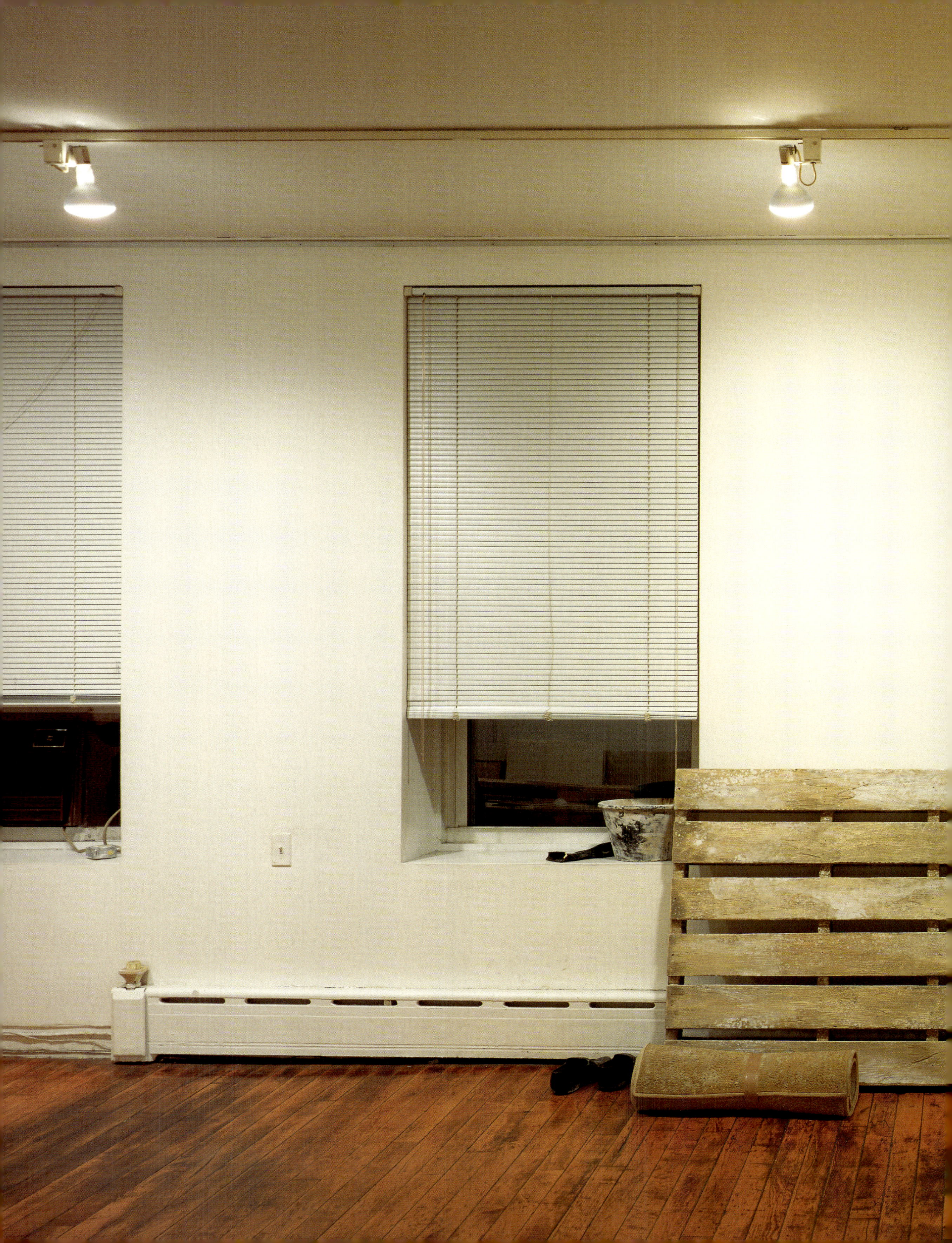

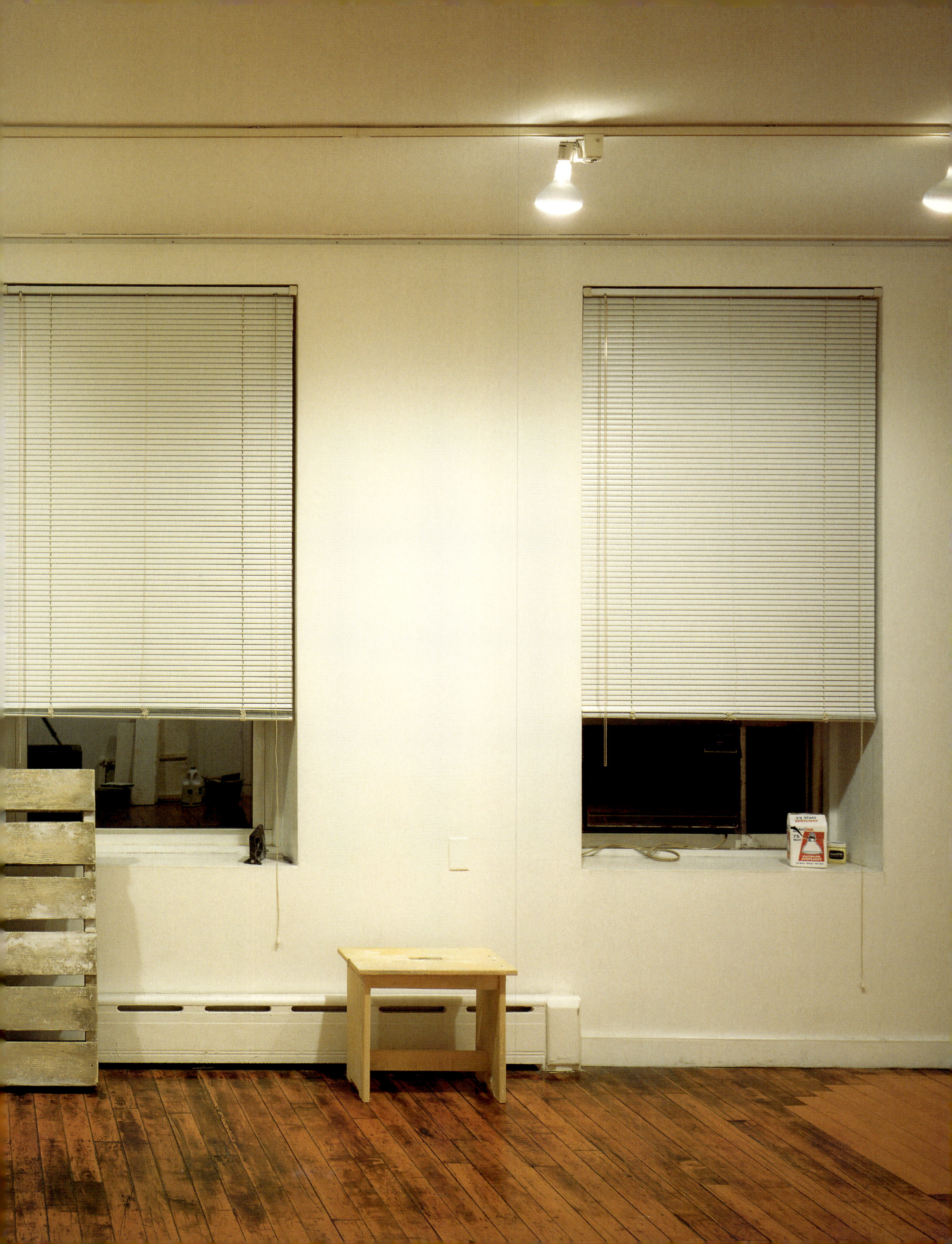
75 Watt
SPOTLIGHT
75
Watt
OUTDOOR
SPOTLIGHT

Vito Acconci

Two or Three Structures That Can Hook on to a Room and Support a Political Boomerang, 1979
Mixed media on board (12 panels)
81 1/8 x 120 in.

Vito Acconci's work *Two or Three Structures That Can Hook on to a Room and Support a Political Boomerang,* 1979, documents the artist's show at the Galleria Mario Diacono in Bologna. *Two or Three Structures* includes five photographs of the Bologna installation taken from various angles and a floor plan of the gallery where it was installed. The structure hooked onto the gallery's doors and windows and traveled between two rooms, creating new partitions within the space. *Two or Three Structures* also features two monochrome panels and two panels of text. In the first text panel, the artist has hand-written I LOVE YOU LOVE ME I LOVE YOU, etc. over and over in rows of white capital letters set against a black background; in the second, the piece's title appears in black stenciled letters on a blue ground. By describing in words what it also represents in an image and by taking a zigzag shape, Acconci's montage mimics the boomerang alluded to in its title.

A boomerang, however, is not simply an instrument designed to return to the person who throws it. More generally, it can also be something that backfires, doing harm to its initiator—a concept that assumes a complex meaning in Acconci's work. Acconci's modular arrangement of plywood ramparts and panels is strongly reminiscent of Minimalist sculpture, the dominant artistic force when he began making performance and video art and large-scale installations in the late 1960s and early 1970s. By using plain materials such as wood and steel in standardized units and repetitive forms, the Minimalists downplayed the role of personal choice and individual expression in the artistic process—shifting the focus of their work instead to the viewer's response. Often forcefully encroaching on the spectator's space, Minimalist sculpture introduced an unprecedented degree of physical awareness to the act of looking at visual art. "Don Judd and others," Acconci has said, "made me think of a room as an art space, rather than just a space that happens to hold art. The notion of being forced to confront that space and the people around the sculpture was exciting to me."[1]

Acconci's photographs, however, stage the gallery as a clean, well-lit space devoid of visitors. The two monochrome panels further reinforce this feeling of stark isolation. By literally embedding his plywood structures in the gallery space, Acconci gives concrete form to the idea that an artwork depends on viewers—as well as on a network of institutions that exhibit and market art. But as we read along the montage, this notion mutates into a narcissistic appeal for the viewer's approval. Just as his structure "needs" the gallery, he needs us, his viewers—demonstrated by the anxious urgency of his hand-scripted entreaty for love. For all their engagement with the viewer, Minimalist sculptors tended to conceive of the spectator as an almost abstract entity whose reactions could be rationally predicted. In Acconci's work, Minimalism's emphasis on objective cognitive response is displaced into the intimate realm of the artist's emotional state. The obsessiveness of his plea leaves us with the uneasy impression that the artist is already aware of its futility. In this way, even as *Two or Three Structures* engages Minimalism's aesthetic, it slyly challenges the movement's fundamental preconceptions about the relation between artist and viewer.

1. Vito Acconci quoted in "Vito Acconci: 'I Want to Put the Viewer on Shaky Ground'" by Ellen Schwartz, *Art News*, Summer 1981, 93–99.

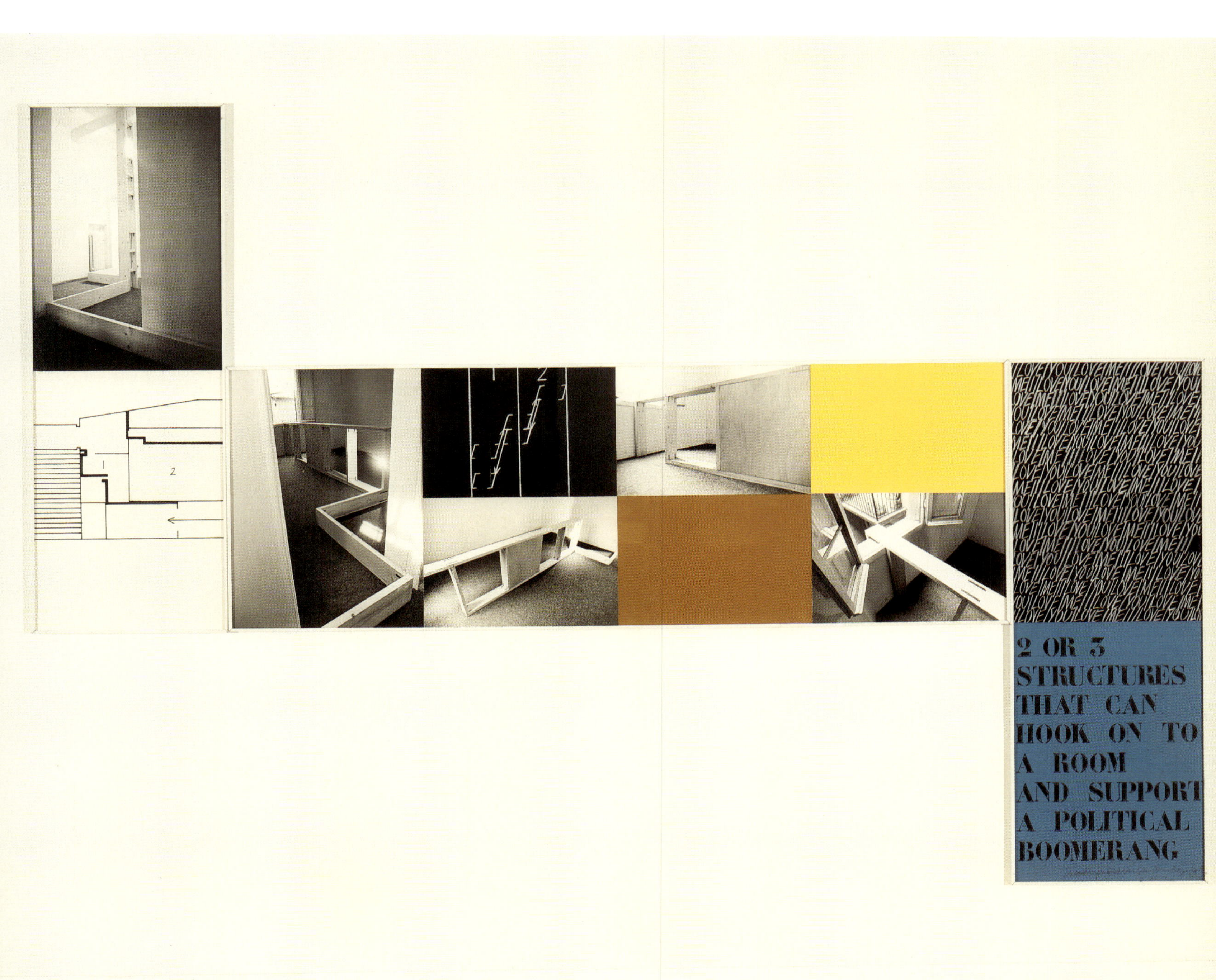
2 OR 3
STRUCTURES
THAT CAN
HOOK ON TO
A ROOM
AND SUPPORT
A POLITICAL
BOOMERANG

John Baldessari

Everything Is Purged..., 1967–68
Acrylic on canvas
68 x 56 in.

EVERYTHING IS PURGED FROM THIS PAINTING BUT ART, NO IDEAS HAVE ENTERED THIS WORK, reads John Baldessari's 1967–68 painting of that title. If Baldessari's work can be included under the rubric "Conceptualism"—a term developed in the late sixties to describe artists' investigations into the concept of art—it also begs recognition for its humanist qualities: wit, warmth, and an overriding desire on the part of its creator to communicate with his audience.

For the "word paintings" Baldessari began making in 1966, the artist chose citations from art books and sought the simplest and most legible lettering—nothing "artful" was to sneak into the works. Baldessari also hired out all the labor: Someone else built and primed the canvases, and sign painters executed the paintings according to his precise instructions. As if in humorous response to his own work's pedantic title, Baldessari has "purged" all the physical and creative engagement with his artwork's materials. What remains is raw information, delivered with negligible aesthetic intervention. The neutral noncolor of his painting's background—a "landlord's color," as he has called it—connotes unqualified banality, matching the deadpan literalism of the citation itself. To say that no ideas have entered the work is to render the painting wholly solipsistic and self-contained. Baldessari, articulating this idea as an irreverent and provocative paradox, contradicts the statement lettered on his own painting. By appropriating, delegating, and radically simplifying, he raises the issue of an artist's material and conceptual involvement in his or her work to a philosophical speculation on the nature of art and authorship.

Baldessari's word paintings led him to experiment with photo-emulsion techniques for printing text in the late 1960s, which in turn paved the way for the photographic collages he began making in the late 1970s. *The Story of One Who Set Out to Study Fear*, 1982, is a grid of twelve cropped photographs, mostly film stills from Baldessari's vast archive of "used" media images. Though the provocative title marches boldly across the work's top margin as if to indicate thematic or narrative structure, Baldessari's cropping techniques and apparently random composition eliminates any such unifying element. By lopping off the heads, bodies, and feet of his human and animal protagonists and by arranging the photographs in a modular grid, Baldessari forcefully accentuates the energy of each picture. Instead of tying the individual images to a developing or sequential structure, Baldessari presents them within a synchronic field where everything happens simultaneously without build-up or aftermath. What can these photographs tell "the one who sets out to study fear"? The fact that they are all "mediated images"—images re- and overprocessed by television, advertising, and cinema—provides a partial answer: To a certain degree, we know fear through our representations of it. The rest of the answer lies in the deliberate excisions of Baldessari's grid: Fear cannot be "learned," and the tools of such a study will always leave out the essential, lived experience.

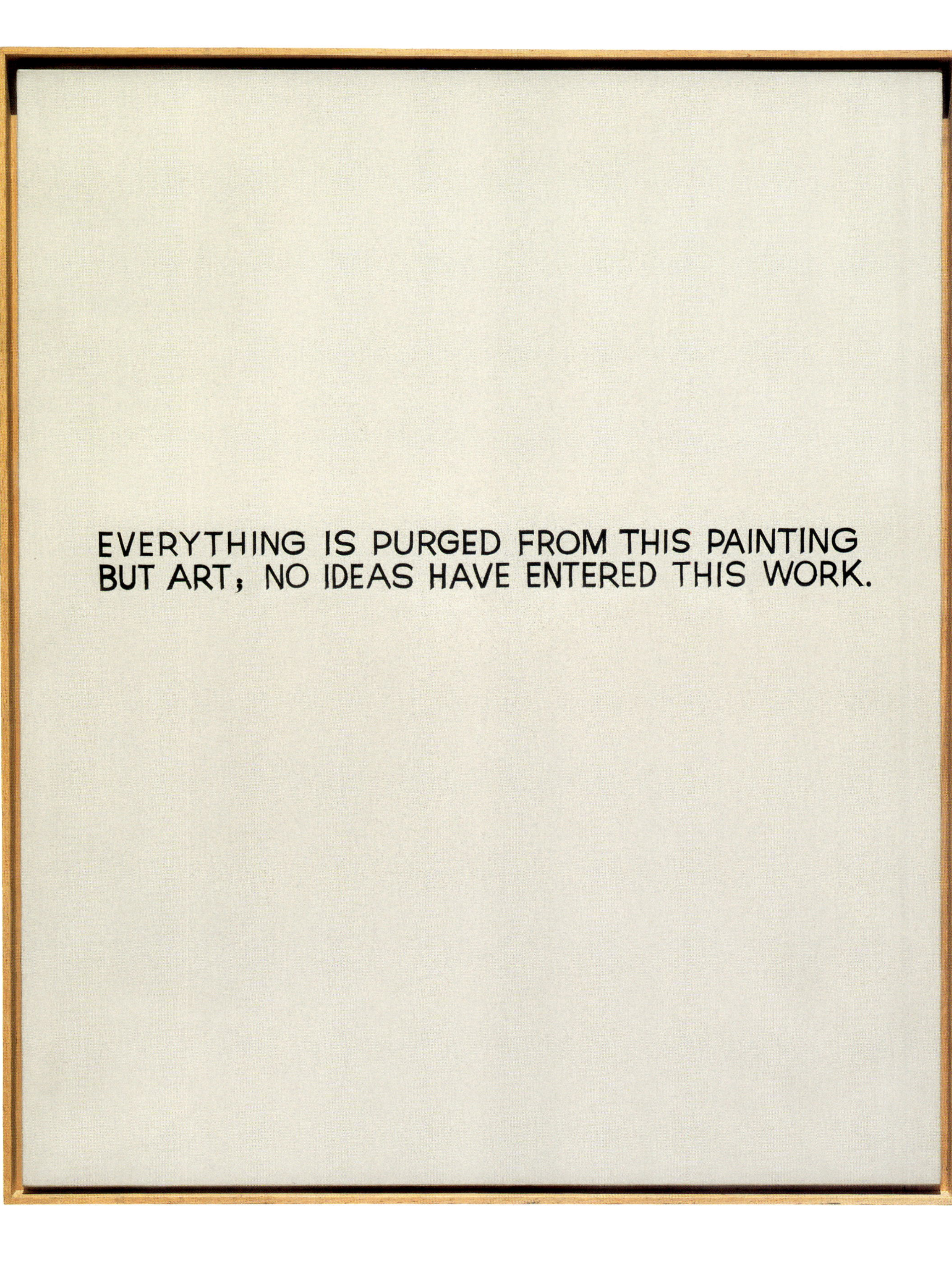
EVERYTHING IS PURGED FROM THIS PAINTING
BUT ART, NO IDEAS HAVE ENTERED THIS WORK.

John Baldessari

The Story of One Who Set Out to Study Fear, 1982

Twelve gelatin silver photographs with text

$83\ ^{7}/_{8}$ x 72 in.

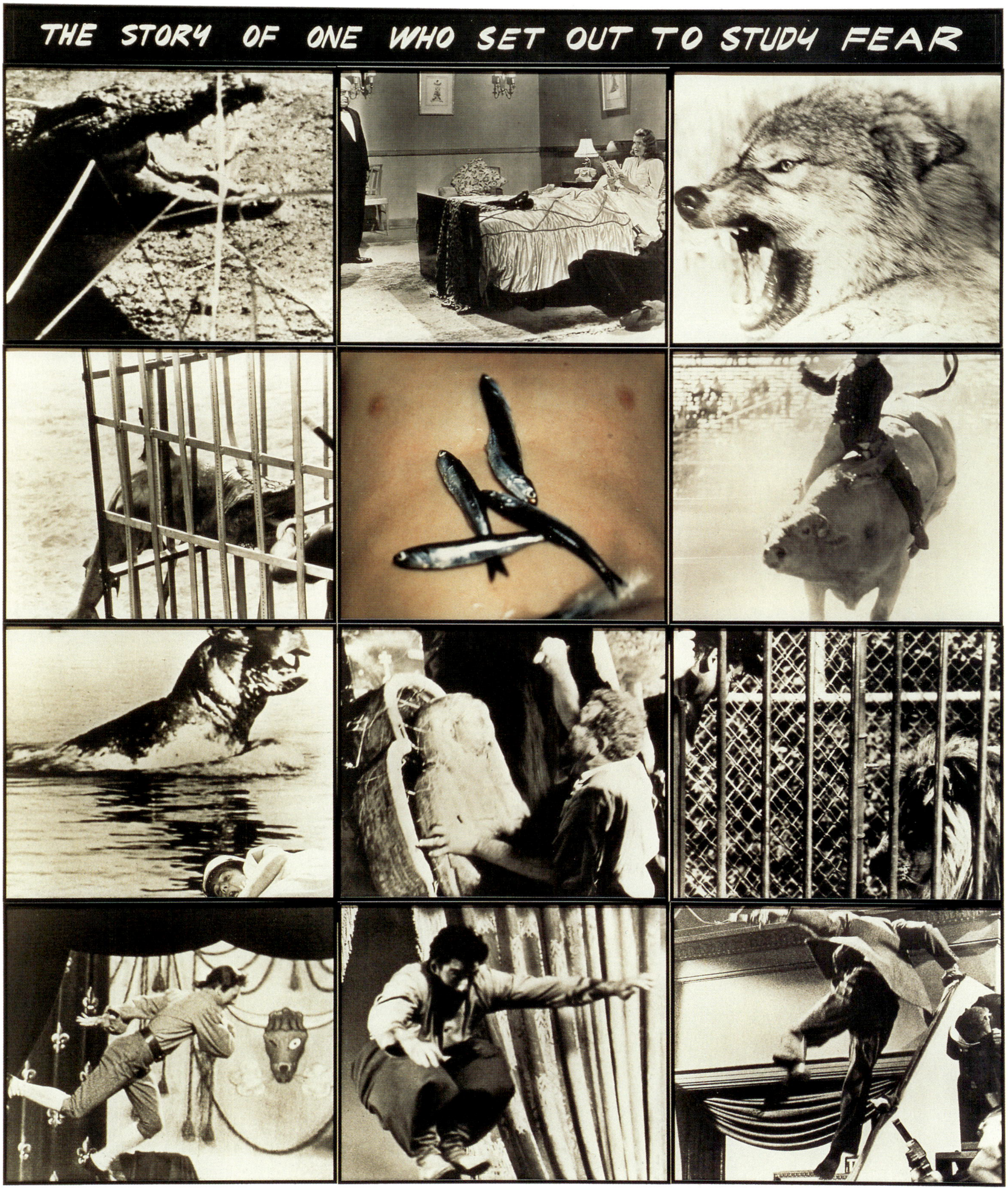

THE STORY OF ONE WHO SET OUT TO STUDY FEAR

Mel Bochner

48" Standards (#24), 1969
Brown wrapping paper, tape, and Letraset on wall
86 3/4 x 98 3/4 in.

When asked about his use of brown paper in *48" Standards (#24)*, 1969, Bochner replied: "[It] began as just a convenience, something that was always around the studio. It came in sizes, three feet by four feet, which are the standard measurements of most building materials. I slowly came to realize that these measurements are so deeply embedded in our experience that they regulate our perception, yet remain completely invisible."[1] In *48" Standards* Bocher stapled two of these sheets of paper directly to the gallery wall. He then measured and notated their length across the same wall in black tape and Letraset. Twelve inches up the longer side of one, Bochner made a thin cut, creating a thirty-six-inch square within his ready-made rectangle. The same twelve-inch distance also separates the two sheets of paper. With this arrangement and the juncture of two strips of black tape in the upper left corner, Bochner created a "phantom" rectangle that, exactly like its brown-paper counterparts, measures three by four feet.

Just as construction paper and tape take the place of traditional artistic materials, like paint and canvas, Bochner's what-you-see-is-what-you-get measurements replace conventional artistic techniques such as illusionism—the appearance of three-dimensional space on a flat surface. Instead, Bochner introduces a set of universal and instantly comprehensible calculations. Many American artists working in the 1960s had come to view artistic illusion as a form of mystification—something that undermined the viewer's capacity to think and perceive independently. *48" Standard* encourages the viewer to consider not only the absence of illusionism but the physical context—here, the gallery wall—on which the convention of illusionism depends.

3 Photographs + 1 Diagram (Row C), was first created in 1966, as part of a larger piece titled *36 Photographs and 12 Diagrams*. As its title suggests, the work features thirty-six photographs and twelve diagrams arranged in a grid. *Three Photographs* consists of three photographs and a diagram hung in a column. The first of Bochner's *3 Photographs* depicts a five-sided pyramidal construction made of cubic wooden blocks. The next presents a side view of the same construction. The final photograph shows an aerial view, so that the descending steps appear to radiate from a protruding center. The schematic drawing at the top of the column employs the numbers one through four, indicating the number of blocks in each vertical stack of the construction. All four images present the same object; the differences between them result entirely from the difference in the photographer's perspective in each of the three shots and, in the case of the drawing, from the exchange of the visual media of sculpture and photography for the language of numbers and graphs.

The gridded display of *36 Photographs* enables the viewer to grasp the pyramid's three-dimensional form from several angles more or less simultaneously. However, as Bochner's work illustrates, no single perspective offers a complete view. But if the diagram demonstrates the rational basis for his work, the photographs themselves subtly reintroduce an element of illusionism—the very thing that Bochner sought to dispel. The photos often create the impression of disorienting bulges and corkscrews; thus perceptual illusions remain despite the work's evident effort to rid itself of optical play. The mixture of photography and sculpture generates perceptual mystery, even in a work that can be diagrammed and explained. As Bochner's procedures become ever more explicit, the odd split between human reason and perception returns with even more subtlety and force.

1. Mel Bochner quoted in a March 1969 interview with Elayne Varian, *Documents* no. 20 (Spring 2001): 4.

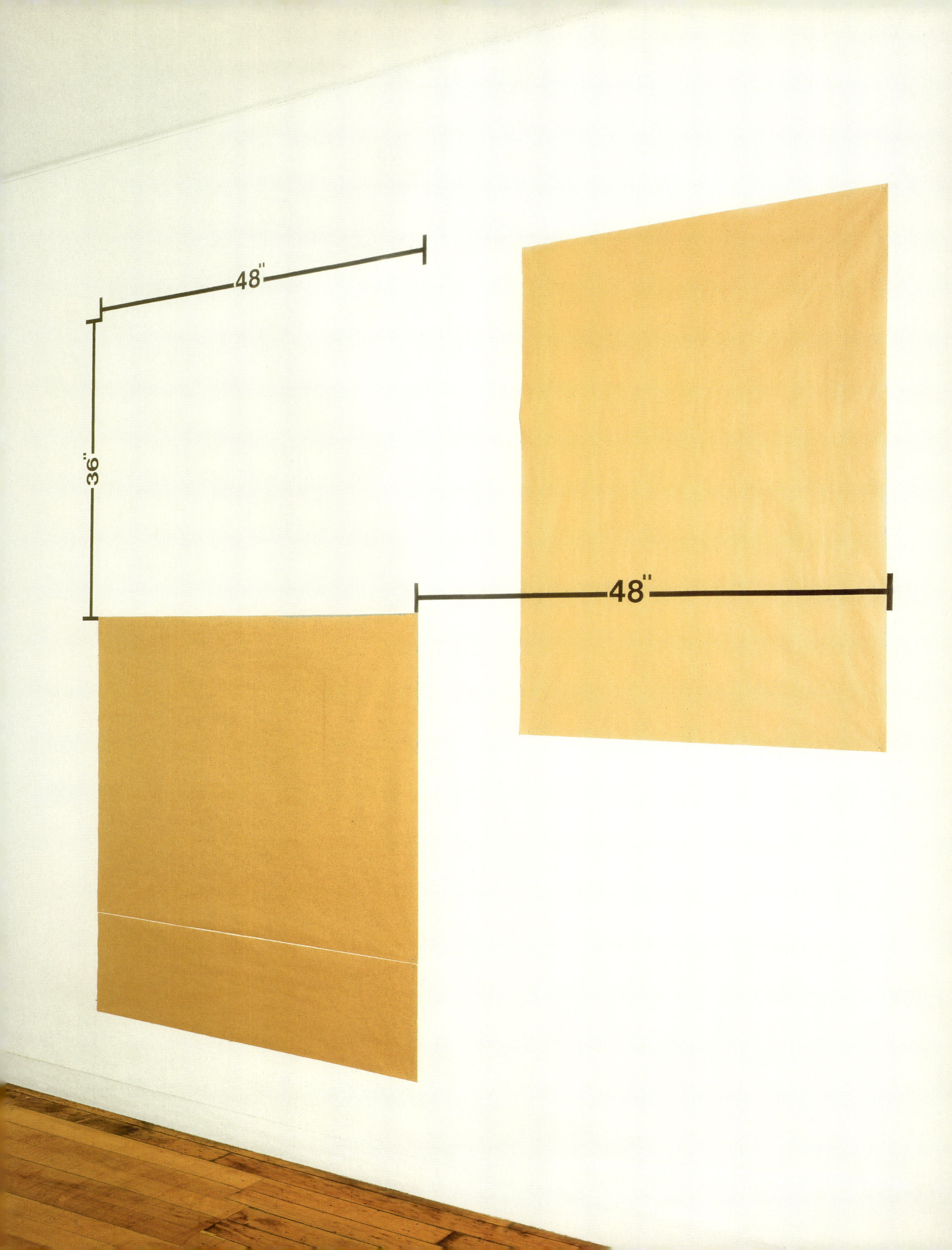
48"
36"
48"

Mel Bochner

3 Photographs + 1 Diagram (Row C), 1968/2001

Four gelatin silver photographs mounted on board

20 x 20 in. each

90 x 20 in. overall

1	2	3	4	3	2	1
2	2	3	4	3	2	2
3	3	3	4	3	3	3
4	4	4	4	4	4	4
3	3	3	4	3	3	3
2	2	3	4	3	2	2
1	2	3	4	3	2	1

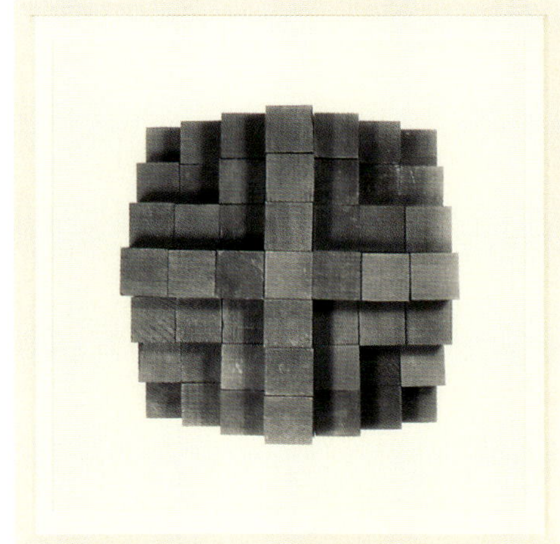

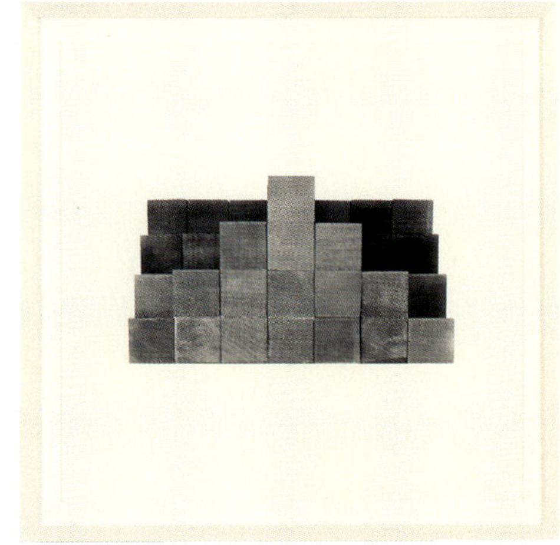

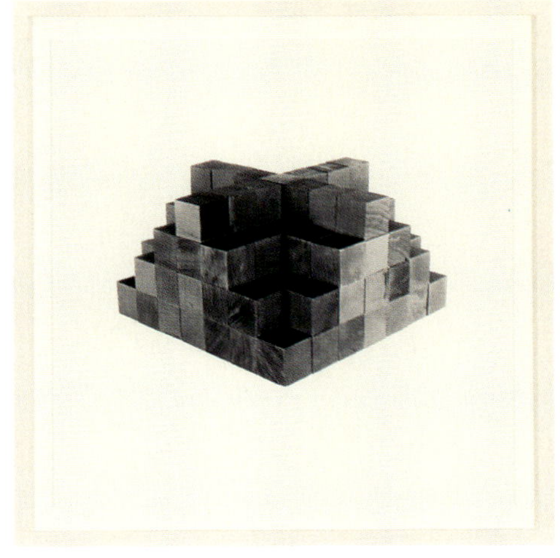

Robert Morris

Nine Fiberglass Sleeves, 1967
Fiberglass
48 1/16 x 24 x 24 in.

Nine Fiberglass Sleeves, 1967, an imposing group of square, open-topped columns, draws out the internal contradictions of medium and process that led to the dramatic transformation in Robert Morris's sculptural work in 1967. In *Nine Sleeves*, the smooth, often reflective industrial surfaces and geometric forms that had characterized Morris's earlier Minimalist vocabulary morph into a highly evocative, slightly sinister suggestiveness. By wrapping fiberglass around metal molds so that its rough side faces out, Morris accentuates his material's inherent qualities—its surface inconsistencies and unevenness. Sharp corners, as in the closed forms of his earlier work, have disappeared; fiberglass, Morris notes, "wants to take curves—in such shapes it is extremely strong."[1] Yet if his material's demands suggested a compromise with the raw angularity of his previous work, the strictly symmetrical grouping of *Nine Sleeves* underscores its arresting architectural presence. Morris's interest in Neolithic building complexes is tangible in the work's stirring, almost tomblike, distinctly anthropomorphic aura.

Nineteen sixty-seven was also the first year Morris began working in felt. The following year he published an article titled "Anti Form," which became a manifesto of the post-Minimalist era. The rigid materials classically used to "perpetuate form," Morris argued, should be replaced with materials that exploit gravity, chance, and indeterminacy. *Untitled*, 1980, belongs to the series Morris began in 1976, mounting twinned rectangles of felt on the wall and pinning them backward to create deep vertical pleats. The erotic charge of the work's languid folds is made even more intimate by the uncanny familiarity of this nostalgic—even childlike—material. Felt's stiffness lends itself to large-scale works, and indeed, the scale of *Untitled* communicates some of the same grandeur as *Nine Sleeves*' totemic solemnity. Hinting at inarticulable emotional, spiritual, or even sexual regressions and revelations, Morris's works evoke the hidden mechanisms of collective and individual memory.

Yet Morris's sculptures also transcend the purely affective space of interiority. His work radically expands the definition of artistic means to encompass abstract concepts and systems. Thus, gravity, uncertainty, and process become not only Morris's objectives but his very *means*—means that rupture the logical austerity of abstract conceptual thought itself. The symmetry of *Nine Sleeves* collides with the freedom of the aleatory, while the uniformity of *Untitled* gives way to minute but exhaustive difference. Morris's art demonstrates that the capacity for logical thinking is both extended and defied by its necessary and inalienable physical dimension. Works like *Untitled* unravel the simplicity and rigor of their formal starting place—and, simultaneously, the reliable consistency of thought itself.

1. Robert Morris quoted in "Robert Morris: Formal Disclosures." Interview with Pepe Karmel in *Art in America*, June 1995, 94.

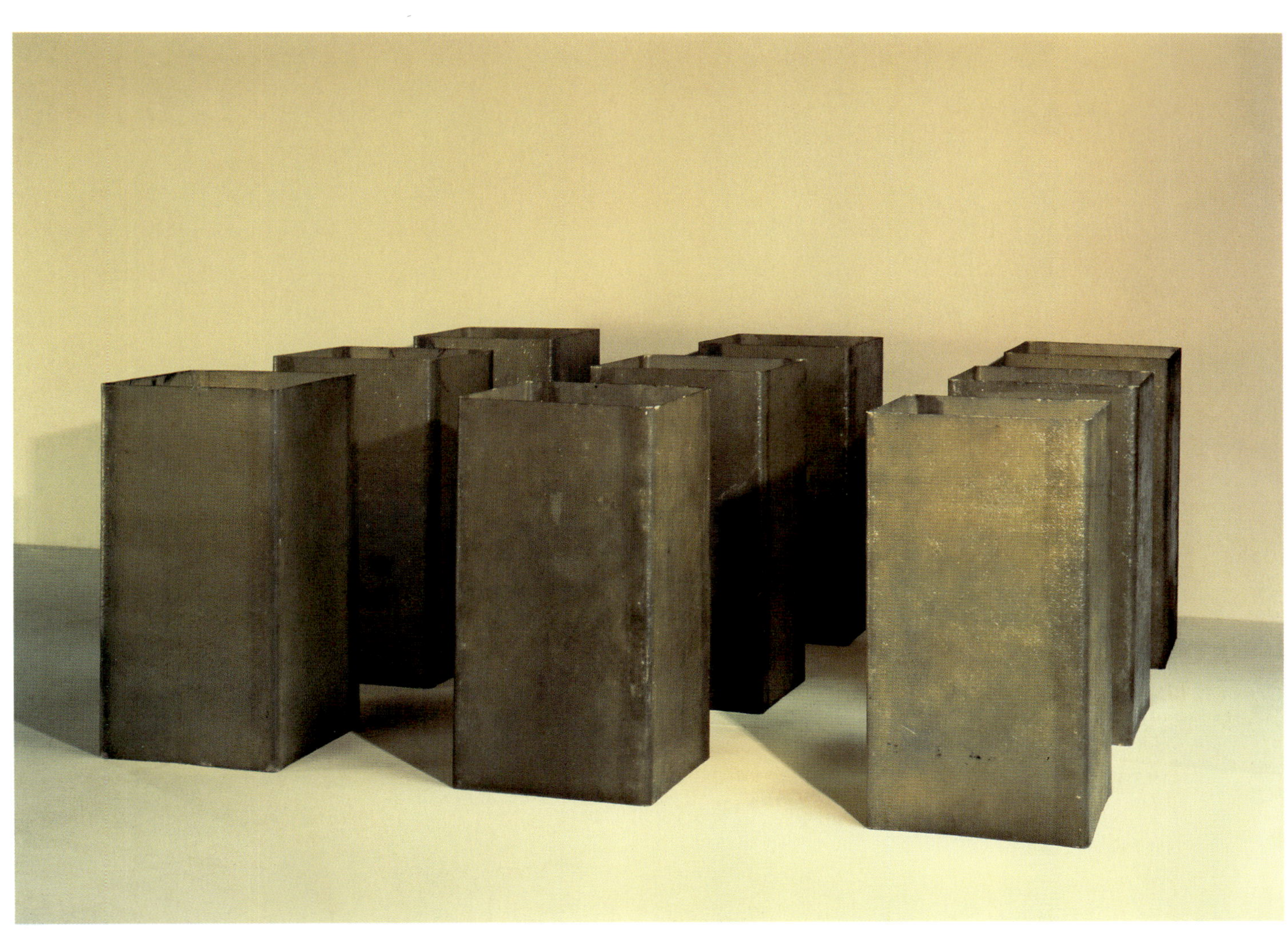

Robert Morris
Untitled, 1980
Felt
98 x 118 in.

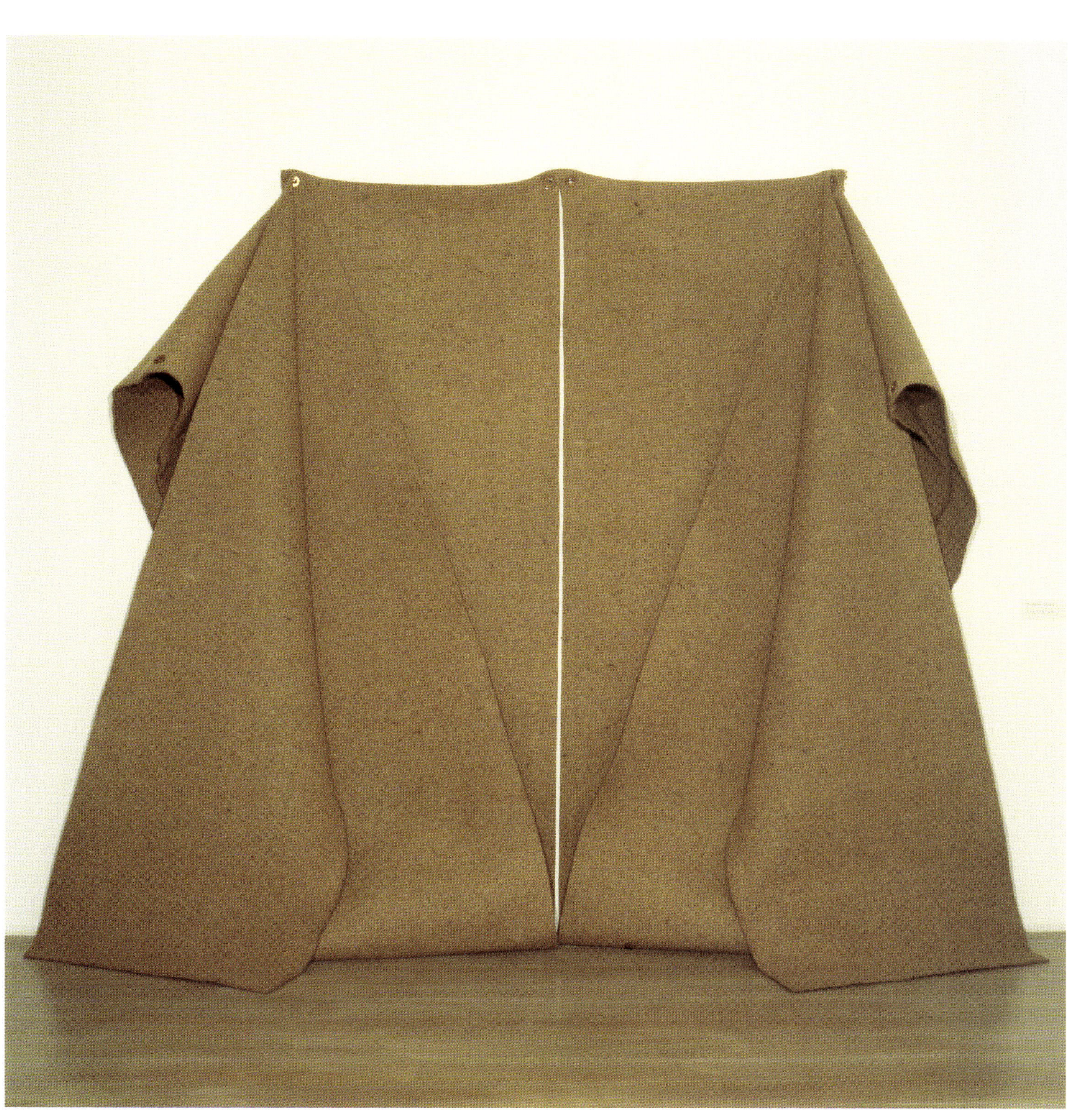

Dan Flavin

Untitled (To the "Innovator" of Wheeling Peachblow), 1966–68
Gold, pink, and daylight fluorescent lights
88 3/16 x 88 3/16 in.

Since his first use of unadorned fluorescent light fixtures in 1963, Dan Flavin has almost exclusively employed standard industrial fluorescent tubing to create his sculptural constructions. Yet within this rigorous limitation Flavin has achieved an extraordinary range of effects. *Untitled*, 1966–68, a seven-foot-square frame installed in the corner of a room, is made of a pair of horizontal "daylight" tubes that face the viewer, while two vertical columns of rose and gold face backward, into the corner. Because the vertical rose and gold tubes are invisible from the front, their warm auburn glow appears to emanate from the corner itself. The subtitle of this work, *To the "Innovator" of Wheeling Peachblow*, alludes to that unearthly glow. Named after a type of Chinese porcelain with similar coloring, Wheeling Peachblow is an American-made glass distinguished by its deep red hue and yellowish-green undertones.

Because of its placement in a corner, *Untitled* draws attention to the kind of ordinary architectural joints that are found in every room. The corner that *Untitled* frames becomes something to be looked at, something deserving of study. This effect—which likens the corner to an abstract painting—is heightened by the work's almost painterly gradation of colors. Western painting from Rembrandt to Vermeer to Seurat to Rothko has treated light as one of its most precious subjects; Flavin continues this tradition but radically alters its terms. His light is severed from any relation to nature, from the temporality of nature's dusks and dawns; it is instead presented as an industrial readymade. Extracted from any interaction with objects that would create shadow play, it is not incorporated into a pictorial composition and replaces the act of representation with the "fact" of light itself.

Yet in Flavin's work light also often seems disconnected from its physical source, for he increases the enveloping or ambient sensations of "bathing light," distancing the viewer from the experience of the actual neon tubes. In *Untitled* this effect is amplified by the blinding brightness of the daylight horizontals and by the invisibility of the source of the reddish peach glow. The light of the rose- and gold-colored tubes spreads and diffuses, creating a fathomless pink vacuum "inside" the square. Despite his preference for industrial, even crude materials, Flavin's art divests light of its materiality, transforming it into something mysterious, even transcendent.

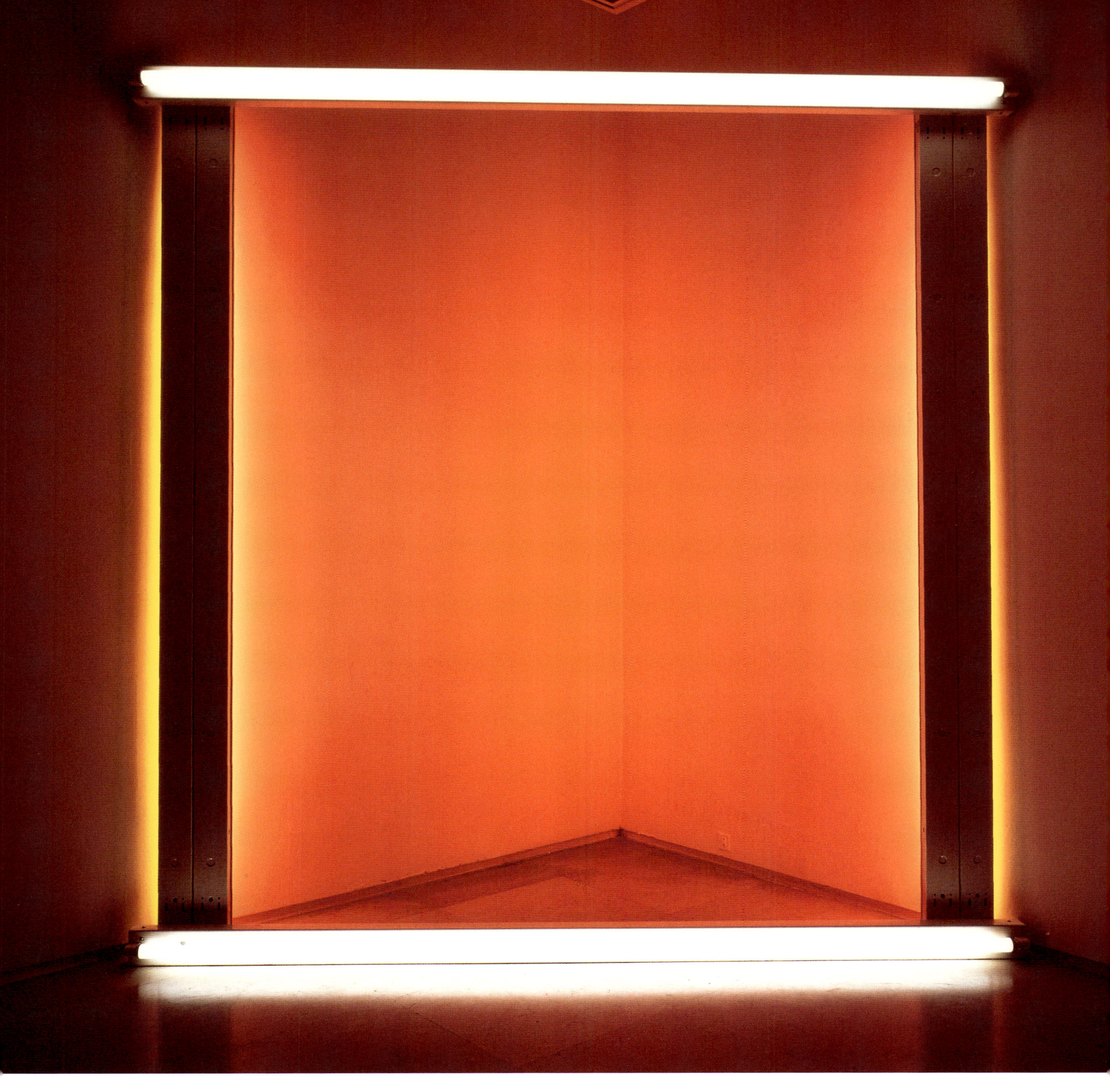

Sol LeWitt

Arcs from Four Corners, 1971
Lead pencil on wall
Dimensions variable

Sol LeWitt's 1971 wall drawing *Arcs from Four Corners* is a dense yet delicate network of penciled lines. On the one hand, it is a work that invites prolonged, almost hypnotic study, only gradually yielding the mysterious properties of its quiet calculus. On the other hand, it is a work that can be fully encapsulated merely by its laconic title and accompanying caption: "Lead pencil on wall, dimensions variable." This oscillation between the lyric and the objective, the dynamic and the inert, the irrationally obsessive and the hyperrationally exact is the hallmark of LeWitt's drawings and wall drawings, paintings and modular structures, prints and books. Created in October 1968, LeWitt's first wall drawing was simply the transposition onto a gallery wall of one page of his *Drawing Project 1968 (Fours)*, a series of after-the-fact drawings in isometric perspective which LeWitt had been making of his three-dimensional structures. By transposing his sheet drawing to the gallery wall, LeWitt withdrew the necessity of canvas or paper support. This revolutionary move extracted both permanence and mobility from the artwork—for a wall drawing cannot be physically moved like a painting or sculpture, and it is painted over at the close of an exhibition, to be redrawn in the next venue.

LeWitt was one of a number of artists in the 1960s who sought to bring the artwork into a more direct engagement with its physical surroundings. He also shared with many of his peers the utopian values articulated in the era's activism and social unrest—in particular, the belief in public space as a site of open exchange, where pamphleteering, debate, and demonstrating could bring new ideas to new audiences. By bringing the wall literally inside the work, *Arcs from Four Corners* introduces a constitutive element of public space to the formerly restricted, elitist arena of the artwork. Moreover, the prospective owner of a wall drawing buys not the physical work itself, but the right to implement it. Indeed, LeWitt himself only conceives and designs his work, leaving the execution to teams of assistants. It is solely LeWitt's conceptual control—not the physical engagement that has always been presumed to be critical to the artist's role—that authenticates his work and lends it its rigor.

Yet the conceptual dimension of LeWitt's work never overshadows its formal complexity. The almost kaleidoscopic density of *Arcs from Four Corners* gives the work a pulsating optical quality and a play between flatness and the suggestion of three dimensions. Sometimes LeWitt's descriptions for a wall drawing can take the form of paragraph-long sentences, which can be exhibited alongside the works or even in place of them: "A rectangle whose left and right sides are two-thirds as long as its top and bottom sides and whose left side is located where a line...."[1] Like the drawings' obdurate patterning, the succinctness of these texts creates a peculiarly musical rhythm; like the serial music of his friends and contemporaries, Steve Reich and Philip Glass, the generative logic and self-exhausting repetition produce uncanny, melodic fluctuations.

1. LeWitt text quoted in Lucy R. Lippard, "The Structures, the Structures and the Wall Drawings, the Structures and the Wall Drawings and the Books," in *Sol LeWitt* (New York: Museum of Modern Art, 1978).

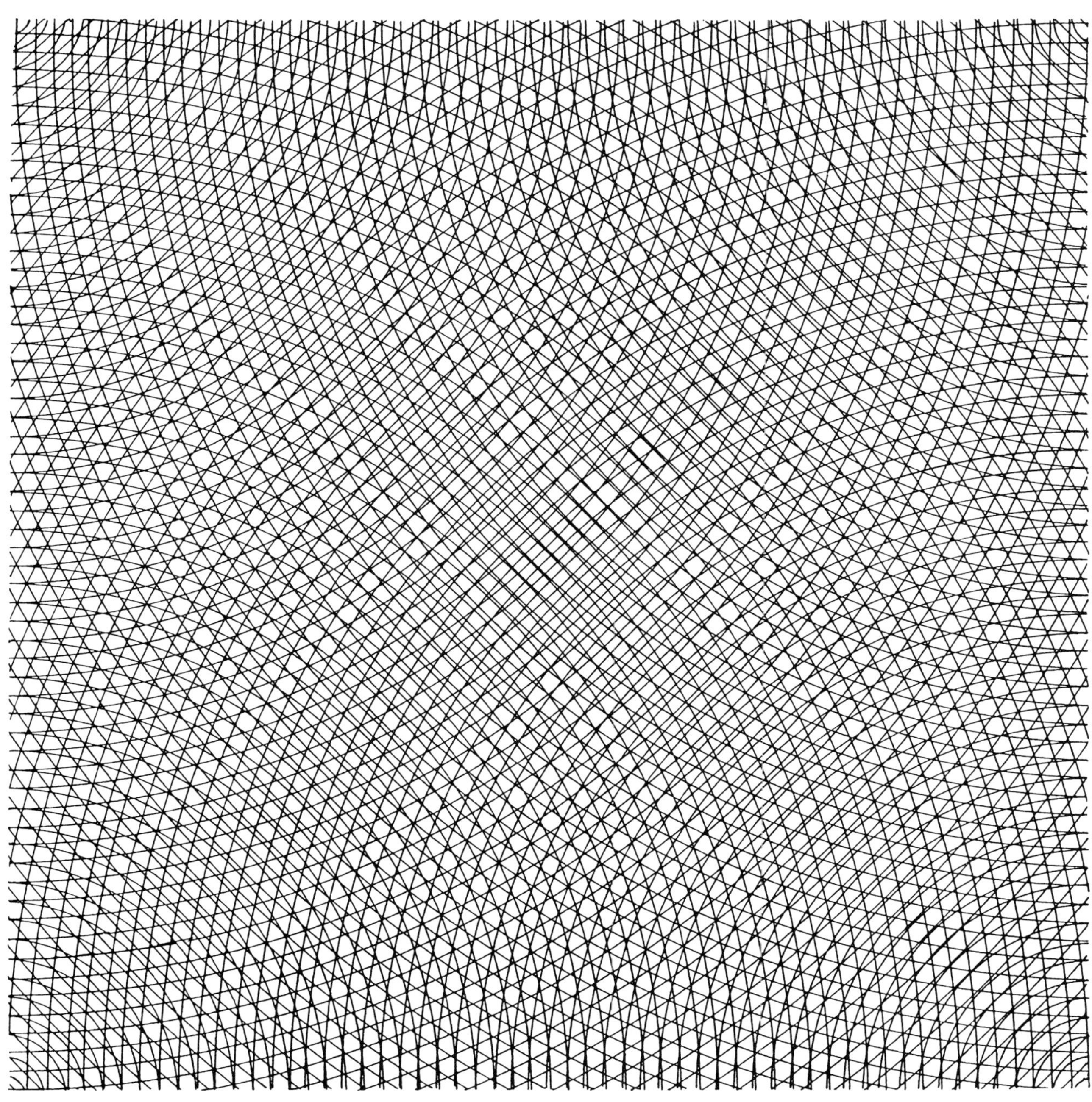

Bruce Nauman

My Name As Though It Were Written On The Surface of the Moon: Bbbbbbbbbbrrrrrrrrrruuuuuuuuuuccccccccccceeeeeeeeee, 1967
Fifteen gelatin silver photographs collaged on paper
12 1/2 x 137 in.

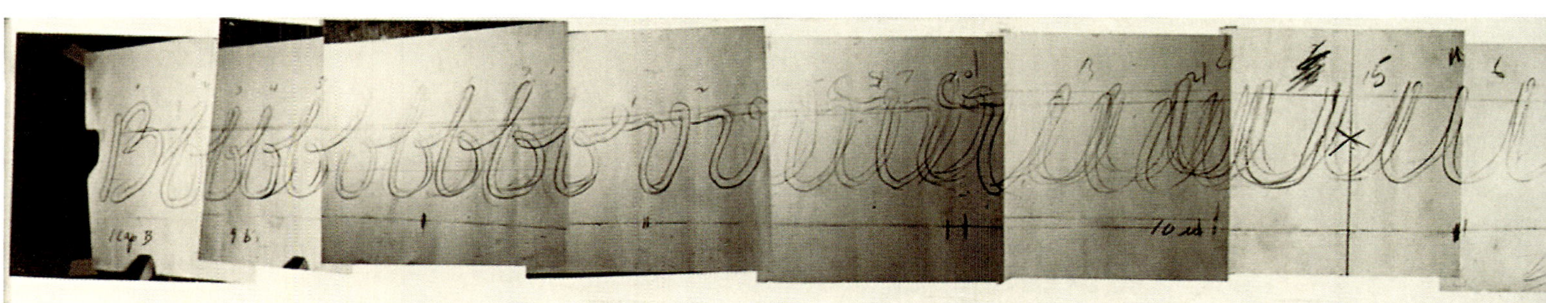

An artist who has worked in video, sculpture, film, performance, photography, set design, printmaking, and painting—and more often than not, in combinations of two or more of these media—Bruce Nauman confounds attempts at categorization and even categorical meaning. He frequently explores the same subject or theme in related pieces, for example in the composite photograph *My Name As Though It Were Written on the Surface of the Moon: Bbbbbbbbbbrrrrrrrrrruuuuuuuuuuccccccccccceeeeeeeeee*, 1967, and the neon sculpture *My Name As Though It Were Written on the Surface of the Moon*, 1968. Both transcribe the artist's first name in handwritten form (albeit almost unrecognizably) into very different media.

Nauman produced the composite photograph by taking successive shots across an expanse of text, elongating it in an unnatural manner underscored by his penciled notations above and below the letters themselves. The work functions almost as a sketch for the sculpture created the following year, which makes a similarly long lateral stretch out of glowing blue neon. The visual impact of elongated writing electrified in neon gives the work an eerie and enigmatic presence. In addition, any easy differentiation between various media and types of representation is challenged: Writing becomes image, sculpture becomes light, and the author's own name is subsumed in a meditation on identity, visibility, and legibility. For Nauman, who frequently documents his own performances and aspects of his private studio space as works of art, the questions of an artist's identity and an artist's process are always closely linked. The unpronounceable "name" in his neon sculpture and composite photograph introduces an element of playful narcissism into Nauman's ongoing investigation of these subjects.

During the late sixties the idea of "writing on the moon" resonated with public significance because of the thousands of pictures returned from the lunar surface by U.S. space probes from 1966–68. More intimately, both the photograph and the neon sculpture play on the

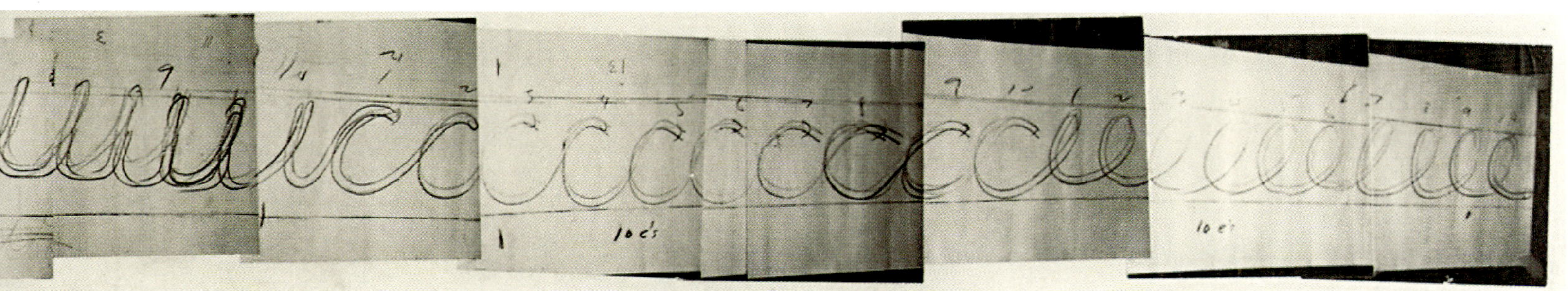

relation between the unyielding physical presence of any artwork and the metaphysical constructs that are equally part of art's makeup. On the one hand, the viewer must decode the bar of undulating graphic rhythm in order to extract the word *BRUCE*. On the other hand, Nauman's work is not reducible to the word it represents any more than it is reducible to his actual identity, as symbolized by his name. An artwork is not simply what we can say it "means," Nauman's elliptical neon sculpture suggests: It is also an indefinable physical and imaginative presence, exceeding even the intentions of its merely mortal maker.

overleaf:
My Name As Though It Were Written On the Surface of the Moon, 1968
Neon tubing
11 x 200 3/4 x 2 in.

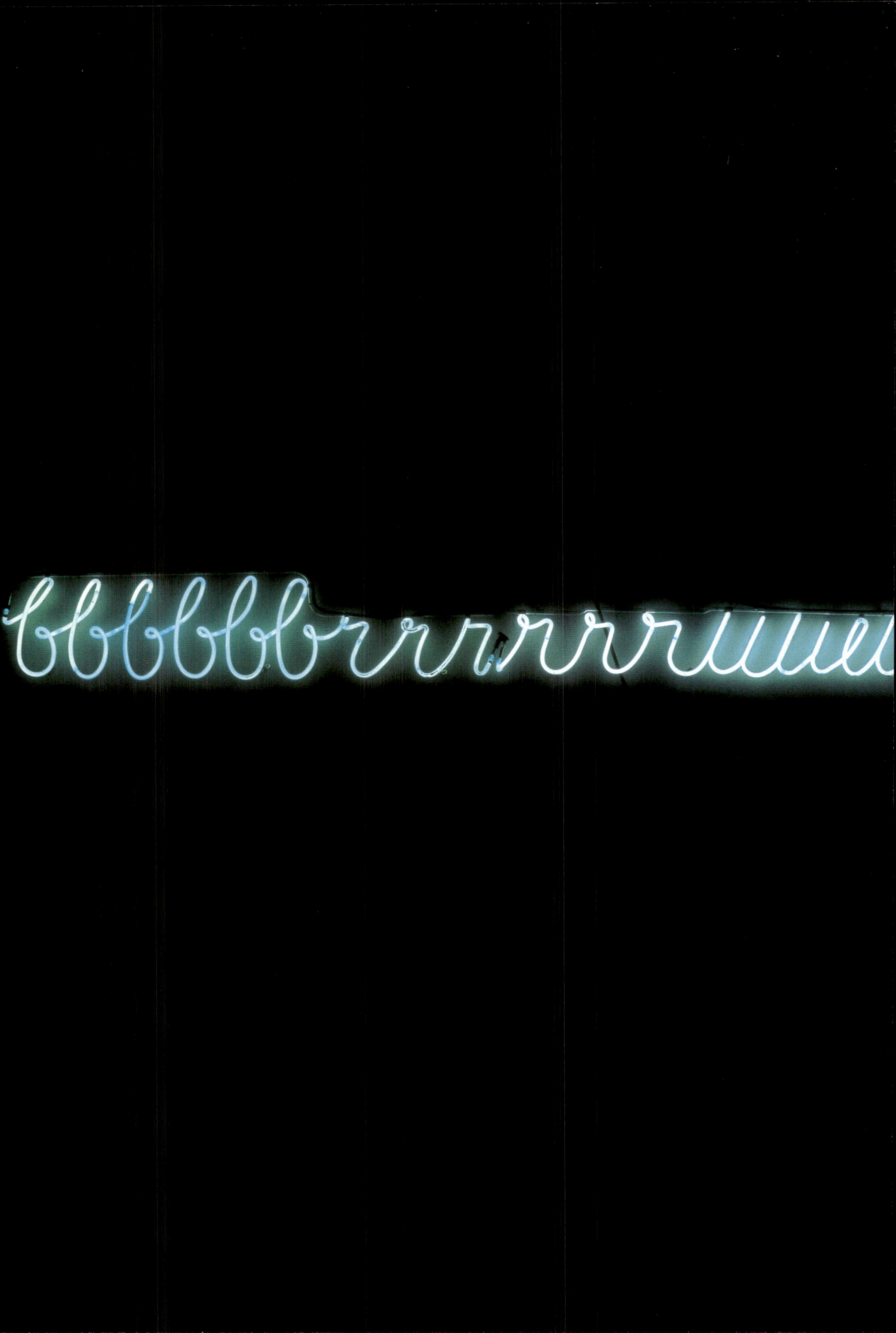

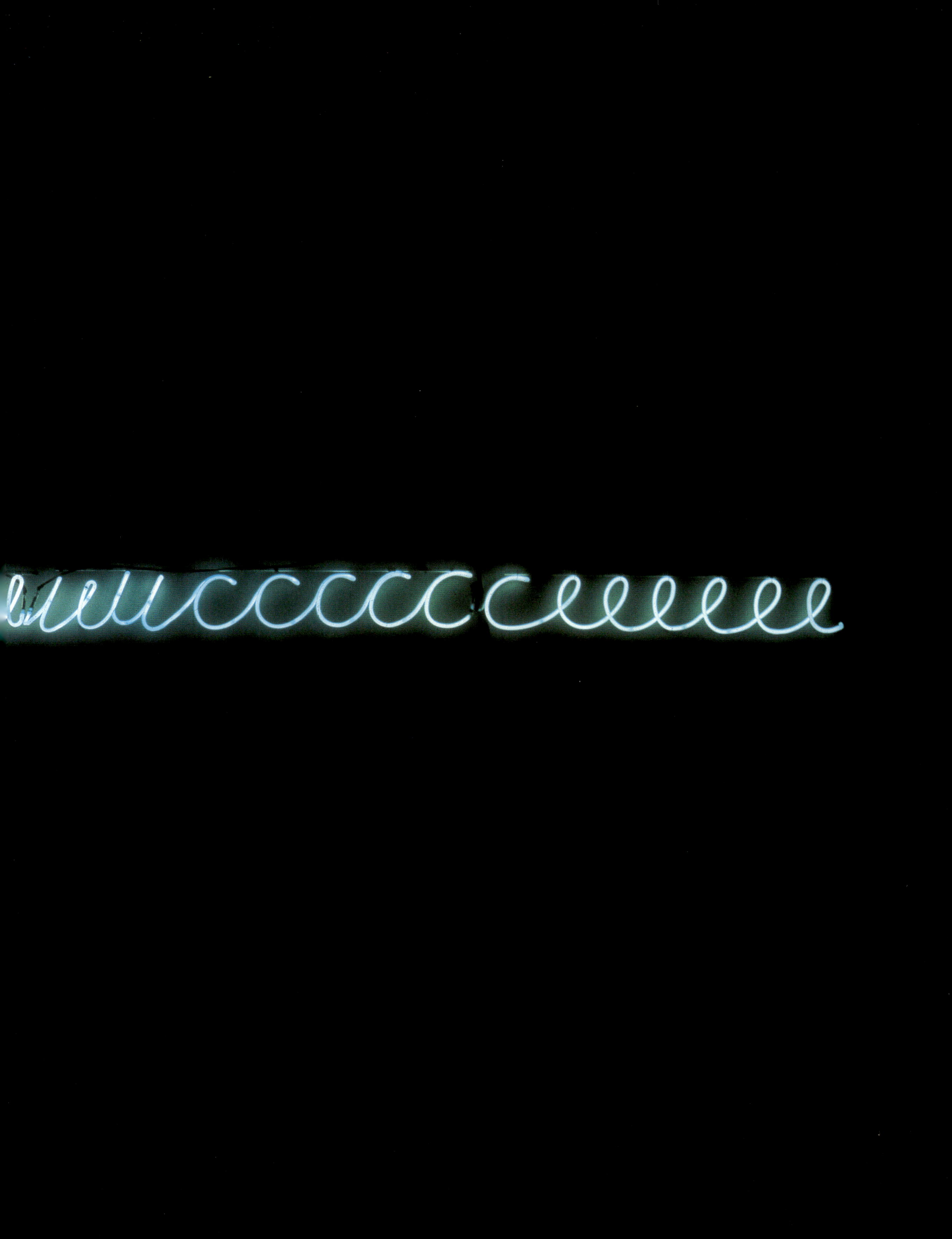

Donald Judd

Untitled, 1967
Blue galvanized steel
5 1/4 x 9 x 24 3/4 in.

These two untitled works from the late 1960s demonstrate the range and complexity of Donald Judd's art. *Untitled*, 1967, is composed of a blue galvanized steel bar to which Judd has attached four blue steel blocks. Although the blocks are arranged in order of decreasing width, the intervals between them remain constant. Known in Judd's work as a "progression," this type of variation uses mathematical calculations to determine the dimensions of the work's elements. *Untitled*, 1968, is a red wooden parallelogram: Both pairs of sides are parallel, but none is at a right angle to another. Grooves line the work; on one side they stop approximately one inch from the edge; on the opposite side they reach the edge, creating a rutted border.

Judd was a leading practitioner and theorist among the American Minimalists, who sought to create art that, as he put it, would depend entirely on "the viewer's knowledge of these objects."[1] To achieve this, they stripped their work of reference, allusion, and visual anecdote, thereby encouraging the viewer to focus on the act of perception itself. In their effort to free sculpture of all symbolic and narrative content, the Minimalists often used serial repetition and mathematical formulas. Not only can these techniques generate spatial variation, they also eliminate much of the spontaneous choice and subjective expression within the artistic decision-making process. In theory, anyone could deduce the mathematical formula used to create one of Judd's sculptures; similarly, since many Minimalist works are made in foundries, anyone could design and order them. In these ways, Judd's work questions traditional assumptions regarding the artist's elevated status as a creative genius and enables viewers to use the same information in judging his works which he himself employed in their construction.

One common misconception about Minimalism is that it sacrificed aesthetic quality for intellectual content; beauty was by no means excluded by the movement's ethos. Rather, artists like Judd redefined aesthetic standards according to the rigor of their means and the workmanlike ordinariness of their chosen materials. Indeed, industrial materials and sober geometric lines are now often considered "beautiful," a broad aesthetic transformation that is largely a by-product of Minimalism's revolution. The visible seams where the four blocks are attached to the long horizontal bar; the mirrorlike finish of the blue galvanized metal; the flat, matte red of the toylike wooden parallelogram and its even, vertical grooves create the model for a stripped-down beauty that is now common in many areas of design. Radically avant-garde and astutely prophetic, Judd's two untitled works blend philosophical rigor with arresting physical authority.

1. Donald Judd, "Specific Objects," *Arts Yearbook* no. 8 (New York: Art Digest, 1965), 74–82.

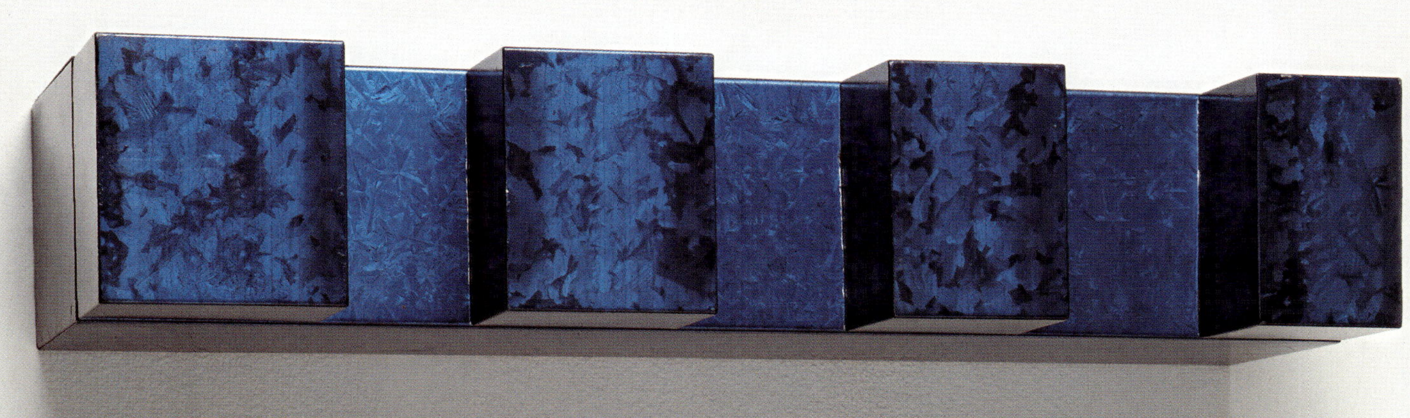

Donald Judd
Untitled (detail), 1968
Painted wood block
25 1/2 x 16 1/4 in.

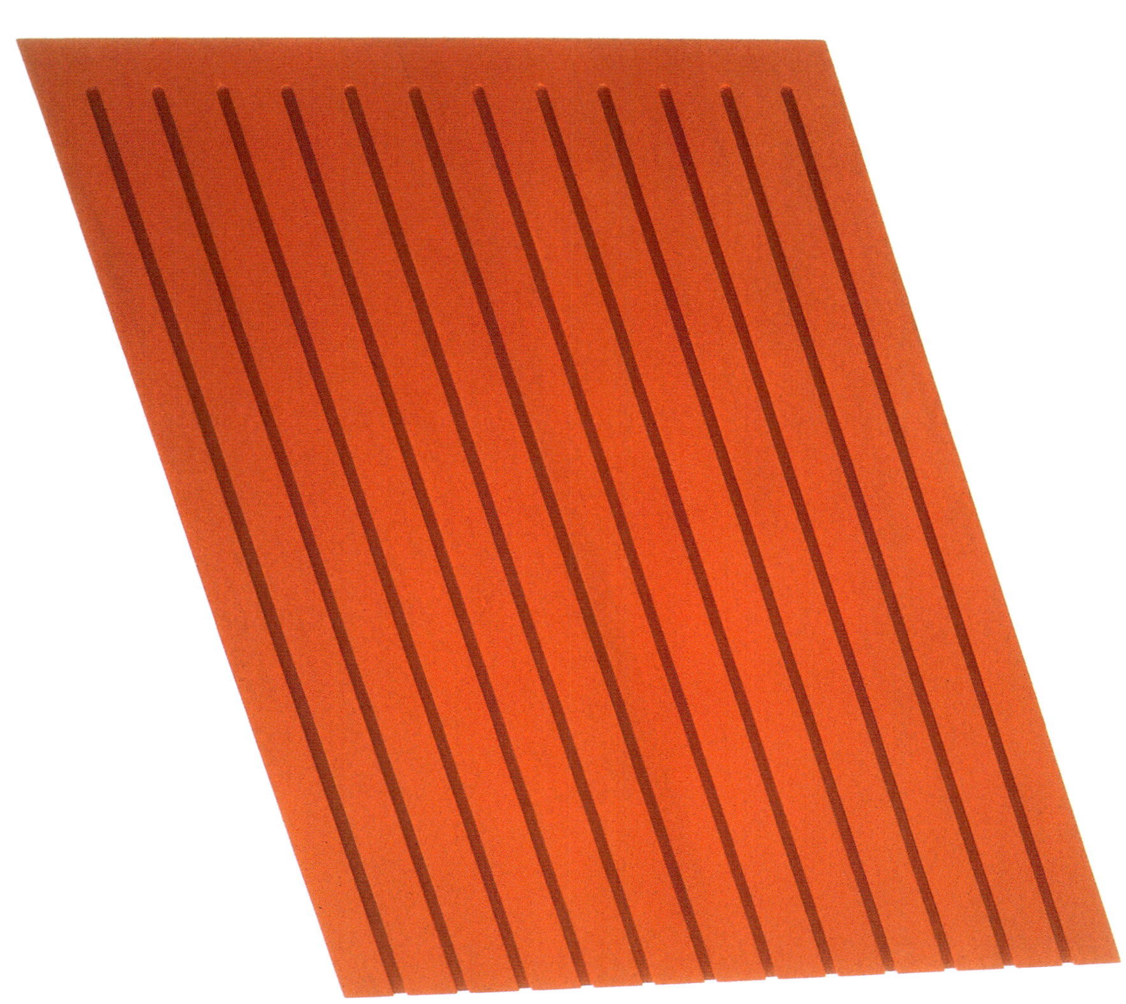

Barry Le Va

Study for Sculpture in Two Parts: Dissected Situations. Arrangements According to Functions (Diagnostics), Variation 8, 1989
Pencil and ink on paper
77 x 50 in.

Barry Le Va's *Study for Sculpture in Two Parts: Dissected Situations. Arrangements According to Functions (Diagnostics), Variation 8,* a 1989 drawing in pencil and ink on two sheets of paper, looks at first glance like a blueprint, and it is, after a fashion. Since 1966 Le Va has used drawings to make sculpture—and sculpture to make drawings. He begins by creating stencils of the forms that he plans eventually to translate into three dimensions. He then cuts out the stencils and begins to move them around on a piece of paper. Different two-dimensional "plottings" are left to rest while he contemplates them; the tracings we see in *Study for Sculpture* are the outlines of such impermanent arrangements. When a certain arrangement strikes Le Va as final, he outlines the shapes in ink, producing arresting modular geometric compositions. The "final" composition receives another transformation when Le Va combines it with a second view of the same subject in a single composite study. In this 1989 work the top drawing presents the front of a projected wall hanging; the bottom drawing displays an aerial view of a freestanding floor sculpture that would accompany the wall hanging in the same space. The paired drawings thus show in two dimensions what they project in three.

The tiny threadlike traces that reflect the stencils' former placement also suggest a sense of movement that cannot be resolved entirely into static form. Movement is crucial in Le Va's work: The viewer's awareness of how his or her body moves through space, and of the chains of cause and effect thereby set in motion, creates the context for Le Va's work. The notion of movement that Le Va engages does not so much erase and replace events lost in time as build on them. "A drawing," he has said, "is a layered map, constructed totally of parts, disconnected time sequences, processes and thoughts...."[1] These "sequences, processes and thoughts" remain abstract and yet palpably real in Le Va's work.

Separated, Catalogued, Sealed, Eventually Joined (Sorted Heads), a work in cast concrete from 1995 that has been recreated for this exhibition, reflects Le Va's ongoing sculptural exploration of the effects of motion and time on perception. Long white cubic rectangles, pointed oblongs, cubes that rest on the floor and atop other pieces—all of slightly varying heights and orientations—are placed in a seemingly haphazard, maze-like configuration. Their interrelationships engage the viewer immediately, issuing an invitation to step among them and conveying the impression of an ongoing process rather than an inert arrangement. But this sense of freedom depends on a rigorous system that is in turn continuously reinvented by the viewer's participation. Le Va's sculpture comes alive in a new way when we allow other possible, imagined arrangements to accumulate amid our perceptions of the objects on the floor before us, creating a fluid and challenging sense of both the artifact and space.

1. Barry Le Va quoted in an interview with Marianne Brouwer, in *Barry Le Va* (Otterlo, Netherlands: Rijksmuseum Kroller-Muller, 1988).

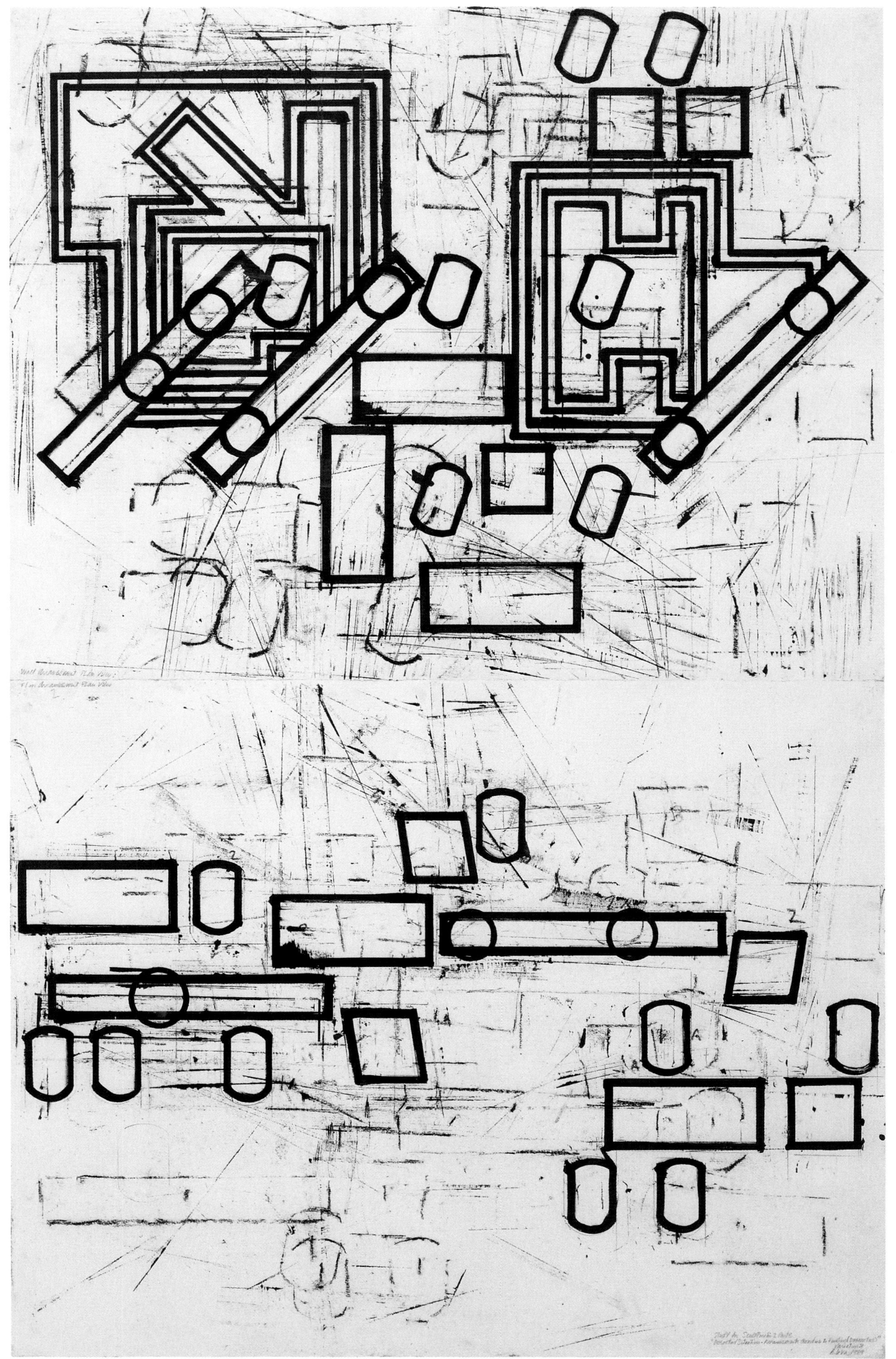

Barry Le Va
Separated, Catalogued, Sealed,
Eventually Joined (Sorted Heads), 1995
Cast cement
Dimensions variable

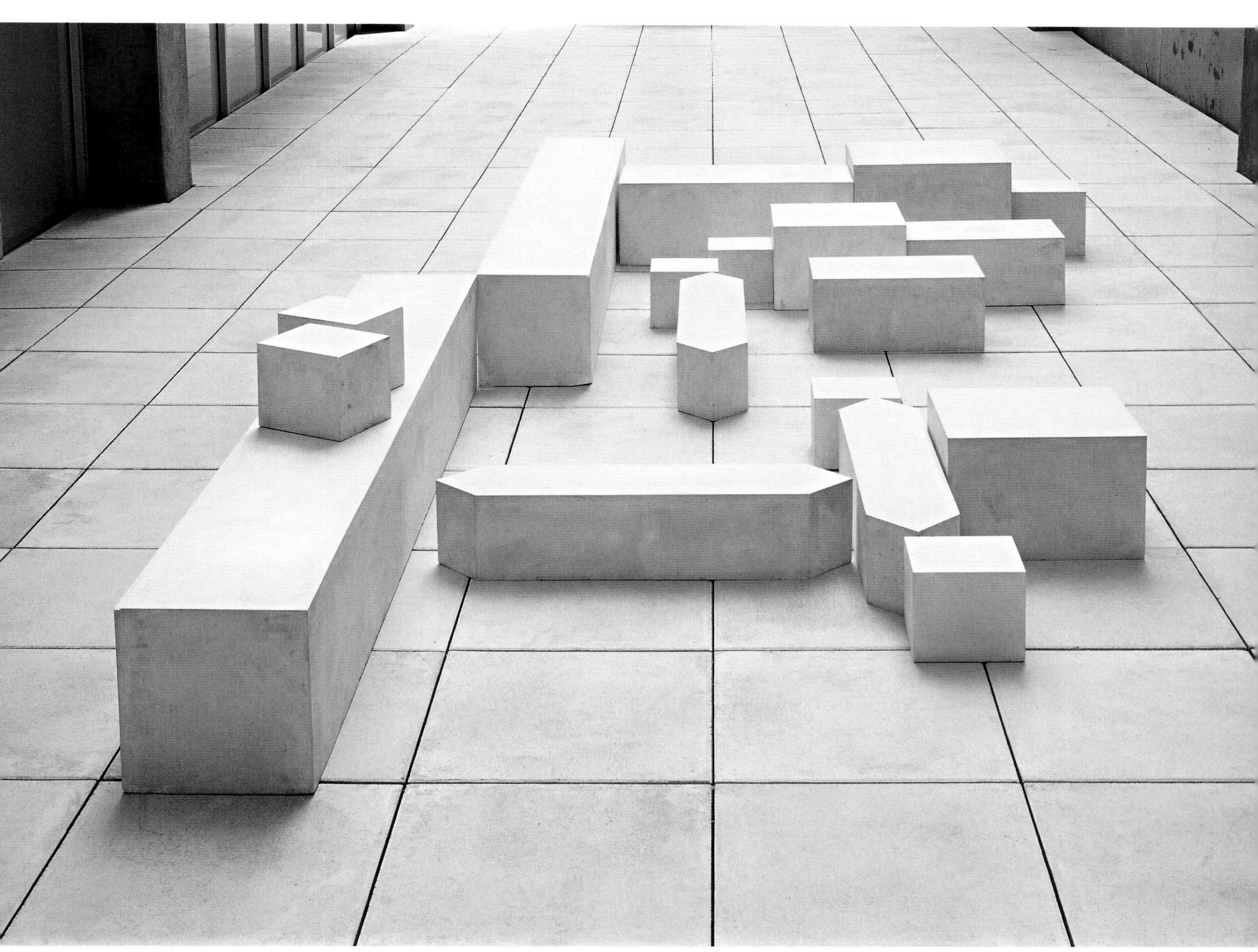

Giovanni Anselmo

Untitled, 1969
Galvanized metal, bricks, water, and chalk
8 5/8 x 51 1/2 x 82 11/16 in.

Giovanni Anselmo's *Untitled*, 1969, begins with a galvanized metal frame measuring approximately six by four feet, which lies flat on the ground. Into this shallow container the artist has poured water and distributed six bricks in an apparently random configuration. Traces of white chalk on the inside and outside edges of the frame interrupt the metal's shiny finish, while the ochre bricks cast shadows on the greenish-gray water, creating subtle color contrasts that harmonize into an almost painterly whole. Instead of framing a picture on a wall, the work contains liquid that is level with the floor; looking into the water we see reflections just as we would in a river's shifting depths or a puddle's still surface. Evoking the meditative tranquility of gazing into a body of water, Anselmo's *Untitled* returns the act of artistic contemplation to its natural origins.

The combination of materials and forms in Anselmo's piece establishes a dialogue between three distinct yet interrelated realms: art, nature, and industry. His arrangement of bricks inside a steel frame alludes to a picture's framing edge and its internal composition even as his use of everyday building materials flouts conventional artistic media such as painting or sculpture. Without detracting from the importance of these traditional forms, Anselmo opposes them to other, nonartistic forces. As the water evaporates, it sinks below the chalked-in section of the metal frame, leaving discolored traces on the bricks. The work gradually and perceptibly alters until someone replenishes the water and the cycle begins anew. This reference to nature's flux is a common theme in Anselmo's oeuvre. For example, natural processes play a central role in two of his works from 1968 (both untitled). In one, he placed absorbent cotton to soak up the water in a steel container; in the second, he wedged lettuce leaves between granite blocks. The tank of water, as with the water in *Untitled*, has to be refilled, and the lettuce has to be replaced or else, as its leaves dehydrate and wilt, the granite blocks will fall.

On one level, Anselmo's work dramatizes the way that all art functions—through the spectator's participation, which typically takes the form simply of viewing. But at the same time, it introduces modes of experience that transcend the realm of art altogether. It is this paradoxical combination that characterizes Anselmo's extremely original, idiosyncratic approach. A piece such as *Untitled* brings acutely focused attention to art's formal and conceptual attributes, in part through the use of nonartistic industrial materials, while simultaneously drawing on the processes and rhythms of the natural world. These apparently distinct or even opposed realms are enfolded into the viewer's experience of the work and thereby appear—however fleetingly—almost reconciled.

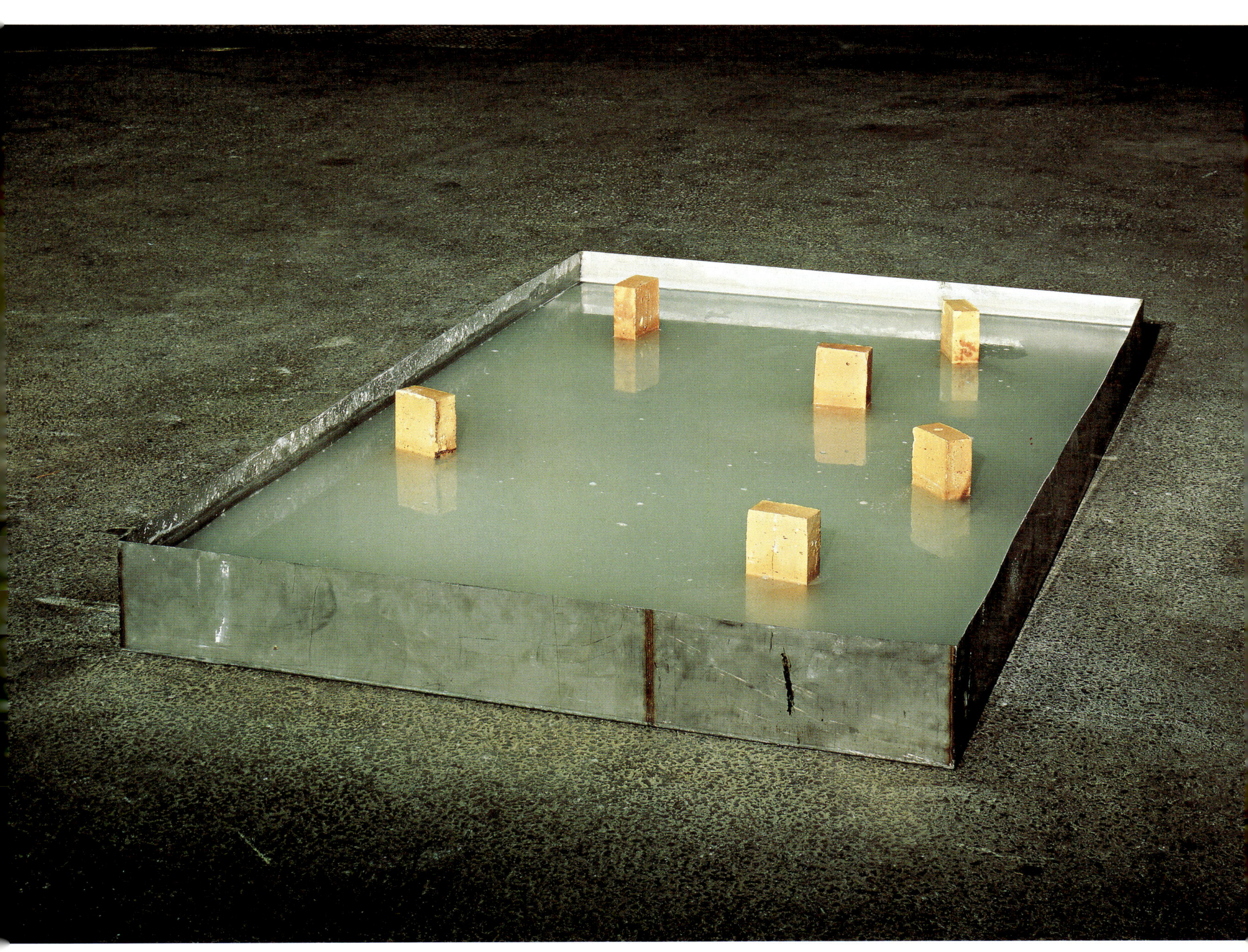

Michelangelo Pistoletto

Biennale 66 (detail), 1966
Silkscreen on metal
90 1/2 x 196 3/4 in.

Michelangelo Pistoletto's *Biennale 66*, from 1966, consists of four enormous plates of mirror-polished stainless steel. Placed side by side and propped against the gallery wall, they together measure over seven by thirteen feet. Pistoletto has collaged life-size painted images of a young boy and several movie-set lights on two of the four plates. In addition, the contents of the room—everything from the visible light fixtures to the other artworks to the gallerygoers—are reflected in the polished steel surface. Thus, while the material components of *Biennale 66* remain constant, the work itself is subjected to constantly shifting external circumstances.

The boy featured in Pistoletto's work would have been familiar to many audiences in 1966, for he was a child actor who appeared in one of the award-winning films shown at that year's Venice Film Biennale. Cinema played an extraordinarily important role in Italy's post-war recovery, renewing the country's sense of cultural identity and bringing international acclaim to such directors as Pier Paolo Pasolini, Federico Fellini, Michelangelo Antonioni, Luchino Visconti, and Bernardo Bertolucci. Throughout the sixties the work of these filmmakers sparked controversy over the appropriate representation of Italian life. But whether romantic, avant-garde, or brutally realistic, their movies afforded momentary escape from an often harsh reality. In *Biennale 66*, cinema's disruption of the everyday is mimicked by the cutout images, which interrupt the reflection of "real life" taking place across its mirrorlike surface.

This emphasis on the gap between representation and reality marks Pistoletto's decade-long experimentation with mirror-polished steel. Many of these works, like *Biennale 66*, incorporate images of people. *Tre ragazze alla balconata* (Three girls on a balcony), 1962–64, for example, features an image of three teenage girls viewed from behind while leaning forward on a horizontal railing, which Pistoletto has cut out of a photograph and silk-screened onto a sheet of stainless steel. Only the girls are visible; whatever they were originally looking at has been eliminated. But because of *Tre ragazze*'s reflective surface, the girls appear to be looking at the very works of art hung on the gallery walls *behind* the work's viewer. In this way, *Tre ragazze*'s inert silhouettes illustrate the isolation that accompanies even live acts of spectatorship. Literally detached—cut off from the viewer as from the audiences of his films and even from the crowds that applauded him at the awards ceremony—Pistoletto's child actor functions in a similar manner. He might stand for the alienation that is inherent in even the most beloved aspects of our contemporary culture or, like the girls in *Tre ragazze*, simply mirror the detachment that accompanies our own act of contemplation.

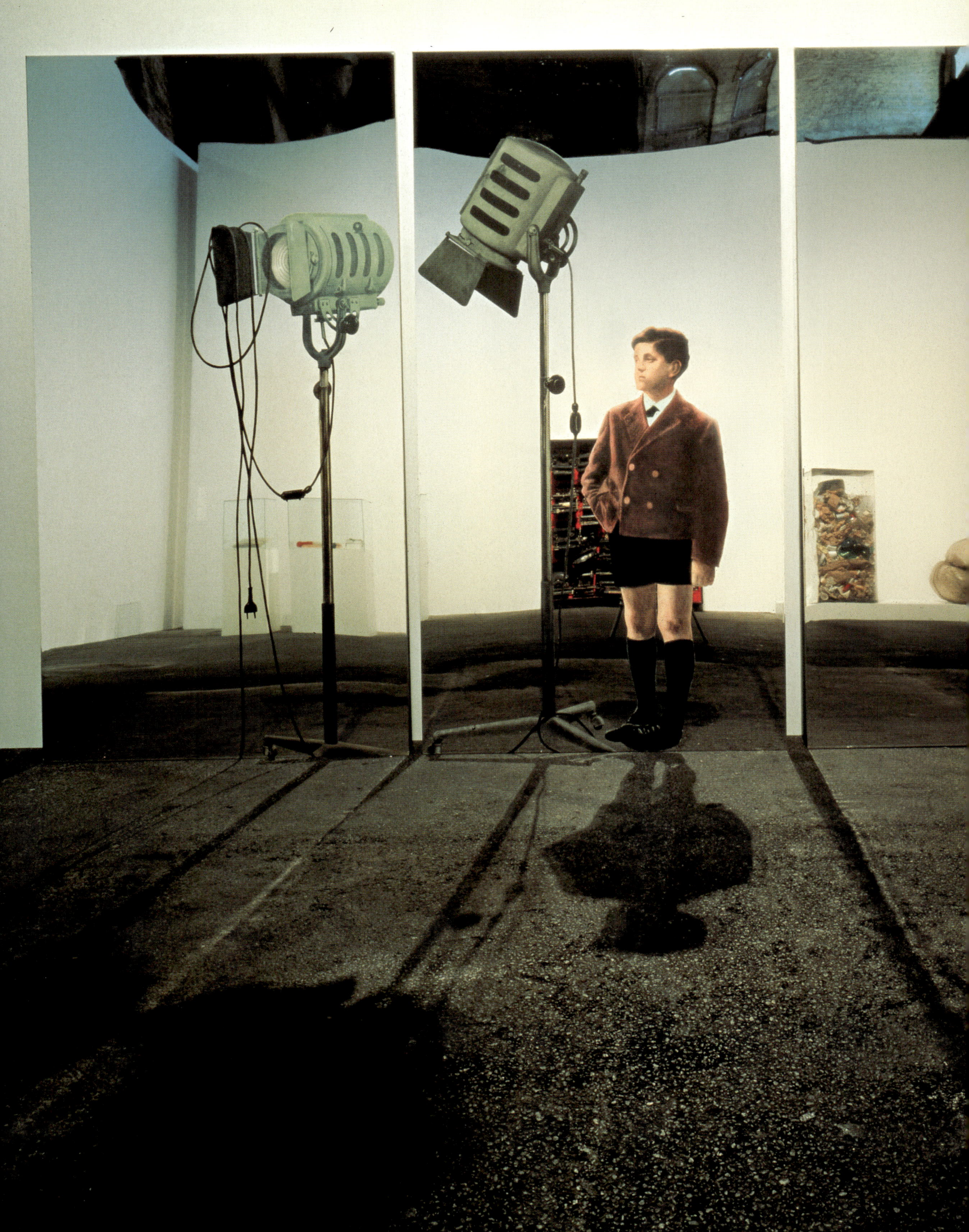

Gilberto Zorio

Untitled, 1968
Canvas, copper, eternit
118 1/8 x 47 1/4 in.

In Gilberto Zorio's *Untitled*, 1968, an apparently hollow copper tube measuring over nine feet is anchored in a paint-spattered canvas base that conceals a stabilizing weight. The broomlike effigy lists slightly, like an oversize domestic implement forgotten in some corner. Both vaguely familiar and vaguely threatening, *Untitled* subtly conjures psychological associations and hints at a suppressed narrative. Indeed, its physical attributes—its improbable scale and lopsided tilt—tip its visual effect into an extraphysical realm. It not only towers above us in height, it intimidates us through its understated yet foreboding suggestiveness.

The investigation of the actual properties of both artistic and nonartistic materials was a principal concern of many of the artists associated with the Italian *arte povera* movement of the 1960s. Some of these artists' most radical moments came when they presented transformations of physical and chemical properties as works of art in themselves. In his work of the 1960s, Zorio frequently explored the coexistence of opposing qualities within a material—density and lightness, impermeability and transparency, rigidity and fluidity, etc. Similarly, he transformed certain materials from one state to another. In *Rosa blu rosa*, 1967, Zorio filled tubes with a chemical substance that changed colors (from pink to blue to pink, as indicated by the title) according to the level of humidity. *Scrittura bruciata* (Burnt writing), 1968–69, used chemical combustion to reveal a text Zorio had written in invisible ink. In each of these pieces Zorio acts in a kind of collaboration with physical and chemical laws. "Authorship" of the work shifts into a fluid partnership in which the artist shares responsibility with his materials and with the physical and chemical laws of nature itself.

In *Untitled* that relationship expands to include the viewer, who is implicated by virtue of the sculpture's overwhelming scale and presence. The viewer assesses *Untitled*'s peculiar imbalance only by confirming, automatically, his or her own balance and bearing. This almost unconscious mental process, which links the viewer's body and awareness to the artwork's physical structure, is a function of each individual's reaction. Yet, it is also an inevitable part of any experience of the artwork proper and, as such, can be considered part of the work itself. The paradox of *Untitled*, however, is that its material properties—despite their power—are utterly ambiguous: Its weight, the source of its stability, and whatever is hidden inside its canvas base remain enigmas. As viewers we are invited to participate in a work that is under wraps, mute and unknowable despite its associative power.

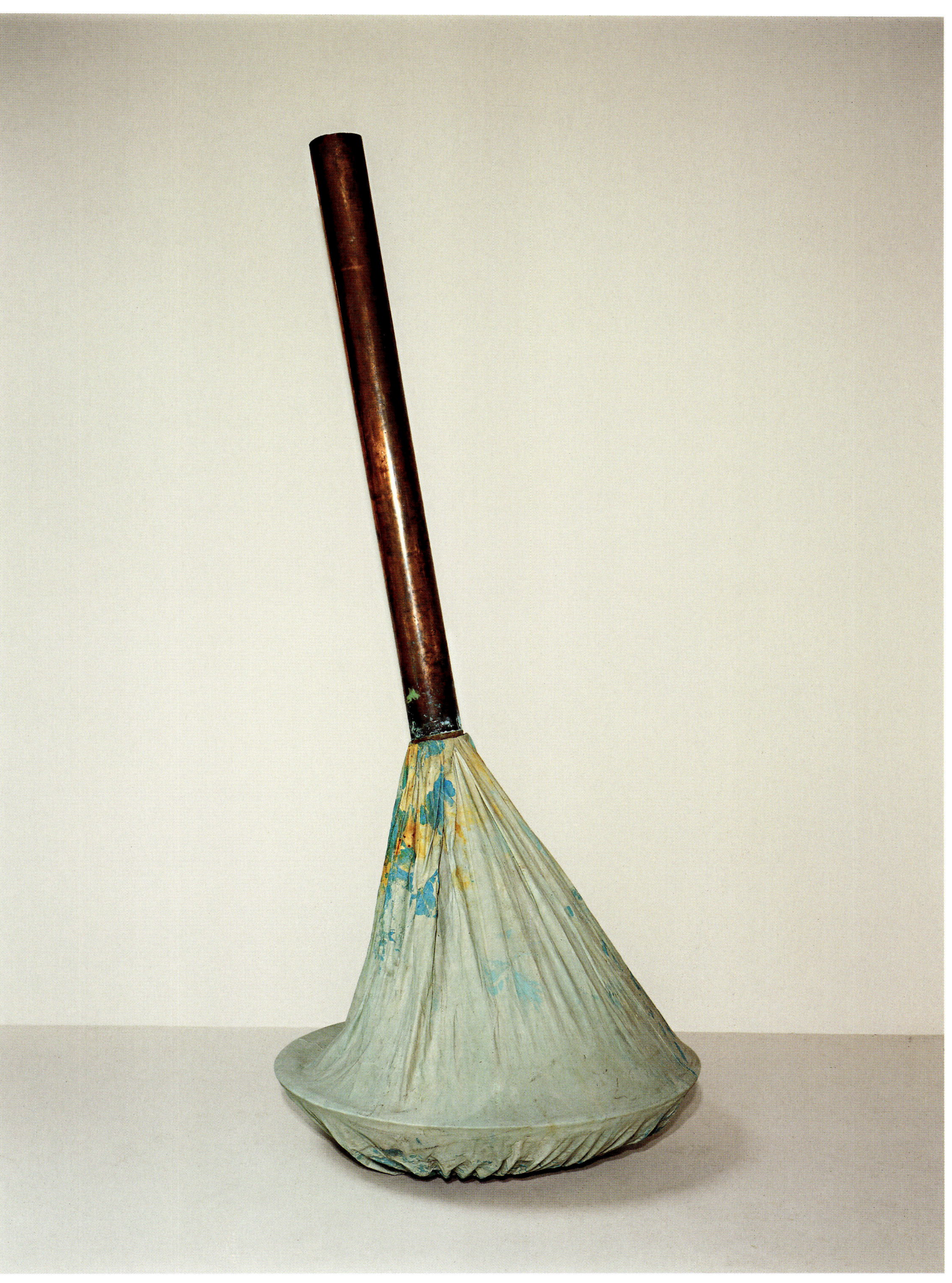

Jannis Kounellis

Untitled, 1985
Oil, metal shelf, egg
72 x 72 in.

Combining minimalism with enigmatic wit, *Untitled*, 1985, by Jannis Kounellis, features a black square painted directly onto the gallery wall. A circular steel plate covered in lush gray brushwork is placed inside the square, and a small horizontal shelf juts out from its center. On that shelf sits a perfectly white, smooth egg.

Kounellis's austere composition succinctly articulates art's most basic formal components: point, line, and plane. Indeed, at first glance, the painted component resembles the purely abstract, nearly monochromatic canvases of Robert Ryman and Ellsworth Kelly. But the introduction of an everyday object aligns *Untitled* more closely to Jasper Johns's targets and Jim Dine's 1960s paintings, which combine simplified abstract forms with found objects hanging from hooks or nestled into cubbyholes. Kounellis's choice of an egg, however, brands the work as uniquely his own. Since the beginning of his career in the early 1960s, Kounellis has consistently incorporated organic elements such as cotton and coffee—and even live parrots and horses—into his work. In his famous 1969 *Senza titolo (12 cavalli)* (Untitled [12 horses]), a dozen horses were led into the Galleria L'Attico in Rome and remained there, tied to the gallery's walls, for three days. By removing any trace of conventional artistic activity, Kounellis refocused the viewer's attention from the contemplation of an aesthetic object to the intellectual problem of what legitimately constitutes a work of art. Particularly in Italy, with its venerable tradition of painting and sculpture, this provocative act represented a veritable artistic coup d'état.

In *Untitled* this revolutionary gesture is given a more understated and elegant form and subtly turned in a new direction. The work's abstract composition mixes luxuriant brushwork with the austerity of a perfect circle—well known as the most difficult shape to draw freehand. Kounellis's circle, however, was not drawn by the artist but cut out of steel using a machine. The black square, according to his instructions, can be made by anyone; in this, *Untitled* recalls the wall drawings and paintings of Sol LeWitt and Lawrence Weiner, who maintained that the artist's hand is inessential to the realization of his work. But Kounellis complicates this rejection of artistic craftsmanship by making an egg the center of his composition. Not only a symbol of natural fertility but a powerful reminder of the eternal, cyclical nature of life and time itself, the egg introduces a new layer of meaning into Kounellis's work. Nature—not an artist—has produced the ultimate, unsurpassable form. Although indifferent to its own perfection, nature, Kounellis suggests, remains the definitive standard to which an artist finally compares his own achievements.

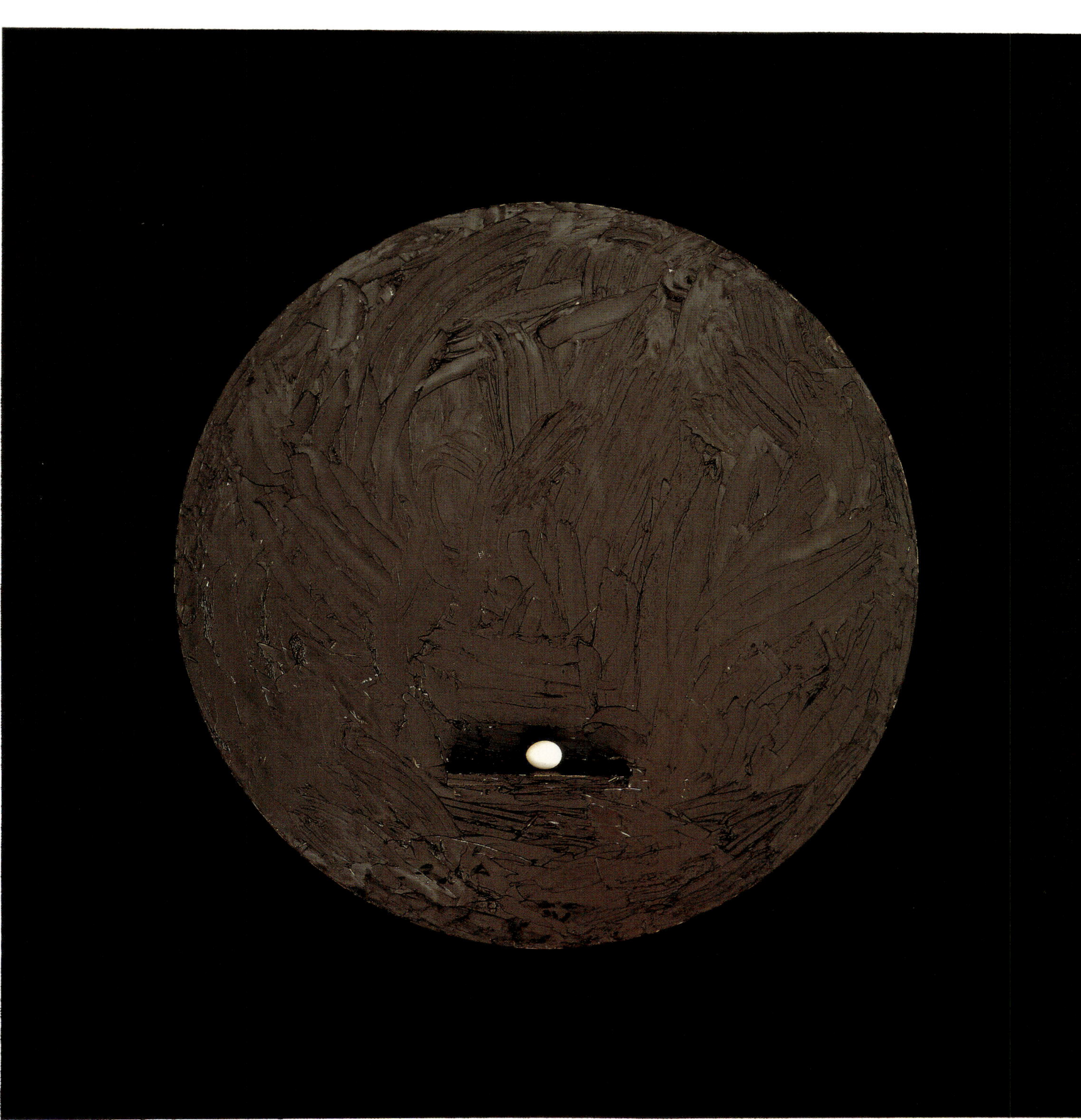

Pier Paolo Calzolari

Portrait, 1969
Steel, copper, flower petals
43 5/16 x 43 3/8 in.

Portrait, a work in steel, copper, and flower petals, from 1969, epitomizes the iconoclastic dimension of Pier Paolo Calzolari's art. This piece consists of a three-and-a-half-foot-square metal plate lying flat on the ground, which the artist has covered with a tight grid of glued, dried flower petals. Nestled among the flowers is a second, smaller plate, engraved with the words SPECCIO (mirror), ARGENTO (silver) and PORTRAIT. The carpet of petals resembles nothing so much as the manicured floral bed of an elegantly austere gravestone. But the dedication inscribed on Calzolari's *Portrait* identifies the things being commemorated as the components of the artwork itself.

Portrait alludes to the artistic developments of its time by evoking the sculpture of Carl Andre, an American Minimalist, and Piero Manzoni, an Italian Conceptualist. Andre's sculptures, composed of grids of steel or copper plates placed directly on the gallery floor, presage the horizontal orientation of Calzolari's *Portrait*. Manzoni's *Socle du monde* (Pedestal of the world), 1961, an iron-and-bronze cube, also rests on the ground. Its title, author, and date are engraved upside down on one side, along with a commemorative inscription, HOMMAGE A GALILEO. In *Portrait*, Calzolari couples the flat horizontality of Andre's sculpture with Manzoni's witty conceptual exploration. But *Portrait*'s memorial aspect puts these references into another perspective.

In their time, Minimalism and Conceptualism were often charged with having demonstrated the finitude, if not the very death, of art. Calzolari's work can be interpreted as a direct parody of such melodramatic pronouncements through its exaggeration of the formal aspects of a commemorative plaque and traditional memorial floral arrangement. But at the same time, *Portrait* is strikingly and undeniably serious. Perhaps more than any other genre, portraiture is an art of memory. Individuals are memorialized through representation for generations to come: Lineage, social and political power, and romantic attachments are fortified through painted or sculpted portraits of ancestors, rulers, and lovers. But since the invention of photography, painted and sculpted portraits only rarely fulfill the same social functions they did in previous centuries. Photography's invention led to the disappearance of a deeply rooted tradition and marked a crucial turning point for many artists. By omitting any pictorial imagery and reducing his artistic means to an austere minimum, Calzolari's *Portrait* mourns art's loss by enacting the very diminishment of its resources. It is a work that, despite its sardonic overtones, shows us the gravity and profundity of loss itself.

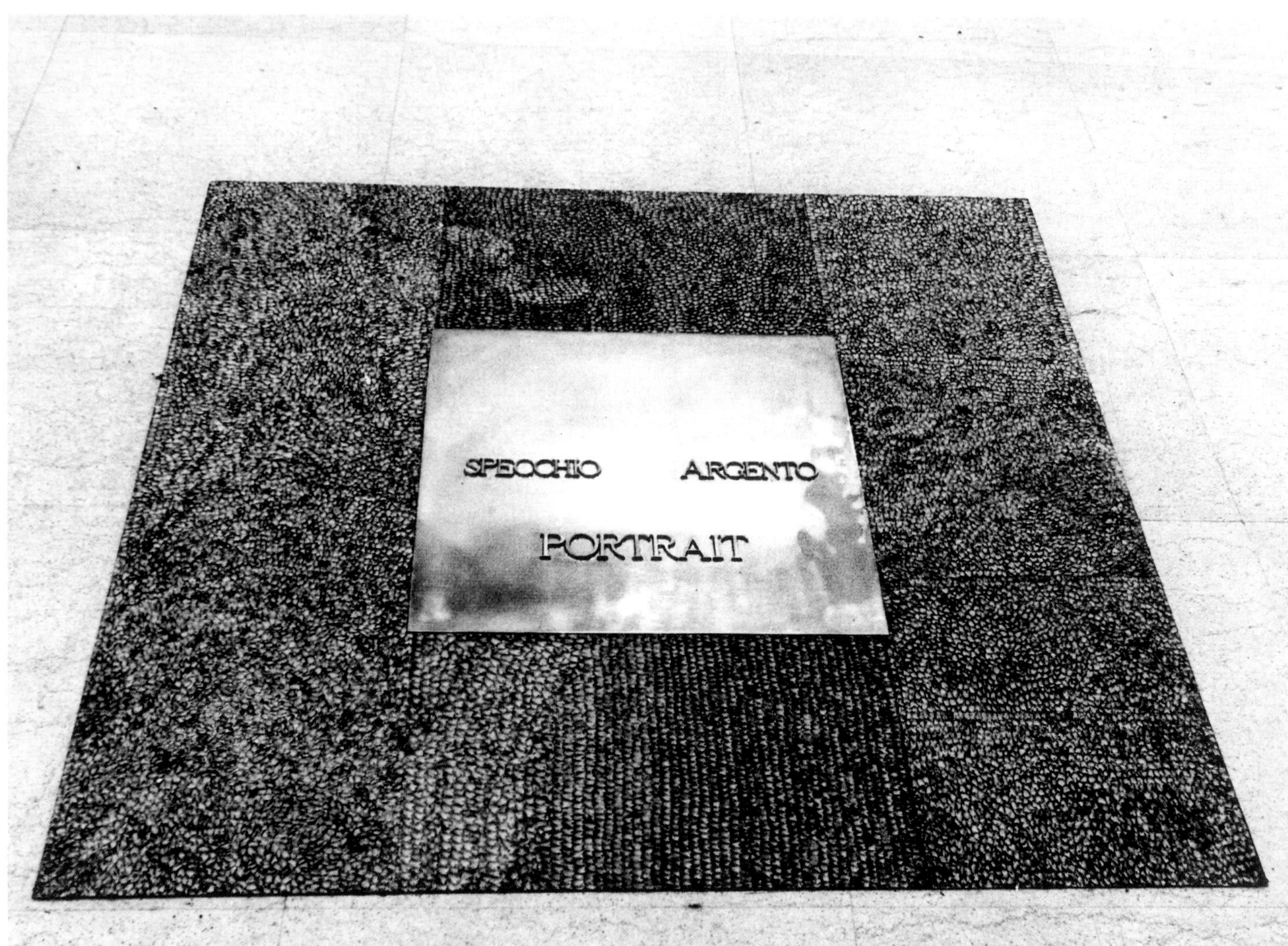
SPECCHIO ARGENTO
PORTRAIT

Keith Sonnier

Lit Square, 1968
Neon, glass
59 7/8 x 59 7/8 x 24 in.

In his 1968 work *Lit Square*, Keith Sonnier placed two square panels of glass against a wall, one in front of the other, connecting them with a sinuous curve of yellow neon tubing. The front panel is corrugated, and its slanting horizontal ridges pick up and reflect the ambient light of the room; the larger square behind is flat and smooth, ever so slightly tinting the wall against which it leans. There is an almost familial quality to the sculpture's configuration; the smaller square nestles into a corner of the larger square, and the umbilical cord of bright yellow neon traverses the depth between them. Landing in front of the smaller square, toward the center of the room, the cordlike neon tubing enters the viewer's space, suggesting the possibility of a physical interaction that would almost transport us "inside" the work.

The same year that he made *Lit Square*, Sonnier also began using flocked latex, a material created by applying colored powdered rayon to latex that has been spread on the floor. The gesture of distributing color over a level horizontal surface links Sonnier's work to Jackson Pollock's revolutionary method, begun in the late 1940s, of dripping paint onto a canvas laid on his studio floor. Pollock's process—the sweeping movement of his arm as he applied paint onto the canvas; the pull of gravity on the paint that drew it to the floor—remains clearly visible in his finished works. As a result, the classical analogy between a painter's physical relationship with the easel and the viewer's position in front of a vertically hung painting is subtly but palpably undermined. In a similar manner, by pushing the plane of the work forward to parallel the wall—but not lie flat against it—Sonnier's glass panels draw attention to the physical relationship between the standing viewer and the traditionally vertical work. The marginal space between the two panels becomes dynamic, literally both electrified and illuminated by the neon tube's supple curve, which extends forward into space in a suggestion of continuous and unbounded movement.

If the smaller panel reflects light and the larger filters it, *Lit Square*'s neon tube, emitting its continual, invariable yellow glow, reminds the viewer of the counterintuitive fact that light is a physical action that takes place over time. Just as the act of looking has duration, even a millisecond of light represents a measure of distance. Sonnier's warping neon tube, a shooting spiral of light, demonstrates for its viewer the importance of that crucial element, time, which links our experienceof a work of art to the rest of our everyday lives.

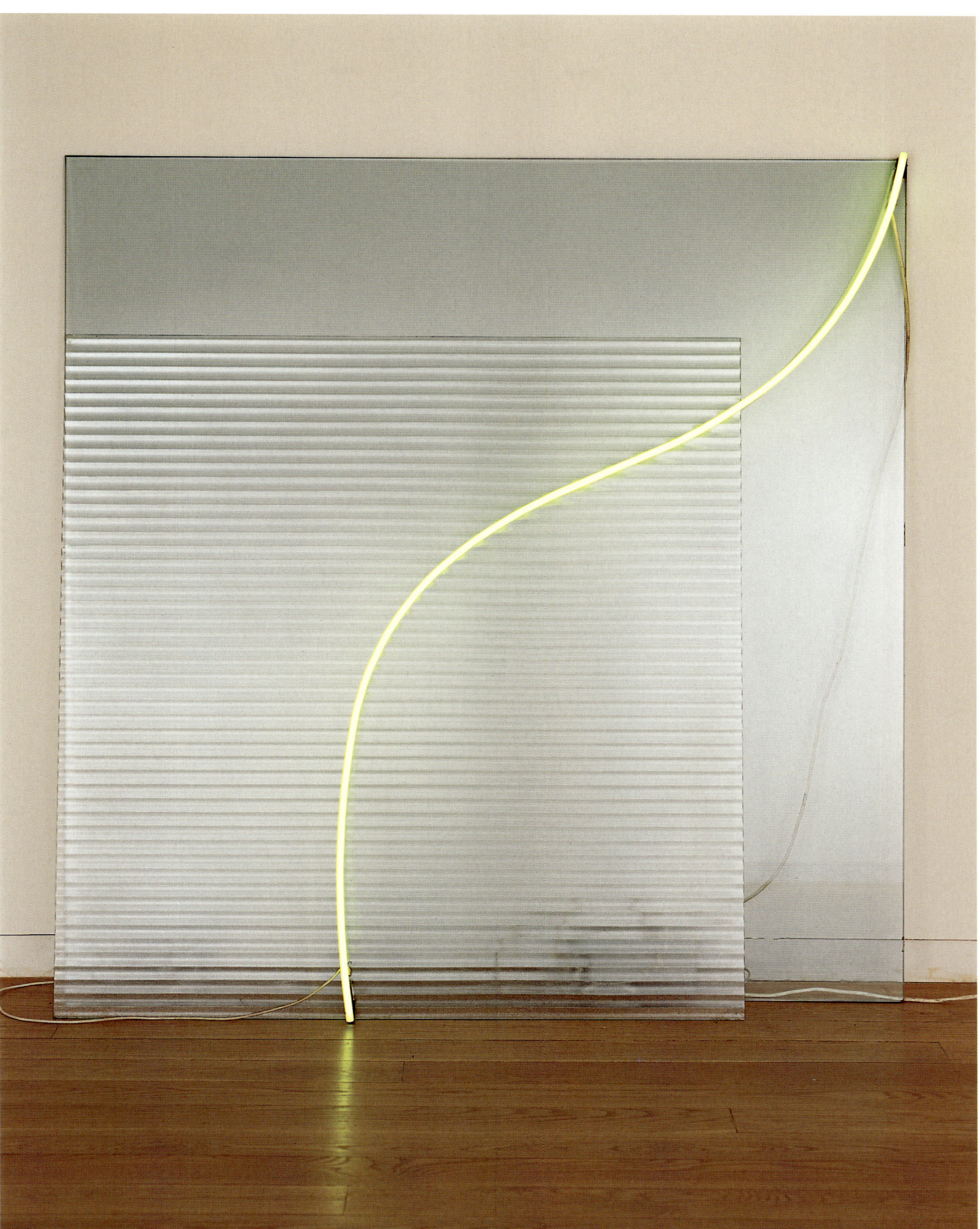

Mario Merz

Cera e gomma, 1966
Metal grill, rubber, wax, and lightbulb
27 9/16 x 53 1/8 x 86 1/2 in.

In *Cera e gomma* (Wax and rubber), 1966, Mario Merz has connected two half-open cylinders in a construction that measures over seven feet long. The cylinder on the left is made of black rubber; the one on the right, of wire mesh covered in wax and lit from within by a single incandescent bulb. A metal frame serves as a skeleton, propping the mesh into a shape similar to the rubber cylinder. Its translucent surface and glowing orange hue contrast strongly with the matte rubber structure, which would hide from view any object placed inside it. Merz's unconventional sculpture makes no pretense of needing a pedestal or base; it stands directly on the same ground as the viewer. Vaguely anthropomorphic in its dimensions, vaguely industrial in its materials, *Cera e gomma* seems half of this world, half of another.

Beginning in the late 1960s, Merz joined his investment in eccentric materials with his fascination with social habitats and processes in a series of works he called igloos. Like whimsical fortresses for a new society, the igloos' infinite variability and incorporation of organic elements made them iconic works in their time. Resembling their real-life counterparts only in their half-spherical form, these constructions are made of everything from iron and neon tubing to plastic bags stuffed with dirt to marble or glass slabs. Their everyday materials and simple forms conjure quotidian acts and needs while projecting buoyantly optimistic views of the possibilities for improving social life. *Cera e gomma* shares many of the artistic concerns and utopian aspirations of Merz's igloos. The rubber's flaccid surface and the wax's grainy permeability suggest a new sort of protection for the human body. As an alternative to the straight-edged designs and polished materials of our sophisticated architecture, Merz's work uses cheap construction materials and plays off the nurturing and protective possibilities of more rounded, organic forms.

With *Cera e gomma*, Merz has created a sculpture that does not hide its materials or their attributes. Rather, his use of a simple incandescent bulb emphasizes the distinction between sturdiness and transparency, delicacy and strength. The contrast between the two cylinders—between the opaque black rubber and the gridded wire mesh—makes us all the more aware of what is taken for granted in certain fundamental oppositions: open and closed, straight and round, light and dark. In *Cera e gomma* Merz holds these oppositions in a complex, sustaining equilibrium. Respecting such balance, his work seems to suggest, might be one way to approach the task of social transformation.

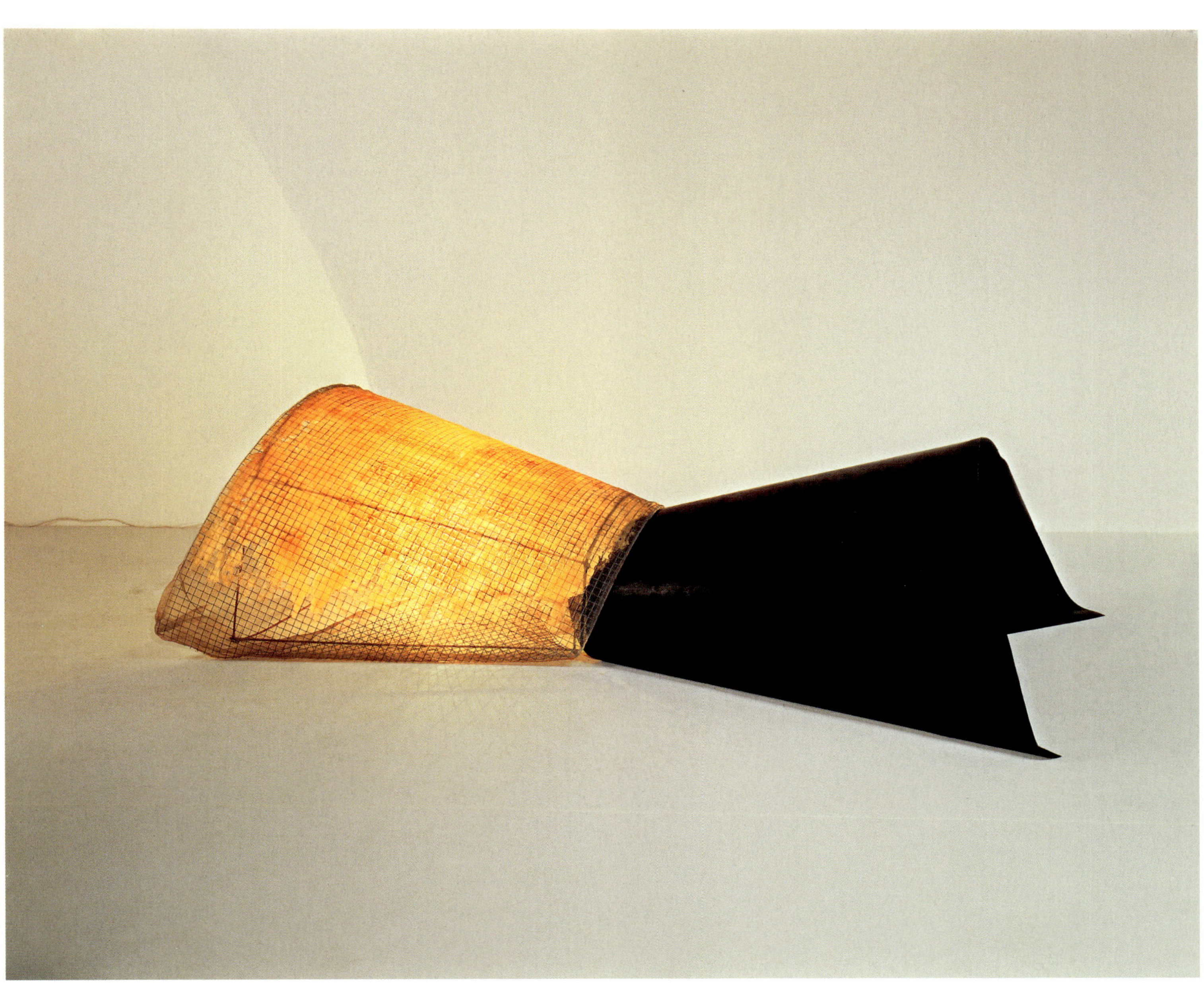

Anselm Kiefer

Baum mit Palette, 1978
Oil and lead on canvas
110 1/4 x 75 in.

The troubled topic of German identity in the second half of the twentieth century—shaped by both the collective remembrance of the Holocaust and the nation's complex postwar reconfiguration—has become a determining matrix for understanding Anselm Kiefer's work. To be so strongly associated with historical forces and events is a rare condition for a living artist, but it is one that Kiefer has courted. His persistent investigation of the legacy of fascism—from his use of Wagnerian iconography to his direct thematic explorations of the Holocaust—has earned him the controversial designation as Germany's "painter of mourning."

Baum mit Palette (Tree with palette), 1978, is one of a number of Kiefer's paintings from the mid-seventies in which an artist's palette is featured in landscapes whose "scorched earth" (as one title describes it), recalls the Nazi military campaigns across Europe. Many of these works are monumental in both their rich layering of thickly applied paint and their size. *Baum mit Palette*, for example, measures more than nine by six feet. Here, a tree trunk bisects the canvas, appearing to continue past the picture frame on both ends. But it is a tree *conveyed* rather than pictorialized, its textures and colors suggested by Kiefer's loose brushstrokes, rich reddish tones, and scratchy, nubby painterly surface. Colossal—in the amount of painting surface that it occupies and in its implied scale—Kiefer's tree is an undeniable symbol of living power and permanence.

The wintry landscape evoked by the surrounding lavender grays and the gleam of light peeking from above, however, suggest a desolate period. The palette, pinned to the tree as if by some mighty natural force, seems to stand in for the painter himself and, by extension, for the regenerative potential of artistic expression. Whether Kiefer's palette represents the painter or, more generally, the predicament of painting "after Auschwitz," its presence is significant. It defines the dilemma of artistic creation after the Holocaust by evoking a tradition as old as painting itself: the symbolic representation of the artist within the work. The emphatic presence of a painter's palette within Kiefer's work insists on the continuing importance of painting even—or *especially*—in a country with a collective identity as scarred and conflicted as Germany's. In this way, *Baum mit Palette* speaks to Kiefer's commitment to the painter's traditional role as the chronicler of momentous or tragic historic events.

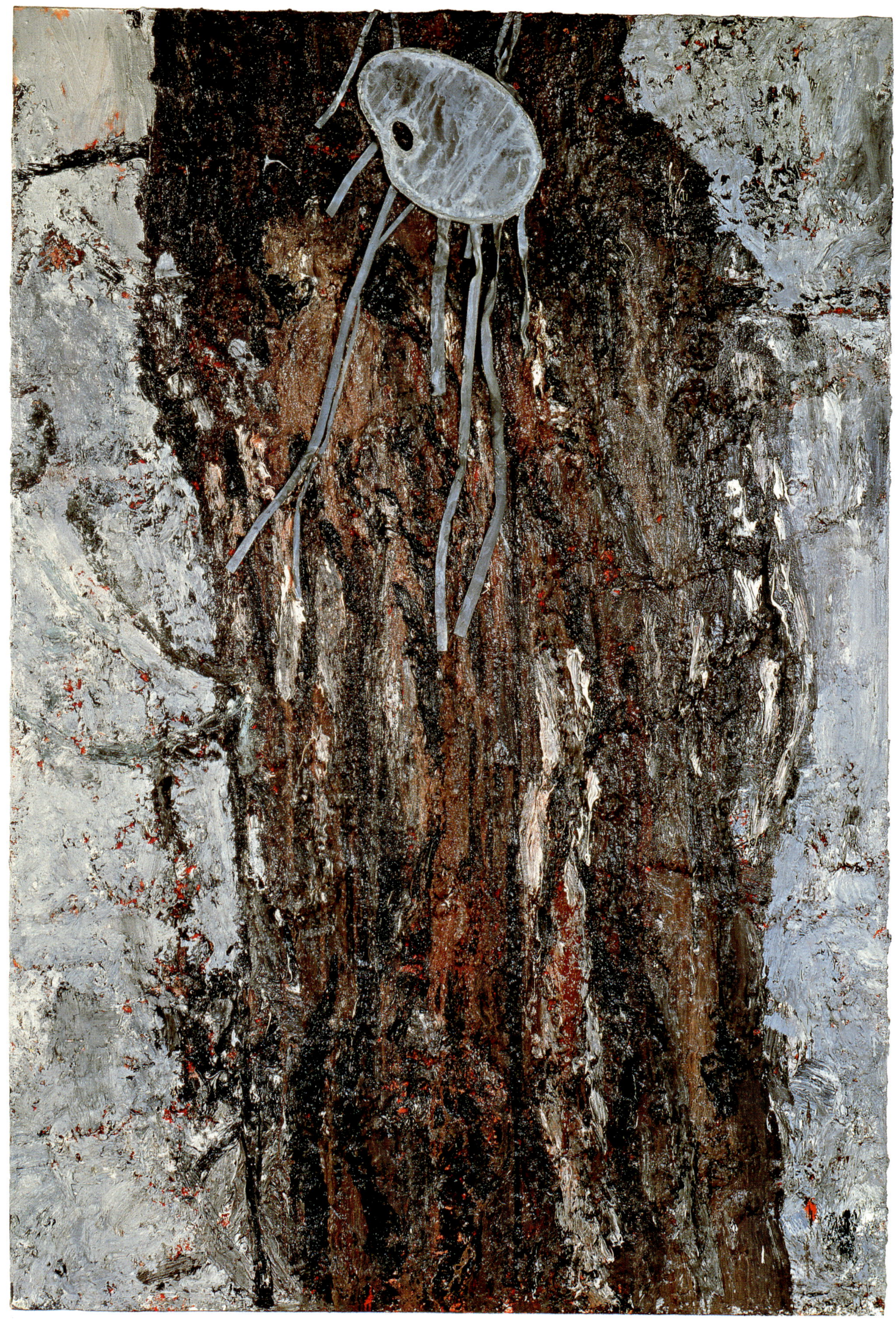

Robert Yarber

Gate (University Park, Texas), 1995
Cibachrome color photograph
30 x 40 in.

Robert Yarber is best known for his paintings of nocturnal landscapes, a subject he also explores in his photographic works. In *Gate (University Park, Texas)*, 1995, the photograph's softly blurred forms offset the acrid, electric-green glow of Dallas's nighttime sky. A metal gate opens on the picture's left while a lake spreads into the distance, reflecting street lamps and the rich foliage of nearby trees. Bright city lights, setting the treetops aglow, remind us of where we are; even amid the quiet rustle of trees, the city's artificial brightness is inescapable. The blurriness of Yarber's image also imparts the feeling of an "instant before," a last glimpse caught before something crucial happens. The trees jutting into the foreground might hide a hostile presence; they also hide the photographer who serves as our eyes, providing our visual access to the scene. In this way, Yarber imbues *his* view—and by extension *our* perspective—with a furtive secrecy.

The notion of the Victorian garden, in which sensuality and danger lurk beneath carefully manicured vines, rare plants, and architectural follies, is one model that Yarber considers in making his nocturnal landscapes. Another is the concept of the modern public park, pioneered by such crucial nineteenth-century figures as Frederick Law Olmsted. Both "natural" and urban, inviting and menacing, such public environments inevitably convey a hint of danger at night, regardless of their daytime serenity. Indeed, the very difference between night and day is blurred in Yarber's *Gate*, in which the nonstop rhythms of urban life imbue this pocket of well-organized nature with a concrete sense of the city that surrounds it.

The visual effects that mark *Gate*—its soft haziness, its extraordinary green glow—derive in part from the physical demands of Yarber's process. Because he uses only available light, his nighttime exposures can easily last two or three minutes. He also does not use a tripod to steady his camera, which results in a slightly blurred image. The fact that Yarber is so literally exposed while taking a picture contributes to the sense of tense premonition in his photographs. The eerie, lurid scenes that he paints contain human figures, narrative elements, and dream-like details. Keeping his photographs almost entirely depopulated and void of anecdotal reference, Yarber restrains their suggestive power. Though the beautiful arc of a tree reflected in a pool of water might easily shift into an ominous, choking tangle of roots and branches, Yarber's image does not forcefully direct our interpretation. Instead, photographs like *Gate* serve as records of a nighttime ramble whose motives and details are left to our imagination.

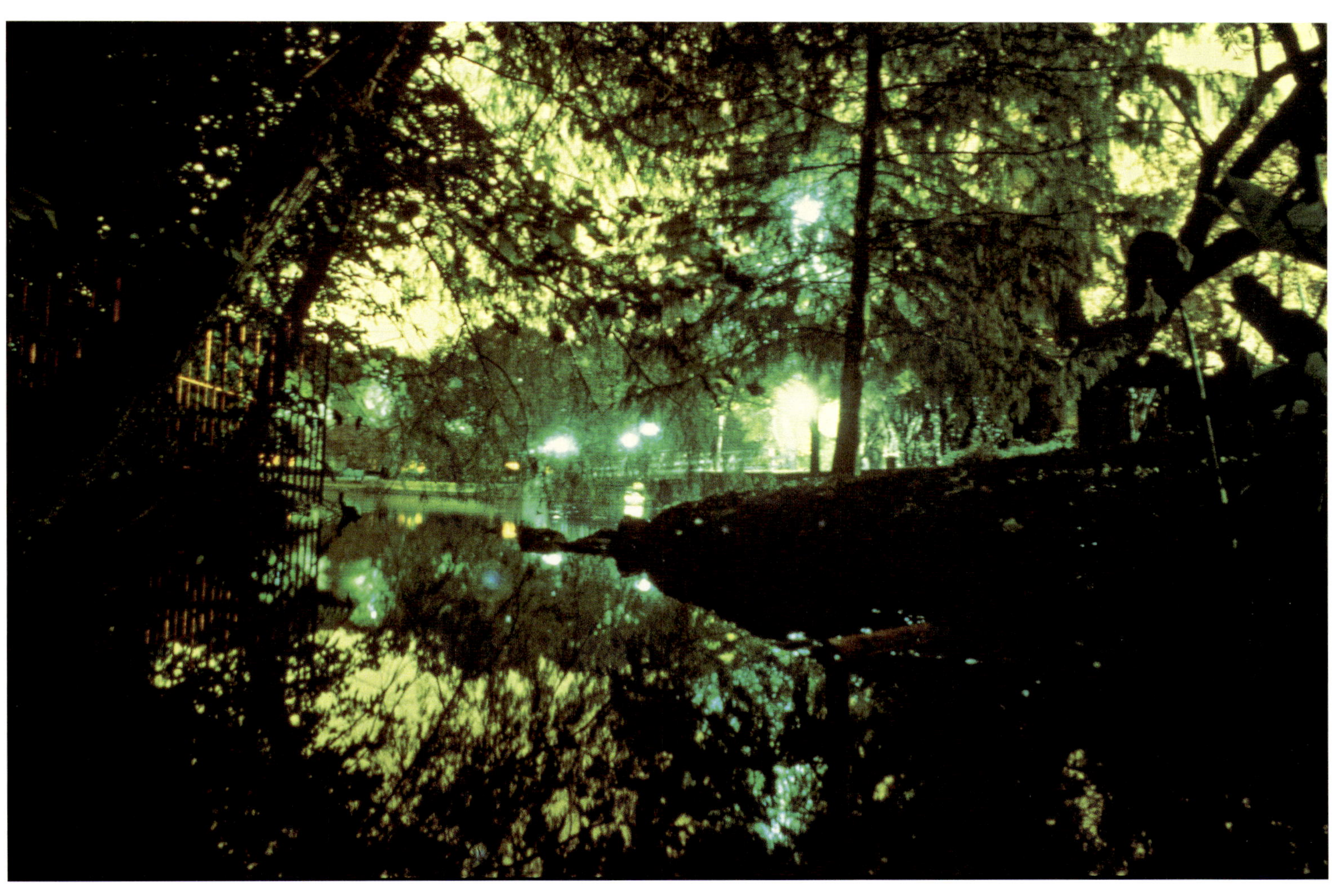

Ashley Bickerton

Green and Brown Box Cantina for Malcolm Lowry and Donald Judd, 1992
Lithographs on avaline-stained wood veneer, acrylic, wood, and canvas
43 x 36 x 12 1/4 in.

Ashley Bickerton's return to painting in the early 1990s surprised many critics who had become accustomed to his acute brand of conceptualist critique, realized in hard-edged sculptural forms and often aimed straight at the art world. But Bickerton's portraits inject a razor-sharp perceptiveness into a medium that has avoided social commentary for decades. With works like *Joan and the Cosmos*, 1996, he decrees a new role and relevance for painting, long excluded from art's "critical" activities.

The subject of *Joan and the Cosmos* is both hyper-individualized and reduced to the lowest common denominator; both superficially highly evolved and spiritually, profoundly regressed. Joan's too impressive musculature, complete with bulging veins, could only come from lifting weights; her tan could only come from overexposure to the sun; her helmet hair, smoldering cigarette, and politically correct T-shirt accessorize her physique. Yet her squatting posture, exposed vagina, and the line of piss extending to her own name stenciled beneath her connect her to a baser level of identity. In this way, *Joan and the Cosmos* expands the themes pursued in the paintings of chimpanzees and vaguely hominoid evolutionary misfits Bickerton began making just after his 1993 move from New York to Indonesia. Self-mastery through exercise, the aping of "natural" beauty through cosmetic enhancements; the activated longing for a lost paradise: These and other addictions become the extreme and exaggerated forms of social behavior that in turn return the subject—in this case, Joan—to the most ignoble and fundamental aspects of our collective humanity.

If Bickerton's luminous, meticulous realism evokes sixteenth-century Dutch painters such as Jan van Eyck, his critical blade suggests another Flemish artist, Pieter Brueghel, whose half-man, half-animal grotesqueries metaphorically represent social injustices as well as the flaws of the human condition. *Green and Brown Box Cantina for Malcolm Lowry and Donald Judd*, 1992, is a stained-wood box decorated with lithographed, Brueghel-esque figures dancing merrily amid symbols of clichéd "tropical" vice: playing cards, mescal, palm trees, and bongo drums. Conjuring the Mexican setting and almost transcendent agonies of drink narrated in Lowry's most famous novel, *Under the Volcano*, these symbols would be barred from the austere, Minimalist style linked to Judd's name and suggested by the sculpture's strict geometry. If Lowry and Judd represent two archetypes for artists—the expatriated misfit and the rigorous intellectual—then Bickerton's homage appears poignantly personal. The message that Bickerton has printed on his OAXACA-DESTINED CARRYING BOX—LA CANTINA DONDE LOS HOMBRES BRAVOS LLORAN (The bar where brave men weep)—uses a faux-nostalgic tone to allude to an elsewhere, a mythically primal site of self-presence, which motivates our tourism as it does our most deep-rooted fantasies.

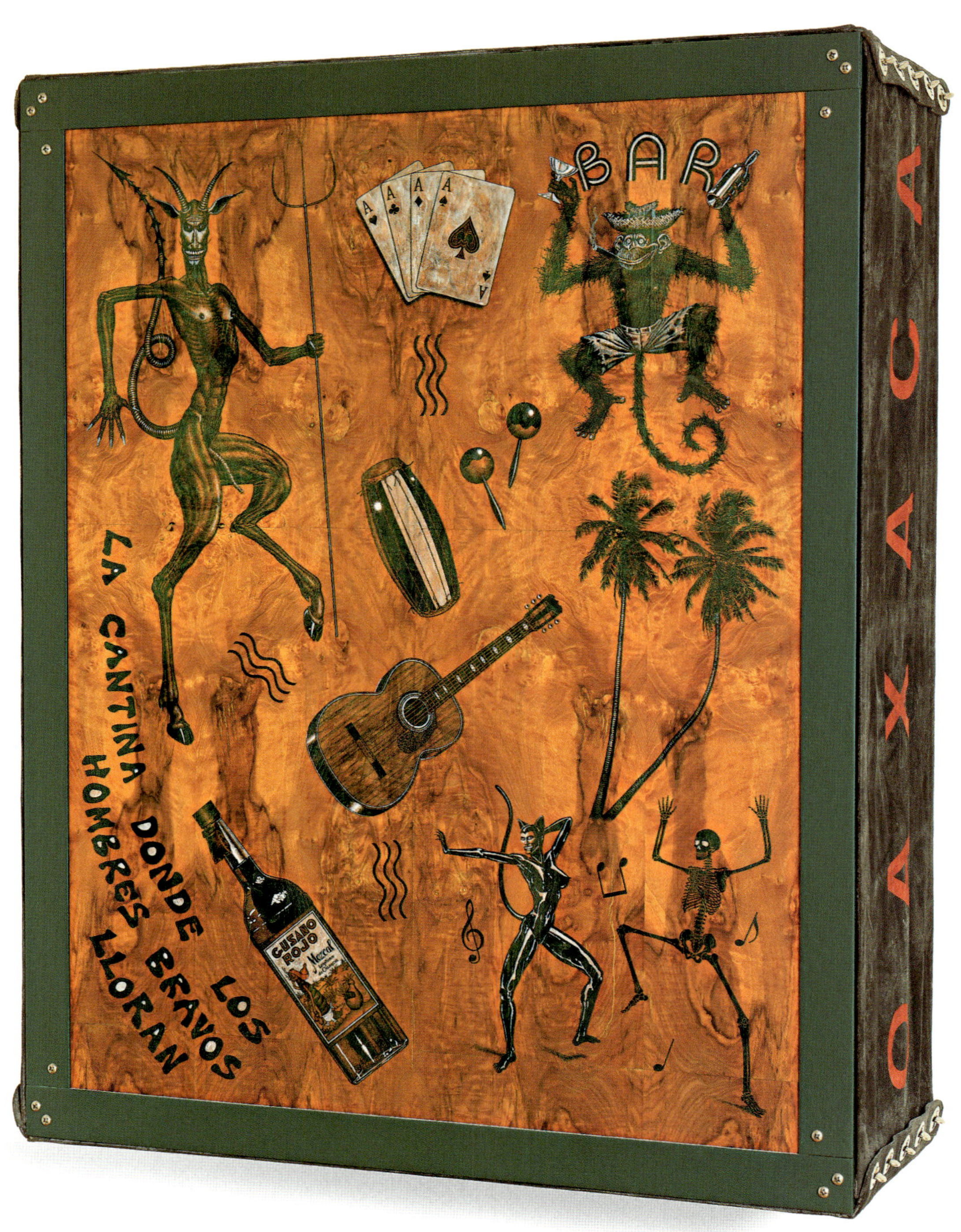
BAR
LA CANTINA DONDE LOS HOMBRES BRAVOS LLORAN
GUSANO ROJO
Mezcal
OAXACA

Ashley Bickerton
Joan and the Cosmos, 1996
Oil, acrylic, and pencil on wood
47 1/4 x 47 1/4 in.

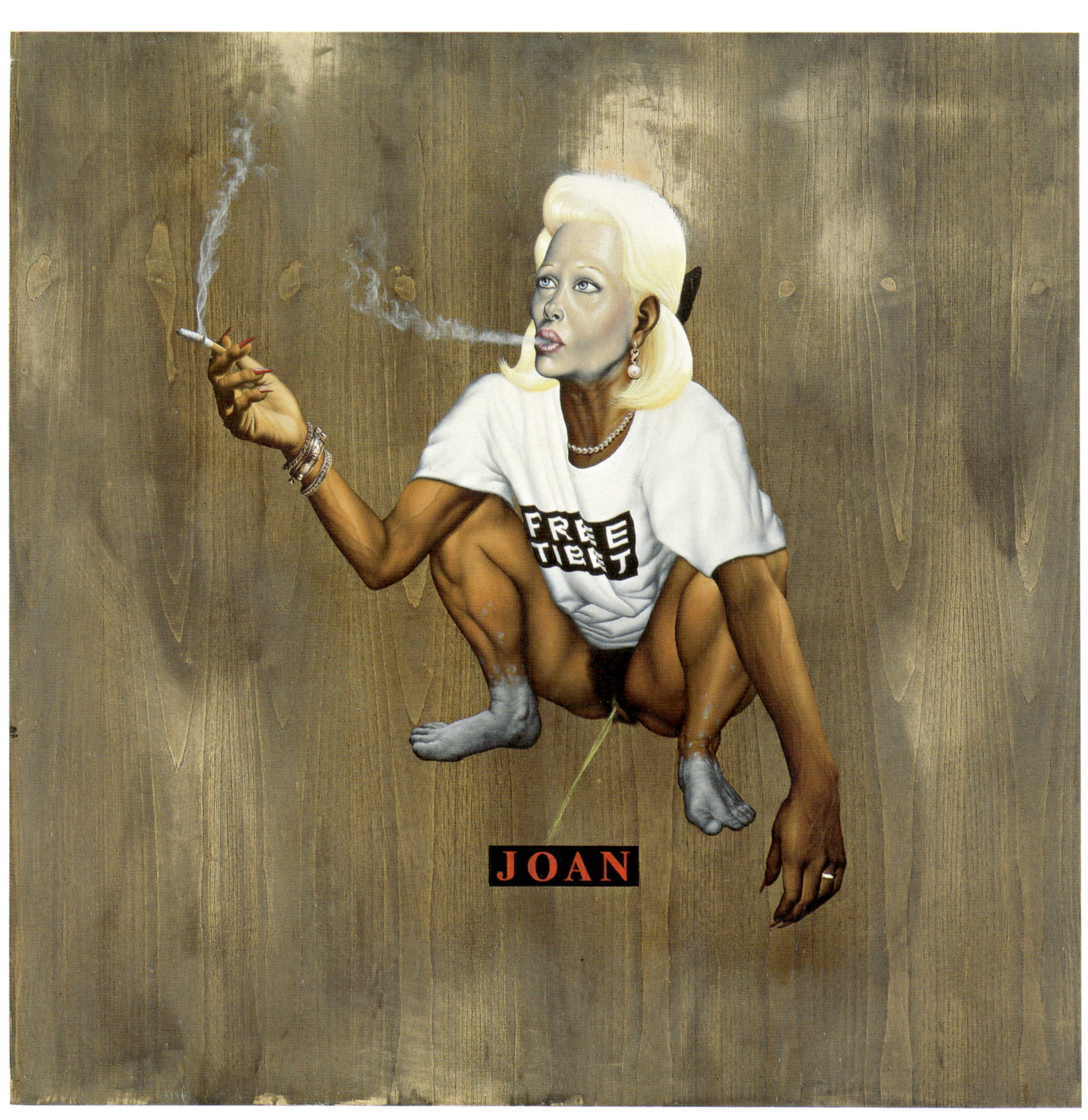
FREE TIBET
JOAN

Haim Steinbach

ultra red no. 1, 1986
Plastic laminated wood shelf, enamel cast-iron pots, digital alarm clocks, and Lava Lites
59 7/8 x 107 x 18 15/16 in.

There are two constants in Haim Steinbach's art: custom-made shelves and ready-made consumer products displayed in their "natural state"—that is, unaltered since the artist purchased them. Both his selection of objects and his issuance of design instructions to a cabinetmaker regarding the size, color, and finish of his shelves bring banal, everyday consumer decisions directly into the artwork, where they are, in turn, transmuted into something mysterious and idiosyncratic. For example, the irregular array of seventeen stacked enamel cast-iron pots, six digital alarm clocks, and four Lava Lites in *ultra red no. 1* implies a kind of mathematics just beyond reach. Any sense of logical order collapses with the objects' careful yet baffling arrangement: While the identical, chorusing clocks zigzag in pairs, the pots are stacked in uneven towers, their sequencing disrupting the "Russian doll" logic they themselves suggest.

The world that Steinbach evokes is that of the commercial display window or vitrine, with its careful, sometimes fetishistic arrangements of products. The artifice involved in such a display might ordinarily employ cheap or temporary materials and constructions, such as those implied by the plywood shelves. Art, we imagine, has deeper ambitions than an arrangement of ready-made materials and a bit of carpentry. Steinbach's work questions just such easy assumptions. In 1912, Constantin Brancusi began incorporating pedestals into his sculptures, making the bases as interesting and important as the sculptures themselves. Two years later, Marcel Duchamp proclaimed an ordinary cast-iron bottle-drying rack an artwork, irrevocably altering existing notions of what constitutes an aesthetic object. Both of these turning points echo in Steinbach's work: His shelves reiterate Brancusi's innovation by importing his work's only properly "sculptural" element under cover of an accessorizing pedestal, while he vaults Duchamp's ordinary consumer product, obtainable by anyone, into the category of art. *ultra red no. 1*, with its classical symmetries surreptitiously disrupted by tiny adjustments—the minutely disordered towers of casseroles, the slightly de-synchronized times shown by the clocks, the ever-so-slowly shifting liquid of the lamps—shows us the artist slipping, almost unnoticed, into a work we hardly recognize as "his."

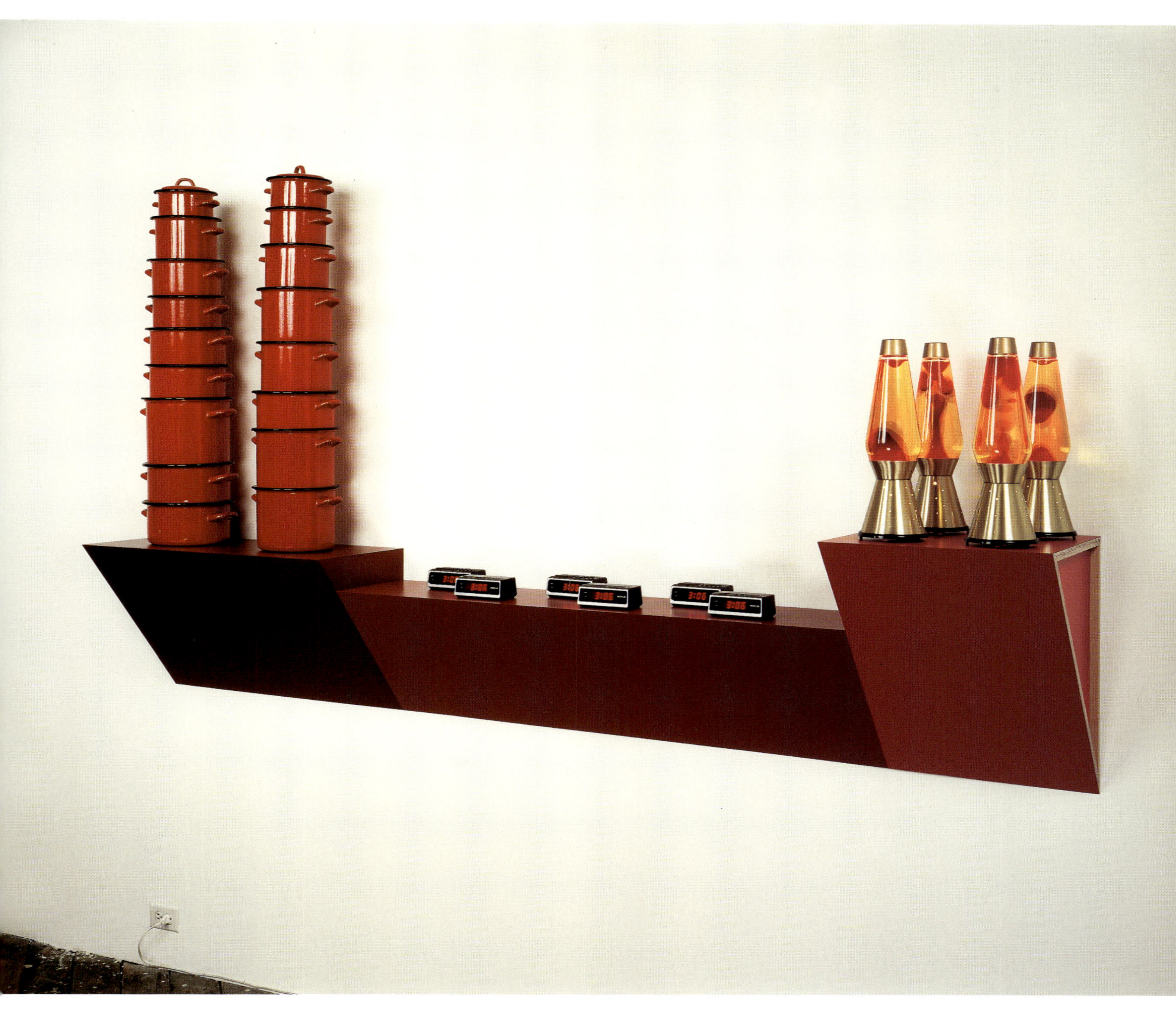

Jeff Koons

New Hoover Convertibles, New Shelton Wet/Dry Displaced Double Decker, 1981–87
Plexiglas, vacuum cleaners, and fluorescent lights
98 1/2 x 41 x 27 1/2 in.

Rabbit, 1986, and *New Hoover Convertibles, New Shelton Wet/Dry Displaced Double Decker*, 1981–87, are quintessential examples of Jeff Koons's very precise—and very controversial—style. With *Rabbit*, Koons has taken a children's toy and, by altering its material and scale, endowed it with a stunningly new presence. *New Hoover Convertibles* appropriates household appliances and leaves them essentially intact, but through the design of the installation, subtly imbues them with an unexpected suggestiveness.

New Hoover Convertibles is one of a group of works that was collectively titled "The New" when Koons began showing them in 1980. The series features ready-made store-bought items—in this case, vacuum cleaners—displayed in Plexiglas. A row of fluorescent lights illuminates each case from below, giving the machines an unearthly glow, as if they had some living, pulsing power. With their self-contained lighting compartments, the clear plastic vitrines resemble portable cages designed to aid in the conservation, transport, and study of precious specimens. They also play a vital role in Koons's displacement of the vacuum cleaners from their original domestic context to that of a museum or art gallery. Once in their new setting and shown off in his discreetly designed viewing cages they reveal formerly hidden qualities. A couple of perky upright *Hoover Convertibles* are paired like innocently matched young twins, and the plastic tube of the Shelton Wet/Dry is draped languidly around its tubular body. "I wasn't showing them with indifference," Koons has said of the cleaners, "I was being very specific. I was showing them for their anthropomorphic quality, their sexual androgyny. They are breathing machines."[1] Unlike Marcel Duchamp, who claimed to practice complete indifference in the selection and exhibition of his ready-mades, Koons does not pretend to reserve aesthetic judgment on these everyday objects. On the contrary, his choice is based on their surreal and erotic dimension, which he draws out through the pristine eeriness of his installation design.

Rabbit is similarly derived from a common mass-produced object—a child's inflatable toy, which the artist has cast in highly polished stainless steel. Magnificently reflective, its oversize surface reflects the surrounding room, literally folding the spectator's image into the work. The rabbit's cocked ear provides Koons's equivalent of classical sculpture's *contrapposto*; the carrot, his update of the attributes and accessories that identify the subjects of traditional portraiture. But where classical sculpture aimed to imitate lifelike movement, Koons's casting process weights down a formerly buoyant form. And where portraiture is historically an art of commemoration reserved for society's elite, Koons presents a universally recognizable and endlessly reproducible subject. An inflatable bunny is already silly; the ironic pretension of Koons's silvery statuary implicates us—the mirrored viewer—in its transformation. Standing almost as tall as a child, Koons's *Rabbit* renders the childlike feelings of ecstasy that we associate with the naive charm of an inflatable toy perverse, even macabre. He also does not hesitate to step over the line that has conventionally been considered the divide between art and industry: A former commodities trader on Wall Street, Koons obtains the legal right to use copyrighted industrial and brand-name forms and orders his cast sculptures from foundries.
In this way, he reproduces the means of mass production within his artistic process and blurs the lines between the invented and the ready-made, the artisanal and the

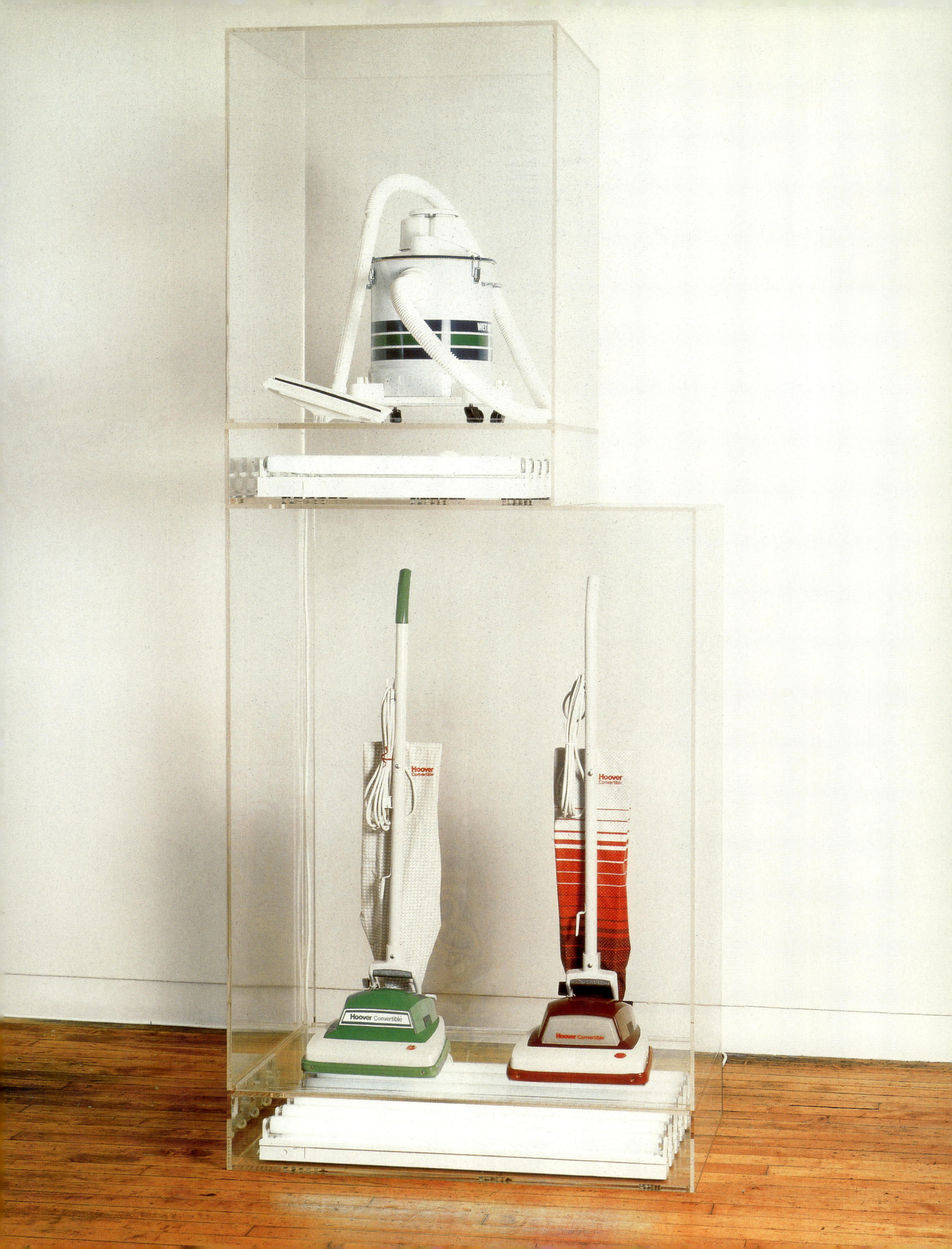
Hoover
Convertible
Hoover
Convertible
Hoover Convertible
Hoover Convertible

industrial, the real and the imitative. The latent morbidity or sexuality of "innocent" consumer forms was a major subject for Pop artists such as Andy Warhol, Tom Wesselmann, and James Rosenquist. But the earlier generation of Pop artists did not imitate and exploit commercial structures within their work to such an extensive degree. Koons's display of vacuum cleaners suggests a new kind of museum—perhaps a museum of the unnatural history of our obsessive, half-blind fascination with consumer objects. The underside of those everyday objects we take for granted comes alive in his work as Koons elicits our unexpected reactions with a gleeful and unmistakable irreverence.

1. Jeff Koons quoted in "Interview: Jeff Koons–Anthony Haden-Guest," in *Jeff Koons* (Cologne, Germany: Benedikt Taschen, 1992), 17.

Jeff Koons
Rabbit, 1986
Stainless steel
41 x 19 x 12 in.

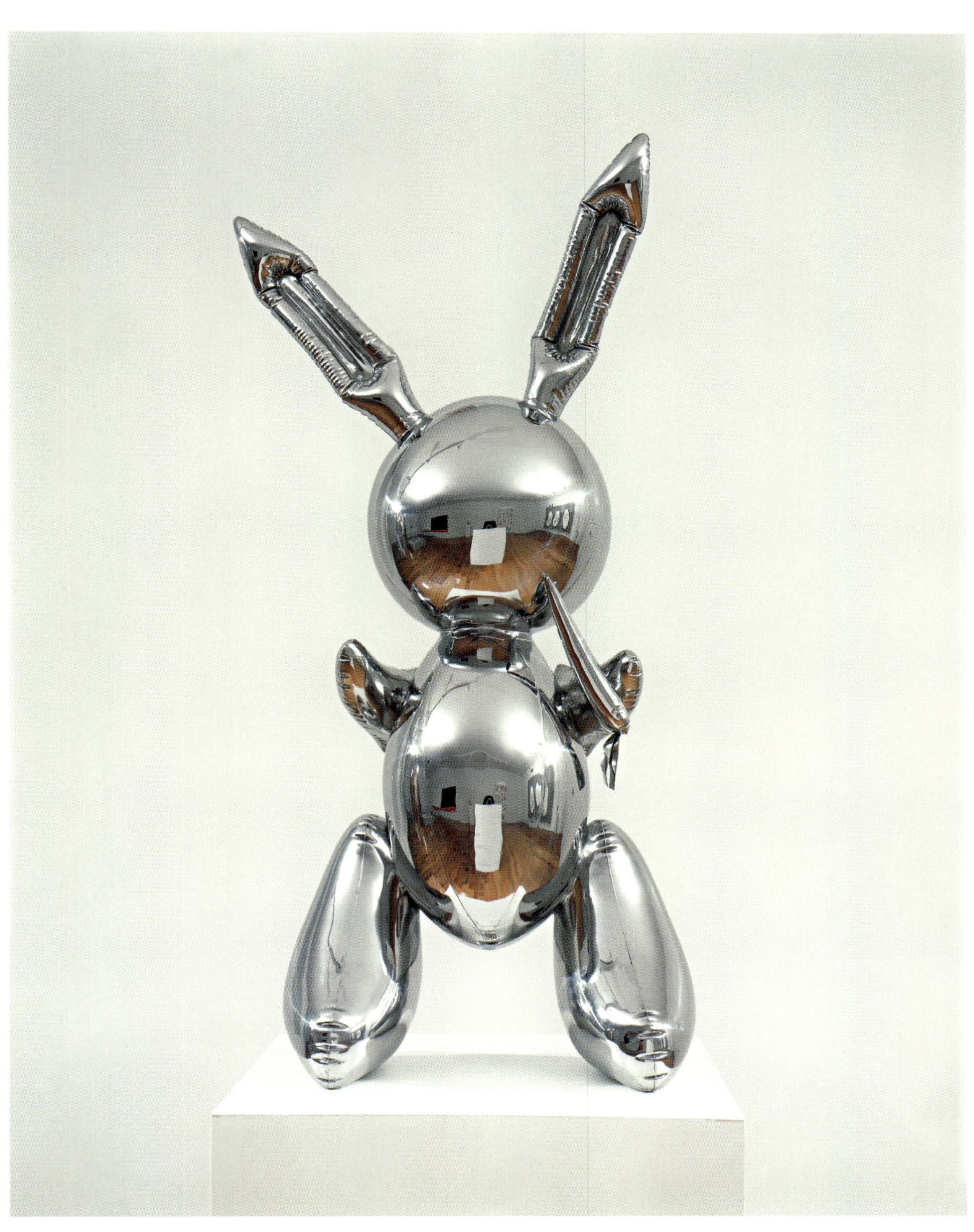

Matthew Weinstein

This Is Not a Love Song, 2000
Bronze, paint, and 14-karat gold-plated barbed wire
54 x 55 x 20 in.

Matthew Weinstein's *This Is Not a Love Song*, 2000, is rich in unusual and even opulent materials—and equally rich in subtle yet profound contradictions. Straight silver rods and gold-plated barbed wire intertwine to form a kinked halo into which Weinstein has inserted ten life-size bronze apples. Four have been electroplated in chrome, and six are hyperrealistically painted, evoking the waxed-to-perfection specimens plucked daily from greengrocers' shelves. Recalling thorns woven into a wreath, *This Is Not a Love Song*'s golden barbed wire instantly conjures an experience of physical pain: like Christ's crown, Weinstein's wreath denotes saintliness and suffering, two concepts whose twinning in Western culture is as enduring as scriptural narrative itself. Similarly, apples have long symbolized Eve's temptation and humanity's ensuing "fall." In Weinstein's work, apples are both seductively proffered in mouthwatering color and inextricably embedded in a threatening web. By introducing symbolism, storytelling, and figuration into his work, Weinstein engages a deep cultural reservoir of audience response and centuries-long traditions within the history of art.

But Weinstein also alludes to more recent artistic precedents, notably the post-Minimalist sculpture of Eva Hesse. Hesse's 1966 *Hang Up*, for example, consists of a thin curving rod that loops several feet out from an empty picture frame hung on the gallery wall; the protruding noose-like wire could almost catch the spectator who stepped inside it. Weinstein's oversize halo engages the viewer in a similar manner. The artist has intentionally created the work so that the apples and wreath cast a strong shadow, as if to remind us that—in spite of their symbolic value—they are nonetheless tangible objects. Despite its somewhat fragile appearance, Weinstein's sculpture has a compelling and forceful physical presence. Hung on the wall with a few delicate pins, *This Is Not a Love Song* projects into the room, encircling the viewer's head and torso. Like the work itself, the viewer casts a shadow on the wall that becomes part of the sculpture's overall effect. Thus, much as in *Hang Up*, Weinstein's viewer is physically implicated in the work. Hesse, however, "represents" desire and suffering abstractly, without images of concrete objects or bodies. Weinstein, on the other hand, not only employs recognizable imagery, he makes the power of representation a principle subject of his work. Indeed, by returning to such age-old symbols as apples and wreaths, Weinstein affirms representation's enduring role in the expression of human desire.

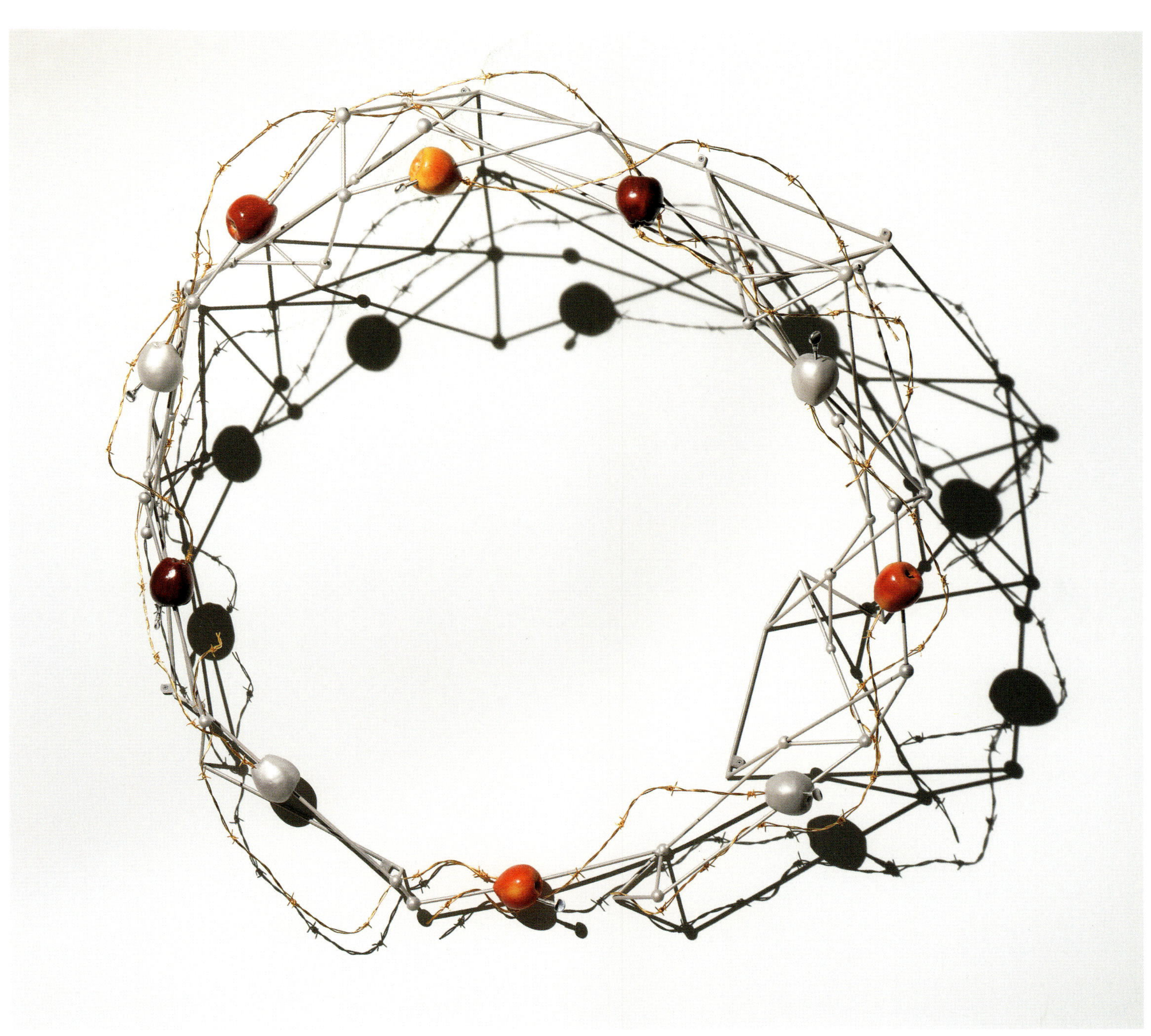

Wim Delvoye

Library I, 1990
45 handsaws, enamel paint, and birch
97 1/2 x 116 x 45 in.

Hanging in each of the forty-five frames of Wim Delvoye's nine-foot-tall folding cabinet of polished birch is a saw whose blade is inscribed with a familiar maxim printed in heraldic lettering: *WELL BEGUN IS HALF DONE*; *A GOOD CONSCIENCE IS A SOFT PILLOW*; *SILENCE IS GOLDEN*. Many are reassuring in tone, but some, like *SAYING AND DOING ARE TWO THINGS*, are slightly menacing, like the saws themselves. *Library I*, 1990, is instantly striking: The incongruity of the disparate elements joins with the work's enfolding architectural construction to amuse—and vaguely threaten—the viewer.

The attention Delvoye lavishes on his spectators' reactions is immediately apparent and is his work's most potent tool. Shock, the alleged trademark of avant-garde art, is itself often parodied in the laconic distance Delvoye builds into his projects. His *Cloaca*, 2000, for example, is an enormous, glistening, high-tech machine that, fed daily by the host museum's staff, creates a chemically engineered substitute for human excrement. Installing a mechanical device that mimics the human body's base functions as a work of art in a museum is a tacit challenge to both "taste" and the official sanctions of tastemaking institutions. In this, *Cloaca* updates Marcel Duchamp's *Fountain*, the store-bought urinal that Duchamp pseudonymously signed and submitted to the committee of an art exhibition in 1917.

Library I serializes and archives the Duchampian readymade. It also gives it an unexpectedly creepy, B-movie feel. The saws, hanging in convenient rows, seem prepared like props for use by the viewer. Delvoye's appropriated pieces of readymade language, printed up as on tourists' souvenirs, are similarly ripe for consumption. If our commodity culture is notorious for controlling consumers' choices, control of language is its most surreptitious and powerful instrument. In collecting the fragments of just such a culture, Delvoye's "library" also underscores the difficulty of fulfilling the avant-garde artist's traditional role as a creator of new languages. His reference to heraldic systems echoes this anxiety—for heraldry, the medieval system of inherited symbols identifying families and individuals, institutionalized the feudal regime through graphic emblems. Just as our own culture reinforces its power through signs—through logos, truisms, and fashions—the contemporary artist, like the medieval herald, is charged with recognizing, devising, and inscribing those signs. The artist neither escapes the system nor overturns it, Delvoye suggests, but his work's importance lies in rendering those operations evident.

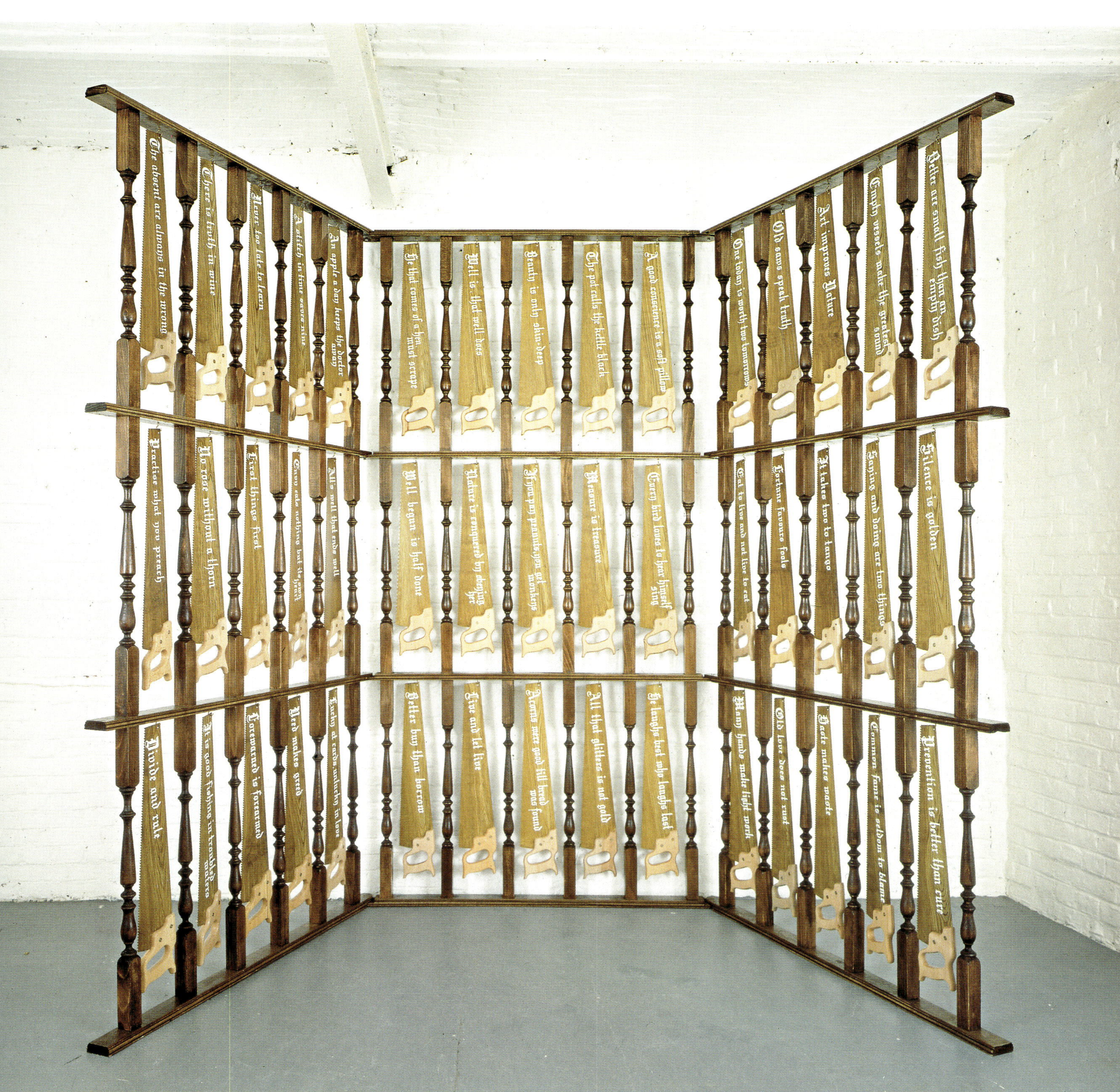
The absent are always in the wrong
There is truth in wine
Never too late to learn
A stitch in time saves nine
An apple a day keeps the doctor away
He that comes of a hen must scrape
Well is that well does
Beauty is only skin-deep
The pot calls the kettle black
A good conscience is a soft pillow
One today is worth two tomorrows
Old saws speak truth
Art improves Nature
Empty vessels make the greatest sound
Better are small fish than an empty dish
Practice what you preach
No rose without a thorn
First things first
Envy eats nothing but its own heart
All's well that ends well
Well begun is half done
Nature is conquered by obeying her
If you pay peanuts you get monkeys
Measure is treasure
Every bird loves to hear himself sing
Eat to live and not live to eat
Fortune favours fools
It takes two to tango
Saying and doing are two things
Silence is golden
Divide and rule
It is good fishing in troubled waters
Forewarned is forearmed
Need makes greed
Lucky at cards, unlucky in love
Better buy than borrow
Live and let live
Acorns were good till bread was found
All that glitters is not gold
He laughs best who laughs last
Many hands make light work
Old love does not rust
Haste makes waste
Common fame is seldom to blame
Prevention is better than cure

Rona Pondick

Dog, 2000
Yellow stainless steel
28 x 16 1/2 x 32 in.

Rona Pondick's *Dog*, 2000, is one of the artist's recent sculptures that use extremely difficult technical processes to produce forms of breathtaking immediacy and surreality. Pondick uses three-dimensional digital technology to create works made of highly polished stainless steel, bronze, aluminum, and industrial rubber. The sculptures combine life casts of the artist's head and body parts with images of animals (as in *Fox*, *Marmot*, *Monkey*, and *Cougar*, to name a few). The unreal smoothness and seamlessly composite form of the pieces bear no trace of the reworkings that are essential to Pondick's uncompromising process. The outstretched arms of *Dog* are oddly out of proportion to the slightly undersize body. Even more jarring is the conjunction of these glistening limbs with the precisely rendered hands and the head, which stares unflinchingly into empty space. This wretched miscreation has been immortalized in sculptural form: *Dog*, a creature that should never have been, is now permanently, glowingly preserved for posterity.

One aspect of sculpture particularly stressed by artists of the Minimalist generation, with whom Pondick received her formal training, is its temporal nature. Traditionally, we perceive sculpture incrementally, its various dimensions and details adding gradually to a bank of perceptual data. In the case of much Minimalist sculpture, however, the use of simple geometric forms allows perception to happen all at once. Either a sculpture distends in time, or it all but erases time. *Dog* does both: It presents itself with a shocking uncanniness, as if somewhere in our mind, we already knew that such a form existed. At the same time it seems to belong to a larger narrative or drama that slowly unfolds in the viewer's imagination. The sculpture looks backward, to the mythological half-man, half-beast hybrids of ancient and classical art and to the childlike visions that belong to our own fabulist infancies. Like a fragment of another world, *Dog* operates in a concentrated, metonymic manner, a part standing in for a whole that, unholy as it might be, feels strangely intimate. By recasting such atavistic visions in contemporary terms, Pondick asks us to consider the origins of culturally conceived fears and desires. Why do mythological beasts still hold a trace of their original power? Why do childhood fantasies recur in mature imaginations? In Pondick's work repressed desires and base impulses are let halfway out, with consequences as familiar as they are frightening.

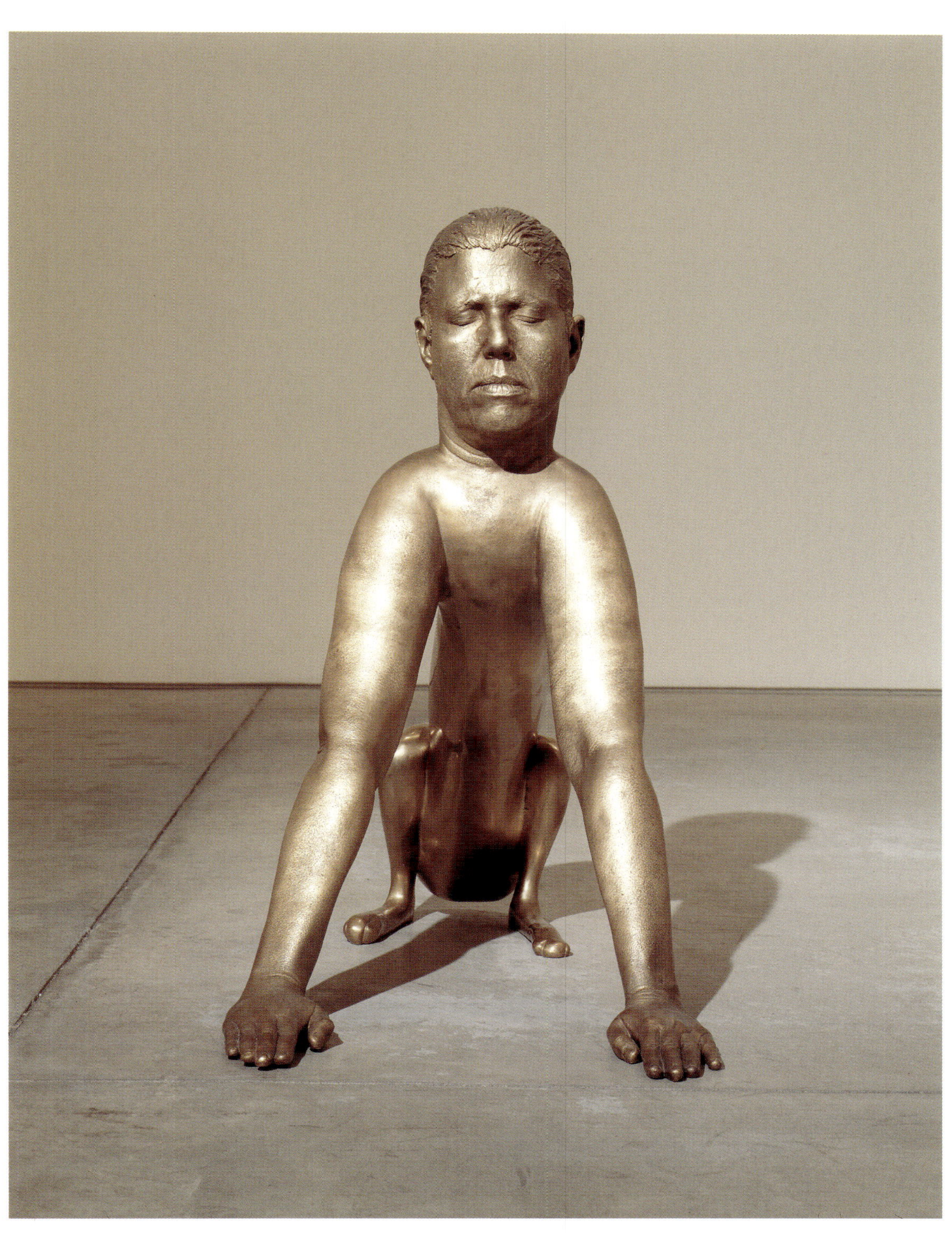

Anne and Patrick Poirier

Fragility (Fragility Series), 1999
Cibachrome color photograph on acrylic
87 x 49 in.

Fragility, 1999, Anne and Patrick Poirier's photograph from the series of the same title presents a single petal of an orchid. Across it, the artists have written the word FRAGILITY, using the flower's own pollen as ink. After photographing their subject, the Poiriers printed the image at monumental proportions. Measuring just over six feet the giant orchid towers over the viewer. Its veiny, skin-like tissue is almost palpable, the curve of its orange pistil almost tenderly erotic. In this manner *Fragility* becomes spectacular, and a slight twinge of embarrassed voyeurism creeps into the act of viewing it. The Poiriers' photograph captures this now immense flower on the brink of imminent decay—its edges are curling and tiny folds shrivel its silky smoothness. The petal indeed seems vulnerable, as its title indicates: Its sinuous curves are beginning to collapse, and the sprinkling of bright orange pollen across its surface resembles a kind of vegetal blood, as if its life were visibly ebbing away. Vague gray shadows darkening the background add a quiet aura of foreboding to the image.

The memento mori—an object, such as a skull, that reminds us of our mortality—is a classic theme in art, especially beloved in the still lifes of seventeenth-century Baroque art. As well as portending its own decay, the ephemeral beauty of a flower inevitably conjures other forms of loss: the turning of seasons, the dissipation of perfume. In their contemporary rendition of the memento mori, the Poiriers infuse a fragment of the natural world with the cultural, allegorical dimensions of a romantic, even erotic, morbidity. This meaning is conveyed in part through their choice of medium, for a photograph registers not only an image but a moment in real time. This interval—the period during which the camera's shutter remains open in front of the subject—gives the photograph its truth-value, guaranteeing the viewer that whatever is pictured actually took place. By showing us a tiny slice of time, *Fragility* bears witness to the real-time decay of the petal. In this way, it can be said to signify death not only because its subject is visibly dying but because it is a photograph, and every photograph, as has been so often remarked, is a reminder of death.

If snapshots of loved ones and even photographs of famous public figures provide us with means of holding onto people—despite the universal fact of mortality—then the sequence of images that the Poiriers have entitled "Fragility" is almost like a family album. With these portraits of flowers, onto which they have written such words as SEX, WOUNDS, and HUNGER, the Poiriers have created an ode to the powerfully romantic and mournful qualities of both the photographic medium and the natural world.

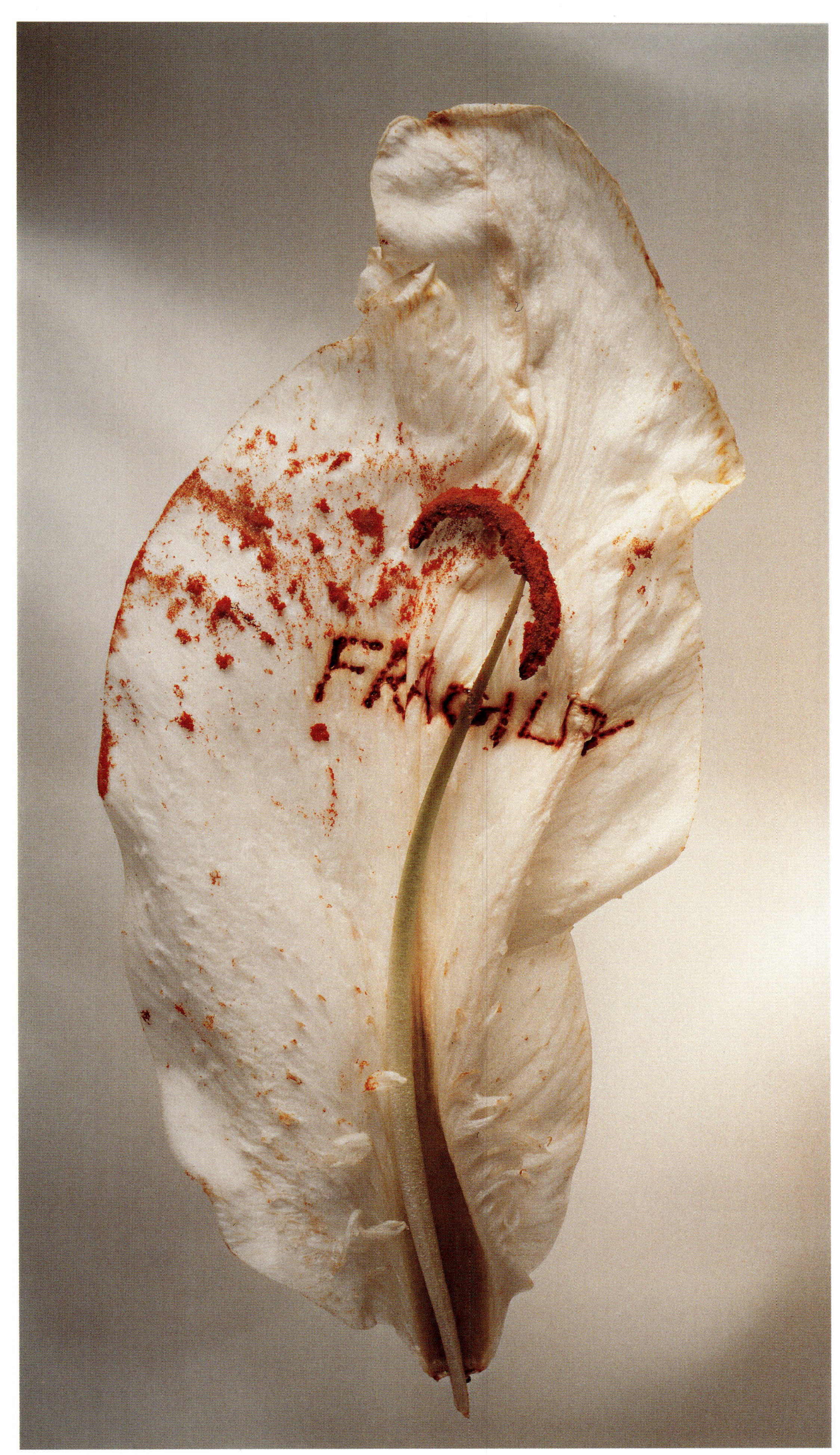
FRAGILITY

Boyd Webb

Terrain, 1995
Unique cibachrome color photograph
33 x 48 in

Boyd Webb's 1995 photograph *Terrain* depicts a strangely alien landscape: A radiant pink surface undulates in smooth curves. Branchlike sticks tumble among the waves, seemingly impervious to gravity's pull. The crevices between the pink folds are illuminated by mysteriously glowing lights. At the bottom of the image, the crests disappear atmospherically into a black background. One senses that unknown rules govern this odd planet: What accounts for the conjunction of its disparate components? What gives them their electric hues? What chemical and physical forces are at play? With a surface that at once resembles a viscous gel and a slippery satin fabric, with elements that seem both organic and entirely synthetic, Webb's *Terrain* edges into the realm of the nightmarish as easily as it conjures fantasies of the microbiological, the extraterrestrial, or the futuristic.

Webb began his career in the early 1970s as a sculptor and performance artist. He first took up photography to document his work in these media and then began making the "staged" photographs like *Terrain* for which he is best known. With these images Webb enters a century-and-a-half-old tradition that began with Julia Margaret Cameron's photographs of young models posing as nymphs or wraiths and includes the more recent efforts of artists such as Jeff Wall and Cindy Sherman. A number of Webb's staged photographs feature actors in theatrical tableaux containing enormous hyperreal props. In others, blobs and squirts resembling bodily fluids and organs are disposed in suggestive arrangements. Webb only very rarely exhibits the objects represented in his images; for the most part, these extremely sophisticated and meticulously constructed scenarios exist only in order to be photographed.

Normally, photographs index the "real" world; Webb's work instead foregrounds the subtle air of unreality that photographic technology brings to objects of scientific study. Microscopes, radiological studies, or telescopic enlargements alter our optical perspective on such seemingly familiar subjects such as human blood or the nighttime sky, until they become unfamiliar, even frighteningly alien. The mysterious beauty of these "new" forms, however, is often overlooked as scientific advancement takes precedence. Webb's photographs act as if to retrain his viewers' eyes, elaborating the foreign universes that can be contained even in ordinary matter. *Terrain*, with its sensuously rippling pink waves and inexplicable lack of gravity, tugs at our imagination while reminding us of the strangeness of the world we believe we know.

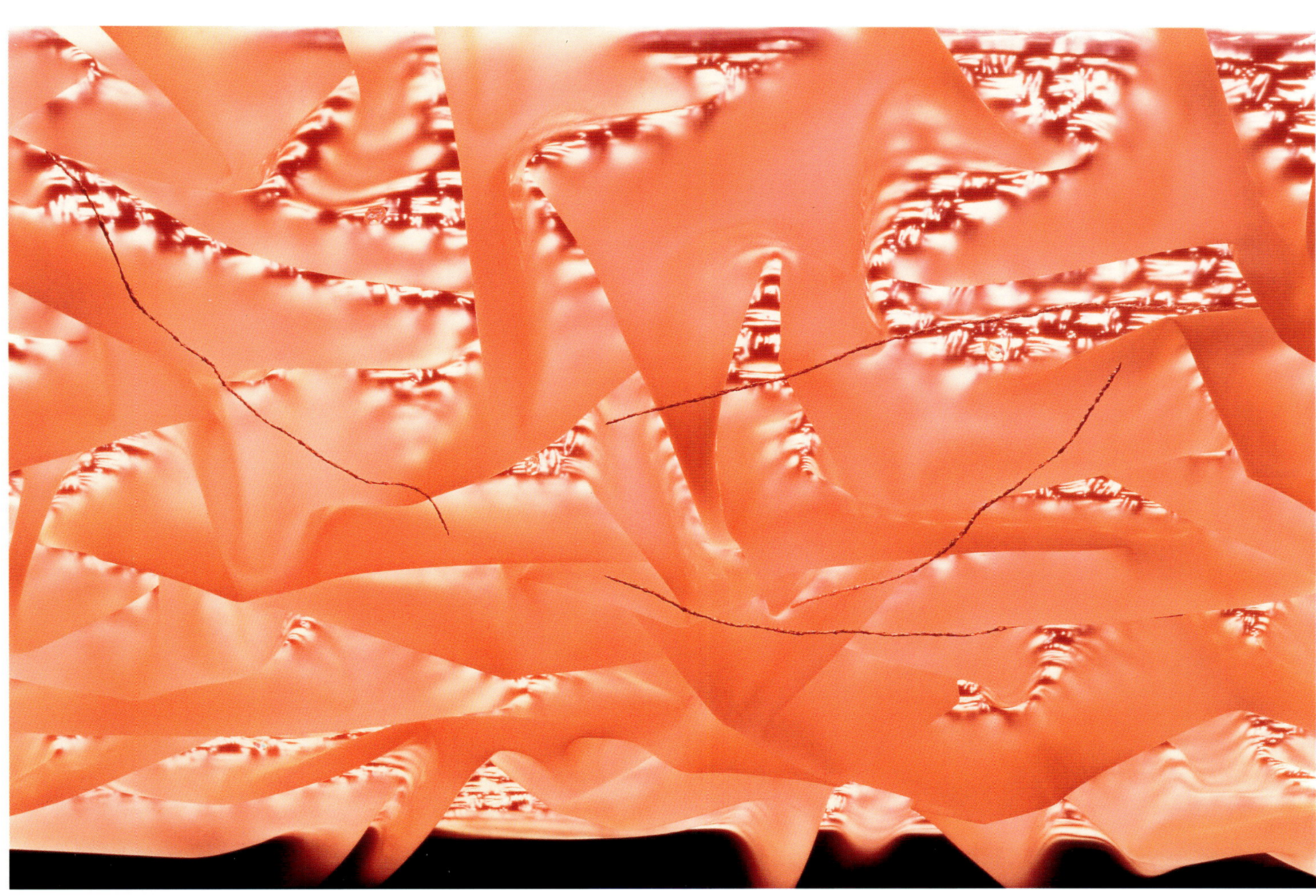

Candida Höfer

Banco de España Madrid III, 2000
Chromogenic color photograph
47 1/4 x 47 1/4 in.

In *Banco de España Madrid III*, a photograph from 2000, Candida Höfer shows us part of the interior lobby of the national bank of Spain. We see a vast marble staircase, baroquely decorated walls and columns, and a classical bust imposingly elevated and flanked by marble statuary glimpsed through the doorway to an adjacent room. The site itself is highly dramatic. But part of the intensity of Höfer's image comes from the unexpected camera angle she has chosen; the view is slightly off center and vaguely incomplete. Her position—behind the marble banister that rings the second-floor landing—would not be the logical choice were she designing a celebratory or even simply complete documentary record of the Banco de España's glorious architecture. Instead, what her photograph reveals is the piercing artificiality of the room's electric lights, the almost absurdly sumptuous scale of its decor, and the extraordinary feeling of isolation it exudes. Nowhere do we find evidence of banking activities: no tellers, vaults, or desks for conferring with clients. Utterly deserted, without a trace of living human presence, the carved marble atrium conveys an unsettling and powerful sense of loneliness.

Höfer typically photographs communal or public spaces, often concentrating on rooms that contain the tools of learning: libraries, museums, archives, lecture halls. One of Bernd and Hilla Becher's students, she has adopted her teachers' methodical approach to subject matter, as well as their reluctance to manipulate photographic images, digitally or otherwise. Whether employing a square or rectangular format, she avoids telephoto and wide-angle lenses and uses only available light, shooting her sometimes cavernous and always vacant interiors just as the human eye perceives them. Höfer deploys these self-imposed technical restrictions to powerfully expressive ends. The off-center perspective in *Banco de España*, for example, presents the site in an extremely specific manner. Institutional spaces like this atrium, which are designed to intimidate and impress, make use of symmetry and elevation to convey a sense of order and timelessness. Any human life feels small, disordered, and extremely finite by comparison—and this disparity is palpable to those who enter the space. But in Höfer's photograph, an almost human vulnerability creeps into the monumental lobby. Its staircase is barren, rows of gargoyles face abandoned rooms, and lights are pointlessly turned on—despite the daylight seen in a distant sliver of window. Though all the intricacy of the bank's heavily ornamented architecture is perfectly in evidence, even precisely focused, what is missing suddenly seems to be its most important element: human usefulness. The bank appears enfeebled by the absence of those subjects it was built to serve. One of those subjects, the photographer, has recorded the fragility behind the institution's imposing façade simply by taking a tiny step to one side before shooting.

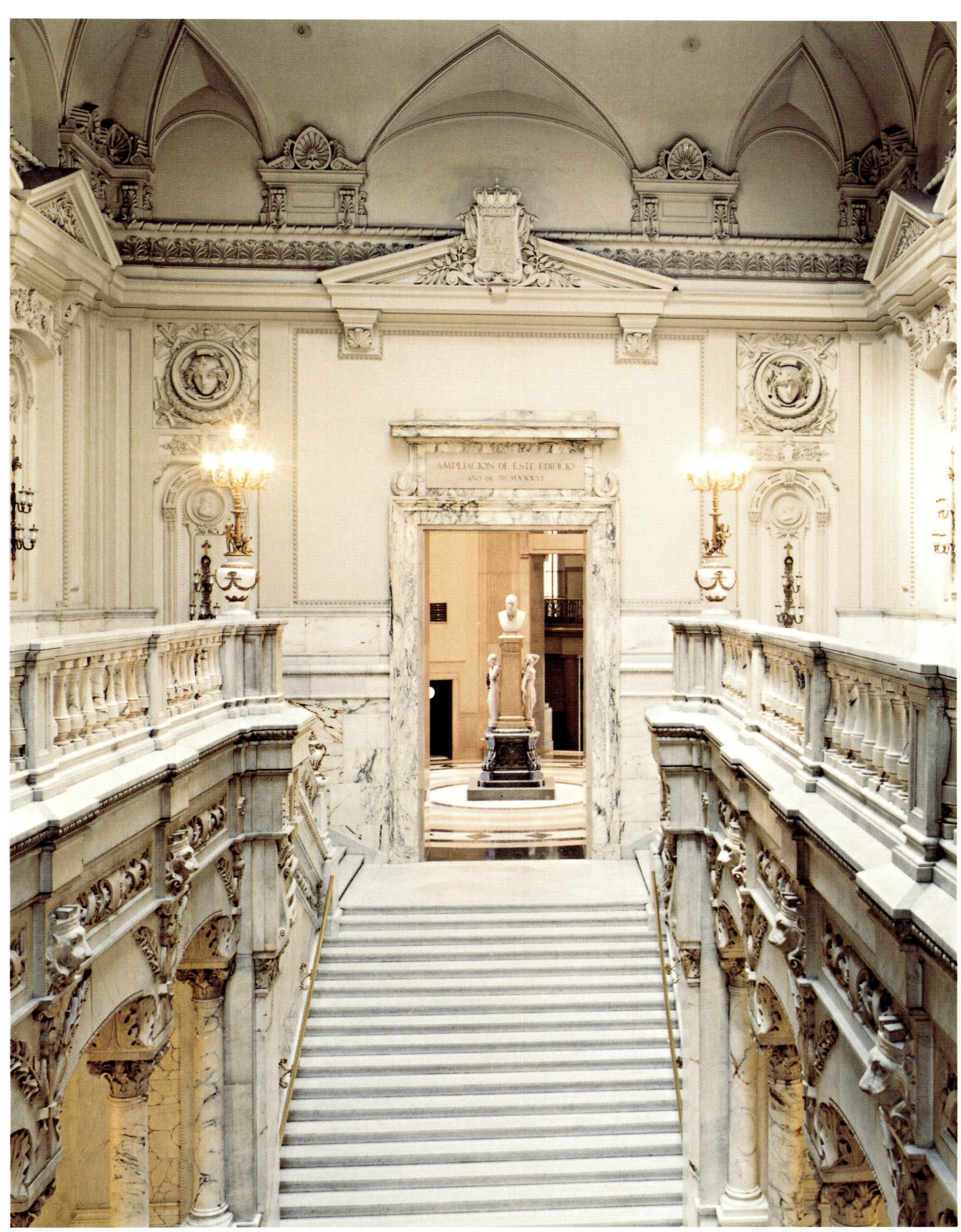
AMPLIACION DE ESTE EDIFICIO

Lawrence Beck

Parc de la Tête d'Or: Sarracenia Catesbaei (detail), 2000
Chromogenic color photograph
30 x 40 in.

Lawrence Beck's *Parc de la Tête d'Or: Sarracenia Catesbaei* and *Parc de la Tête d'Or: Drosera Binata*, are two photographs from a series shot in 2000 in Lyon's public botanical gardens. Displayed together, they form a kind of casual diptych; the tall yellow stems in the right edge of the former peek into the tufts of rose and green spikes of the latter. A stunning amount of visual information is conveyed in Beck's crystalline images, giving each the feel of an intimate portrait of a particular botanical family. The plants' wild colors and textures, their peculiar individuality and variety, seem nearly as palpable and perfumed as if one were standing before them in the garden itself. *Drosera*'s voluptuous, bushy mass is at once fragile and rough, silky and spiny; the bowed petals topping *Sarracenia Catesbaei*'s elegant, long-stemmed necks gaze down at its spiraling, deep red leaves. And yet, with an almost antiseptic effect, Beck includes in each photograph the identifying plaque that advertises the plant's genus, Latin name, and place of origin.

In the background of these two photographs we also see a windowpane's rusty edges. In featuring such a detail, Beck alludes to a tradition of self-referentiality within figurative painting. Looking at a painting is classically likened to gazing out a window; the inclusion of a "window within a window" draws attention to this analogy and, by extension, to the act of representation itself. Like the labels, this architectural element disrupts an apparently natural world, reminding the viewer of the degree of human intervention that both makes possible and interrupts the "natural" beauty of the scene. Since 1992, when he first began photographing the artificial flowers left by mourners in Italian cemeteries, Beck has studied the contrivances and manipulations that characterize society's response to the natural world. In every social, scientific, and artistic realm, from botany to public parks, from biologically-engineered food to still life painting, social relations with nature seem to take the form of either careful imitation or controlling administration. If nature inspires fear in its mimics and managers, however, it also provokes fierce longing. This duality seems captured by *Drosera*'s feathery mass, spilling forward with luxuriant immoderacy against freshly painted walls.

Beck's technical virtuosity begins with his use of large, eight-by-ten negatives, which demand extremely precise planning and allow microscopic details to come into focus. The resulting hyperreal effects resemble the sensuous immediacy of the still life paintings by eighteenth-century French artist Jean-Baptiste Chardin. Like Chardin, Beck creates compositions that, although carefully considered, appear spontaneous and unplanned. This uncontrived effect, heightened by Beck's preference for straightforward, frontal views, contributes to the sense of ease and intimacy in his work. In locations like botanical gardens and greenhouses, intellect and reason organize our collective relationship to plants and flowers. Exploring this aspect of our complex connection to nature through his rigorous conceptual wit, Beck couples it with a profound sensuous enjoyment of his subject.

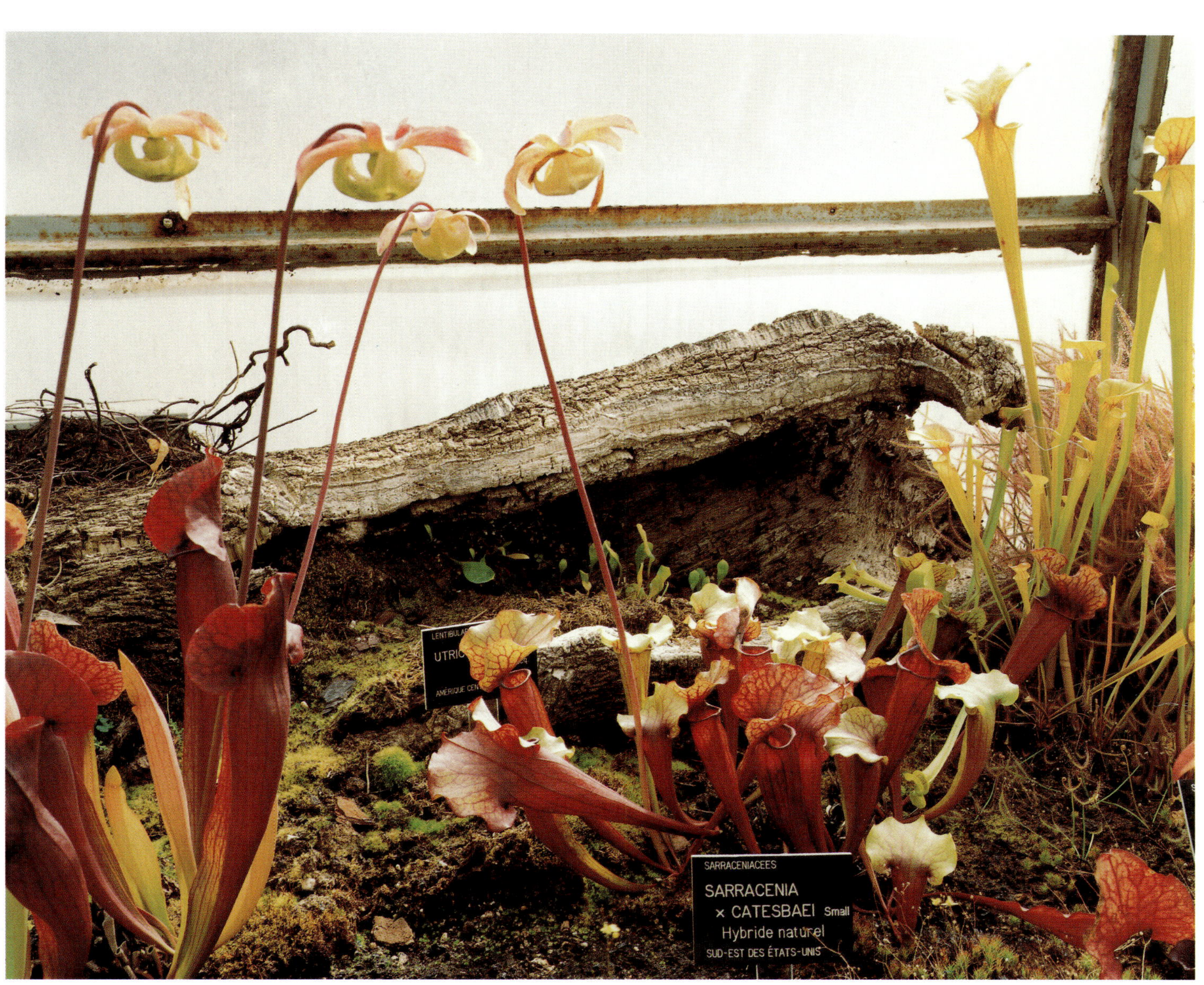
SARRACENIACEES
SARRACENIA
× CATESBAEI Small
Hybride naturel
SUD-EST DES ÉTATS-UNIS

Andrea Robbins and Max Becher

German Indians: Chief, 1998
Chromogenic color photograph
20 x 16 in.

In *German Indians: Chief*, 1998, an archetypal German face stares out from beneath a "typical" Native American headdress, and a vividly colorful pattern decorates his tunic. Details jump out: his pixieish expression, slightly mischievous despite its seriousness; the American flags beaded onto his sleeves; the furry strap across his chest. His blue green gaze is directed meaningfully and forcefully at the viewer, enhanced by the regal plumage he has appropriated for his role as "chief." The utter dedication that has gone into his role-playing costume is unmistakable. Its specific historical origin lies in the best-selling western novels of Karl May,[1] the nineteenth-century writer who introduced generations of Europeans, and especially Germans, to Native American folklore and became a veritable cult hero in the process. *Chief* was shot at the annual festival celebrating May's birthday that features encampments and lifestyle reenactments, and which draws thousands of participants to his hometown. But the process of mimicry and wish fulfillment, the sense of liberation from the confines of one's own identity that comes with the elaboration of a fantasy identity, is a psychic phenomenon that traverses every culture on record as well as every age, sex, and class. With *Chief*, Robbins and Becher document what is at once a timeless psychological process and a particular perversity of our contemporary global culture.

In their ongoing project, titled "Co-Locations," the notion of globalization takes a different turn. This diptych from the series pairs two blandly generic and virtually identical desert landscapes that seem almost to continue each other. In the photograph on the left, a cloudless sky shimmers above a vast plain, and cacti dot a sloping clay-colored hillside in the foreground. On the right, a crested hill continues the same arc beneath a gray blue sky; tiny yellow flowers and scorched, fanning bushes are interspersed along its ground. The two hills look uncannily similar, as if both photographs had been taken in the same mountain range, if not on the same mountain.

In fact they were shot in two extremely different, distant locations, as the work's title, *Co-Landscape, Arizona and Namibia*, 2002, indicates. Once the viewer becomes aware of this fact, knowledge of the vast social differences between the two sites—in terms of economic wealth, political stability, and local history and culture—becomes an integral if invisible component of Robbins and Becher's piece. Their seemingly impassive documentary style carefully sidesteps any element that would indicate the location of either image: people, landmarks, architecture, and signage are entirely absent. Presenting two scenes that are both extremely similar and extremely bland, Robbins and Becher form this diptych out of their subjects' shared neutrality. This neutrality, however, turns into a powerful tool when we learn the identity of the two sites pictured. The photographs' visual interchangeability points to the vast apparatus of globalization that connects the two geographically disparate landscapes. Yet, just as happens "in reality," the causal chain that links global commerce and banking to local political and social forces—which keeps an African country economically dependent and politically volatile while its twin enjoys relative serenity and wealth—leaves no visible trace in the images themselves. In this respect, Robbins and Becher's diptych speaks to the limitations of their medium as poignantly as to the injustice of the world. Though generations of documentary photographers have used cameras to bring social issues to view, it is just as easy, the artists demonstrate, to mute or silence the realities that haunt our society.

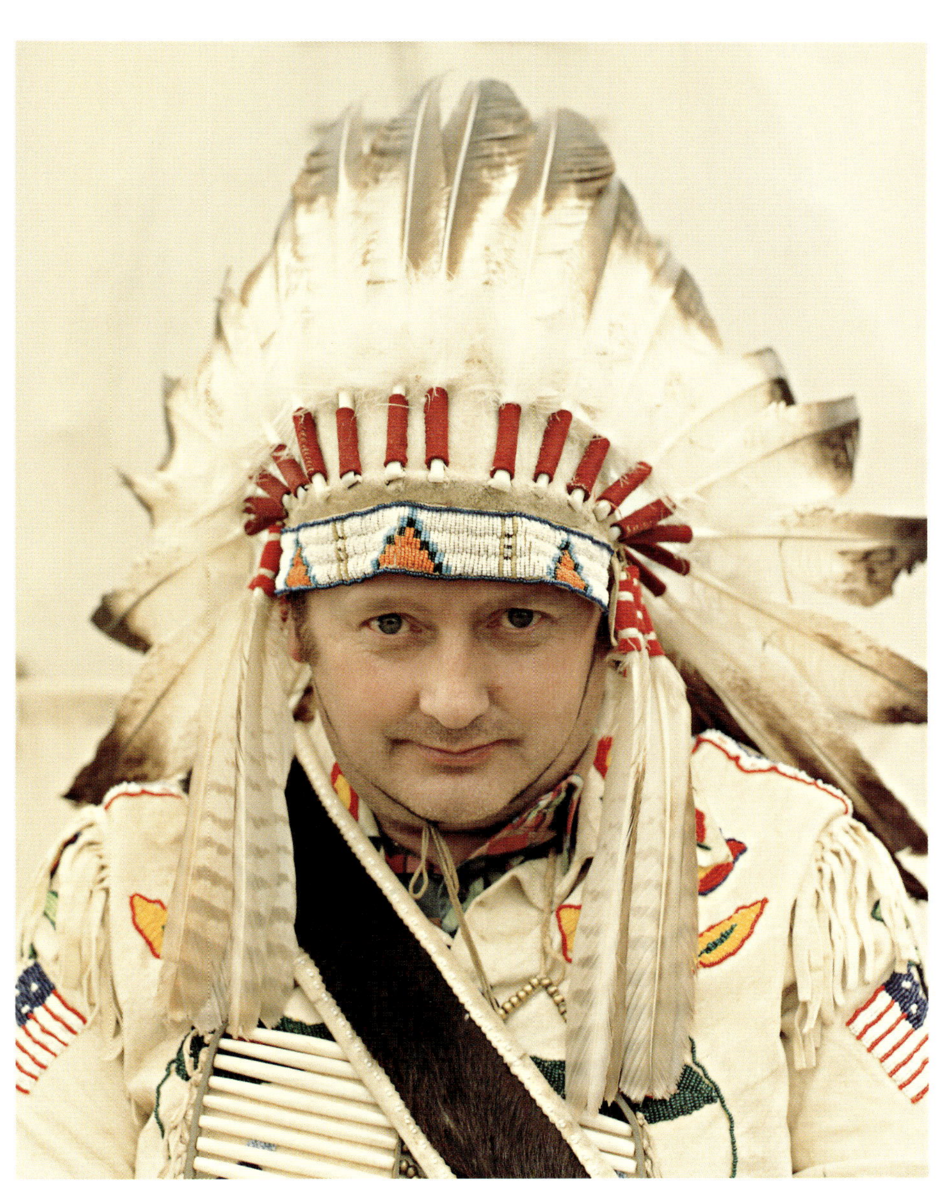

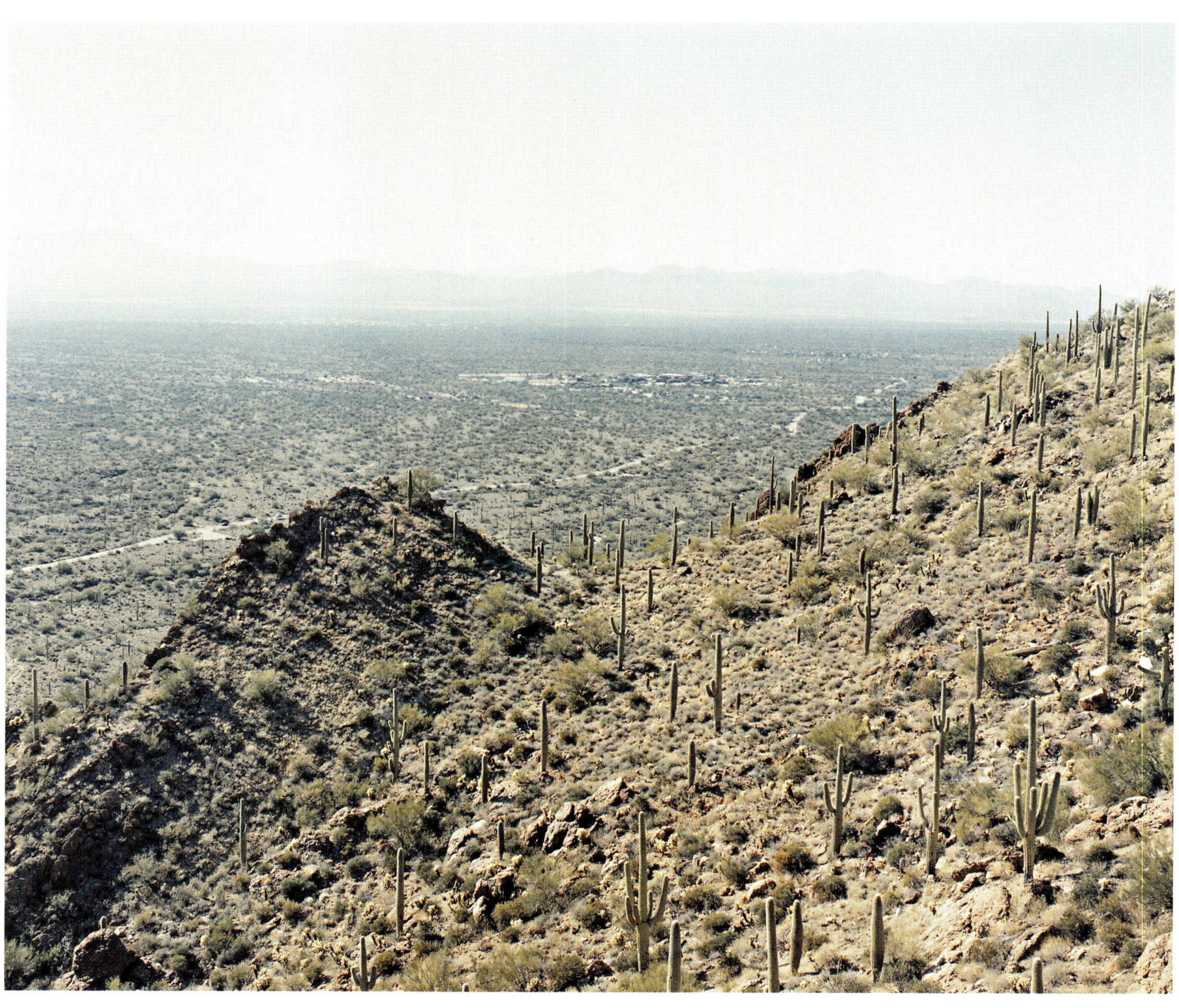

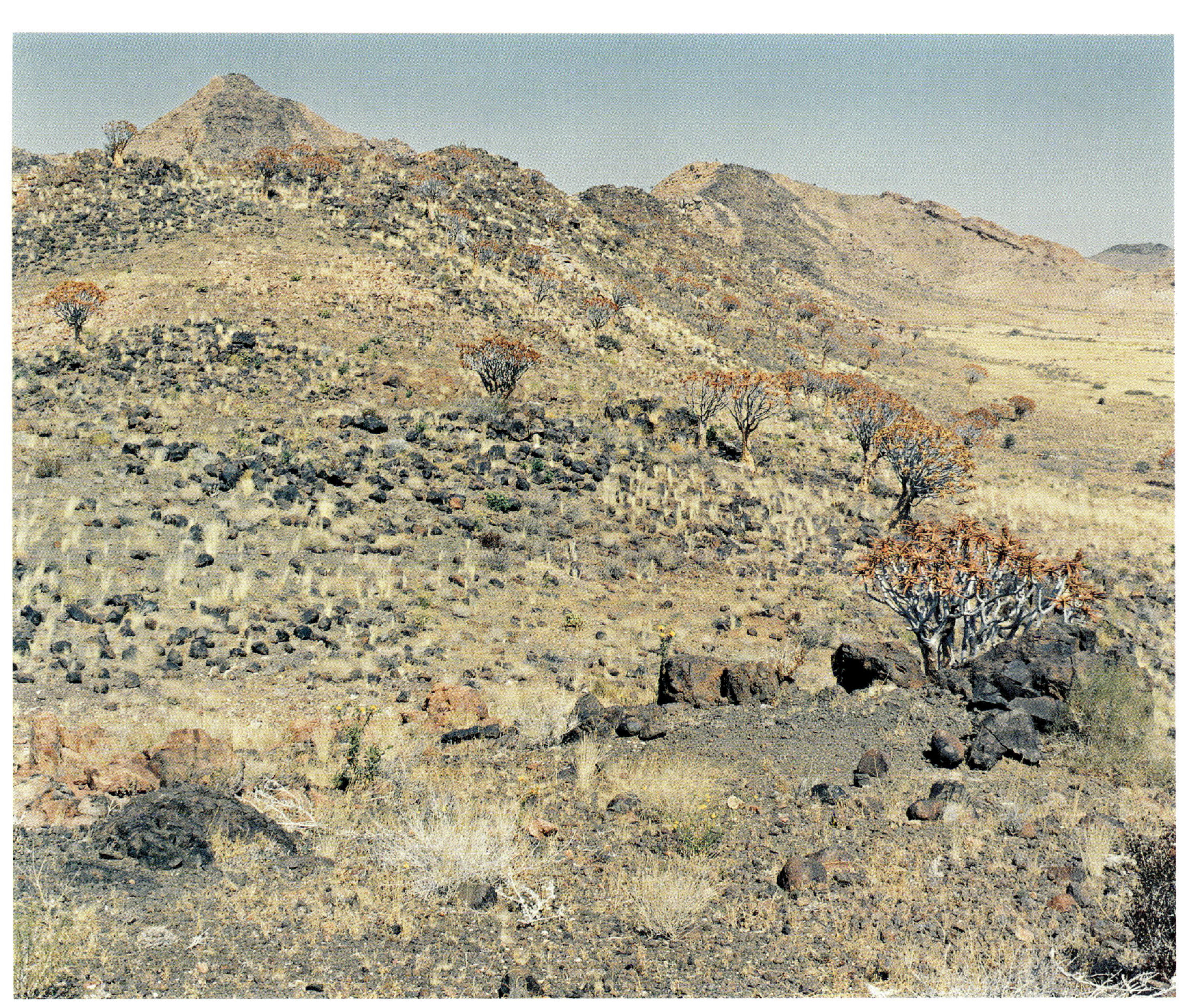

Andrea Robbins and Max Becher
Co-Landscape, Arizona and Namibia, 2002
Two chromogenic color photographs
30 1/8 x 34 3/4 in. each
30 1/8 x 70 1/2 in. overall

Clifford Ross

Hurricane XXIV, 2000
Gelatin silver photograph
46 x 56 5/8 in.

Clifford Ross's 2000 photograph *Hurricane XXIV* shows a pair of cresting waves beneath a nearly black sky and a white expanse of ocean stretching all the way to the foreground's edge. The larger wave, which forms the picture's horizon, appears to be closing in on the smaller one, almost like a pair of giant jaws clamping down on its prey. Captured in a state of majestic chaos, the sea seems unusually exposed, as if caught by an intruder. Yet after one views several photographs from Ross's ongoing "Hurricane" series, it becomes clear that these extraordinary natural forces continually escape "capture." Ross's work instead testifies to an enduring, intense relationship with an unknowable partner.

Ross began his "Hurricane" series in 1998 when, upon hearing of Hurricane Bonnie's proximity to Long Island, the New York–based artist took an impromptu trip to the beach and came home with almost two hundred and fifty negatives. Since then he has tracked the progress of hurricanes around eastern shores, experimenting with different cameras but retaining essentially the same format. Ross always presents waves in a frontal composition, from the shore-side; yet the range of visual possibilities he extracts is astonishing. Some of his photographs seem strikingly sculptural, others pictorial; in some, the waves resemble Bernini's statues, their white curves as hard and polished as marble, while in others the surf's spray seems to imitate Jackson Pollock's splatters and drips. Ross himself is a painter who came of age in the 1950s during the reign of American Color Field painting, and the tripartite composition of *Hurricane XXIV*, with the unfurling waves serving as its middle section, could indeed be compared to Mark Rothko's somberly beautiful canvases.

But despite its affinity to painterly abstraction, *Hurricane XXIV* is first and foremost a representational image. The more the picture gains concrete character, the more difficult it is to imagine how the photograph was taken; how the camera was held steady or level enough, how the lens stayed clear of surf spray, where the artist stood. And yet Ross's technique is remarkably simple: He uses a medium-format camera, available light, and rarely employs assistants or props. It is the very simplicity of his approach that leads to the slight sense of encroaching danger characteristic of the "Hurricane" series. Perhaps it is ultimately the venerable, even mythical relation between man and the sea that surfaces in Ross's work, imbuing it with a drama that is at once intensely personal and profoundly universal.

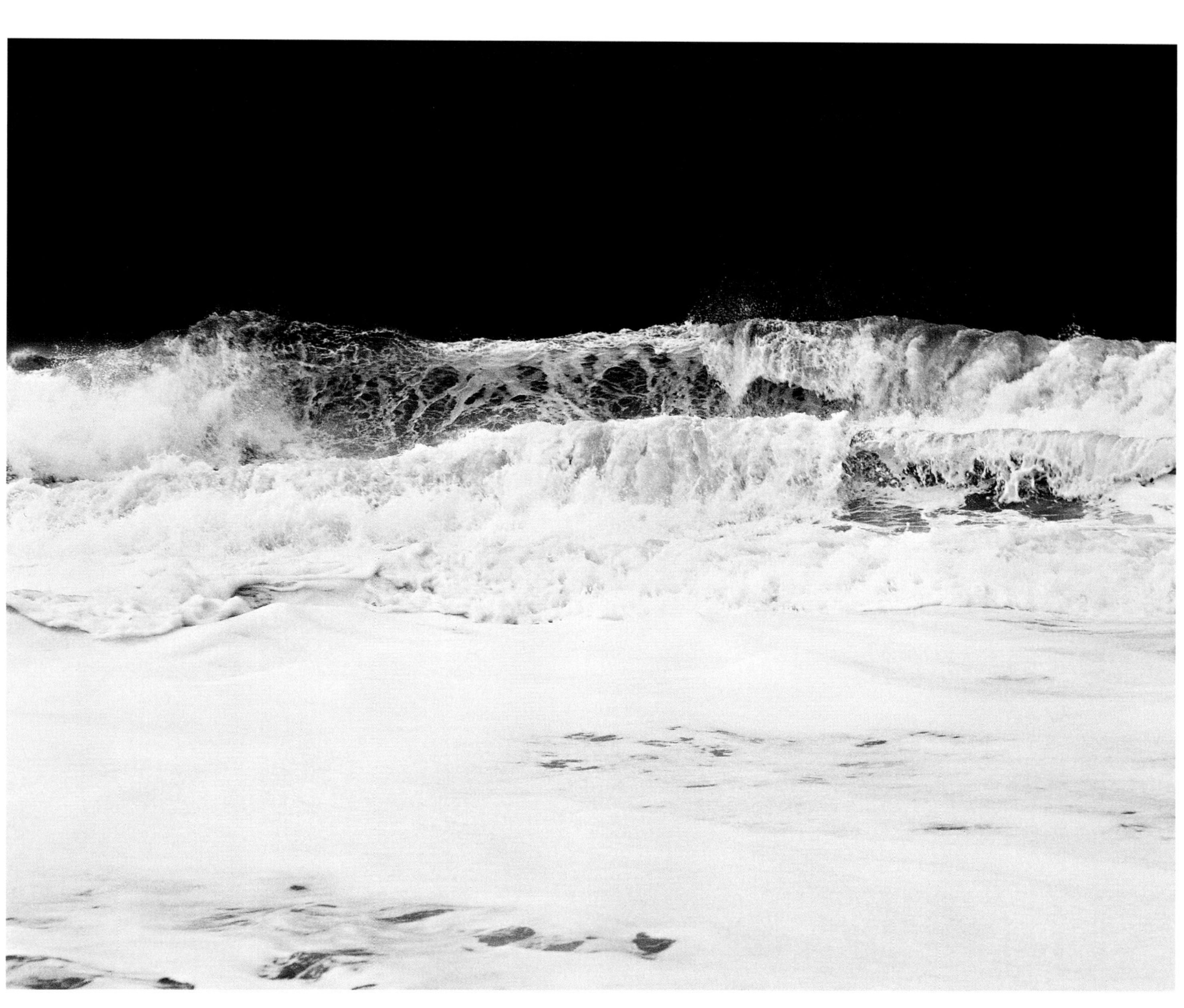

ARTISTS' BIOGRAPHIES

Vito Acconci

Born in the Bronx, New York, in 1940, Vito Acconci studied at Holy Cross College, Worcester, Massachusetts (B.A., 1962) and at the University of Iowa, Iowa City (M.F.A., 1964).

After exhibiting and performing the notorious *Seedbed* during his solo exhibition at Sonnabend Gallery, New York (1971), Acconci began to exhibit regularly in New York and Europe at such venues as John Gibson Gallery, New York (1971); Sonnabend Gallery, New York (1972, 1973, 1975, 1976, 1979, 1989); Galerie Sonnabend, Paris (1972, 1977, 1979); and California Institute of the Arts, Valencia, California (1972).

Important early group exhibitions include "Information," Museum of Modern Art, New York (1970); "American Drawings 1963–1973," Whitney Museum of American Art, New York (1973); "Video Art," Museum of Modern Art, New York (1975); "Bodyworks," Museum of Contemporary Art, Chicago (1975); and the Venice Biennale, Venice, Italy (1976).

More recently, Acconci's work has appeared in the following group exhibitions: "Heaven," P.S. 1, New York (1997); Documenta X, Kassel, Germany (1997); "Room with a View: Environments for Video," Solomon R. Guggenheim Museum, New York (1997); and "Out of Actions: Between Performance and the Object, 1949–1979," Museum of Contemporary Art, Los Angeles (1998).

In 1980, the Museum of Contemporary Art, Chicago, organized "Vito Acconci: A Retrospective, 1969 to 1980." Recent solo exhibitions include "Theater Project for a Rock Band," Dia Center for the Arts/BAM Visual Arts Initiative, New York (1995); "Acconci: Old, Refreshed & Re-viewed," Stroom, The Hague, Netherlands (1997); "Vito Acconci: Public Art," Rosenwald-Wolf Gallery, University of the Arts, Philadelphia, (1999); and "Vito Acconci: Skatepark," Institut Français d'Architecture, Paris (2000).

Vito Acconci lives and works in Brooklyn, New York.

Selected Further Readings

Acconci, Vito. *Pulse (For My Mother)*. Paris: Multiplicata, 1973.

_____. *Think/Leap/Re-think/Fall*. Dayton. Ohio: University Art Galleries, Wright State University, 1976.

Vito Acconci: A Retrospective 1969–1980 (exhibition catalogue). Chicago: Museum of Contemporary Art, 1980.

Machineworks, Vito Acconci, Alice Aycock, Dennis Oppenheim (exhibition catalogue). Philadelphia: The Institute, 1981.

Visions of Paradise: Installations by Vito Acconci, David Ireland, and James Surls (exhibition catalogue). Cambridge, MA: MIT Press, 1984.

Vito Acconci: The House and Furnishings as Social Metaphor (exhibition catalogue). Tampa, FL: University of South Florida, 1986.

Vito Acconci: Domestic Trappings (exhibition catalogue). La Jolla, CA: La Jolla Museum of Contemporary Art, 1987.

Vito Acconci, Public Places (exhibition catalogue). New York: Museum of Modern Art, 1988.

Making Public (exhibition catalogue). The Hague, Netherlands: Stroom, 1993.

Acconci, Vito, and Kate Linker. *Vito Acconci*. New York: Rizzoli, 1994.

Moure, Gloria, ed. *Vito Acconci: Writing, Works, Projects*. Barcelona, Spain: Ediciones Poligrafa, 2001.

Taylor, Mark, et. al. *Vito Acconci (Contemporary Artists Series)*. London: Phaidon, 2002.

Giovanni Anselmo

Born in Borgofranco d'Ivrea, Italy, in 1934, Giovanni Anselmo began exhibiting as an important member of the *arte povera* group at such venues as the Instituto di Storia del'Arte, Universita di Genova (1967); Galleria de Foscherari, Bologna, Italy (1968); Centro Arte Viva, Trieste, Italy (1968); Galleria del Deposito, Gian Enzo Sperone, Turin, Italy (1968). Other important early group shows included "Nine at Castelli," Leo Castelli Warehouse, New York (1968); "Conceptual Art–Arte Povera–Land Art," Galleria Civica d'Arte Moderna, Turin, Italy (1970); "*Arte Povera: 13 Italienische Kunstler*," Kunstverein, Munich, Germany (1970); Documenta 5, Kassel, Germany (1972); Venice Biennale, Venice, Italy (1979); "Idea and Image in Recent Art," Art Institute of Chicago, Chicago (1974); "Arte in Italia 1960–1970," Galleria Civica d'Arte Moderna, Turin, Italy (1977); "Europe in the '70s: Aspects of Recent Art," Art Institute of Chicago, Chicago (1977).

Anselmo's first solo exhibition was at Galleria Gian Enzo Sperone, Turin, Italy (1968). Other important early solo exhibitions were mounted at Galerie Sonnabend, Paris (1969); John Weber Gallery, New York (1972); Kunstmuseum Luzern, Switzerland (1973); Sperone Gallery, New York (1974); Sperone Westwater/Fischer Gallery, New York (1978); Kunsthalle Basel, Switzerland (1979); and Stedelijk van Abbemuseum, Eindhoven, Netherlands (1980).

In the past twenty years, Anselmo has participated in major international group shows such as Documenta 7, Kassel, Germany (1982); "An International Survey of Recent Painting and Sculpture," Museum of Modern Art, New York (1984); "The Knot: Arte Povera at P.S. 1," P.S. 1, New York (1985); "Transformations in Sculpture—Four Decades of American and European Art," Solomon R. Guggenheim Museum, New York (1985); "Italian Art in the Twentieth Century," Royal Academy of Arts, London (1989); Venice Biennale, Venice, Italy (1990); and "Zero to Infinity: Arte Povera 1962–1972," Tate Modern, London (2001).

Anselmo's solo exhibitions have taken place at Centre d'Arte Contemporain, Geneva (1993); Centro Galego de Arte Contemporánea, Santiago de Compostela, Spain (1995); Musée d'Art Moderne et d'Art Contemporain, Nice, France (1996).

Giovanni Anselmo lives and works in Turin, Italy.

Selected Further Readings

Giovanni Anselmo (exhibition catalogue). New York: Sonnabend Gallery, 1969.

Giovanni Anselmo (exhibition catalogue). Lucerne, Switzerland: Kunstmuseum Luzern, 1973.

Ammann, Jean-Christophe, and Rudi Fuchs. *Giovanni Anselmo* (exhibition catalogue). Basel, Switzerland: Kunsthalle, 1979.

Celant, Germano. *Arte Povera.* Milan, Italy: Electra, 1985.

Giovanni Anselmo (exhibition catalogue). Florence, Italy: Hopefulmonster, 1989.

Moure, Gloria. *Giovanni Anselmo.* Barcelona, Spain: Ediciones Polígrafa, S.A., 1996.

Gilman, Claire. *Arte Povera: Selections from the Sonnabend Collection* (exhibition catalogue). New York: Miriam & Ira D. Wallach Art Gallery, Columbia University, 2001.

Arman

Born in Nice, France, in 1928, Arman (Armand Pierre Fernandez) studied at the Ecole Nationale d'Art Décoratif, Nice, France (1946–49), and the Ecole du Louvre, Paris (1949–51).

Early solo exhibitions were mounted at Sidney Janis Gallery, New York (1962); Walker Art Center, Minneapolis (1964); Stedelijk Museum, Amsterdam, (1964); and Galerie Sonnabend, Paris (1967, 1969, 1970). Arman was included in numerous group exhibitions during the 1960s. Early group exhibitions include "The Art of Assemblage," Museum of Modern Art, New York (1961); "The New Realists," Sidney Janis Gallery, New York (1962); Venice Biennale, Venice, Italy (1968); and Documenta 4, Kassel, Germany (1968).

Arman participated in group exhibitions such as "*L'Ivresse du Réel,*" Carré d'Art, Musée d'Art Contemporain, Nîmes, France, (1993); "Garbage!," Real Art Ways, Hartford, Connecticut (1994); "The Gun: Icon of Twentieth Century Art," Ubu Gallery, New York (1996); and "Feminine Image," Nassau County Museum of Art, Roslyn Harbor, New York (1997).

Arman has had midcareer retrospectives mounted at the Centre d'Art et de Culture, Flaine, France, (1980); Ulrich Museum of Arts, Wichita State University, Wichita, Kansas (1986); and Galerie Pavillon Werd, Zurich, Switzerland (1986). More recent retrospectives include "A Retrospective: 1955–1991," Museum of Fine Arts, Houston (1991), which traveled to the Brooklyn Museum of Art, New York (1992) and the Detroit Institute of Arts, Detroit (1992).

Solo exhibitions in the last decade include Sonnabend Gallery, New York (1992, 1997); Mayor Gallery, London (1997); Galerie Nationale du Jeu de Paume, Paris (1998); Ludwig Museum, Koblenz, Germany (2000–2001); and Marlborough Gallery, New York (2001).

Arman lives and works in New York City and Paris.

Selected Further Readings

Arman: Retrospektive (exhibition catalogue). Zurich, Switzerland: Die Galerie, 1986.

Arman 1955–1991: A Retrospective (exhibition catalogue). Houston: Museum of Fine Arts, 1991.

Arman in Italy (exhibition catalogue). Milan, Italy: Fondazione Mudima, 1991.

Arman and Otto Hahn. *Mémoires accumulés: Entretiens avec Otto Hahn.* Paris: P. Belfond, 1992.

Arman (exhibition catalogue). Paris: Galerie Nationale du Jeu de Paume, 1998.

Arman: La Traversée des objets (exhibition catalogue). Vence, France: Château de Villeneuve, 2000.

Arman and Tita Reut. *Il y a lieux : l'Album Arman.* Paris: Hazan, 2000.

Arman: Werke auf papier. Bielefeld, Germany: Kerber, 2000.

Arman, New Works: "Sandwich Combos" Series (exhibition catalogue). New York: Marlborough Chelsea, 2001.

Arman: Passage à l'acte (exhibition catalogue). Milan, Italy: Skira, 2001.

Richard Artschwager

Born in Washington, D.C., in 1923, Richard Artschwager studied at Cornell University, in Ithaca, New York (1941–1948). In 1950, Artschwager moved to New York City, where he soon established his career after his first solo exhibition was mounted at Leo Castelli Gallery, New York (1965). Subsequently, Artschwager was included in numerous prestigious group exhibitions including Documenta, Kassel, Germany (1968, 1972, 1982, 1987); "Contemporary American Painting," Whitney Museum of American Art, New York (1972); "American Pop Art," Whitney Museum (1974); Venice Biennale, Venice, Italy (1980); and Whitney Biennial, Whitney Museum of American Art (1983).

Major solo exhibitions took place at such venues as Museum of Contemporary Art, Chicago (1973); Whitney Museum of American Art, New York (1988); San Francisco

Museum of Modern Art (1988); and Museum of Contemporary Art, Los Angeles (1989).

More recent group exhibitions include Documenta 9, Kassel, Germany (1992); the Forty-fourth Biennial Exhibition of Contemporary American Painting, "Painting Outside Painting," Corcoran Gallery, Washington, D.C. (1995); and "The American Century: Art and Culture, 1900–2000," Whitney Museum, New York (1999).

Major solo exhibitions were held at Fondation Cartier pour l'Art Contemporain, Paris (1994); Herbert F. Johnson Museum of Art, Cornell University, Ithaca, New York (1998); Whitney Museum (1998); and Kunsthalle Nuremburg, Germany (2001).

Richard Artschwager lives and works in Hudson, New York.

Selected Further Readings

Halbreich, Kathy. *Corners: Painterly and Sculptural Work (Richard Artschwager, Jennifer Bartlett, Anthony Caro, Don Dudley, James Ford, Bryan Hunt, Patrick Ireland, Marilyn Lenkowsky, John Avery Newman).* Cambridge, MA: MIT Press, 1979.

Parkett, no. 23, Richard Artschwager (with David Byrne). Zurich, Switzerland: Parkett Verlag, 1990.

Richard Artschwager: Fondation Cartier pour l'Art Contemporain (exhibition catalogue). Paris: Fondation Cartier, 1994.

Parkett, no. 46, Richard Artschwager, Cady Noland, Hiroshi Sugimoto. Zurich, Switzerland: Parkett Verlag, 1996.

Richard Artschwager (exhibition catalogue). New York: Whitney Museum of American Art, 1998.

Richard Artschwager (exhibition catalogue). Ithaca, New York: Herbert F. Johnson Museum of Art at Cornell University, 1998.

Richard Artschwager: Up and Across (exhibition catalogue). Nuremburg, Germany: Verlag für Moderne Kunst, 2001.

John Baldessari

Born in National City, California, in 1931, John Baldessari studied art at San Diego State College, San Diego, California (1949–57). Baldessari's early paintings, which incorporated text and photographs, were first exhibited at Molly Barnes Gallery, Los Angeles (1968), after which he had a one-person exhibition at Richard Feigen Gallery, New York (1970). Selected one-person exhibitions include Galerie Sonnabend, Paris (1973, 1975); Sonnabend Gallery, New York (1973, 1975, 1978, 1980, 1981, 1984, 1986, 1987, 1990, 1992, 1994, 1997, 1998); "*Ni Por Esas*—Not Even So: John Baldessari," Centro de Arte Reina Sofia, Madrid (1989); "John Baldessari: Recent Work," Margo Leavin Gallery, Los Angeles (1988); "The Information Age," Susan Inglett Gallery, New York (1998); "Artist's Choice: John Baldessari," Museum of Modern Art, New York (1994); and "Exposition, 4 RMS W VU: Wallpaper, lamps, and plants," Witte de With Center for Contemporary Art, Rotterdam (1998).

A selection of Baldessari's group exhibitions includes the Whitney Biennial, Whitney Museum of American Art, New York (1985); "Group Exhibition," Sonnabend Gallery, New York (1989, 1994, 1995, 2001); "California Photography: Remaking the Make Believe," Museum of Modern Art, New York (1989); "Invention and Continuity in Contemporary Photographs," Metropolitan Museum of Art, New York (1989); "L.A. Pop in the Sixties," Newport Harbor Art Museum, Newport Beach, California (1989); "Word as Image: American Art 1960–1990, Milwaukee Art Museum, Milwaukee (1990); "Breakthroughs: Avant-Garde Artists in Europe and America 1950–1990," Wexner Center for the Arts, Columbus, Ohio (1991); "Special Collections: The Photographic Order from Pop to Now," International Center of Photography, New York (1992); "Altered States," Charles Cowles Gallery, New York (1999); "Drawings 2000," Barbara Gladstone Gallery, New York (2000); and "Snapshot," Aldrich Museum of Contemporary Art, Ridgefield, Connecticut (2002). In 1990, the Museum of Contemporary Art, Los Angeles, organized a retrospective of Baldessari's work.

John Baldessari lives and works in Santa Monica, California.

Selected Further Readings

John Baldessari (exhibition catalogue). New York: Museum of Modern Art, 1981.

John Baldessari (exhibition catalogue). Santa Barbara, California: Santa Barbara Museum of Art, 1986.

van Bruggen, Coosje. *John Baldessari/Coosje van Bruggen.* New York: Rizzoli International Artist Books, 1990.

Baldessari, John. *The Telephone Book: (With Pearls).* Ghent, Belgium: Imschoot, Uitgevers for IC, 1992.

This Not That (exhibition catalogue). Manchester, England: Cornerhouse, 1995.

John Baldessari: National City (exhibition catalogue). San Diego: Museum of Contemporary Art, 1997.

John Baldessari: The Goya Series (exhibition catalogue). Los Angeles: Margo Leavin Gallery, 1997.

Baldessari, John, Hans Ulrich-Obrist. *Zorro.* Cologne, Germany: Oktagon, 1998.

Baldessari, John. *The Metaphor Problem: Again.* Zurich, Switzerland: Mai 36 Galerie, 1999.

Baldessari, John. *Two Gestures and One Mark.* Cologne, Germany: Oktagon, 1999.

John Baldessari: While Something Is Happening Here, Something Else Is Happening There: Works 1988–1999 (exhibition catalogue). Cologne, Germany: Verlag der Buchhandlung Walther König, 1999.

Tetrad Series (exhibition catalogue). New York: Marian Goodman Gallery, 1999.
John Baldessari (exhibition catalogue). Milan, Italy: Skira, 2000.
Baldessari, John. *Brown and Green and Other Parables.* Reykjavík, Iceland: Reykjavík Art Museum, 2001.

Bernd and Hilla Becher

Bernd Becher, born in the Siegen District, Germany, in 1931, studied at the Kunstakademie Stuttgart and the Kunstakademie Düsseldorf, Germany. He began photographing industrial buildings in 1956. Hilla Becher, born in Berlin, in 1934, studied at the Kunstakademie Düsseldorf. Bernd and Hilla Becher began working together in 1959.

Early important group exhibitions include "Prospect '69," Stadtische Kunsthalle, Düsseldorf (1969); "*Konzeption*," Stadtische Museum, Leverkusen, Germany (1969); "Information," Museum of Modern Art, New York (1970); "Idea and Image," Art Institute of Chicago, Chicago (1974); "New Media," Malmö Kunsthalle, Malmö, Sweden (1975); XIV International São Paulo Biennale, São Paulo, Brazil (1977); and Documenta, Kassel, Germany (1972, 1977, 1982). Early solo exhibitions were held at Moderna Museet, Stockholm, Sweden (1970); Galerie Konrad Fischer, Düsseldorf, Germany (1970); Sonnabend Gallery, New York (1972, 1974, 1977, 1978, 1981, 1983, 1985, 1988, 1990, 1993, 1995, 1999); and Galerie Sonnabend, Paris (1973, 1975, 1979).

Over the past thirty years, their work has been included in numerous group exhibitions, such as "Big Pictures," Museum of Modern Art, New York (1983); "Another Objectivity," Institute of Contemporary Arts, London (1988); "German Photography: Documentation and Introspection," Aldrich Museum of Contemporary Art, Ridgefield, Connecticut (1990); "Special Collections: The Photographic Order from Pop to Now," International Center of Photography, New York (1992); "Out of Sight, Out of Mind," Lisson Gallery, London (1993); "The Epic and the Everyday: Contemporary Photographic Art," Hayward Gallery, London (1994); "*Sammlung Sonnabend*," Deichtorhallen, Hamburg, Germany (1996); Photographische Sammlung/SK Stiftung Kultur im Media Park, Cologne, Germany (1997); and "Views from the Edge of the World," Marlborough Gallery, New York (1999).

In 1991, the Kolnischer Kunstverein, Cologne, Germany, organized a retrospective exhibition of their work. More recent solo exhibitions include "Typologies," Ydessa Hendeles Foundation, Toronto (1994); Centre d'Art Contemporain, Fribourg, Switzerland (1994); Daniel Weinburg Gallery, San Francisco (1996); Albright-Knox Art Gallery, Buffalo, New York (1996); and Sonnabend Gallery, New York (1999).

Bernd and Hilla Becher live and work in Düsseldorf, Germany.

Selected Further Readings

Bernd and Hilla Becher (exhibition catalogue). La Jolla, CA: La Jolla Museum of Contemporary Art, 1974.
Photographs of Hilla and Bernd Becher (exhibition catalogue). Milwaukee: Milwaukee Art Center, 1978.
Becher, Bernd and Hilla. *Watertowers.* Cambridge, MA: MIT Press, 1988.
Assembled: Works of Art Using Photography as a Construction Element (exhibition catalogue). Dayton, OH: University Art Galleries, Wright State University, 1990.
Becher, Bernd, and Hilla Becher. *Blast Furnaces.* Cambridge, MA: MIT Press, 1990.
Becher, Bernd, and Hilla Becher. *Gastanks.* Cambridge, MA: MIT Press, 1993.
Bernd and Hilla Becher (exhibition catalogue). Buffalo, NY: Buffalo Fine Arts Academy, 1996.
Becher, Bernd, and Hilla Becher. *Typologien* (Typologies). Munich, Germany: Schirmer/Mosel Verlag, 1999.
Becher, Bernd, and Hilla Becher. *Zeche Hannibal* (Hannibal mine). Munich, Germany: Schirmer/Mosel Verlag, 2000.
Becher, Bernd, and Hilla Becher. *Framework Houses.* Cambridge, MA: MIT Press, 2001.

Lawrence Beck

Born in New York City, in 1962, Lawrence Beck studied at the State University of New York, Purchase, New York (B.A. 1984). Beck began his career after participating in the group exhibition "Europa/America," Pino Molica Gallery, New York (1992). He continued with other group exhibitions including "Black and White," 123 Watts Gallery, New York (1995); "Fantastic Imagery: Lawrence Beck, Nancy Lawton, Dennis Masback," Nancy Solomon Gallery, Atlanta (1995); and "Works on Paper (Old Masters to Contemporary)," Park Avenue Armory, New York (1996).

Beck had his first solo show in New York at Sonnabend Gallery (1998), followed by an exhibition at Metropolis, Lyon, France (1999). He recently mounted another show at Sonnabend Gallery, New York (2002).

Recent group exhibitions include "Bernd & Hilla Becher, Lawrence Beck, Hiroshi Sugimoto," Galerie Rodolfe Janssen, Brussels, Belgium (1999); "Lawrence Beck, Elger Esser, Hiroshi Sugimoto," Sonnabend Gallery, New York (1999); "The Chicago Art Fair," Sonnabend Gallery, New York (1999); "Lawrence Beck, Elger Esser, Candida Höfer," Thomas Segal Gallery, Baltimore (2000); "Group Exhibition," Galerie

Metropolis, Lyon, France (2000); and "Bernd & Hilla Becher, Lawrence Beck, Hiroshi Sugimoto," Galerie Ziegler, Zurich, Switzerland (2000).

Lawrence Beck lives and works in New York City and Italy.

Selected Further Readings

Hobbs, Sarah. "Black and White Unfixed," *Art Papers*, May–June 1997: 51.

Meyer, James. "The Macabre Museum," *Frieze*, January–February 1997: 56–61.

Three dimensions: 9 Pacific Northwest Artists (exhibition catalogue). Eugene, OR: University of Oregon, 1996.

Wolin, Joseph. "High Anxiety," *Photography Quarterly*, No. 69: 4–9, 13.

Ashley Bickerton

Born in Barbados, West Indies, in 1959, Ashley Bickerton studied at the California Institute of the Arts, Valencia, California (B.F.A., 1982), before entering the Whitney Museum Independent Study Program, New York (1985). His first solo exhibition was at White Columns, New York, in 1984. Other early solo exhibitions include Artists Space, New York (1984); Cable Gallery, New York (1986); Donald Young Gallery, Chicago (1987); Daniel Weinburg Gallery, Los Angeles (1988); Sonnabend Gallery, New York (1988, 1989, 1991, 1993, 1999); and Donald Young Gallery, Chicago (1990).

Early group exhibitions include "Seven Young Painters," Holly Solomon Gallery, New York (1985); "Surfboards," Michael Kohn Gallery, Los Angeles (1986); "Currents, Simulations, New American Conceptualism," Milwaukee Art Museum, Milwaukee (1987); and the Whitney Biennial, Whitney Museum of American Art, New York (1989).

Recent solo exhibitions have been mounted at venues such as White Cube, London (1997); and No Limits Event Gallery (N.E.G.) Milan, Italy (2000). Recent group exhibitions include "American Art of the '80s," Museo d'Arte Moderna e Contemporanea di Trento e Rovereto, Trento, Italy (1992); "Extravagant: The Economy of Elegance," Russisches Kulturzentrum, Berlin (1993); Sonnabend Gallery, New York (1994, 2001); "Border Crawl," Kukje Gallery, Seoul, Korea (1995); "Garbage," Thread Waxing Space, New York (1995); "Pop-Surrealism," Aldrich Museum of Contemporary Art, Ridgefield, Connecticut (1998); and "Face to Face," Vancouver Art Gallery, Vancouver, British Columbia (1999).

Ashley Bickerton lives and works in Bali, Indonesia.

Selected Further Readings

New York in View: Ashley Bickerton, Jeff Koons, Allan McCollum, Haim Steinbach, Meyer Vaisman (exhibition catalogue). Munich, Germany: Kunstverein München, 1988.

Biggs, Melissa E. *In the Vernacular: Interviews at Yale with Sculptors of Culture*. Jefferson, NC: McFarland, 1991.

Object Lessons (exhibition catalogue). Portland, OR: Portland Art Museum, 1991.

Ashley Bickerton (exhibition catalogue). Oslo, Norway: Kunstnernes Hus, 1992.

Some Went Mad, Some Ran Away (exhibition catalogue). London: Serpentine Gallery, 1995.

Ashley Bickerton (exhibition catalogue). Santander, Spain: Autoridad Portuaria de Santander, 1996.

Natural Spectacles (exhibition catalogue). Providence, RI: David Winton Bell Gallery, Brown University, 1996.

Pollution: Ashley Bickerton (exhibition catalogue). Milan, Italy: Galleria C. Gian Ferrari Arte Contemporanea, 1998.

Mel Bochner

Born in Pittsburgh, in 1940, Mel Bochner studied at the Carnegie Institute of Technology, Pittsburgh (B.F.A., 1962). Bochner's early contribution to the Conceptual Art movement began in the early 1960s with his solo exhibition at the School of Visual Arts Gallery, New York (1966). Subsequent solo shows were held at such venues as Museum of Modern Art, New York (1971); Lisson Gallery, London (1972); Galerie Sonnabend, Paris (1972, 1973, 1974); Sonnabend Gallery, New York (1972, 1973, 1975, 1976, 1978, 1980, 1982, 1983, 1985, 1987, 1989, 1993, 1996, 2000); Schema Gallery, Florence, Italy (1974); Ricke Gallery, Cologne, Germany (1975); Baltimore Museum of Art, Baltimore (1976); Art in Progress Gallery, Düsseldorf, Germany (1979); Carnegie Mellon University Art Gallery, Pittsburgh (1985); Kunstmuseum Luzern, Lucerne, Switzerland (1986); David Nolan Gallery, New York (1988); Galleria Primo Piano, Rome (1990); Galerie Arnaud Lefebvre, Paris (1994); and Musée d'Art Moderne et Contemporain, Geneva (1997).

Bochner participated in numerous early group exhibitions including "*Konzeption*," Museum Leverkusen, Leverkusen, Germany (1969); "Using the Walls," Jewish Museum, New York (1970); "Information," Museum of Modern Art, New York (1970); Documenta 5, Kassel Germany (1972); "American Drawings," Whitney Museum of American Art, New York (1973); "Idea and Image," Art Institute of Chicago, Chicago (1974); "Drawing Now," Museum of Modern Art, New York (1976); Whitney Biennial, Whitney Museum, New York (1977,

1979); "Minimalism to Expressionism," Whitney Museum, New York (1983); *"L'Art Conceptual, Une Perspective,"* Musée d'Art Moderne de la Ville de Paris, Paris (1989).

Bochner's recent comprehensive exhibitions include "Mel Bochner: Thought Made Visible, 1966–1973," Yale University Art Gallery, New Haven, Connecticut (1995); "Constants & Variables 1966–96," Sonnabend Gallery, New York (1996); "Mel Bochner: Drawings, 1966–1973," Lawrence Markey Gallery, New York (1998); "Mel Bochner, Counting and Measuring Pieces 1966–1998," Akira Ikeda Gallery, AIG Exhibition, Taura, Japan (1999); and "Mel Bochner Photographs: 1966–1969," Arthur M. Sackler Museum, Harvard University, Cambridge, Massachusetts (2002).

Mel Bochner lives and works in New York City.

Selected Further Readings

Bochner, Mel. *Misunderstanding: A Theory of Photography.* New York: Multiples, Inc., 1970.

_____. *Primer: The Complete Catalog of Twenty-one Demonstrations from a Theory of Sculpture: (Counting).* Milan, Italy: Flash Art Edizione, 1973.

(Toward) Axiom of Indifference: 1971–1973 (exhibition catalogue). New York: Sonnabend Gallery, 1974.

Mel Bochner: Number and Shape (exhibition catalogue). Baltimore: Baltimore Museum of Art, 1976.

Mel Bochner: Twenty-five Drawings 1973–1980 (exhibition catalogue). Cleveland: New Gallery of Contemporary Art, 1980.

Mel Bochner: 1973–1985 (exhibition catalogue). Pittsburgh: Carnegie Mellon University Press, 1985.

Mel Bochner: Thought Made Visible 1966–1973 (exhibition catalogue) New Haven, CT: Yale University Art Gallery, 1995.

Mel Bochner: Drawings, 1966–1973 (exhibition catalogue). New York: Lawrence Markey Gallery, 1998.

Mel Bochner: Counting and Measuring Pieces, 1966–1998 (exhibition catalogue). Taura, Japan: Akira Ikeda Gallery, 1999.

Rothkopf, Scott, and Elisabeth Sussman. *Mel Bochner Photographs: 1966–1969.* New Haven, CT: Yale University Press, 2002.

Christian Boltanski

Born in 1944 in Paris, Christian Boltanski began painting in 1958 without formal art training.

In 1968 he had his first one-person exhibition, *"La Vie impossible de Christian Boltanski,"* Cinema le Ranelagh, Paris, and in 1971 he exhibited at Galerie Sonnabend, Paris (subsequent solo exhibitions: 1974, 1975, 1976, 1977, 1979, 1980). His first New York exhibition took place at Sonnabend Gallery, New York (subsequent solo exhibitions: 1973, 1975, 1979, 1982).

Retrospectives of Boltanski's work have been mounted at the National Museum of Contemporary Art, Oslo, Norway, (1994) and "Christian Boltanski So Far," Kemper Museum of Contemporary Art, Kansas City, Missouri (1998).

Recent one-person exhibitions include *"Dernières années,"* Musée d'Art Moderne de la Ville de Paris (1998); "Christian Boltanski: Loss of Innocence," Bates College Museum of Art, Lewiston, Maine (2000). "Reflexion," Museum of Fine Arts, Boston (2000); "Coming and Going," Marian Goodman Gallery, New York (2001); "Lessons of Darkness," Museum of Contemporary Art, Chicago (traveling exhibition, 2001); and *"Christian Boltanski: Les Abonnés du Téléphone,"* South London Gallery, London (2002).

Boltanski's recent participation in group exhibitions includes "Temporarily Possessed: The Semi-Permanent Collection, New Museum of Contemporary Art, New York (1995); "Group Show," Marian Goodman Gallery, New York (1996); *"Colección: Últimos años,"* Museu d'Art Contemporani, Barcelona, Spain (1998); "The Museum as Muse: Artists Reflect," Museum of Modern Art, New York (1999); and "A Work in Progress," New Museum of Contemporary Art, New York (2002).

Christian Boltanski lives and works in Malakoff, France.

Selected Further Readings

Essais de reconstitution d'objets ayant appartenu à Christian Boltanski entre 1948–1954 (exhibition catalogue). Paris: Galerie Sonnabend, 1971.

Christian Boltanski: Lessons of Darkness. (exhibition catalogue). Chicago: Museum of Contemporary Art, 1988.

Christian Boltanski—Reconstitution (exhibition catalogue). London: Whitechapel Art Gallery, 1990.

Boltanski, Christian. *Le Club Mickey.* Ghent, Belgium: Imschoot, Utigevers, 1991.

Sans-Souci. Frankfurt am Main, Germany: Portikus, 1991.

La Maison manquante. Paris: La Hune, 1992.

Flay, Jennifer, ed. *Christian Boltanski: Books, Printed Matter, Ephemera 1966–1991.* Cologne, Germany: Verlag der Buchhandlung Walther König, 1992.

Gumpert, Lynn. *Christian Boltanski.* Paris: Flammarion, 1994.

Christian Boltanski: Advent and Other Times (exhibition catalogue). Barcelona, Spain: Poligrafa, 1996.

Boltanski, Christian, Tamar Garb, Donald B. Kuspit, and Didier Semin. *Christian Boltanski.* London: Phaidon, 1997.

Boltanski, Christian. *Inventaire du cabinet d'art graphique, 1977–1998.* Paris: Centre Georges Pompidou, 1999.

Boltanski, Christian. *Vie impossible.* Cologne, Germany: Verlag der Buchhandlung Walther König, 2001.

Pier Paolo Calzolari

Born in Bologna, Italy, in 1943, Pier Paolo Calzolari spent his childhood in Venice and his early adulthood in Bologna, where he began to exhibit in the 1960s. At this time Calzolari was regularly included in important *arte povera* group exhibitions including "*Op losse schroven: situaties en cryptostructuren,*" Stedelijk Museum, Amsterdam, (1969); "*Verbogne Strukturen,*" Essen, Germany (1969); and "*Konzeption,*" Leverkusen, Germany (1969). Calzolari had his first solo exhibition that same year at the Galleria Gian Enzo Sperone, Turin, Italy, which led to solo exhibitions at Galerie Sonnabend, Paris, (1970, 1971), and Sonnabend Gallery, New York (1971). He later exhibited regularly with Modern Art Agency, Naples, Italy; Toselli Gallery, Milan, Italy; Giorgio Persano Gallery, Turin, Italy; Tucci Rosso Gallery, Turin, Italy (1975); and Barbara Gladstone Gallery, New York (1988).

A recent retrospective was organized collaboratively by the Galerie Nationale du Jeu de Paume, Paris, and the Castello di Rivoli, Turin, Italy (1994). A 1999 solo exhibition was mounted at Galleria d'Arte Moderna di Bologna, Italy. Calzolari participated in the recent group exhibition, "Zero to Infinity: Arte Povera 1962–1972," organized collaboratively by the Walker Art Center, Minneapolis and the Tate Modern, London (2001), which traveled to the Museum of Contemporary Art, Los Angeles (2002), and the Hirshhorn Museum and Sculpture Garden, Washington, D.C. (2002–2003).

Pier Paolo Calzolari lives and works in Urbino, Italy.

Selected Further Readings

Pier Paolo Calzolari (exhibition catalogue). New York: Barbara Gladstone Gallery, 1988.

Celant, Germano. *Arte povera: Giovanni Anselmo, Alighiero Boetti, Pier Paolo Calzolari.* Turin, Italy: U. Allemandi, 1989.

Calzolari, Pier Paolo, Catherine David, Bruno Corà, et al. *Day After Day* (exhibition catalogue). Turin, Italy: Canale, Pedrini, Persano, 1994.

Pier Paolo Calzolari (exhibition catalogue). Paris: Galerie Nationale du Jeu de Paume, 1994.

Guidieri, Remo. *Le livre d'or. Pier Paolo Calzolari.* Arles, France: Le Crestet, 1999.

Pier Paolo Calzolari (exhibition catalogue). Bologna, Italy: Galleria d'Arte Moderna di Bologna, 1999.

Wim Delvoye

Born in Wervik, Germany, in 1965, Wim Delvoye's first solo exhibition was mounted at the Galerie Plus-Kern in Brussels, Belgium (1986). Other early solo exhibitions include "This Side of Paradise," Riekje Swart Galerij, Amsterdam (1988), and "1968–1989," Galerie Bebert, Rotterdam, (1989).

More recent solo exhibitions have taken place at Art Gallery of New South Wales, Sydney, Australia (1991); Galerie Faust, Geneva (1991); and Sonnabend Gallery, New York (1991, 1992, 1998).

By the late 1980s, Delvoye had participated in numerous important group exhibitions, such as "*Confrontatie & Confrontaties,*" Museum voor Hedendaagase Kunst, Ghent, Belgium (1988); "Six Flemish Artists," Jack Tilton Gallery, New York (1989); "*Confrontaciones,*" Museo Español de Arte Contemporaneo, Madrid, Spain (1990); "Cartographic Paintings," Gallerie Murnik, Milan, Italy (1990); "History as Fiction," Meyers Bloom Gallery, Santa Monica, California (1991); "*Buchstaeblich,*" Van der Heydtmuseum, Wuppertal, Germany (1991); and Documenta 9, Kassel, Germany (1992).

Recent solo exhibitions have been mounted at such venues as Galerie Lehmann, Lausanne, Switzerland (1993); Modulo, Centro Difusor de Arte, Lisbon, Portugal (1994); Gallery Tanit, Munich, Germany (1995); Anders Tonberg Gallery, Lund, Sweden (1995); Gandy Gallery, Prague, Czech Republic (1996); Galeria Luisa Strina, São Paulo, Brazil (1997); Delfina Gallery, London (1997); Galleria Gian Enzo Sperone, Turin, Italy (1999); Galerie Krinzinger, Vienna, Austria (2000); and Musee National d'Art Moderne, Centre Georges Pompidou, Paris (2000). Delvoye's most recent solo exhibition, "Cloaca," was mounted at the New Museum of Contemporary Art, New York (2002).

Additional group exhibitions include "Post Human," Deichtorhallen, Hamburg, Germany; Israel Museum, Jerusalem (1993); "Everything That's Interesting Is New/ The Dakis Joannou Collection," Athens School of Fine Arts, Athens (1996); "*Sammlung Sonnabend,*" Deichtorhallen, Hamburg, Germany (1996); Kwangju Biennale, Kwangju, South Korea (1997); Biennale de Cetinje, Cetinje, Montenegro (1997); "Patchwork in Progress 3," Geneva Museum of Modern and Contemporary Art (MAMCO), Geneva (1998); "Dust and Dirt," Witte Zeal, Ghent, Belgium (2000); and "Give and Take," Victoria and Albert Museum, London (2001).

Wim Delvoye lives and works in Ghent, Belgium.

Selected Further Readings

Wim Delvoye: Fünf Arbeiten ((exhibition catalogue). Nuremberg, Germany: Verlag für Moderne Kunst, 1992.

Wim Delvoye (exhibition catalogue). Limoges, France: CRAFT, 1995.
Wim Delvoye (exhibition catalogue). London: Delfina, 1996.
Wim Delvoye (exhibition catalogue). Antwerp, Belgium: Openluchtmuseum voor beeldhouwkunst Middelheim, 1997.
Atlas Wim Delvoye (exhibition catalogue). Nantes, France: Fonds Régional d'Art Contemporain (FRAC) des Pays de la Loire, 1999.
Delvoye, Wim. *Pigs*. Ghent, Belgium: Cultureel Ambassadeur van Vlaanderen, 1999.
American Bricolage (exhibition catalogue). New York: Sperone Westwater, 2000.
Fresh Cream: Contemporary Art in Culture. London: Phaidon, 2000.
Wim Delvoye: New and Improved, Cloaca (exhibition catalogue). New York: New Museum of Contemporary Art in association with Rectapublishers, 2001.

Jim Dine

Born in Cincinnati, in 1935, Jim Dine studied at the Cincinnati Art Academy, Cincinnati (1953), while a senior in high school. In 1954, Dine enrolled at the University of Cincinnati. The following year he spent a semester at the Boston Museum School and later transferred to Ohio University, Athens, where he received his B.F.A. in 1957.

Dine had his first New York solo exhibition at the Rueben Gallery (1960). His many subsequent solo exhibitions have included Galerie Sonnabend, Paris (1963, 1969, 1970, 1972, 1975); Galerie Sonnabend, Geneva (1974); Sonnabend Gallery, New York (1970, 1973, 1974, 1984); Galeria Gian Enzo Sperone, Turin, Italy (1965); Andrew Dickinson White Museum of Art, Cornell University, Ithaca, New York (1967); Institute of Contemporary Art, London (1973); Williams College Museum of Art, Williamstown, Massachusetts (1976); Pace Gallery, New York (1977); Museum of Modern Art, New York (1978); Waddington Galleries, London (1989); Pace Gallery, New York (1991); Residenzgalerie, Salzburg, Austria (1994); Civico Museo Revoltella, Trieste, Italy (1996); and Richard Gray Gallery, Chicago (1998).

Dine has participated in numerous groundbreaking group exhibitions, including the Venice Biennale, Venice, Italy (1964, 1970, 1972); "American Pop Art," Stedelijk Museum, Amsterdam (1964); Whitney Biennial, Whitney Museum of American Art, New York (1965, 1966, 1967, 1973); Documenta, Kassel, Germany (1968, 1977); "Prints by Five New York Painters: Jim Dine, Roy Lichtenstein, Robert Rauschenberg, Larry Rivers, James Rosenquist," Metropolitan Museum of Art, New York (1969); "The Painterly Print: Monotypes from the Seventeenth to the Twentieth Century," Metropolitan Museum of Art, New York (1980); "Blam! The Explosion of Pop, Minimalism and Performance, 1958–64," Whitney Museum, New York (1984); "Hand-Painted Pop, American Art in Transition, 1955–1962," Museum of Contemporary Art, Los Angeles (1993).

Retrospectives have been held at the Whitney Museum, New York (1970); Walker Art Center, Minneapolis (1984); Galleria d'Arte Moderna Ca' Pesara, Venice, Italy (1988); and Isetan Museum of Art, Shinju-ku, Tokyo (1990).

Jim Dine lives and works in New York City and London.

Suggested Further Reading

Fahlstrom, Oyvind. *New Paintings by Jim Dine*. New York: Sidney Janis, 1963.
Gordon, John. *Jim Dine*. New York: Whitney Musem of American Art, 1970.
Shapiro, David. *Jim Dine: Painting What One Is*. New York: Henry N. Abrams, 1981.
Beal, Graham. *Jim Dine: Five Themes*. New York: Abbeville Press, 1984.
Oberhuber, Konrad. *Jim Dine: Youth and Maiden*. London, Waddington, Gallery, 1989.
Jim Dine: The Four Continents. London: Waddington Gallery, 1993.
Feinberg, Jean. *Jim Dine*. New York: Abbeville Press, 1995.
Celant, Germano, and Clare Bell. *Jim Dine: Memory, 1959–1969*. New York: Solomon R. Guggenheim Museum, 1999.
Livingstone, Marco. *Jim Dine: Subjects*. London: Alan Cristea Gallery, 2000.

Elger Esser

Born in Stuttgart, Germany, in 1967, Elger Esser spent his early childhood in Rome. He studied at the Kunstakademie Düsseldorf (1991–97) with Bernd Becher.

Esser first exhibited his large-scale photographs at the Kulturbahnhof Eller, Düsseldorf, Germany, in 1995 and had numerous one-person exhibitions at European venues such as the Kunstverein, Hagen, Germany (1997); Andreas Grimm, Palma, Spain (1997); Galerie 213, Paris (1998); De Zaal Gallery, Delft, Netherlands (1998); and at Sonnabend Gallery, New York (1999).

Esser has participated in numerous group exhibitions since the mid '90s, including "*Auslöser*," Düsseldorf, Germany (1996); "*Landschaftsbilder*," Stadtische Galerie, Tuttlingen, Germany (1998); and "Lawrence Beck, Elger Esser, Hiroshi Sugimoto," Sonnabend Gallery, New York (1999). In 2001,

Esser mounted a solo exhibition at Sonnabend Gallery, New York.

Elger Esser lives and works in Düsseldorf, Germany.

Selected Further Readings

Kino, Carol. "Elger Esser at Sonnabend." *Art in America*, June 1999: 120.

Pollack, Barbara. "Lawrence Beck, Elger Esser, Hiroshi Sugimoto." *Art News*, December 1999: 173–74.

Esser, Elger, and Manfred Esser. *Nach Italien: Reisebeschreibungen und Fotografien*. Heidelberg, Germany: Kehrer, 2000.

Esser, Elger. *Veduten und Landschaften 1996–2000*. Munich, Germany: Schirmer/Mosel, 2001.

Eakin, Hugh. "Photographing Non-Places." *Art News*, March 2002: 98.

Gigliotti, Guglielmo. "Elger Esser." *Tema Celeste*, January/February 2002: 52–55.

Peter Fischli and David Weiss

Peter Fischli and David Weiss were born in Zurich, Switzerland (1952 and 1946 respectively). Fischli studied at the Accademia Belle Arti Bologne (1975–76). Weiss attended Kunstgewerbeschule Zurich (1963–64) and Kunstgewerbeschule Basel, Switzerland (1964–65).

Fischli and Weiss have been collaborating on sculpture, photography, film, video, and installation art since the late 1970s. Their extensive exhibition history includes shows at such venues as Musée National d'Art Moderne, Paris (1992); the Venice Biennale, Venice, Italy (1995); Sonnabend Gallery, New York (1985, 1986, 1989, 1994, 1995, 1998); Kunsthaus Zurich, Zurich, Switzerland (1996); Museum of Modern Art, San Francisco (1997); White Cube, London (1998); ARC Musée d'Art Moderne de la Ville de Paris, Paris (1999); Matthew Marks Gallery, New York (2001, 2002); and Monika Spruth/Philomene Magers, Munich, Germany (2001).

Fischli and Weiss's participation in group exhibitions includes Documenta X, Kassel, Germany (1997); "Group Exhibition," Sonnabend Gallery, New York (1997); "Eight people from Europe," Museum of Modern Art Gunma, Gunma, Japan (1998); the Eleventh Biennale of Sydney, Sydney, Australia (1998); "Maisons/Häuser: Carsten Höller, Rosemarie Trockel, Peter Fischli & David Weiss," Musée d'Art Moderne de la Ville de Paris, Paris (1999); "Europeans," Zwirner and Wirth, New York (2000); and "Restaging the Everyday: Recent Work by Beat Streuli and Fischli/Weiss," San Francisco Museum of Modern Art, San Francisco, California (2002). Their first North American survey exhibition took place in 1996 at the Walker Art Center in Minneapolis and traveled to several American cities and Wolfsburg, Germany.

Peter Fischli and David Weiss live and work in Zurich, Switzerland.

Selected Further Readings

Parkett, no. 17, Peter Fischli & David Weiss (with Louise Bourgeois). Zurich, Switzerland: Parkett Verlag, 1988.

Airports (exhibition catalogue). Zurich, Switzerland: P. Frey, 1990.

Projekt Schweiz: Amiet, Fischli & Weiss, Giacometti, Hahn, Manz, Mariétan, Meier, Rist, Schnyder (exhibition catalogue). Basel, Switzerland: Kunsthalle Basel, 1992.

Peter Fischli, David Weiss: In a Restless World. Minneapolis: Walker Art Center, 1996.

Peter Fischli, David Weiss (exhibition catalogue). New York: Matthew Marks Gallery, 1999.

Mike Kelly, Peter Fischli, David Weiss (exhibition catalogue). Munich, Germany: Sammlung Goetz, 2000.

Sichtbare Welt (exhibition catalogue). Cologne, Germany: W. Konig, 2000.

Groys, Boris. *Peter Fischli, David Weiss*. New York: Distributed Art Publishers, Inc., 2001.

Dan Flavin

Born in Jamaica, Queens, New York, in 1933, Dan Flavin studied at the University of Maryland Extension Program in Korea while serving in the army from 1954 to 1955. He continued his studies in New York at the Hans Hofmann School of Fine Arts and Columbia University as well as the New School for Social Research.

Flavin was included in the groundbreaking 1966 Minimalist exhibition, "Working drawings and other visible things on paper not necessarily meant to be viewed as art," held at the School of Visual Arts, New York. Subsequently Flavin participated in the important group exhibition "Electric Art," Galerie Sonnabend, Paris (1966), and began to exhibit regularly at Leo Castelli Gallery, New York (1968–89), where he had a retrospective in 1995.

Flavin also exhibited in numerous international group exhibitions including Documenta 4, Kassel, Germany (1968); "New York Painting and Sculpture: 1940–1970," Metropolitan Museum of Art, New York (1969); National Gallery of Canada, Ottawa (1969); and CAPC Musée d'Art Contemporain, Bordeaux, France (1985).

In 1983, Dia Center for the Arts opened the Dan Flavin Art Institute in Bridgehampton, New York, which houses a permanent collection of his works. In 1989, Flavin was honored with a large solo exhibition, "'Monuments' for V. Tatlin from Dan Flavin 1964–1982," organized collaboratively by the Donald Young Gallery for the Museum of Contemporary Art, Chicago, and by the Leo Castelli Gallery, New York (1989). That same year, Flavin exhibited "New Uses for Fluorescent Light with Diagrams, Drawings, and Prints from Dan Flavin" at Staatliche Kunsthalle, Baden-Baden, Germany. In 1992, a monumental installation of Flavin's work was organized by the Solomon R. Guggenheim Museum, New York. More recent solo exhibitions include "Dan Flavin: "Monuments" for V. Tatlin," Danese Gallery, New York (1997); Fondazione Prada, Milan (1997–98); "Light Pieces," Forum d'Art Contemporain, Casino Luxembourg, Belgium (2000); and "*Dan Flavin: die Architektur des Lichts*," Deutsche Guggenheim, Berlin (2000).

Dan Flavin died on November 29, 1996.

Selected Further Readings

Dan Flavin, Fluorescent Light, etc. (exhibition catalogue). Ottawa: National Gallery of Canada, 1969.

Dan Flavin: Drawings, Diagrams, and Prints, 1972–1975 (exhibition catalogue). Fort Worth, TX: Fort Worth Art Museum, 1977.

"Monuments" for V. Tatlin from Dan Flavin 1964–1982 (exhibition catalogue). Chicago: Donald Young Gallery for the Museum of Contemporary Art, Los Angeles, in collaboration with the Leo Castelli Gallery, New York, 1989.

Poetter, Jochen, Madeleine Deschamps, et al. *Original Title (New Uses for Fluorescent Light with Diagrams, Drawings and Prints from Dan Flavin)* (exhibition catalogue). Baden-Baden, Germany: Staatliche Kunsthalle, 1989.

Dan Flavin (exhibition catalogue). Munich, Germany: Städtische Galerie im Lenbachhaus, 1994.

Ragheb, J. Fiona, ed. *Dan Flavin: Architecture of Light* (exhibition catalogue). New York: Solomon R. Guggenheim Museum, 1999.

Gilbert & George

Gilbert Proesch, born in Dolomites, Italy, in 1943, and George Passmore, born in Devon, England, in 1942, have been working together since 1967, when they were students at St. Martin's School of Art, in London.

Gilbert & George's career began when they performed *Underneath the Arches*, their first performance as "Singing Sculptures." As early as 1969, the London-based team were invited to perform their living sculpture at the Stedelijk Museum, Amsterdam, Netherlands, and began showing frequently with such galleries as Galleria Sperone, Turin, Italy (1971); Whitechapel Art Gallery, London (1971); Sonnabend Gallery, New York (1971, 1973, 1976, 1977, 1978, 1980, 1983, 1985, 1987, 1991, 1997); Galerie Sonnabend, Paris (1975, 1977); Galerie Sonnabend, Geneva (1975); and Galerie Konrad Fischer, Düsseldorf, Germany (1970).

Gilbert & George were included in pivotal exhibitions such as "Information," Museum of Modern Art, New York (1970); Documenta, Kassel, Germany (1972, 1977, 1982); "Prospect," Kunsthalle, Düsseldorf, Germany (1974); Stedelijk Museum, Amsterdam, Netherlands (1978); "Europe in the '70s," Contemporary Art Center, Cincinnati (1979); "On Walks and Travels," Bonnefantenmuseum, Maastricht, Netherlands (1979); "Trends in Post War American and European Art," Solomon R. Guggenheim Museum, New York (1983); Sixteenth International São Paulo Biennale, São Paulo, Brazil (1981); "New Art," Tate Gallery, London (1983); "The Critical Eye," Yale Center for British Art, Yale University, New Haven, Connecticut (1984); "Artistic Collaboration in the Twentieth Century," Hirshhorn Museum and Sculpture Garden, Washington, D.C. (1984). In 1980, the Stedelijk van Abbemuseum, Eindhoven, Netherlands, organized a midcareer retrospective that traveled to the Kunsthalle Düsseldorf, Germany; Kunsthalle Bern, Switzerland; Musée National d'Art Moderne, Centre Georges Pompidou, Paris; and Whitechapel Art Gallery, London. In 1987, Gilbert & George mounted a major retrospective at the Hayward Gallery, London. Gilbert & George have had solo exhibitions at National Art Gallery, Beijing; Art Museum, Shanghai, China (1993); and Museo d'Arte Moderna, Lugano, Switzerland (1994). Recent retrospectives were held at the Musée d'Art Moderne de la Ville de Paris, Paris (1997); Ministério da Cultura, Lisbon, Portugal (2000); and Milton Keynes Exhibition Gallery, Milton Keynes, England (1999–2000) which traveled to the Gagosian Gallery, Los Angeles (2000).

Gilbert & George live and work in London.

Selected Further Readings

Carter, Ratcliff. *Gilbert & George 1968 to 1980* (exhibition catalogue). Eindhoven, Netherlands: Stedelijk van Abbemuseum, 1980.

Gilbert & George, 1968 to 1980 (exhibition catalogue). Eindhoven, Netherlands: Municipal van Abbemuseum, 1980.

Gilbert & George (exhibition catalogue). Baltimore: Baltimore Museum of Art, 1984.

Gilbert & George. *Gilbert & George: The Complete Pictures 1971–1985*. New York: Rizzoli, 1986.

Gilbert & George: The Charcoal on Paper Sculptures, 1970–1974 (exhibition catalogue). Bordeaux, France: CAPC Musée d'Art Contemporain de Bordeaux, 1986.
Jahn, Wolf. *The Art of Gilbert & George, or, An Aesthetic of Existence.* New York: Thames and Hudson, 1989.
Gilbert & George, Robert Rosenblum. *Worlds and Windows.* New York: Robert Miller, 1990.
Gilbert & George Postcard Sculptures and Ephemera, 1969–1981 (exhibition catalogue). New York: Hirschl & Adler Modern, 1990.
Farson, Daniel. *With Gilbert & George in Moscow.* London: Bloomsbury, 1991.
Kold, Anders, Andrew Wilson, Lars Morell. *Gilbert & George: New Democratic Pictures* (exhibition catalogue). Aarhus, Denmark: Aarhus Kunstmuseum, 1992.
Gilbert & George. *Gilbert & George: The Singing Sculpture.* London: Thames and Hudson, 1993.
_____. *The World of Gilbert & George: The Storyboard.* London: Enitharmon, 2001.

Candida Höfer

Born in Eberswalde, Germany, in 1944, Candida Höfer studied at the Kunstakademie Düsseldorf (1973–76) under Bernd Becher. Höfer's thirty-year career began in the 1970s when her work was exhibited at such prestigious galleries as Galerie Konrad Fischer, Düsseldorf, Germany (1975); Museum für Volkerkunde, Hamburg, Germany (1978), and Art Galaxy, New York (1982).

Höfer has exhibited at numerous galleries throughout Germany, Italy, France, and Switzerland during the 1980s and had many one-person exhibitions at such venues as Nicole Klagsbrun Gallery, New York (1992), Hamburger Kunsthalle, Hamburg, Germany (1994); Rena Bransten Gallery, San Francisco, California (1996); Sonnabend Gallery, New York (1996, 2001); Power Plant, Toronto (2000); and Museum of Contemporary Photography, Chicago (2000). Höfer was featured in the 1990 exhibition, "Gunther Forg, Andreas Gursky, Candida Höfer, Thomas Ruff," Kunstverein, Ulm, Germany.

Höfer has participated in numerous group exhibitions in the United States over the past ten years, including "German Photography: Documentation and Introspection," Aldrich Museum of Contemporary Art, Ridgefield, Connecticut (1990); "Making Pictures: Women and Photography, 1975–Now," Nicole Klagsbrun Gallery, New York (1996); "Women Photographers of the Twentieth Century," Saint Louis Art Museum, St. Louis, Missouri (1997); "Museum Studies: Eleven Photographers' View," High Museum of Art, Atlanta (1997); "Reconstructing Space: Architecture in Recent German Photography," Architectural Association, London (1999); and "The Museum as Muse: Artists Reflect," Museum of Modern Art, New York (1999).

Candida Höfer lives and works in Cologne, Germany.

Selected Further Readings

Candida Höfer, Innenraum: Fotografien 1979–1984 (exhibition catalogue). Cologne, Germany: Rheinland-Verlag, 1984.
Humpty Dumpty's Kaleidoscope (exhibition catalogue). Sydney, Australia: Museum of Contemporary Art, 1992.
Höfer, Candida. *Photographie.* Munich, Germany: Schirmer/Mosel, 1998.
Candida Höfer: Orte Jahre/Photographien 1968–1999. Munich, Germany: Schirmer/Mosel, 1999.
Lucinda Devlin/Andreas Gursky/Candida Höfer: Raume (exhibition catalogue). Bregenz, Austria: Kunsthaus Bregenz, 2000.
Moure, Gloria. *La Arquitectura sin sombra.* Barcelona, Spain: Ediciones Polígrafa, 2000.
Candida Höfer: Douze (exhibition catalogue). Calais, France: Musée des Beaux Arts de Calais, 2001
Höfer, Candida. *Candida Höfer.* Munich, Germany: Schirmer/Mosel, 2001.
Zwischen Schönheit und Sachlichkeit: Boris Becker, Andreas Gursky, Candida Höfer, Axel Hütte, Thomas Ruff, Thomas Struth (exhibition catalogue). Heidelberg, Germany: Edition Braus, 2002.

Jasper Johns

Born in Augusta, Georgia, in 1930, Jasper Johns attended the University of South Carolina for a year and a half in the early 1950s, followed by two years in the army, after which he settled in New York in 1953.

Johns's first solo exhibition was held at the Leo Castelli Gallery, New York (1958). Three years later, Johns had a solo exhibition at Galerie Sonnabend, Paris (1962, 1966). Soon after, Johns was included in the Venice Biennale, Venice, Italy (1964), and had a solo exhibition at Whitechapel Art Gallery, London (1964). In 1988, Johns won the Grand Prix at the Venice Biennale. He participated in the 1991 Whitney Biennial, the Whitney Museum, New York.

Johns has had midcareer retrospectives at the Jewish Museum, New York (1964), Pasadena Art Museum, Pasadena, California (1965); and Whitney Museum of American Art, New York (1977).

A recent solo exhibition, "Jasper Johns: The Seasons (Prints and Related Works)," was mounted at Brooke Alexander Editions, New York (1991–92). Recent retrospectives include

"Retrospective of Jasper Johns Prints from the Leo Castelli Collection," Visual Arts Center, Brenau College, Gainesville, Georgia (1991), a show that traveled to Israel and Belgium; "*Jasper Johns: Gravures et Dessins de la Collection Castelli, 1960–1991*" and "*Portraits de l'artiste Hans Namuth, 1962–1989*," Fondation Vincent van Gogh, Palais de Luppé, Arles, France (1992); "Jasper Johns: 35 Years with Leo Castelli," Leo Castelli Gallery, New York (1993).

Jasper Johns lives and works in Sharon, Connecticut.

Selected Further Readings

Johns, Jasper. *17 Monotypes*. West Islip, NY: Universal Limited Art Editions, 1982.

Bernstein, Roberta. *Jasper Johns: Paintings and Sculptures 1954–1974: The Changing Focus of the Eye*. Ann Arbor, MI: UMI Research Press, 1985.

Boudaille, Georges. *Jasper Johns*. New York: Rizzoli, 1989.

Rosenthal, Mark. *Jasper Johns: Work since 1974* (exhibition catalogue). Philadelphia: Philadelphia Museum of Art, 1989.

Johns, Jasper. *Jasper Johns: Printed Symbols*. Minneapolis: Walker Art Center, 1990.

Johns, Jasper. *Jasper Johns*. New York: Rizzoli Art Series, 1992.

Orton, Fred. *Figuring Jasper Johns*. Cambridge, MA: Harvard University Press, 1994.

Jasper Johns Flags, 1955–1994 (exhibition catalogue). London: Anthony d'Offay Gallery, 1996.

Varnedoe, Kirk. *Jasper Johns: A Retrospective* (exhibition catalogue). New York: Museum of Modern Art, 1996.

Rosenblum, Richard, and Markus Bruderlin. *Jasper Johns: Loans from the Artist*. Ostfildern-Ruit, Germany: Hatje Cantz, 2002.

Donald Judd

Born in Excelsior Springs, Missouri, in 1928, Donald Judd studied briefly at the Art Students League of New York in 1948 before enrolling at the College of William and Mary, Wiliamsburg, Virginia. In 1949, Judd returned to New York, where he studied philosophy and art history at Columbia University and took additional art courses at the Art Students League.

In 1957, Judd had his first one-person exhibition of painting at the Panoramas Gallery. By 1966, Judd had begun exhibiting regularly at the Leo Castelli Gallery, New York, as well as at numerous museums and galleries in Europe such as the Moderna Museet, Stockholm, Sweden (1966); Galerie Sonnabend, Paris (1969); Documenta 4, Kassel, Germany (1968); and the Venice Biennale, Venice, Italy (1972). Judd participated in numerous important group exhibitions in the U.S. during the 1960s and '70s, including "The Art of the Real: USA 1948–1968," Museum of Modern Art, New York (1968), which traveled to the Centre National d'Art Contemporain, Paris. Other group exhibitions include "Painting and Sculpture: 1940–1970," Metropolitan Museum of Art, New York (1969); "Whitney Biennial," the Whitney Museum (1973); and "Drawing Now," Museum of Modern Art, New York (1976).

In 1986, the Chinati Foundation, which Judd designed as a permanent museum for his artwork and that of other Minimalist artists, opened in Marfa, Texas. Judd's first retrospective was organized by the Whitney Museum in 1968. In 1987, the Stedelijk van Abbemuseum, Eindhoven, Netherlands, organized an expansive collection of his works for an exhibition which traveled to Düsseldorf, Germany; Paris; Barcelona, Spain; and Turin, Italy. The Whitney Museum of American Art mounted a traveling retrospective exhibition in 1988. The Museum of Modern Art, Saitama, Japan, organized a retrospective of Judd's work in 1999.

Donald Judd died on February 12, 1994.

Selected Further Readings

Donald Judd (exhibition catalogue). New York: Whitney Museum of American Art, 1968.

Judd, Donald. *Complete Writings, 1959–1975: Gallery Reviews, Book Reviews, Articles, Letters to the Editor, Reports, Statements, Complaints*. Halifax, Nova Scotia: Press of the Nova Scotia College of Art and Design, 1975.

Donald Judd (exhibition catalogue). New York: Whitney Museum of American Art, 1988.

Donald Judd Furniture (exhibition catalogue). St. Louis: Saint Louis Art Museum, 1991.

Donald Judd: Large Scale Works (exhibition catalogue). New York: Pace Gallery, 1993.

Donald Judd, Prints and Works in Editions: A Catalogue Raisonné (exhibition catalogue). New York: Edition Schellmann, 1993.

Judd, Donald. *Some Aspects of Color in General and Red and Black in Particular*. Rotterdam, Netherlands: Sikkens Foundation, 1993.

Kunst + Design: Donald Judd (exhibition catalogue). Stuttgart, Germany: Cantz Verlag, 1993.

Donald Judd: Selected Works 1960–1991 (exhibition catalogue). Saitama, Japan: Museum of Modern Art, 1999.

Elger, Dietmar. *Donald Judd: Colorist*. Ostfildern-Ruit, Germany: Hatje Cantz, 2000.

Clay Ketter

Born in Brunswick, Maine, in 1961, Clay Ketter studied at the State University of New York in Purchase, New York (B.F.A., 1985).

Early one-person exhibitions were mounted at such venues as Galleri Andreas Brandstrom, Stockholm, Sweden (1994); and White Cube/Jay Jopling, London (1996). Early group exhibitions include "Floor Show," Galleri Anders Tornberg, Lund, Sweden (1993); "Interiors," Galerie Chantel Crousel, Paris (1996); "Abstract/Real," Museum Moderner Kunst/Stiftung Ludvig, Vienna, Austria (1996); and "Thomas Demand + Clay Ketter," Galerie Peter Kilchmann, Zurich, Switzerland (1997).

Recent one-person exhibitions have been mounted at the Sonnabend Gallery, New York (1999, 2002); Galleri Andreas Brandstrom, Stockholm, Sweden (1999); Galleri Specta, Copenhagen, Denmark (2000); Angles Gallery, Santa Monica, California (2000), and Daniel Templon, Paris (2001).

Recent group exhibitions include "Young Americans 2," Saatchi Gallery, London (1998); "Fischli & Weiss, Clay Ketter, Jeff Koons," Sonnabend Gallery, New York (1998); "Hvid," Charlottenborg, Copenhagen, Denmark (1999); "Impostures: Clay Ketter and George Stoll," Rose Art Museum, Brandeis University, Waltham, Massachusetts (2000); and "Painting Degree Zero," Independent Curators International, New York, which traveled to Cranbrook Museum of Art, Bloomfield Hills, Michigan; Fred Jones Jr. Art Museum, University of Oklahoma, Norman, Oklahoma; and Norman Cleveland Center for Contemporary Art, Cleveland.

Clay Ketter lives and works in Lilla Uppakra, Sweden.

Selected Further Readings

Brooks, Adam, and Lisa Liebmann. *Young Americans 2* (exhibition catalogue). London: Saatchi Gallery, 1998.

Ketter, Clay. *Labors of Love, Love's Labor Lost.* Malmö, Sweden: Propexus, 1999.

Basualdo, Carlos, and Ellen Tepfer. *Painting Degree Zero.* New York: Independent Curators International, 2000.

Fergusson, Bruce. *Clay Ketter.* Malmö, Sweden: Propexus, 2000.

Nacking, Åsa, and Bo Nilsson. *Century of Innocence: The History of White Monochrome* (exhibition catalogue). Malmö, Sweden; Rooseum, 2000

Robert Ryman: Retrospektive mit Raumen von Ariane Epars, Clay Ketter, Albert Weis und Beat Zoderer (exhibition catalogue). Ostfildern-Ruit, Germany: Edition Tertium, 2000.

Anselm Kiefer

Born in Donaueschingen, Baden-Wurttemburg, Germany, in 1945, Anselm Kiefer studied at the Albert-Ludwigs-Universität Freiburg, Freiburg, Germany (1965), and the Akademie der Bildenden Künste Karlsruhe, Karlsruhe, Germany (1966–68). By the early 1970s, Kiefer had begun to exhibit regularly in Europe and the U.S. at such venues as Galerie Michael Werner, Cologne, Germany (1973); Kunstverein, Bonn, Germany (1977); Kunsthalle, Bern, Switzerland (1978); Stedelijk van Abbemuseum, Eindhoven, Netherlands (1979); Galerie Paul Maenz, Cologne, Germany (1981); Marian Goodman Gallery, New York (1981); Mary Boone Gallery, New York (1982); Anthony d'Offay Gallery, London (1983); and Louisiana Museum of Modern Art, Humlebaek, Denmark (2001).

Significant early group shows include "*Beuys und seine Schuler,*" Frankfurter Kunstverein, Frankfurt, Germany (1976); Documenta, Kassel, Germany (1977, 1982, 1987); Venice Biennale, Venice, Italy (1980, 1997); "A New Spirit in Painting," Royal Academy of Arts, London (1981); "Survey of Recent Painting and Sculpture," Museum of Modern Art, New York (1984); "Content: A Contemporary Focus 1974–1984," Hirshhorn Museum and Sculpture Garden, Washington, D.C. (1984); "German Art in the Twentieth Century: Painting and Sculpture 1905–1985," Royal Academy of the Arts, London (1985); "Forty Years of Modern Art 1945–1985, Tate Gallery, London (1986); and Guggenheim Museum, Bilbao, Spain (1997).

Recent major one-person exhibitions were mounted at Art Institute of Chicago, Chicago (1987); which traveled to the Philadelphia Museum of Art, Philadelphia, the Museum of Contemporary Art, Los Angeles, and the Museum of Modern Art, New York; Neue Nationalgalerie, Berlin (1991); Museo Correr, Venice, Italy (1997); Gagosian Gallery, New York (1998), and the Metropolitan Museum of Art, New York (1999).

Anselm Kiefer lives and works in Barjac, France.

Selected Further Readings

Watercolors 1970–1982 (exhibition catalogue). London: Anthony d'Offay, 1983.

Kiefer, Anselm. *Anselm Kiefer: Lilith.* New York: Marian Goodman Gallery, 1992.

Anselm Kiefer (exhibition catalogue). Milan, Italy: Charta, 1997.

Anselm Kiefer: Your Age and Mine and the Age of the World (exhibition catalogue). New York: Gagosian Gallery, 1998.

Kiefer, Anselm, Jürgen Harten, and Theodore E. Stebbins. *A Book by Anselm Kiefer*. New York: G. Braziller, in association with Museum of Fine Arts, Boston, 1998.
Anselm Kiefer, Works on Paper (exhibition catalogue). New York: Metropolitan Museum of Art, 1999.
Anselm Kiefer: Let a Thousand Flowers Bloom (exhibition catalogue). London: Anthony d'Offay Gallery, 2000.
Biro, Matthew. *Anselm Kiefer and the Philosophy of Martin Heidegger*. Cambridge, England: Cambridge University Press, 2000.
Saltzman, Lisa. *Anselm Kiefer and Art After Auschwitz*. Cambridge, England: Cambridge University Press, 2000.
Arasse, Daniel. *Anselm Kiefer*. New York: Harry N. Abrams, 2001.
Anselm Kiefer: The Seven Heavenly Palaces, 1973–2001 (exhibition catalogue). Ostfildern-Ruit, Germany: Hatje Cantz, 2001.

Jeff Koons

Born in York, Pennsylvania, in 1955, Jeff Koons studied at the Maryland Institute College of Art for two years before transferring to the Art Institute of Chicago, where he earned his B.A. in 1976. After moving to New York (in 1976), Koons began exhibiting widely as a member of the neo-geo movement and had one-person shows at the New Museum of Contemporary Art, New York (1980); International with Monument, New York (1985); and Sonnabend Gallery, New York (1988, 1991, 1999).

Koons also participated in numerous prestigious group exhibitions, including the groundbreaking "New Concepts: Ashley Bickerton, Peter Halley, Jeff Koons, Meyer Vaisman," at Sonnabend Gallery, New York (1986); Whitney Biennial, Whitney Museum of American Art, New York (1987); "Post-Abstract Abstraction," Aldrich Museum of Contemporary Art, Ridgefield, Connecticut (1987); "Carte Blanche," Musée National d'Art Moderne, Centre Georges Pompidou, Paris (1987); "Altered States," Kent Fine Art, New York (1988); Carnegie International, Carnegie Museum of Fine Art, Pittsburgh (1988); "Horn of Plenty: Sixteen Artists from NYC," Stedelijk Museum, Amsterdam (1989); Whitney Biennial, Whitney Museum, New York (1989); "A Forest of Signs: Art in the Crisis of Representation," Museum of Contemporary Art, Los Angeles (1989); "Image World: Art and Media Culture," Whitney Museum, New York (1989); "Culture and Commentary: An Eighties Perspective," Hirshhorn Museum and Sculpture Garden, Washington, D.C. (1990); "Aperto 90," at the Venice Biennale, Italy (1990); and "High & Low: Modern Art and Popular Culture," Museum of Modern Art, New York (1990).

A major retrospective was organized by the San Francisco Museum of Modern Art and the Stedelijk Museum, Amsterdam (1992–93). Recent exhibitions include "Jeff Koons: Made in Heaven," Galerie Max Hetzler, Cologne, Germany (1991), which traveled to Sonnabend Gallery, New York (1992); and "Jeff Koons: Easyfun–Ethereal," Solomon R. Guggenheim Museum, Berlin (2000–2001).

Jeff Koons lives and works in New York City.

Selected Further Readings

New Sculpture: Robert Gober, Jeff Koons, Haim Steinbach (exhibition catalogue). Chicago: The Renaissance Society, University of Chicago, 1986.
Jeff Koons (exhibition catalogue). Chicago: The Museum, 1988.
Jeff Koons (exhibition catalogue). San Francisco: San Francisco Museum of Modern Art, 1992.
Koons, Jeff. *The Jeff Koons Handbook*. New York: Rizzoli, 1993.
Koons, Jeff. *The Jeff Koons Daybook*. New York: Distributed Art Publishers, 1994.
Parkett, No. 50/51, Collaborations: John Armleder, Jeff Koons, Jean-Luc Mylayne, Thomas Struth, Sue Williams. Zurich, Switzerland: Parkett Verlag, 1997.
Hypermental: Rampant Reality, 1950–2000, From Salvador Dali to Jeff Koons (exhibition catalogue). Ostfildern-Ruit, Germany: Hatje Cantz, 2000.
Jasper Johns to Jeff Koons: Four Decades of Art from the Broad Collections (exhibition catalogue). New York: Harry N. Abrams, 2001.
Jeff Koons: Easyfun–Ethereal (exhibition catalogue). Berlin: Solomon R. Guggenheim Museum, 2001.
Gingera, Alison, and Eckard Schneider. *Jeff Koons*. New York: Distributed Art Publishers, 2002.

Jannis Kounellis

Born in Piraeus, Greece, in 1936, Jannis Kounellis moved to Rome in 1956, where he studied at the Accademia di Belle Arti. In 1969, Kounellis mounted his groundbreaking exhibition "Untitled (12 horses)" at Attico Gallery, Rome.

Subsequently Kounellis was included in important *arte povera* group exhibitions such as *"Arte povera—IM spazio,"* Galleria La Bertesca, Genoa, Italy (1967); "Live in Your Head: When Attitudes Become Form," Bern, Switzerland, Krefeld, Germany, and London (1969); and *"Op losse schroven: situaties en cryptostructuren,"* Stedelijk Museum, Amsterdam, Netherlands (1969). Kounellis had solo exhibitions in New York at the Sonnabend Gallery (1972, 1974, 1980, 1983, 1984, 1987).

During the 1970s and '80s, Kounellis exhibited extensively in the U.S. and Europe, including an early 1980s solo exhibition mounted at the Stedelijk van Abbemuseum, Eindhoven, Netherlands, which traveled to Obra Social, Caja de Pensiones, Madrid, Whitechapel Art Gallery, London, and the Staatliche Kunsthalle, Baden-Baden, Germany. Among the many museums to have held a major exhibition of Kounellis's work are Kunstmuseum Luzern, Switzerland (1977); CAPC Musée d'Art Contemporain, Bordeaux, France (1985); Museum of Contemporary Art, Chicago (1986–87); Museo Nacional Centro de Arte Reina Sofia, Madrid, Spain (1996); and Museum Ludwig, Cologne, Germany (1997).

Jannis Kounellis lives and works in Rome.

Selected Further Readings

Kounellis, Jannis. *Jannis Kounellis.* Baden-Baden, Germany: Staatliche Kunsthalle, 1982.

Celant, Germano. "The Collision and the Cry: Jannis Kounellis." *Artforum*, October 1983: 61–67.

Jacob, Mary Jane, and Thomas McEvilley. *Jannis Kounellis* (exhibition catalogue). Chicago: Museum of Contemporary Art, 1986.

Kounellis, Jannis. *Kounellis.* Chicago: Museum of Contemporary Art/Arnoldo Mondadori Editore, 1986.

Jones, Alan. "Kounellis Unbound: Dialogue of the Old World and the New. "*Arts Magazine*, February 1990: 21–22.

Moure, Gloria, ed. *Kounellis.* New York: Rizzoli, 1990.

Kounellis, Jannis. *Editions 1972–1990.* Munich/New York: Schellmann & Schirmer Mosel Verlag, 1991.

Barry Le Va

Born in Long Beach, California, in 1941, Barry Le Va studied at California State University, Long Beach, as well as Los Angeles College of Art & Design, and received his M.F.A. from Otis Art Institute of Los Angeles County (1967).

By the late 1960s, Le Va had begun to participate regularly in group exhibitions, such as "Anti-Illusion: Procedure and Materials," Whitney Museum of American Art, New York (1969); "Information," Museum of Modern Art, New York (1970); "Group Exhibition," Rene Block Gallery, Berlin (1976); and Documenta 6, Kassel, Germany (1978). Early solo exhibitions were mounted at Walker Art Center in Minneapolis (1969); and the Minneapolis Institute of Art (1969). In subsequent years, Le Va exhibited at Ricke Gallery, Cologne, Germany (1970–73, 1976); and Bykert Gallery, New York (1972–75).

In 1976, Barry Le Va had his first show with Galerie Sonnabend, Paris, and in 1978, at Sonnabend Gallery, New York, where he exhibited regularly for the next twenty years (1978, 1979, 1981, 1983, 1986, 1991, 1995, 1998). Other solo exhibitions were held at such venues as P.S. 1, New York (1982); Daniel Weinberg Gallery, Los Angeles (1980); David Nolan Gallery, New York (1989); and Nolan/Eckman Gallery, New York (1995).

Recent retrospectives include "Barry Le Va: 1966–1988," Carnegie Mellon University Art Gallery, Pittsburgh (1988), and "Smatterings: Works on Paper 1967–1998," Sonnabend Gallery, New York (1998). Recent group exhibitions include "Europe/America," Museum Ludwig, Cologne, Germany (1986); "*Entre et le Geste,*" Galerie Georges-Philippe Vallois Paris (1990); "American Art 1930–70," Lingotto, Turin, Italy (1992); the Whitney Biennial, Whitney Museum, New York (1995); "*Sammlung Sonnabend,*" Deichtorhallen, Hamburg, Germany (1996); and "Laying Low," Kunstnernes Hus, Oslo, Norway (1997).

Barry Le Va lives and works in New York City.

Selected Further Readings

Bochner, Le Va, Rochburne, Tuttle (exhibition catalogue). Cincinnati: Contemporary Arts Center, 1975.

Le Va, Barry. *Accumulated Vision: Extended Boundaries.* Dayton, Ohio: Wright State University Art Gallery, 1977.

Four Consecutive Installations & Drawings, 1967–1978 (exhibition catalogue). New York: New Museum, 1978.

Barry Le Va (exhibition catalogue). Otterlo, Netherlands: Rijksmuseum Kroller-Muller, 1988.

Barry Le Va: 1966–1988 (exhibition catalogue). Pittsburgh: Carnegie Mellon Press, 1988.

Barry Le Va: Dreaded Intrusions–Institutional Templates (exhibition catalogue). Munich, Germany: Verlag Fred Jahn, 1992.

Barry Le Va (exhibition catalogue). New York: Nolan/Eckman Gallery, 1996.

Sol LeWitt

Born in Hartford, Connecticut, in 1928, Sol LeWitt studied at Syracuse University in Syracuse, New York (1945–1949). LeWitt moved to New York City in the mid-1950s, where he worked for the architect I.M. Pei (1955–1956) and for the Museum of Modern Art (1960).

LeWitt made his first wall drawing (*Wall Drawing #1*) in pencil on plaster at the Paula Cooper Gallery (1968). His long career has included exhibitions at major international galleries and museums, shows such as Documenta, Kassel Germany (1968, 1977); "The Art of the Real," Museum of Modern Art (1968–69); and "Special Collections: The Photographic Order from Pop to Now," International Center of Photography, New York (1992). LeWitt was honored with a midcareer retrospective at the Museum of Modern Art, New York (1978–79).

LeWitt has mounted numerous one-person exhibitions at such venues as Protetch McIntosh Gallery, Washington, D.C. (1980); Museum of Modern Art, New York (1980); Whitney Museum, New York (1984); Tate Gallery, London (1986); and the Addison Gallery of American Art, Phillips Academy, Andover, Massachusetts (1993).

He had a major one-person exhibition at the Wadsworth Atheneum Museum of Art, Hartford, Connecticut (2001), and a traveling retrospective at three locations, including the San Francisco Museum of Modern Art (2000), the Museum of Contemporary Art, Chicago (2000), and the Whitney Museum in New York (2000–2001).

Sol LeWitt lives in Chester, Connecticut, New York City, and Spoleto, Italy.

Selected Further Readings

LeWitt, Sol. *Five Structures*. New York: Hammarskjold Sculpture Garden, 1976.

Sol Prints 1970–86. New York: Rizzoli, 1978.

Geometric Figures and Color. New York: Harry N. Abrams, 1978.

Prints 1970–86. London: Tate Gallery, 1986.

Sol LeWitt: Drawings 1958–1992 (exhibition catalogue). The Hague, Netherlands: Haags Gemeentemuseum, 1992.

Sol LeWitt: Structures 1962–1993 (exhibition catalogue). Oxford, England: Museum of Modern Art, 1993.

Sol LeWitt: Twenty-Five Years of Wall Drawings, 1968–1993 (exhibition catalogue). Andover, MA: Addison Gallery of American Art, Phillips Academy, 1993.

Garrels, Gary, ed. *Sol LeWitt: A Retrospective* (exhibition catalogue). New Haven, CT: Yale University Press, 2000.

Sol LeWitt: Incomplete Open Cubes (exhibition catalogue). Hartford, CT: Wadsworth Atheneum Museum of Art, 2001.

Roy Lichtenstein

Born in New York, in 1923, Roy Lichtenstein studied under Reginald Marsh at the Art Students League while still in high school. Lichtenstein completed undergraduate and graduate studies at Ohio State University, Columbus, Ohio (M.F.A., 1949).

The artist mounted his first major exhibition in New York at the Leo Castelli Gallery (1962), followed by one-person exhibitions in Europe at Galerie Sonnabend, Paris, France (1963, 1965, 1966, 1970, 1972, 1975). Subsequently, Lichtenstein began to show widely in Europe at group exhibitions including "*Vingtième Salon de Mai,*" Musée d'Art Moderne de la Ville de, Paris (1964); Gemeente Museum, The Hague, Netherlands (1964); "American Pop Art," Stedelijk Museum, Amsterdam (1964); Palais des Beaux-Arts, Brussels, Belgium (1965); Venice Biennale, Venice, Italy (1966, 1968, 1970); and Documenta 4, Kassel, Germany (1968).

Concurrently, Lichtenstein participated in prestigious group exhibitions, such as "Six Painters and the Object," at the Solomon R. Guggenheim Museum, New York (1963); "The 1965 Annual Exhibition of Contemporary American Painting," Whitney Museum of American Art, New York (1965); and "The Current Moment in Art: Exhibition: East," San Francisco Museum of Art, San Francisco (1966).

Lichtenstein exhibited internationally, at illustrious venues, throughout his career. His work was the subject of two mid-career retrospectives, at the Pasadena Art Museum, Pasadena, California (1967–68); and the Solomon R. Guggenheim Museum, New York (1969). More recent retrospectives have been held at the Saint Louis Art Museum, St. Louis, which toured the United States, Europe, and Japan in 1981; the Museum of Modern Art, New York (1987); and Kunsthalle, Frankfurt, Germany (1988), culminating in a retrospective at the Solomon R. Guggenheim Museum, New York, in 1994.

Roy Lichtenstein died on September 30, 1997.

Selected Further Readings

Waldman, Diane. *Roy Lichtenstein* (exhibition catalogue). New York: Solomon R. Guggenheim Museum, 1969.

Coplans, John, ed. *Roy Lichtenstein*. New York: Praeger, 1972.

Alloway, Lawrence. *Lichtenstein*. New York: Abbeville Press, 1983.

Tomkins, Calvin, and Bob Adelman, *Roy Lichtenstein: Mural with Blue Brushstrokes*. New York: Harry N. Abrams, 1987.

Waldman, Diane. *Roy Lichtenstein* (exhibition catalogue). New York: Solomon R. Guggenheim Museum, 1993.

Corlett, Mary Lee. *The Prints of Roy Lichtenstein: A Catalogue Raisonné 1948–1993*. New York: Hudson Hills Press, 1994.

Brown, David J. *Roy Lichtenstein: Man Hit by the Twenty-first Century* (exhibition catalogue). Cincinnati: Contemporary Arts Center, 1997–1998.

Roy Lichtenstein: Interiors (exhibition catalogue). Chicago: Museum of Contemporary Art, 1999.

Hickey, Dave. *Roy Lichtenstein: Brushstrokes, Four Decades*. New York: Mitchell-Innes & Nash, 2001

Lobel, Michael. *Image Duplicator: Roy Lichtenstein and the Emergence of Pop Art*. New Haven, CT: Yale University Press, 2002.

Mario Merz

Born in Milan, Italy, in 1925, Mario Merz attended medical school at the Università degli Studi di Torino in Turin for two years. Merz had his first solo exhibition of oil paintings at Galleria La Bussola, Turin, Italy (1954).

By 1969, Merz had been included in major group exhibitions featuring *arte povera* artists, such as "*Arte povera + azioni povera,*" at the Arsenali dell'Antica Repubblica, Amalfi, Italy (1969); "Live in Your Head: When Attitudes Become Form," Bern, Switzerland, London, and Krefeld, Germany (1968–69); "Prospect '68," Düsseldorf, Germany (1968); Documenta 5, Kassel, Germany (1972); and "*Positionen heutiger Kunst,*" National Gallery, Berlin (1988).

Merz exhibited in New York City for the first time at Sonnabend Gallery, New York (1970, 1972). Subsequently he was honored with solo museum exhibitions at the Walker Art Center, Minneapolis (1972), and Kunsthalle Basel, Switzerland (1975).

More recent large one-person exhibitions have been mounted at the Solomon R. Guggenheim Museum, New York (1989); Museum of Contemporary Art, Los Angeles (1989); Castello di Rivoli, Turin, Italy (1990); Galleria Civica d'Arte Moderna, Turin, Italy (1995); and W. Lehmbruck Museum, Duisburg, Germany (1996).

Mario Merz lives and works in Milan, Italy.

Selected Further Readings

Merz, Mario. *Fibonacci.* Turin, Italy: Sperone Editore, 1970.

Mario Merz (exhibition catalogue). Stockholm, Sweden: Moderna Museet, 1983.

Collaboration Mario Merz. Zurich, Switzerland: Parkett-Verlag, 1988.

Mario Merz (exhibition catalogue). Nagoya, Japan: Institute of Contemporary Arts, Nagoya, 1988.

Corà, Bruno, and Mary Jane Jacob. *Mario Merz at* MoCA (exhibition catalogue). Los Angeles: Museum of Contemporary Art, 1989.

Mario Merz (exhibition catalogue). New York: Solomon R. Guggenheim Museum, 1989.

Moure, Gloria. *Configuraciones urbanas.* Barcelona, Spain: Ediciones Polígrafa, 1994.

Mario Merz: Selected Works 1967–1982 (exhibition catalogue). New York: Sperone Westwater, 1995.

Merz, Mario, and Beatrice Merz. *Voglio fare subito un libro.* Florence, Italy: Hopefulmonster, 1999.

Robert Morris

Born in Kansas City, Missouri, in 1931, Robert Morris attended graduate classes in art history at Hunter College (1962–63). Morris also wrote numerous important essays on Minimal art, including "Notes on Sculpture" (1968), "Anti Form" (1968), and "Aligned with Nazca" (1975).

Morris's illustrious forty-year career began in the late 1960s with solo exhibitions at galleries and museums such as Galerie Sonnabend, Paris (1968, 1971, 1973, 1977, 1979, 1975); Galerie Sonnabend, Geneva (1975); Sonnabend Gallery, New York (1974, 1976, 1979, 1983, 1988, 2001); Whitney Museum of American Art, New York (1970); Art Institute of Chicago (1980); Chicago Museum of Contemporary Art (1986); and Corcoran Gallery of Art, Washington, D.C. (1990).

Morris also participated in numerous group exhibitions, such as "Art of the Real: USA 1948–1968," Museum of Modern Art, New York (1968); "Anti-Illusion: Procedures/Materials," Whitney Museum of American Art, New York (1969); Whitney Biennial, Whitney Museum, New York (1973); "Postminimalism," Aldrich Museum, Ridgefield, Connecticut (1982); Biennale d'Art Contemporain, Lyon, France (1993); and "Attitudes/Sculptures, 1963–1972," CAPC, Musée d'Art Contemporain, Bordeaux, France (1995).

Morris's midcareer retrospective, "Works from 1967 to 1984," was collaboratively organized by Leo Castelli Gallery, New York, and Sonnabend Gallery, New York (1985). More recent retrospectives were mounted by the Solomon R. Guggenheim Museum, New York (1994), which traveled to the Deichtorhallen Museum, Hamburg, Germany; Musée National d'Art Moderne, Paris; and Instituto Valenciano de Arte Moderno, Valencia, Spain (2000).

Robert Morris lives and works in New York City and Gardiner, New York.

Selected Further Readings

Morris, Robert, and Marcia Tucker. *Robert Morris* (exhibition catalogue). New York: Whitney Museum of American Art, 1970.

Compton, Michael, and David Sylvester. *Robert Morris* (exhibition catalogue). London: Tate Gallery, 1971.

Morris, Robert. *Robert Morris Retrospective.* London: Tate Gallery, 1971.

Mayo, Marti. *Robert Morris: Selected Works 1970–1980* (exhibition catalogue). Houston: Contemporary Arts Museum, 1982.

Berger, Maurice. *Labyrinths: Robert Morris, Minimalism, and the 1960s.* New York: Harper & Row, 1989.

Karmel, Pepe, and Maurice Berger. *Robert Morris: The Felt Works* (exhibition catalogue). New York: Grey Art Gallery and Study Center, New York University, 1989.
Krauss, Rosalind E., Maurice Berger, David Antin, et al. *Robert Morris: The Mind/Body Problem* (exhibition catalogue). New York: Solomon R. Guggenheim Museum, 1994.
Morris, Robert. *Continuous Project Altered Daily: The Writings of Robert Morris*. Cambridge, MA, and London: MIT Press; and New York: Solomon R. Guggenheim Museum, 1993.
Tsouti-Schillinger, Nena. *Robert Morris and Angst*. New York: Braziller, 2000.

Bruce Nauman

Born in Fort Wayne, Indiana, in 1941, Bruce Nauman studied at the University of Wisconsin, Madison (B.S., 1964), and the University of California at Davis (M.F.A., 1966).

Nauman began to exhibit nationally in the mid-1960s and had solo exhibitions at Nicholas Wilder Gallery, Los Angeles (1966); Leo Castelli Gallery, New York (1968); Galerie Konrad Fischer, Düsseldorf, Germany (1968); Galerie Sonnabend, Paris (1969, 1971, 1974); Galleria Gian Enzo Sperone, Turin, Italy (1970); and Sonnabend Gallery, New York (1976).

Nauman participated in numerous prestigious group exhibitions including Documenta 4, Kassel, Germany (1968); "Thirty-first Biennial of American Painting," Corcoran Gallery of Art, Washington, D.C. (1969); "Live in Your Head, When Attitude Becomes Form," Kunsthalle, Bern, Switzerland (1969); "*Op losse schroven: situaties en cryptostructuren*," Stedelijk Museum, Amsterdam, (1969); "Nine Young Artists," Solomon R. Guggenheim Museum, New York (1969); "Anti-Illusion: Materials/Procedures," Whitney Museum of American Art, New York (1969); and "Kompas 4 West Coast U.S.A.," Stedelijk van Abbemuseum, Eindhoven, Netherlands (1969–70).

Nauman's first museum retrospective was co-organized by the Los Angeles County Museum of Art, Los Angeles, and the Whitney Museum, New York (1973), and traveled throughout Europe and the United States. A ten-year retrospective was mounted at the Rijksmuseum, Kroller-Muller, Otterlo, Netherlands, an exhibition that traveled to the Staatliche Kunsthalle Baden-Baden, Germany (1981). Twenty-year retrospectives followed at the Museum für Gegenwartkunst, Basel, Switzerland, which traveled throughout Europe and the U.S. in 1986; University Art Museum, University of California at Berkeley (1986); and Museum of Contemporary Art, Los Angeles (1986).

Recent retrospectives include one collaboratively organized by the Walker Art Center, Minneapolis, and the Hirshhorn Museum and Sculpture Garden, Washington, D.C., which traveled throughout America and Europe (1993–95); "Bruce Nauman 1985–1996: Drawings, Prints, and Related Works," Aldrich Museum of Contemporary Art, Ridgefield, Connecticut, which traveled to the Cleveland Center for Contemporary Art, Cleveland (1997); and "Bruce Nauman: Image/Text 1966–1996," Kunstmuseum Wolfsburg, Germany, which traveled to the Musée National d'Art Moderne, Centre Georges Pompidou, Paris; Hayward Gallery, London; and Museum of Contemporary Art, Helsinki, Finland (1997).

Recent one-person exhibitions have been mounted at Museum für Neue Kunst, MNK/ZKM, Karlsruhe, Germany (1999–2000); Kunsthalle Wien, Vienna, Austria (2000); Wilhelm Lehmbruck Museum Duisburg, Germany (2000); and Zwirner & Wirth, New York (2001).

Bruce Nauman lives and works in Galisteo, New Mexico.

Selected Further Readings

Nauman, Bruce. *Clear Sky, New York*. New York: Leo Castelli Gallery, 1969.
Nauman, Bruce, and Brenda Richardson. *Bruce Nauman: Neons*. Baltimore: Baltimore Museum of Art, 1982.
Van Bruggen, Coosje. *Bruce Nauman*. New York: Rizzoli, 1988.
Bruce Nauman, Prints 1970–89: A Catalogue Raisonné (exhibition catalogue). New York: Castelli Graphics, 1989.
Bruce Nauman (exhibition catalogue). Minneapolis: Walker Art Center, 1994.
Nauman, Bruce. *Fingers and Holes*. Los Angeles: Gemini G.E.L., 1994.
Bruce Nauman: 1985–1996 Drawings, Prints, and Related Works. Ridgefield, CT: Aldrich Museum of Contemporary Art, 1997.
Bruce Nauman (exhibition catalogue). London: Hayward Gallery, 1998.
Von Bismarck, Beatrice. *Bruce Nauman: The True Artist*. Ostfildern-Ruit, Germany: Cantz Verlag, 1998.
Samuel Beckett, Bruce Nauman (exhibition catalogue). Vienna, Austria: Die Kunsthalle, 2000.
Fischer, Peter, Hans-Michael Herzog, and Nicholas Serota. *Nauman, Kruger, Jaar*. London: Thames and Hudson, 2002.

Claes Oldenburg

Born in Stockholm, Sweden, in 1929, Claes Oldenburg spent his early childhood in the United States and Norway before his family settled in Chicago in 1936. From 1946 to 1950, Oldenburg attended Yale University in New Haven, Connecticut where he studied literature and art history. He then attended the Art Institute of Chicago from 1950 to 1954. Oldenburg became a U.S. citizen in 1953.

Oldenburg's first monumental outdoor sculpture, *Lipstick (Ascending) on Caterpillar Tracks* was installed at Yale University in 1969. From this period on, Oldenburg exhibited widely at an international level, participating in the Venice Biennale, Venice, Italy (1964, 1968), and Documenta, Kassel, Germany (1968, 1972, 1977, 1982). Oldenburg was honored with numerous early solo exhibitions at such venues as Galerie Sonnabend, Paris (1964); Pace Gallery, Boston (1964); and Moderner Museet, Stockholm, Sweden (1966).

In 1969, Oldenburg had a midcareer retrospective at the Museum of Modern Art, followed by a retrospective at the Stedelijk Museum, Amsterdam in 1970. From 1976, Oldenburg collaborated on most of his large-scale projects with art critic Coosje van Bruggen, whom he married in 1977. His most recent retrospective, "Claes Oldenburg: An Anthology," was organized by the National Gallery of Art, Washington, D.C., and the Solomon R. Guggenheim Museum, New York, in 1995.

Claes Oldenburg lives and works in New York City.

Selected Further Readings

New Work by Oldenburg at Sidney Janis (exhibition catalogue). New York: Sidney Janis Gallery, 1966.

Rose, Barbara. *Claes Oldenburg* (exhibition catalogue). New York: Museum of Modern Art, 1970.

Oldenburg, Claes, and Coosje van Bruggen. *Claes Oldenburg, Large-Scale Projects, 1977–1980 : Based on Notes, Statements, Contracts, Correspondence, and Other Documents Related to the Works: A Chronicle.* New York: Rizzoli, 1980.

A Bottle of Notes: Claes Oldenburg, Coosje van Bruggen: Claes Oldenburg, Drawings, Sculptures, and Large-Scale Projects with Coosje van Bruggen (exhibition catalogue). New York: Rizzoli, 1988.

Van Bruggen, Coosje. *Claes Oldenburg* (exhibition catalogue). Frankfurt am Main, Germany: Museum für Moderne Kunst, 1991.

Oldenburg, Claes, Thomas Lawson, Arthur Solway, et al. *Multiples in Retrospect, 1964–1990.* New York: Rizzoli, 1991.

Celant, Germano, Dieter Koepplin, et al. *Claes Oldenburg: An Anthology* (exhibition catalogue). New York: Solomon R. Guggenheim Museum, 1995.

Claes Oldenburg: The Multiples Store (exhibition catalogue). Manchester, England: National Touring Exhibitions, 1996.

Printed Stuff: Prints, Posters, and Ephemera by Claes Oldenburg: A Catalogue Raisonné 1958–1996 (exhibition catalogue). New York: Hudson Hills Press in association with Madison Art Center, Wisconsin, 1997.

Celant, Germano, ed. *Claes Oldenburg, Coosje van Bruggen* (exhibition catalogue). Milan, Italy: Skira, 1999.

Michelangelo Pistoletto

Born in Biella, Turin, Italy, in 1933, Michelangelo Pistoletto began his career as a painter in the 1950s and later became one of the central figures of the *arte povera* movement. His early one-person exhibition was mounted at Galleria Galatea, Turin, Italy (1960). Pistoletto began to exhibit frequently during the early 1960s with Galleria Sperone, Turin, Italy, and Galerie Sonnabend, Paris (1964, 1967). Pistoletto was included in seminal group exhibitions "*Arte povera + azioni povera*" Arsenali dell'Antica Repubblica, Amalfi, Italy (1969); "Live in Your Head, When Attitude Becomes Form," Bern, Switzerland, which traveled to London and Krefeld, Germany (1968–69); "Information," Museum of Modern Art, New York (1970); and Documenta, Kassel, Germany (1982, 1992, 1997).

Recent solo exhibitions include "*Michelangelo Pistoletto–Zeit Raume,*" Museum Moderner Kunst Stiftung Ludwig, Vienna, Austria (1995); "*Memoria, Intelligentia, Praeventia,*" Kunstbau Lenbachhaus, Munich, Germany (1996). Recent retrospectives were held at Galerie im Taxispalais, Innsbruck, Germany (1999), and Museu d'Art Contemporani de Barcelona (2000).

Michelangelo Pistoletto lives and works in Turin, Italy.

Selected Further Readings

Pistoletto (exhibition catalogue). Paris: Sonnabend, 1964.

Pistoletto, Michelangelo. *A Minus Artist.* Florence, Italy: Hopefulmonster, 1988.

Pistoletto: Division and Multiplication of the Mirror (exhibition catalogue). New York: P. S. 1 Institute for Contemporary Art, 1988.

Celant, Germano. Translated by Joachim Neugroschel. *Pistoletto.* New York: Rizzoli, 1989.

Pistoletto, Michelangelo, and Jan Fonce. *Michelangelo Pistoletto.* Brussels, Belgium: Xavier Hufkens, 1989.

Le Porte di Palazzo Fabroni (exhibition catalogue). Milan, Italy: Charta, 1995.

Michelangelo Pistoletto: Shifting Perspective ("I am the other") (exhibition catalogue). Oxford, England: Museum of Modern Art, 1999.

Michelangelo Pistoletto (exhibition catalogue). Barcelona, Spain: Museu d'Art Contemporani de Barcelona, 2000.

Continents of Time: Michelangelo Pistoletto (exhibition catalogue). Lyon, France: Musée d'Art Contemporain, 2001.

Anne and Patrick Poirier

Anne and Patrick Poirier, born in Marseilles and Nantes, France, respectively, in 1942, studied at the Ecole Nationale Supérieure des Arts Décoratifs in Paris from 1963 to 1966 and married in 1968. The Poiriers began exhibiting in the early 1970s with solo shows at Galerie Sonnabend, Paris (1973, 1975, 1977, 1978, 1979); Galerie Sonnabend, Geneva (1974); Sonnabend Gallery, New York (1974, 1978, 1980, 1982, 1984, 1988, 1991, 1995); Musée National d'Art Moderne, Centre Georges Pompidou, Paris (1978); Museum of Modern Art, New York (1978); and "Wandering into Memory," Storm King Art Center, Mountainville, New York (1989). Numerous group exhibitions during this time include "Project 74," Kunsthalle Cologne, Germany (1974); Venice Biennale, Venice, Italy (1976, 1980, 1984); Documenta 6, Kassel, Germany (1977); and "Autoportraits Photographiques," Musée National d'Art Moderne, Centre Georges Pompidou, Paris (1981).

More recent solo exhibitions were mounted at Museum Moderner Kunst, Vienna, Austria (1993); Gulbenkian Foundation, Lisbon, Portugal (1996); Galerie Thaddaeus Ropac, Paris (1998); Fondation Mont Blanc, New York (1999); Getty Research Institute, Los Angeles (1999); Fondation Européenne pour la Sculpture, Brussels, Belgium (2000); and Galerie Sfeir-Semler, Hamburg, Germany (2001).

Recent group exhibitions include "Contemporary Classicism," Neuberger Museum of Art, Purchase, New York (1999), and "Mitologie individuali," Padiglione d'Arte Contemporanea, Milan, Italy (2002).

Anne and Patrick Poirier live and work in Trevi, Italy and Paris.

Selected Further Readings

Poirier, Anne, and Patrick Poirier. *A La Mémoire de Romulus.* Liège, France: Yellow Now Editions, 1974.

_____. *Les Paysages revolus.* New York: Sonnabend Editions, 1975.

_____. *Les Realités incompatibles.* Copenhagen, Denmark: Martin Berg Editions, 1975.

Anne et Patrick Poirier: Domus Aurea: Fascination des Ruines (exhibition catalogue). Paris: Centre National d'Art et de Culture Georges Pompidou, Musée National d'Art Moderne, 1978.

Anne et Patrick Poirier: Voyages...et Caetera 1969–1983 (exhibition catalogue). Paris: Chapelle de la Salpetrière, 1983.

Lost Archetypes (exhibition catalogue). Bath, England: Artsite Gallery, 1986.

Poirier, Anne, and Patrick Poirier. *Wandering into Memory: Sculpture by Anne and Patrick Poirier* (exhibition catalogue). Mountainville, New York: Storm King Art Center, 1989.

_____ and André Ménard. *Anima Mundi: Lettres.* Montreal: S. Lallouz, 1991.

Anne and Patrick Poirier (exhibition catalogue). Milan, Italy: Electa, 1994.

Anne and Patrick Poirier: Fragility (exhibition catalogue). New York: Sonnabend Gallery, 1997.

Rona Pondick

Born in Brooklyn, New York, in 1952, Rona Pondick studied at Queens College, Flushing, New York (B.A., 1974) and at Yale University, New Haven, Connecticut (M.F.A., 1977).

Pondick's first site-specific installation, *Beds*, was presented at the Sculpture Center in New York (1988). Subsequent one-person exhibitions/installations include "Currents," Institute of Contemporary Art, Boston (1989); "Bed Milk Shoe, Fiction/Nonfiction," New York (1989); Asher-Faure Gallery, Los Angeles (1990, 1991); "Pink and Brown," Israel Museum, Jerusalem (1992); "New Art 4," Cincinnati Art Museum, Cincinnati (1995); "MINE," Brooklyn Museum, Brooklyn, New York (1996–97); "Tree Head Room," Sidney Janis Gallery, New York (1997); and Patricia Faure Gallery, Santa Monica (1996, 2001). Pondick recently mounted a solo exhibition at Sonnabend Gallery, New York (2002).

A selection of Pondick's numerous group exhibitions includes the Whitney Biennial, Whitney Museum, New York (1991); "Power Play," Gallery of the Art Institute of Chicago, Chicago (1992); "Altered and Irrational," Whitney Museum, New York (1995); "Home/Salon," Institute of Contemporary Art (Clocktower Gallery), New York (1996); "Comfort Zone: Furniture by Artists," PaineWeber Art Gallery, New York (1999); and Sonnabend Gallery, New York (2001).

Rona Pondick lives and works in New York City.

Selected Further Readings

Pondick, Rona. *Rona Pondick* (exhibition catalogue). New York: Fiction/Nonfiction, 1991.

Rona Pondick, Pink and Brown (exhibition catalogue). Jerusalem: Israel Museum, 1992.

Feinberg, Jean E. *A Conversation between Rona Pondick and Jean Feinberg.* Cincinnati: Cincinnati Art Museum, 1995.

Kotik, Charlotta. *Mine* (exhibition catalogue). New York: Brooklyn Museum of Art, 1996.

Deans, Jeanie. *Tree Head Room* (exhibition catalogue). New York: Sidney Janis Gallery, 1997.

Pondick, Rona. *12345.* Boston: Howard Yezerski Gallery, 1998.

Capasso, Nick. *Rona Pondick: New Work* (exhibition catalogue). Lincoln, Nebraska: De Cordova Museum and Sculpture Park, 2002.

Rona Pondick (exhibition catalogue). New York: Sonnabend Press, 2002.

Robert Rauschenberg

Born in Port Arthur, Texas, in 1925, Robert Rauschenberg studied at the Kansas City Art Institute, Kansas City, Missouri (1947–1948); Black Mountain College, North Carolina (1948–1952); and the Art Students League, New York (1949–1951).

Rauschenberg's first one-person exhibition took place at Betty Parsons Gallery, New York, in 1951. Other solo exhibitions were held at such venues as Leo Castelli Gallery, New York (1958); Sonnabend Gallery, New York (1974, 1977, 1979, 1981, 1982, 1983, 1984, 1996); Galerie Sonnabend, Paris (1963, 1964, 1966, 1968, 1971, 1972, 1975, 1977, 1978, 1980); Galerie Sonnabend, Geneva (1974); the Whitney Museum of American Art, New York, (1961–62); Whitechapel Art Gallery, London (1964); Contemporary Arts Museum, Houston (1965); Stedelijk Museum, Amsterdam (1968); and Museum of Modern Art, New York (1968–1969).

Since the late 1950s, Rauschenberg has participated in numerous group exhibitions such as Documenta 2, Kassel, Germany (1959); São Paulo Biennale, São Paulo, Brazil (1959); and the Venice Biennale, Venice, Italy (1964), for which he was the first American to receive the prestigious Grand Prix.

Midcareer retrospectives were mounted at international venues including Minneapolis Institute of Arts, Minneapolis (1970); Smithsonian Institution, Washington, D.C. (1976); Visual Arts Museum, School of Visual Arts, New York (1975), and Staatliche Kunsthalle, Berlin (1980), an exhibition that traveled to Kunsthalle, Düsseldorf, Germany (1980); Louisiana Museum for Modern Art, Humlebaek, Copenhagen, Denmark (1980); Stadelsches Kunstinstitut, Frankfurt, Germany (1980–1981); Stadelsches Galerie im Lenbachhaus, Munich, Germany (1981); and the Tate Gallery, London (1981).

Recent one-person exhibitions were mounted at such venues as the Whitney Museum, New York (1990); the National Gallery of Art, Washington, D.C. (1991); Hiroshima City Museum of Contemporary Art, Hiroshima, Japan (1993–94); and Sonnabend Gallery, New York (1996). A major retrospective of Rauschenberg's fifty-year career was organized by Solomon R. Guggenheim Museum, New York, in 1998.

Robert Rauschenberg lives in New York City, and Captiva Island, Florida.

Selected Further Readings

Rauschenberg, Robert. *Rauschenberg: XXXIV Drawings for Dante's Inferno.* New York: Harry N. Abrams, 1965.

Forge, Andrew. *Rauschenberg.* New York: Harry N. Abrams, 1972.

Tomkins, Calvin. *Off the Wall: Robert Rauschenberg and the Art World of Our Time.* Garden City, NY: Doubleday, 1980.

Rauschenberg, Robert. *Photos In + Out of City Limits: Boston.* West Islip, NY: Universal Limited Art Editions (ULAE), 1981.

Robert Rauschenberg Photographs (exhibition catalogue). New York: Pantheon Books, 1981.

Kotz, Mary Lynn. *Rauschenberg: Art and Life.* New York: Harry N. Abrams, 1990.

Rauschenberg Overseas Culture Interchange (exhibition catalogue). Washington, D.C.: National Gallery of Art, 1990.

Hopps, Walter. *Robert Rauschenberg: The Early 1950s* (exhibition catalogue). Houston: Menil Collection and Houston Fine Arts, 1991.

Hopps, Walter, Susan Davidson, et al. *Robert Rauschenberg: A Retrospective* (exhibition catalogue). New York: Solomon R. Guggenheim Museum, 1997.

Andrea Robbins and Max Becher

Born in Boston in 1963, Andrea Robbins studied at Cooper Union School of Art, New York (B.F.A., 1986), and Hunter College School of Art, New York (1987–89). Born in Düsseldorf, Germany, in 1964, Max Becher studied at Cooper Union School of Art, New York (B.F.A., 1986), and Mason Gross School of the Arts, Rutgers University, New Brunswick, New Jersey (M.F.A., 1990).

Robbins and Becher began collaborating in 1986 and had their first solo exhibition, "Portrait of Felix Buchloh," at Arthur A. Houghton Gallery in New York (1986). Other early solo exhibitions include "Still-Life Maintenance," Hunter Gallery, Hunter College, New York (1989); "Wall Street in Cuba/ Colonial Remains," Kanaal Art Foundation, Kortrijk, Belgium (1994); "Holland," Basilico Fine Arts, New York (1995); and "Shrinking People, Exiled Cigars and Galloping Dinosaurs," Basilico Fine Arts, New York (1996).

Early group exhibitions include *"Jardin Secret,"* Arca Centre d'Art Contemporain, Marseilles, France (1986); "Green Acres: Neocolonialism in the U.S.," Washington University Gallery of Art, St. Louis (1992); "In the Field: Landscape in Recent Photography," Margo Leavin Gallery, Los Angeles (1994); and "Western Views: A Photographic History of Land Use in the West," San Francisco Museum of Modern Art, San Francisco (1996).

Robbins and Becher recently mounted solo exhibitions at Basilico Fine Arts, New York (1997); American Fine Arts, New York (1999); Gallerie Windows, Brussels, Belgium (1999); Yerba Buena Center for the Arts, San Francisco (2000); Sonnabend Gallery, New York (2001); and Museum of Contemporary Photography, Chicago (2002).

Recent group exhibitions include "The Cultured Tourist," Leslie Tonkonow Artworks & Projects, New York (1998); "Photography: An Expanded View," Solomon R. Guggenheim Museum, New York (1999); *Biennale de Lyon d'Art Contemporain*, Lyon, France (2000); "Documentary Processes," Museum of Contemporary Art, Barcelona, Spain (2001); and "*Bal-Arts '02*," Palma de Mallorca, Spain (2002).

Andrea Robbins and Max Becher live and work in New York City.

Selected Further Readings

Van Winkel, Camiel. "Vestiges of Utopia, The Düsseldorf School," *Archis*, October 1995: 65–80.

Karmel, Pepe. "Andrea Robbins and Max Becher: Shrinking People, Exiled Cigars and Galloping Dinosaurs," *New York Times*, February 2, 1996: C26.

Boxer, Sarah. "The Guggenheim Sounds the Alarm: It Ain't Necessarily So," *New York Times*, March 19, 1998: C37.

Goldberg, Vicki. "Of Fairies, Free Spirits and Outright Frauds," *New York Times*, February 1, 1998: Sec. 2, 48–49.

James Rosenquist

James Rosenquist was born in Grand Forks, North Dakota, in 1933. He studied at the University of Minnesota and then briefly at the Art Students League in New York. His first one-person exhibition was at the Green Gallery, New York (1962). Other early solo exhibitions include Galerie Sonnabend, Paris (1965, 1968, 1974); Dwan Gallery, Los Angeles (1964); Leo Castelli Gallery, New York (1965); Galerie Rolf Ricke, Cologne, Germany (1971); Whitney Museum of American Art, New York (1972); Castelli Feigen Corcoran Gallery, New York (1982); Gallerie Daniel Templon, Paris (1987); and Wetterling Gallery, Stockholm, Sweden (1989).

Rosenquist's first participation in a group exhibition was at Green Gallery, New York (1961). Other early group exhibitions include "*Pop Art Américain*," Galerie Sonnabend, Paris (1963); "Americans 1963," Museum of Modern Art, New York (1963); "New York Painting and Sculpture 1940–1970," Metropolitan Museum of Art, New York (1969); "American Pop Art," Whitney Museum of American Art, New York (1974); "Pop Art: Evolution of a Generation," Palazzo Grassi, Venice, Italy (1980); and "High and Low: Modern Art and Popular Culture," Museum of Modern Art, New York (1990).

Retrospective exhibitions include "James Rosenquist" at Denver Art Museum, which traveled to Houston, Des Moines, Iowa, New York, and Washington, D.C. (1985); and "James Rosenquist: Time Dust: The Complete Graphics 1962–1992," Walker Arts Center, Minneapolis (1993).

Recent solo exhibitions include "Rosenquist: Moscow/USA," Trtyakov Museum, Moscow (1991); "James Rosenquist," Galeria Weber Alexander Cobo, Madrid, Spain (1992); and "James Rosenquist, Recent Work," Portland Art Museum, Portland, Oregon (1995).

Group exhibitions include "Twentieth Century Collage," Margo Leavin Gallery, Los Angeles (1991); "*Le Portrait dans l'art contemporain*," Musée d'Art Moderne et d'Art Contemporain, Nice, France (1992); "The Pop Show," Richard Green Gallery, Santa Monica, California (1992); and Bobbie Greenfield Fine Art, Venice, California (1993).

James Rosenquist lives and works in Aripeka, Florida.

Selected Further Readings

James Rosenquist: The National Gallery of Canada (exhibition catalogue). Ottawa: Queen's Printer, 1968.

James A. Rosenquist (exhibition catalogue). Paris: Galerie Ileana Sonnabend, 1968.

Tucker, Marcia. *James Rosenquist* (exhibition catalogue). New York: Whitney Museum of American Art, 1972.

Rosenquist, James. *Drawings While Waiting for an Idea.* New York: Lapp Princess Press, 1979.

Goldman, Judith. *James Rosenquist.* New York: Viking, 1985.

Time Dust: James Rosenquist Complete Graphics 1962–1992 (exhibition catalogue). New York: Rizzoli, 1993.

Rosenquist, James, and Leo Castelli. *James Rosenquist: The Big Paintings: Thirty Years.* New York: Rizzoli International Publications, 1994.

Clifford Ross

Born in New York, in 1952, Clifford Ross attended Skowhegan School of Painting and Sculpture in New York, New York (1973), and Yale University in New Haven, Connecticut (1974).

Ross began his career with a solo exhibition at the Tibor de Nagy Gallery, New York (1976). He later exhibited with William Edward O'Reilly Gallery, New York (1977); Byck Gallery,

Louisville, Kentucky (1981); Salander-O'Reilly Galleries, New York (1984); and Corcoran Gallery of Art, Washington, D.C. (1988). Ross was soon included in prestigious group exhibitions such as "Twelve in New York," Yale School of Art, New Haven, Connecticut (1986), and "The 1980s: A New Generation," Metropolitan Museum of Art, New York (1988).

More recent one-person exhibitions include Salander-O'Reilly Galleries, New York (1994); Glenn Horowitz Gallery, East Hampton, New York (1995); Houk Friedman Gallery, New York (1997); Edwynn Houk Gallery, New York (1999); and Sonnabend Gallery, New York (2001, 2002).

Ross's recent group exhibitions include "Something Old, Something New: Contemporary Artists Reflect on the Past," Renée Foutouhi Gallery, East Hampton, New York (1995); "Water," Hamiltons Gallery, London (1997); "Waterproof," Centro Cultural de Belem Expo '98, Lisbon, Portugal (1998); "Surroundings: Responses to the American Landscape," San Jose Museum of Art, San Jose, California (1999).

Clifford Ross lives and works in New York City.

Selected Further Readings

Ross, Clifford. *Phantasmagorey: The Work of Edward Gorey* (exhibition catalogue). New Haven, CT: Yale University Library, 1974.

Clifford Ross: Sculpture & Paintings (exhibition catalogue). New York: Salander-O'Reilly Galleries, 1984.

Ross, Clifford. *Abstract Expressionism: Creators and Critics, an Anthology*. New York: Harry N. Abrams, 1990.

Ross, Clifford, Karen Wilkin, Ruth Peltason, eds. *The World of Edward Gorey*. New York: Harry N. Abrams, 1996.

Chase, Linda. "Water World–Photography of Clifford Ross." *Seasons*, Summer 1999: 42–51.

Keith Sonnier

Born in Mamou, Louisiana, in 1941, Keith Sonnier earned his B.A. at the University of Southwestern Louisiana, Lafayette (1963), and his M.F.A. at Rutgers University, New Brunswick, New Jersey (1966). Sonnier gained recognition for his wall reliefs and floor-based sculptures in the late 1960s and early '70s, with important group exhibitions such as "When Attitude Becomes Form," Kunsthalle, Bern, Switzerland (1969); "Anti-Illusion: Procedures/Materials," Whitney Museum of American Art, New York (1969); "Information," Museum of Modern Art, New York (1970); Venice Biennale, Italy (1972, 1982); Documenta 5, Kassel, Germany (1972); Whitney Biennial, Whitney Museum, New York (1973); and Sonnabend, Gallery, New York (1977). During this time, Sonnier's numerous one-person exhibitions at prestigious galleries and museums included "Projects: Keith Sonnier," Museum of Modern Art, New York (1971); "Keith Sonnier Live and Channel Video," Leo Castelli Gallery, New York (1972); and "*Keith Sonnier: Porte Vue*," Musée National d'Art Moderne, Centre Georges Pompidou, Paris (1979).

Sonnier continued to exhibit widely in Europe and the U.S. during the next thirty years, including one-person exhibitions at the Hirshhorn Museum and Sculpture Garden, Washington, D.C. (1989); Barbara Gladstone, New York (1989); Musée Château d'Annecy, Annecy, France (1992); and group exhibitions such as "Drawing Distinctions: American Drawings of the Seventies," Louisiana Museum of Modern Art, Humlebaek, Copenhagen, Denmark (1981); "Lightworks," Australian National Gallery, Canberra, Australia (1985); and "Gravity and Grace," Hayward Gallery, London (1993). More recent one-person exhibitions include "Alternating Currents," Leo Castelli Gallery, New York (1997); "Channel Mix," Nicole Klagsbrun Gallery, New York (1997); "Keith Sonnier: New Work" and "Keith Sonnier: Sculpture 1966–1998," Marlborough Gallery, New York (1998, 2000).

Keith Sonnier lives and works in New York City.

Selected Further Readings

Blagg, Max, Robert Roos. *Keith Sonnier: The Experience of Space* (exhibition catalogue). Brussels, Belgium: Liverpool Gallery, 1990.

Casorati, Cecilia, Linda McGreevy. *Keith Sonnier* (exhibition catalogue). Rome: Galleria Il Ponte, 1990.

Keith Sonnier: Expanded File Series 1969–1989 (exhibition catalogue). Hamburg, Germany: Galerie Jürgen Becker, 1990.

Keith Sonnier: Werke (Works) (exhibition catalogue). Stuttgart, Germany: Edition Cantz, 1993.

Keith Sonnier: Sculpture, 1966–1998 (exhibition catalogue). New York: Marlborough Gallery, 1998.

Keith Sonnier: Sculpture 1966–1998 (exhibition catalogue) New York: Marlborough Gallery, 1999.

Keith Sonnier: New Work 2000 (exhibition catalogue). New York: Marlborough Chelsea, 2000.

Köb, Edelbert, ed. *Keith Sonnier: Public Commissions in Architecture 1990–1999*. Ostfildern-Ruit, Germany: Hatje Cantz, 2000.

Haim Steinbach

Born in Rehovot, Israel, in 1944, Haim Steinbach became a U.S. citizen in 1962 and attended Pratt Institute, in Brooklyn, New York from 1962 to 1968 (B.F.A., 1968). Steinbach also attended the Université d'Aix, in Marseilles, France (1965–66) and Yale University, New Haven, Connecticut (M.F.A., 1973).

Steinbach's early group exhibitions include "New Sculpture: Robert Gober, Jeff Koons, Haim Steinbach," Renaissance Society at the University of Chicago (1986); "Damaged Goods: Desire and the Economy of the Object," New Museum of Contemporary Art, New York (1986); "*Les Courtiers du Désir*," Musée National d'Art Moderne Centre Georges Pompidou, Paris (1987); Documenta 7 and Documenta 8, Kassel, Germany (1987, 1992); "Horn of Plenty," Stedelijk Museum, Amsterdam, Netherlands (1989); Venice Biennale, Venice, Italy (1997); "Around 1984: A Look at Art in the Eighties," P.S. 1 Contemporary Art Museum, New York (2000).

Since the early 1980s, Steinbach has mounted one-person exhibitions regularly in Europe and the U.S., at Sonnabend Gallery, New York (1987, 1990, 1993, 1997); Jay Gorney Modern Art, New York (1988); Castello di Rivoli, Museo d'Arte Contemporanea, Rivoli-Torino, Italy (1995); and Museum Moderner Kunst Stiftung Ludwig, Vienna, Austria (1997).

Haim Steinbach lives and works in Brooklyn, New York.

Selected Further Readings

Haim Steinbach: Oeuvres récentes (exhibition catalogue). Bordeaux, France: CAPC Musée d'Art Contemporain de Bordeaux, 1988.

No Rocks Allowed (exhibition catalogue). Rotterdam, Netherlands: Witte de With Center for Contemporary Art, 1992.

Osmosis: Ettore Spalletti–Haim Steinbach (exhibition catalogue). New York: Solomon R. Guggenheim Museum, 1993.

Haim Steinbach (exhibition catalogue). Klagenfurt, Germany: Kunsthalle Ritter Klagenfurt, 1995.

Haim Steinbach (exhibition catalogue). Milan, Italy: Edizioni Charta, 1995.

Haim Steinbach (exhibition catalogue). Vienna, Austria: Triton, 1997.

Steinbach, Haim. *0%*. Vienna, Austria: Triton, 1997.

Haim Steinbach (exhibition catalogue). Milan, Italy: Edizioni Charta, 1999.

Hiroshi Sugimoto

Born in Tokyo, Japan, in 1948, Hiroshi Sugimoto studied sociology and politics at Saint Paul's University, Tokyo (B.A., 1970) before studying art at the Art Center College of Design, Los Angeles (B.F.A., 1972). Sugimoto moved to New York in 1974.

Sugimoto has been creating black-and-white photographic series, such as "Dioramas," "Seascapes," "Theatres," and "Portraits," since 1976. Since this time, Sugimoto has exhibited regularly in numerous important group exhibitions in Europe, Japan, and the U.S., including "The Art of Memory, The Loss of History," New Museum of Contemporary Art, New York (1986); "Reorienting: Looking East," Third Eye Center, Glasgow, Scotland (1990); "The Twenty-First Century: Into the Future with Paracelsus," Kunsthalle Basel, Switzerland (1993); "Art in Japan Today: 1985–1995," Museum of Contemporary Art, Tokyo (1995); "Evidence: Photography and Site," Wexner Center for the Arts, Columbus, Ohio (1997), which traveled to Cranbrook Art Museum, Bloomfield Hills, Michigan (1998); "The Museum as Muse: Artists Reflect," Museum of Modern Art, New York (1999); and "Small World: Dioramas in Contemporary Art," Museum of Contemporary Art, San Diego (2000).

One-person exhibitions have been mounted at the Sonnabend Gallery, New York (1981, 1983, 1988, 1992, 1994, 1995, 1997, 1998, 2001); CAPC Musée d'Art Contemporain, Bordeaux, France (1992); Museum of Contemporary Art, Los Angeles (1994); Metropolitan Museum of Art, New York (1995); and Moderna Museet, Stockholm, Sweden (1996).

Recent one-person exhibitions have taken place at the San Francisco Museum of Modern Art, San Francisco (2000); Solomon R. Guggenheim Museum SoHo, New York (2001); and Sonnabend Gallery, New York (2001).

Hiroshi Sugimoto lives and works in New York City.

Selected Further Readings

Sugimoto (exhibition catalogue). Los Angeles: Museum of Contemporary Art, 1993.

Sugimoto, Hiroshi, David Britt, and Thomas Kellein. *Hiroshi Sugimoto: Time Exposed*. New York: Thames and Hudson, 1995.

Sugimoto. Houston and Tokyo: Contemporary Arts Museum and Hara Museum, 1996.

Hiroshi Sugimoto (exhibition catalogue). Norwich, England: Sainsbury Centre for Visual Arts, University of East Anglia, 1997.

Sugimoto, Hiroshi. *Sea of Buddha*. New York: Sonnabend Sundell Editions, 1997.

Sugimoto (exhibition catalogue). Madrid, Spain: Fundación "la Caixa," 1998.
Sugimoto, Hiroshi. *In Praise of Shadows*. Kitakyushu, Japan: Korinsha Press, 1999.
Ferguson, Russell, ed. *Sugimoto* (exhibition catalogue). New York: Fotofolio, 1999.
Bashkoff, Tracey, and Nancy Spector. *Sugimoto: Portraits*. New York: Solomon R. Guggenheim Museum, 2000.
Sugimoto, Hiroshi. *Theaters*. New York: Sonnabend Sundell Editions, 2000.

Cy Twombly

Born in Lexington, Virginia, in 1928, Cy Twombly studied at the School of the Museum of Fine Arts, Boston (1947–49); the Art Students League, New York (1950–51), and Black Mountain College, North Carolina (1951–52). Twombly moved to Italy in 1957.

His early paintings were exhibited at the Kotz Gallery, New York (1951); Stable Gallery, New York (1953); and the Leo Castelli Gallery, New York (1964). In 1964, Twombly was invited to participate in the Venice Biennale, Venice, Italy (1964), and began to exhibit widely throughout the U.S. and Europe.

Twombly was honored with several retrospectives early on in his career at prestigious venues such as the Milwaukee Art Center, Milwaukee (1968); Kunstmuseum Basel, Switzerland (1973); Kunsthalle Bern, Switzerland (1973); and "Cy Twombly: Paintings, Drawings, Constructions, 1951–1974," Institute of Contemporary Art, University of Pennsylvania, Philadelphia, which traveled to San Francisco Museum of Art (1975); *"Cy Twombly: Dessins 1954–1976,"* Musée d'Art Moderne de la Ville de Paris, Paris (1976); and "Cy Twombly, Paintings and Drawings, 1954–1977," Whitney Museum of American Art, New York (1979).

Recent retrospectives have been mounted at CAPC Musée d'Art Contemporain, Bordeaux, France (1984); Kunsthaus, Zurich, Switzerland (1987); Hirschl & Adler Modern, New York (1984); Musée National d'Art Moderne, Centre Georges Pompidou, Paris (1988); and Museum of Modern Art, New York (1994). The Menil Collection, in collaboration with Twombly and Dia Center for the Arts, opened the Cy Twombly Gallery in Houston in 1995. The gallery houses a permanent installation of the artist's work.

Recent one-person exhibitions include "The Imagined World," Nolan/Eckman Gallery, New York (1998); "Cy Twombly: Coronation of Sesostris," Gagosian Gallery, New York (2000–2001); "Cy Twombly: The Sculpture," Kunstmuseum Basel, Switzerland (2000), which traveled to the Menil Collection, Houston (2000–2001); and "Thirty-five Drawings," Richard Gray Gallery, New York (2001).

Cy Twombly lives and works in Rome and Gaeta, Italy and Lexington, Virginia.

Selected Further Readings

Cy Twombly: Paintings and Drawings 1965–1977 (exhibition catalogue). New York: The Museum, 1979.
Cy Twombly: Paintings and Drawings, 1952–1984 (exhibition catalogue). New York: Hirschl & Adler Modern, 1984.
Twombly, Cy. *Cy Twombly Photographs*. New York: Matthew Marks Gallery, 1993.
Cy Twombly: A Retrospective (exhibition catalogue). New York: Museum of Modern Art, 1995.
Del Roscio, Nicola, and Arthur C. Danto. *Cy Twombly: Catalogue Raisonné of Sculpture*. Munich, Germany: Schirmer/Mosel, 1997.
Cy Twombly (exhibition catalogue). Ostfildern-Ruit, Germany: Hatje Cantz, 2000.
Cy Twombly: The Sculpture (exhibition catalogue). Ostfildern-Ruit, Germany: Hatje Cantz, 2000.
Kennison, Donald, ed. *Cy Twombly: Coronation of Sesostris* (exhibition catalogue). New York: Gagosian Gallery, 2001.

Andy Warhol

Born in Pittsburgh, Pennsylvania, in 1928, Andy Warhol began his career as a commercial illustrator in New York after receiving his B.F.A. from the Carnegie Institute of Technology, Pittsburgh, Pennsylvania (1949).

Warhol exhibited *Fifteen Drawings Based on Truman Capote* at the Hugo Gallery, New York in 1952. Ten years later, he exhibited at Ferus Gallery, Los Angeles (1962). Additional early one-person exhibitions were mounted at Galerie Sonnabend, Paris (1964, 1965, 1967, 1974); Galerie Sonnabend, Geneva (1974); Leo Castelli Gallery, New York (1966); and Whitney Museum of American Art, New York (1979).

More recent one-person exhibitions include "Andy Warhol Stitched Photographs," Paul Kasmin Gallery, New York (1999); "Andy Warhol Photography," Andy Warhol Museum, Pittsburgh (1999–2000); "Andy Warhol: A Factory," Solomon R. Guggenheim Museum, New York (2000); "The Warhol Look: Glamour, Style, Fashion," Andy Warhol Museum, Pittsburgh (2000); "Andy Warhol Photographs," International Center of Photography, New York (2001); "Queer(ing) Warhol: Andy Warhol's (Self-) Portraits," University of California, Riverside/California Museum of Photography, Riverside (2001–2002).

Warhol's participation in group exhibitions includes "The Photographic Image," Solomon R. Guggenheim Museum,

New York (1966); "New York Painting and Sculpture: 1940–70," Metropolitan Museum of Art, New York (1969); Whitney Biennial, Whitney Museum of American Art, New York (1969); "Pop Art," Whitney Museum, New York (1974); "Warhol, Basquiat: Paintings," Tony Shafrazi Gallery, New York (1985); "Special Collections: The Photographic Order from Pop to Now," International Center of Photography, New York (1992); "Fame after Photography," Museum of Modern Art, New York (1999); and "Nadar, Warhol: Paris, New York," J. Paul Getty Museum, Los Angeles (1999).

In 1970, the Pasadena Art Museum, in Pasadena, California, organized "Andy Warhol," which traveled to Chicago, Eindhoven, Paris, London, and New York. A major posthumous retrospective was mounted at the Museum of Modern Art, New York, in 1989.

Andy Warhol died on February 22, 1987.

Selected Further Readings

Coplans, John. *Andy Warhol.* New York: Graphic Society, 1970.

Warhol, Andy. *The Philosophy of Andy Warhol (From A to B and Back Again).* New York: Harcourt Brace Jovanovich, 1975.

Rosenblum, Robert. *Andy Warhol: Portraits of the '70s.* New York: Random House/Whitney Museum of American Art, 1979.

Printz, Neil. *Andy Warhol: Death and Disasters* (exhibition catalogue). Houston: Menil Collection and Fine Art Press, 1988.

Bourdon, David. *Warhol.* New York: Harry N. Abrams, 1989.

McShine, Kynaston, ed. *Andy Warhol: A Retrospective* (exhibition catalogue). New York: Museum of Modern Art, 1989.

Warhol, Andy, and Pat Hackett, ed. *Andy Warhol Diaries.* New York: Warner Books, 1989.

Yau, John. *In the Realm of Appearances: The Art of Andy Warhol.* Hopewell, NJ: Ecco Press, 1993.

Andy Warhol 1956–1986: Mirror of His Time (exhibition catalogue). Pittsburgh: Andy Warhol Museum, 1996.

Warhol, Andy, and Pat Hackett. *POPism: The Warhol '60s.* London: Pimlico, 1996.

Feldman, Frayda. *Andy Warhol Prints: A Catalogue Raisonné 1962–1987.* Munich, Germany: Edition Schellmann, 1997.

Francis, Mark, and Margery King, eds. *The Warhol Look: Glamour, Style, Fashion* (exhibition catalogue). Boston: Bulfinch Press, 1997.

Warhol, Andy. *a: a novel.* New York: Grove Press,1998.

Photography: Andy Warhol (exhibition catalogue). Pittsburgh: Andy Warhol Museum, 1999.

Michelson, Annette, ed. *Andy Warhol.* Cambridge, MA: MIT Press, 2001.

Warhol, Andy. *Andy Warhol: Catalogue Raisonné vol. 1: Paintings and Sculpture 1961–1963.* New York: Phaidon, 2002.

Boyd Webb

Born in Christchurch, New Zealand, in 1947, Boyd Webb studied at the Ilam School of Art in Christchurch (1968–71) and at the Royal College of Art (1972–75) in London, where he settled. Webb gained recognition for his staged color photographs in the late 1970s, with numerous one-person exhibitions at prestigious European galleries, such as Whitechapel Art Gallery, London (1978, 1987); Konrad Fischer Gallery, Düsseldorf, Germany (1978); Galerie Sonnabend, Paris (1979); and Sonnabend Gallery, New York (1979, 1981, 1985, 1989, 1995). During the 1980s, Webb mounted numerous one-person exhibitions in the United States and Europe, including shows at Anthony d'Offay Gallery, London (1981); Stedelijk van Abbemuseum, Eindhoven, Netherlands (1983), which traveled to Kunsthalle, Bern, Switzerland; Le Nouveau Musée, Villeurbanne, France; Leeds City Art Gallery, Leeds, England; and Musée Principale, La Roche-sur-Yon, France. Additional one-person shows have been mounted at the Centre Georges Pompidou, Paris (1983); Hirshhorn Museum and Sculpture Garden, Washington, D.C. (1990); and Centre d'Art Contemporain, Geneva (1993).

Webb has been featured in numerous important group exhibitions since the 1980s, including Documenta 7, Kassel, Germany (1982); "Sculpture into Photography," Walker Art Center, Venice Biennale, Venice, Italy (1986); "Prospect 86," Frankfurter Kunstverein and Schirn Kunsthalle, Frankfurt, Germany (1986); "Doubletake: Collective Memory and Current Art," Hayward Gallery, London, and Kunsthalle, Vienna, Austria (1992); "VIII Indian Triennale," New Delhi, India (1994), where he won first prize; and "Spellbound," Hayward Gallery, London (1996).

Boyd Webb lives and works in London.

Selected Further Readings

Boyd Webb (exhibition catalogue). London: Whitechapel Art Gallery, 1978.

Boyd Webb (exhibition catalogue). Eindhoven, Netherlands: Stedelijk van Abbemuseum, 1983.

Boyd Webb (exhibition catalogue). London: Whitechapel Art Gallery, 1987.

Boyd Webb: Oeuvres-Works, 1988–90 (exhibition catalogue). Limoges, France: Fonds Régional d'Art Contemporain du Limousin, 1990.

Boyd Webb: VIII Indian Triennale: 16 February–15 March 1994 (exhibition catalogue). New Delhi, India: Lalit Kala Akademi, 1994.

William Wegman

Born in Holyoke, Massachusetts, in 1943, William Wegman studied at the Massachusetts College of Art, Boston (B.F.A., 1965), and the University of Illinois, Chicago (M.F.A., 1967).

His conceptual videos of the early 1970s evolved into a lifetime involvement with photography, notably his use of the large-format Polaroid, as early as 1979. His first one-person exhibition at Galerie Sonnabend, Paris (1971) was followed by a series of one-person exhibitions at Sonnabend Gallery, New York (1972, 1977) and The Kitchen, New York (1976). In 1979, a midcareer retrospective was organized by Fine Arts Galleries, University of Wisconsin, Milwaukee.

Group exhibitions include "Big Pictures," Museum of Modern Art, New York (1983); "Image World," Whitney Museum of Art, New York (1989); and "Reconsidering the Object of Art: 1965–1975, Museum of Contemporary Art, Los Angeles (1995).

Recent solo exhibitions have been mounted at the Whitney Museum, New York (1990); Carnegie Museum of Art, Pittsburgh (1993); Museum of Contemporary Art, San Diego (1993); Museo de Monterrey, Mexico (1993); Aspen Art Museum, Aspen, Colorado (1995); Pace Wildenstein MacGill, Los Angeles (1995); Montgomery Museum of Fine Arts, Montgomery (1996); Fraenkel Gallery, San Francisco (1997); and the Isetan Museum of Art, Tokyo (1997).

William Wegman lives and works in New York City and Maine.

Selected Further Readings

Wegman, William. *William Wegman: Paintings, Drawings, Photographs, Videotapes* (exhibition catalog). New York: Harry N. Abrams, 1990.

William Wegman (exhibition catalogue). New York: Holly Solomon Gallery, Pace/MacGill Gallery, 1992.

Wegman, William. *Cinderella*. New York: Hyperion, 1993.

William Wegman: Photographic Works, 1969–76 (exhibition catalogue). Limoges, France: Fonds Régional d'Art Contemporain (FRAC), 1993.

Wegman, William. *1,2,3*. New York: Hyperion, 1995.

Fay's Friends. New York: Chronicle, 1995.

Triangle, Circle, Square. New York: Hyperion, 1995

Puppies. New York: Hyperion, 1997.

William Wegman (exhibition catalogue). Boston: Massachusetts College of Art, 1998.

Fashion Photographs (exhibition catalogue). New York: Harry N. Abrams, 1999.

Fay. New York: Hyperion, 1999.

Wegmanology. New York: Hyperion, 2001.

Matthew Weinstein

Born in New York, in 1964, Matthew Weinstein studied at Columbia University (B.A., 1987).

His first one-person exhibition was mounted at Daniel Weinberg Gallery, Los Angeles (1989). Subsequent solo exhibitions were held at Postmasters Gallery, New York (1990, 1991); Sonnabend Gallery, New York (1992, 1994, 1996); and most recently, Greene Gallery, Geneva (2000).

Weinstein was featured in group exhibitions at the Sonnabend Gallery, New York (1995, 1997, 2000). Additional group exhibitions include "Chance Choice and Irony," Todd Gallery, London (1994); "What I Did on My Summer Vacation," White Columns, New York (1996); and "Power by Consent: Thoughts on Desire, Consumption, and the Market," Art Center, Miami (1998).

Matthew Weinstein lives and works in New York City.

Selected Further Readings

Hirsh, David. "Art of Crisis." *New York Native*, March 4, 1991.

Bleckner, Ross. "Independents: Emerging Artists," *Out Magazine*, Fall 1992: 41–49.

Myers, Terry, R. "Abstraction Gets a Life," *Tema Celeste*, Summer 1993.

Saltz, Jerry. "Matthew Weinstein at Sonnabend Gallery, *Art in America*, February 1993: 104–105.

Siegel, Jeanne. "Unveiling the Male Body," *Artpress*, September 1993: E12–E15.

Holland, Cotter. "Matthew Weinstein: Sonnabend Gallery," *New York Times*, April 29, 1994: C24.

Kuspit, Donald. "Matthew Weinstein: Sonnabend Gallery," *Artforum*, October 1994: 101–102.

Tom Wesselmann

Born in Cincinnati, in 1931, Tom Wesselmann attended Hiram College, Hiram, Ohio (1949–1951), University of Cincinnati (B.A., 1956), the Art Academy of Cincinnati (1954–1956), and Cooper Union School of Art and Architecture, New York (1956–1959).

Wesselmann's early one-man exhibitions were mounted at such venues as the Tanager Gallery, New York (1961); Green Gallery, New York (1962); Sidney Janis Gallery, New York (1968, where he exhibited regularly until 1992); Galerie Sonnabend, Paris (1966); F.A.I.C. Grand Palais, Paris (1979); Galerie de France, Paris (1987); Galerie Tokyo, Tokyo (1988); and Mayor Gallery, London (1988).

Early important group exhibitions include "The Figure," Museum of Modern Art, New York (1962); "*Pop Art Américain*,"

Galerie Sonnabend, Paris (1963); "Young America 1965," Whitney Museum of American Art, New York (1965); "Electric Art," Galerie Sonnabend, Paris (1966); São Paulo Biennale, São Paulo, Brazil (1967); Documenta, Kassel, Germany (1968, 1977); and "American Pop Art," Whitney Museum of American Art, New York (1974).

More recent group exhibitions include "Pop Art," Royal Academy of Arts, London (1991); "Group Show," Avanti Galleries, New York (1996); "Modern and Contemporary Masters: Paintings, Sculpture, Works on Paper," Sidney Janis Gallery, New York (1997); "Inaugural Exhibition: 68 Years/68 Masters," ACA Galleries, New York (2000); "Evidence of Love, Romance, Desire & Fantasy," Jack Rutberg Fine Arts, Los Angeles (2001); and "Images of Women," Jack Rutberg Fine Arts, Los Angeles (2002).

More recent solo exhibitions include "Tom Wesselmann: New Abstract Metal Paintings," Sidney Janis Gallery, New York (1996); "Tom Wesselmann: Abstract Maquettes," Galerie Benden & Klimczak, Vierseen, Germany (1999); "Tom Wesselmann, Prints," Galerie Kaess-Weiss, Stuggart, Germany (1999); and "Tom Wesselmann: Blue Nudes," Joseph Heldman Gallery, New York (2000). Recent retrospectives include "Tom Wesselmann, Paintings 1962–1986," Mayor Gallery, London (1988); "Tom Wesselmann, A Survey, 1959–1995," Fred Hoffman Fine Art, Santa Monica, California (1996); and "Tom Wesselmann: A Retrospective Survey, 1959–1992," Isetan Museum of Art, Shinju-ku, Japan (1993).

Tom Wesselmann lives and works in New York City.

Selected Further Readings

Wesselmann, Tom. *Tom Wesselmann, Early Still Lifes: 1962–1964.* New York: Nelson Doubleday, 1971.

Tom Wesselmann, Paintings 1962–1986 (exhibition catalogue). London: Mayor Gallery, 1988.

Tom Wesselmann: A Retrospective Survey, 1959–1992 (exhibition catalogue). Tokyo: Art Life, Ltd., 1993.

Hunter, Sam. *Tom Wesselmann.* New York: Rizzoli, 1994.

Tom Wesselmann, 1959–1993 (exhibition catalogue). Ostfildern-Ruit, Germany: Hatje Cantz, 1994.

Hunter, Sam. *Tom Wesselmann.* Barcelona, Spain: Ediciones Poligrafa, 1995.

Tom Wesselmann (exhibition catalogue). Ostfildern-Ruit, Germany: Hatje Cantz, 1996.

Tom Wesselmann, A Survey, 1959–1995 (exhibition catalogue). Santa Monica, CA: Fred Hoffman Fine Art, 1996.

Robert Yarber

Born in Dallas in 1948, Robert Yarber studied at Cooper Union College, New York (B.F.A., 1971), and Louisiana State University, Baton Rouge, Louisiana (M.F.A., 1974).

Yarber's early solo exhibitions were mounted at Bowery Gallery, New York (1970); Simon Lowinsky Gallery, Los Angeles (1981); and Steven Lieber Gallery, San Francisco (1983).

Yarber's first group exhibition was "Texas Painting and Sculpture Exhibition," organized by the Dallas Museum of Fine Arts, Dallas (1967). Other early group exhibitions include Bowery Gallery, New York (1969); George Goodenow Gallery, Dallas (1975); Open Studio, San Francisco (1977); "Humor in Art," Los Angeles Institute of Contemporary Art, Los Angeles (1981); "The Impolite Figure," Southern Exposure Gallery, San Francisco (1983); "Five From Austin," Waco Art Center, Waco, Texas (1983); "Outside New York," New Museum of Contemporary Art, New York (1984); and the Forty-first Venice Biennale, Venice, Italy (1984).

By the early '90s, Yarber began exhibiting regularly in the United States and Europe, at such venues as Sonnabend Gallery, New York (1990, 1993, 1995, 1998); Marella Arte Contemporanea, Sarnico, Italy (1996); Nevada Institute of Contemporary Art, Las Vegas (1995); and Patricia Faure Gallery, Santa Monica, California (1995).

Yarber also participated in numerous group exhibitions, including "The New Portrait," P.S. 1, New York (1984); the Whitney Biennial, Whitney Museum of American Art, New York (1985); Sonnabend Gallery, New York (1989, 1994, 1995, and 1997); "*Sélection*," FAE, Musée d'Art Contemporain, Lausanne, Switzerland (1991); "The Fluorescent Collection," Deichtorhalle in Hamburg, Germany (1996); and "Zero G: When Gravity Becomes Form," Whitney Museum at Champion, Stamford, Connecticut (1999).

Robert Yarber lives and works in Julian, Pennsylvania.

Selected Further Readings

Locations (exhibition catalogue). San Bernardino, California: California State College, San Bernardino, 1981.

Robert Yarber Paintings: 1980–1988 (exhibition catalogue). University Park, PA: Palmer Museum of Art, Pennsylvania State University, 1989.

Robert Yarber: New Works (exhibition catalogue). Turin, Italy: Galleria In Arco, 1992.

Crone, Rainer, and David Moos. *The Fluorescent Conscious* (exhibition catalogue). Munich, Germany: Galerie Pfefferle, 1993.

Moos, David. *Painting in the Age of Artificial Intelligence.* London: Academy Group Ltd., 1996.

Robert Yarber: Paintings, 1988–1996 (exhibtion catalogue). Sarnico, Italy: Marella Arte Contemporanea, 1996.

Gilberto Zorio

Born in Andorno Micca, Turin, Italy, in 1944, Gilberto Zorio studied at the Accademia di Belle Arti (1963–70) where he concentrated on painting and sculpture.

Zorio had his first solo exhibition of sculptural works at Galleria Sperone, Turin, Italy (1967). Zorio's work became known shortly after his exhibition/performance, *Scrittura bruciata* (Burnt writing), at Galerie Sonnabend, Paris (1968). Zorio was given one-person exhibitions at Kunstmuseum Luzern, Switzerland (1976), and Sonnabend Gallery, New York (1981, 1988), and a midcareer retrospective at Stedelijk Museum, Amsterdam, Netherlands (1979).

Zorio participated in numerous seminal *arte povera* exhibitions including "*Op losse schroven: situaties en cryptostructuren*," Stedelijk Museum, Amsterdam, Netherlands (1968); "Nine Young Artists: Theodoron Awards," Solomon R. Guggenheim Museum, New York (1969); Documenta 5, Kassel, Germany (1972); and the Venice Biennale, Venice, Italy (1978, 1980, 1986, 1995, 1997).

In 1985, a major retrospective of Zorio's work was organized by the Kunstverein Stuttgart, Germany, which traveled to the Musée National d'Art Moderne, Paris; Centre d'Art Contemporain, Geneva; and Stedelijk van Abbemuseum, Eindhoven, Netherlands. A retrospective was organized by the Instituto Valenciano de Arte Moderno, Valencia, Spain (1991), which traveled to Prato, Centro per L'Arte Contemporanea Luigi Pecci (1992), and Galleria Civica di Arte Contemporanea, Trento, Italy (1996).

Gilberto Zorio lives and works in Turin, Italy.

Selected Further Readings

Zorio, Gilberto. *Gilberto Zorio* (exhibition catalogue). Paris: Galerie Ileana Sonnabend, 1970.

Gilberto Zorio (exhibition catalogue). Lucerne, Switzerland: Kunstmuseum Luzern, 1976.

Gilberto Zorio (exhibition catalogue). Ravenna, Italy: Essegi, 1982.

Gilberto Zorio (exhibition catalogue). Stuttgart, Germany: Der Kunstverein, 1985.

Gilberto Zorio: Opere 1967–1984 (exhibition catalogue). Modena, Italy: Panini, 1985.

Gilberto Zorio (exhibition catalogue). Paris: Editions du Centre Pompidou/M.N.A.M., 1986.

Gilberto Zorio (exhibition catalogue). Valencia, Spain: IVAM Centre del Carme, 1991.

Zorio, Gilberto. *Gilberto Zorio*. Amsterdam: Institute of Contemporary Art, 1992.

Gilberto Zorio (exhibition catalogue). Turin, Italy: Hopefulmonster, 1996.

ACKNOWLEDGMENTS

From Pop to Now: Selections from the Sonnabend Collection is strikingly representative of the monumental changes in the American and international art world that began over four decades ago with the emergence of Pop art. The realization of any exhibition and publication—large or small, contemporary or historical—depends on a diverse group of artists and the support, advice, and assistance of countless individuals. In this case, when we are talking about an exhibition of some of the greatest artworks of the twentieth century, the prospect of adequately acknowledging those involved is at once breathtaking and humbling.

At the Frances Young Tang Teaching Museum and Art Gallery at Skidmore College we are indebted to many individuals who contributed their time and talents to this exhibition. On behalf of everyone at Skidmore College, I must first express my profound gratitude and most heartfelt thanks to Ileana Sonnabend for giving the Tang Museum the opportunity to present this remarkable collection. It seems in keeping with so many other decisions she has made during the past half century that she would choose a new and little-known museum to showcase her beloved collection. I must also extend a most generous thank you to Antonio Homem of the Sonnabend Gallery for so graciously and freely sharing his knowledge of the collection and for his wise suggestions on so many aspects of this project from beginning to end. I would also be remiss if I did not thank the numerous artists, too many to name here, who assisted at every stage.

Without the advice, help, and commitment of many people this exhibition and accompanying catalogue would not have been possible. For the ultimate success of this publication I am enormously indebted to Helaina Blume, Rachel Haidu, Bethany Johns, and Margaret Sundell. Helaina Blume did an amazing job of culling massive amounts of research, managing an array of day-to-day details and calming many frayed nerves; Rachel Haidu wrote the succinct and eloquent texts; Bethany Johns (who has designed a number of Tang catalogues) has once again worked her magic with great aplomb and humor and made this publication one of the most beautiful I have ever been a part of; and Margaret Sundell worked tirelessly in making sure that every aspect of the catalogue was perfect. Copy editor Emily Votruba and proofreaders Jeanine Herman and Apollinaire Scherr assured the clarity and consistency of the words we have chosen.

At Sonnabend Gallery, we thank Laura Bloom, Xan Price, Nick Sheidy, Queenie Wong, Gabriella Artinian, Jeff Byrd, and Jason Ysenburg for their patience in assisting with a seemingly never-ending stream of questions and requests.

The very small Tang staff has risen to meet a very big challenge and proved that there is no such thing as an insignificant detail. I thank Barbara Rhodes, Brian Caverly, Jill Cohan, Lori Geraghty, Allison Hunter, Susi Kerr, Barbara Schrade, and Tyler Auwarter. I am particularly grateful to three key people on staff: Gayle King, Chris Kobuskie, and Ian Berry, who not only with this project but on a daily basis make sure that the Tang lives up to the expectations of everyone who supports our programs and that the museum pushes the envelope of its own potential. Pearl Rucker, Liz Blum, Steve Martonis, Shaw Fici, Abe Ferraro, Alex Roediger, and Jefferson Nelson worked with tremendous care to install the works in the Tang and they deserve a special note of appreciation.

I would also like to acknowledge the work of our student interns: Crystal Daigle, Dan Byers, Doria Santofler, Gillian Roberts, Kristina Podesva, and Justin Rogers-Cooper. Their assistance made all the difference, and their youthful energy was infectious.

At Skidmore College I would like to thank Robert Kimmerle, Barbara Melville, Michael Casey, Mary Jo Driscoll, Barbara Casey, Barry Pritzker, Susan Bender, and Chuck Joseph for all their efforts, both large and small, in ensuring the overall success of this endeavor. I must also express my gratitude for the support of Jamienne Studley, president of Skidmore College, and the entire administration of the college. In the short time I have been here, they have allowed the Tang and me to explore and embrace the notion of experimentation and discovery in the best tradition of a small progressive liberal arts college.

I also want to call attention to the numerous individuals who have in many ways contributed to the project: Frazer Ward, Robert Beach and Lane Press, Thomas O'Connor at Mohawk Paper, Daniela Oliveira at Fundação de Serralves Museu de Arte Contemporânea, Porto, Portugal; Susanna Singer and Tomas Ramberg at the Sol LeWitt Studio; Kara Kirk at San Francisco Museum of Modern Art; Ann Schapps Schaffer; Argie Tang; Gail Peters Beits; Meg Reitman Jacobs; Beverly Mastrianni; Katherine Michaelson; Beth Mohel Siskind; Leslie Tonkonow; Janet Lucas Whitman; Allison Derusha; Elizabeth Chapman; and Fred Schroeder. And most important, a heartfelt thanks to my wife Kitty Bowe Hearty for her wise words and patient ear.

Finally, special thanks to Lane Press and Mohawk Paper for their donations. On behalf of Skidmore College and the Frances Young Tang Teaching Museum and Art Gallery I want especially to thank Mr. and Mrs. Edgar Wachenheim III, Beverly Beaston Grossman '58 and Felix T. Grossman, the Edward J. Noble Foundation, the AT&T Foundation, and the Friends of the Tang for their generous support of this publication and the exhibition, *From Pop to Now: Selections from the Sonnabend Collection*.

CHARLES ASHLEY STAINBACK
Dayton Director
The Frances Young Tang Teaching Museum and Art Gallery
at Skidmore College